Theology and Science in the Thought of Ian Barbour

Theology and Science
in the Thought of Ian Barbour

This book is part of the Peter Lang Humanities list.
Every volume is peer reviewed and meets
the highest quality standards for content and production.

PETER LANG
New York • Bern • Berlin
Brussels • Vienna • Oxford • Warsaw

Joseph R. Laracy

Theology and Science
in the Thought of Ian Barbour

A Thomistic Evaluation
for the Catholic Doctrine of Creation

PETER LANG
New York • Bern • Berlin
Brussels • Vienna • Oxford • Warsaw

Library of Congress Cataloging-in-Publication Control Number: 2021025168

Bibliographic information published by **Die Deutsche Nationalbibliothek**.
Die Deutsche Nationalbibliothek lists this publication in the "Deutsche
Nationalbibliografie"; detailed bibliographic data are available
on the Internet at http://dnb.d-nb.de/.

ISBN 978-1-4331-9005-6 (hardcover)
ISBN 978-1-4331-9006-3 (ebook pdf)
ISBN 978-1-4331-9008-7 (epub)
DOI 10.3726/b18601

© 2021 Peter Lang Publishing, Inc., New York
80 Broad Street, 5th floor, New York, NY 10004
www.peterlang.com

For my parents, Paul and Catherine Laracy, with love.

Table of Contents

Foreword

We live in a scientific age. The discoveries made by science in the fields of physics (the structure of reality in the Standard Model), astrophysics (a vast expanding universe), computer science (the possibility of AI), and in the biological sciences (genetics) have opened up a universe and a micro-universe vast and infinitesimal in scale, respectively. They have also challenged human beings to think about their place in the cosmos as well as to reflect on their own self-understanding and identity, given their cultures, philosophies, and religious faiths. At the nexus of where these currents meet stands the relationship between religion and science. The interaction between these two spheres of human activity can be characterized as one of either conflict, compartmentalization (mutually exclusive domains), or some form of engagement and dialogue and integration emphasizing a common sphere of influence. The last few decades have been rich in exploring the interaction between faith and science in different ways, for example, as seen in the work of figures such as Pierre Teilhard de Chardin, Arthur Peacock, John Polkinghorne, Stanley Jaki, George Coyne, William Stoeger, Peter Hodgson, John Haught, Ian Barbour, not to mention the perennial, centuries-old influence of St. Thomas Aquinas, just to name a few. Here in this book, Fr. Joseph Laracy explores the immense contribution made to the interaction between faith and science by Ian Barbour, a prodigious, prolific, and gifted scholar (a physicist and a theologian). He examines what Catholic theology and philosophy (especially when seen from a Thomistic point of view) can learn from Barbour's Protestant Christian approach, which has also appropriated certain aspects of process philosophy, especially from Whitehead, and process theology. In particular, this is done by examining the faith/science dialectic when applied to the Catholic doctrine of Creation.

A point of common ground between science and faith is to be found in an acceptance of the natural world as a primary object of study—the reality of the cosmos and of the truths that emerge from what is observed and what is experienced by human beings. They are both truth-seeking endeavors. This is certainly a quintessential starting point for Catholic theology (such as that of St. Thomas Aquinas), which is why there is great potential always to be seen in its dialogue with science and the physical reality that it seeks to describe. Both domains assume the intelligibility of such a reality and of the capacity of human reason to know it. It is on this point that Fr. Laracy, along with many other scholars, indicates the important contribution that Barbour's "critical realism" provides to the commonality (e.g., same structures) between faith and science—a bridge between the two domains. Observing the dynamism of the world of science (such as in evolution) and in human life (including faith), Barbour attempts to employ process philosophy in establishing a common metaphysical framework for both domains, thus accounting for the subjective and objective. In so doing, Barbour wishes to highlight the aspect of "becoming" rather than ontological "being" as the underlying principle that drives our reality and from which truths emerge. Important to this venture is how both science and faith must account for the "data" of reality, coherence, and comprehensiveness in which they describe. Articulating a four-fold typology for the interaction of science and faith (conflict, or independence, or dialogue, and/or integration), Barbour favors dialogue and integration as the best way to facilitate a "culture of encounter" between both domains.

In many ways, there is much that Barbour's work can contribute to Catholic methodology of the interaction of faith and science, which is also one of engagement and integration, though proceeding along different fundamental criteria than those that he uses. As he studies this point in systematic detail, Fr. Laracy uses three basic criteria to evaluate Barbour's contribution to the Catholic understanding of integration of faith and science: (1) fidelity to divine revelation and interpretation in the Church, (2) a suitable epistemology and metaphysics for both science and Catholic theology that respects both domains, and, (3) consistency with, respect for, and concordance with solid science. In particular, the Catholic doctrine of Creation is the lens through which Fr. Laracy investigates how Barbour's integration of faith and natural sciences may be attempted, given the understandings of God, of the natural world, and of human beings that are implicit in such a doctrine.

Not surprisingly, Barbour's methodology, especially with his use of process philosophy/theology, does not entirely harmonize with the Catholic understanding of God, of creation ex nihilo, of how God relates to creation, of truth as a way of knowing, and of actuality in God. These incompatibilities notwithstanding, Fr. Laracy's investigation is a valuable and necessary exercise in how other currents of thought can contribute to and enrich the Catholic understanding of the interaction between faith and science. Crucial to deepening the ability of faith and science to interact with and to enrich one another is the ability to engage and to dialogue with rigor and honesty and openness, even if differences in philosophies and theologies are evident. This will always be a constructive exercise. We will have deepened our understanding of the truth.

Fr. David A. Brown, SJ, DPhil (Oxon)
Vatican Observatory
Solemnity of St. Joseph
March 19, 2021

Acknowledgments

I would like to express my great gratitude to Father Paul M. Haffner, STD, my doctoral dissertation director, for his valuable and constructive suggestions during the planning and development of this research. His willingness to give his time so generously is very much appreciated. I would like to offer my special thanks as well to Father Matthew Baldwin, STD, Father Thomas K. Macdonald, STD, John T. Laracy, PhD, Father Matthew Rolling, PhD, Thomas Marlowe, PhD, Father Douglas Milewski, STD, and Monsignor Thomas G. Guarino, STD for their insightful feedback on my research as it developed.

I also must acknowledge my late Archbishop Emeritus, His Grace, John J. Myers, JCD, DD, (1941–2020) for appointing me to seminary studies, ordaining me a deacon and a priest, and first assigning me to ministry in higher education. I am also very grateful to His Eminence, Joseph W. Cardinal Tobin, CSsR, DD, Archbishop of Newark, for appointing me to doctoral studies in theology and continuing to support my priestly ministry at Seton Hall University.

The spiritual accompaniment of Monsignor Gerard H. McCarren, STD and Father Brendan Hurley, SJ, MDiv has been a tremendous blessing. I also thank my family, friends, and brother priests, for their support.

Most of all, *Deo gratias*!

List of Abbreviations

al.	*alii* (that is, "others")
bk.	book
cf.	*confer* (that is, "compare with")
chap.	chapter
ed.	edition
e.g.,	*exempli gratia* (that is, "for example")
etc.	*et cetera* (that is, "and so forth")
Ibid.	*Ibidem* (that is, "at the same place")
i.e.	*id est* ("that is")
N.B.	*nota bene* (that is, "note well")
pg.	page
par.	paragraph
trans.	translator
vol.	volume

CHAPTER ONE

Ian Barbour:
Life and Works

1. Introduction

In his Apostolic Exhortation, *Evangelii Gaudium*, Pope Francis, offers a timely reminder to the universal Church on the importance of relating the Christian faith and the natural sciences. He writes,

> Dialogue between science and faith also belongs to the work of evangelization at the service of peace. Whereas positivism and scientism "refuse to admit the validity of forms of knowledge[1] other than those of the positive sciences,"[2] the Church proposes another path, which calls for a synthesis between the responsible use of methods proper to the empirical sciences and other areas of knowledge such as philosophy, theology, as well as faith itself, which elevates us to the mystery transcending nature and human intelligence.[3]

---

1   While the natural sciences are oriented toward *empiriological* knowledge, metaphysics, for example, is interested in *ontological* knowledge (which studies being and the intelligible structure of reality). For more on this distinction, see Jacques Maritain, *Philosophy of Nature*, trans. Imelda C. Byrne (New York: Philosophical Library, 1951), 73ff.
2   John Paul II, *Fides et Ratio*, 1998, 74.
3   Francis, *Evangelii Gaudium*, 2013, 242.

Two paragraphs later, the Holy Father echoes the Catholic commitment to ecumenical dialogue that received great emphasis at the Second Vatican Council.[4] A stance of humility and openness is important for Catholics when relating to other Christians because, as Francis writes, "We must never forget that we are pilgrims journeying alongside one another."[5]

Similarly, Pope Saint Paul VI declared that "dialogue ... is a recognized method of the apostolate. It is a way of making spiritual contact."[6] In this monograph, we strive to adhere to his four principles for dialogue: *perspicuitas, lenitas, fiducia, et prudentia.* Paul VI encourages clarity in expression, Christ-like meekness and the avoidance of all arrogance, trust in God and confidence in the good will of the other, and prudence in how one engages the partner in dialogue. The Second Vatican Council's Decree on Ecumenism, *Unitatis Redintegratio,* teaches that there exists a "lawful variety" of "differences in theological expression of doctrine."[7] In addition, the Pastoral Constitution on the Church in the Modern World, *Gaudium et Spes,* exhorts theologians to "seek continually for more suitable ways of communicating doctrine to the men of their times; for the deposit of Faith or the truths are one thing and the manner in which they are enunciated, in the same meaning and understanding, is another."[8] This important relationship of unity and plurality in faith was also a topic of a 1972 document of the International Theological Commission.[9]

The highly influential German philosopher and theologian, Karl Rahner, SJ, in his 1981 essay, "Naturwissenschaft und vernünftiger Glaube," later published in English as, "Natural Science and Reasonable Faith: Theological Perspectives for Dialogue with the Natural Sciences,"[10] expresses regret that "in recent decades, theology has not occupied itself very intensively with borderline questions between the natural sciences and itself."[11] As a first step toward facilitating a dialogue, Rahner suggests that fundamental theology must engage in a serious conversation with the natural sciences on essential epistemological issues. (In addition, we

---

4 Second Vatican Council, *Unitatis Redintegratio,* 1964, 4, 6.

5 Francis, *Evangelii Gaudium,* 244.

6 Paul VI, *Ecclesiam Suam,* 1964, 81.

7 Second Vatican Council, *Unitatis Redintegratio,* 17.

8 Second Vatican Council, *Gaudium et Spes,* 1964, 62.

9 International Theological Commission, *Unity of the Faith and Theological Pluralism,* 1972.

10 The original German essay was published in Karl Rahner, "Naturwissenschaft und vernünftiger Glaube," in *Christlicher Glaube in Moderner Gesellschaft,* ed. A. Battke, vol. 3, Weltall—Erde— Mensch 2 (Freiburg im Breisgau: Herder, 1981), 34–78.

11 Karl Rahner, "Natural Science and Reasonable Faith: Theological Perspectives for Dialogue with the Natural Sciences," in *Theological Investigations,* trans. Hugh M. Riley, vol. 21 (New York: Crossroad, 1988), 16.

would add inquiry into *metaphysical* questions.) Rahner's perspective is hopeful for a harmonious relationship. In his view, science and theology cannot, in principle, contradict each other as their areas of investigation and methodologies are distinct.[12]

In light of the recent Papal and Conciliar Magisterium, and given the scope of fundamental theology to cast its gaze not merely within the confines of the Catholic Church, but also to engage truth wherever it may be found, we strive to carry out a substantial study in the thought of the late Professor Ian Graeme Barbour. In this book, we analyze Ian Barbour's distinctive approach to the relationship of theology and science, largely unexplored in the Catholic tradition, according to fundamental theological criteria. Our goal is to investigate the possibility for Barbour's epistemic, metaphysical, and theological principles to enrich the *dialogue* and *integration* (to use Barbour's terms) of the Catholic doctrine of creation with the natural sciences. Barbour's corpus and contributions are vast, so we use the theology of creation as a lens, or "limit," to focus this research.[13]

Ian Graeme Barbour (1923–2013) was a prominent American theologian and physicist who served for many years on the faculty of Carleton College, Northfield, Minnesota, USA. As a scholar, Ian Barbour has a certain *je ne sais quoi*. His highly significant research on the relationship of theology and science led to an invitation to deliver the esteemed Gifford Lectures in Scotland (1989–1991) and won him the prestigious Templeton Prize in 1999. Born in Beijing, the son of an American Episcopalian mother and a Scottish Presbyterian father, Barbour eventually found his ecclesial home in the United Church of Christ.[14]

Barbour's quest begins in an Anglophonic, Protestant world still deeply influenced by the "conflict" hypothesis between Christianity and science instigated in the nineteenth century by John William Draper and Andrew Dickson White. Draper, a distinguished chemist and physician who was also virulently anti-Catholic, published *History of the Conflict between Religion and Science* in 1874.[15] In

---

12 Ibid., 19. As will be seen later in the explication of Barbour's thought, Barbour suggests conceptual and methodological parallels between the natural sciences and theology.

13 Anne E. Clifford, CSJ notes that "since the nineteenth century, the doctrine of creation has been enmeshed in questions about the relationship of theology and science." Anne M. Clifford, "Creation," in *Systematic Theology: Roman Catholic Perspectives*, ed. Francis Schüssler Fiorenza and John P. Galvin, vol. 1 (Minneapolis: Fortress Press, 1991), 225.

14 For a collection of essays on the roots, polity, ministry, worship, and theology of the United Church of Christ, see Daniel L. Johnson and Charles Hambrick-Stowe, eds., *Theology and Identity: Traditions, Movements, and Polity in the United Church of Christ*, Revised. (Cleveland: United Church Press, 2007).

15 John William Draper, *History of the Conflict between Religion and Science* (CreateSpace Independent Publishing Platform, 2014).

this work, Draper posits that his perceived conflict between religion and science in the United States was a direct result of the Catholic Church's perpetual battle against reason and science. Not surprisingly, this anti-historical work was placed on the *Index Librorum Prohibitorum* in 1876.[16]

White was a historian, politician, and co-founder of Cornell University. In 1896, he published *A History of the Warfare of Science with Theology in Christendom*.[17] Although baptized an Episcopalian, he became extremely hostile to any form of "revealed religion." Regrettably, White's book became enormously popular in the United States and was eventually translated into German, French, Italian, Swedish, and Japanese. *A History of the Warfare of Science with Theology in Christendom* greatly popularized the conflict hypothesis.

Emerging as an enthusiastic, young scholar in the mid-twentieth century, one of Barbour's goals was to revive and reposition the reputation of the natural sciences among American and British Protestant Christians. He approached this task with great *élan*. A fundamental principle for Barbour is that theology and science are separate *truth-producing* activities that can be considered in varying forms of relationship to one another. Barbour's work in theology and science has had a profound impact on the field and stimulated scholarly work throughout the United States, the United Kingdom, and beyond.

Barbour's four-fold typologies of interaction between theology and science, his development of a common epistemological approach of "critical realism," and his metaphysical commitment to Whiteheadian process thought indubitably merit an evaluation according to the methods and principles of Catholic theology. Given his epistemic, metaphysical, and ultimately theological foundations, what are the implications for a Catholic reception of his thought? The fundamental research question is: Can Ian Barbour's approach for the interaction of theology and science promote a more fruitful dialogue and integration between the natural sciences and the Catholic doctrine of creation?

The metaphysical concept of *creation* has been a subject of reflection by the most inquisitive minds since the great, ancient pre-Christian civilizations to the present.[18] It is also very germane to the contemporary theological engagement with the natural sciences. For example, two distinguished physicists, James

---

16 Francis S. Betten, ed., *The Roman Index of Forbidden Books*, 5th ed. (London: B. Herder Book Co., 1920), 66.

17 Andrew D. White, *A History of the Warfare of Science with Theology in Christendom* (Buffalo: Prometheus Books, 1993).

18 See Stanley L. Jaki, *Science and Creation* (Lanham: University Press of America, 1990) and Stanley L. Jaki, *The Savior of Science* (Grand Rapids: Wm. B. Eerdmans Publishing Company, 2000) for a detailed analysis.

Hartle and Stephen Hawking, developed a well-known cosmic origin hypothesis that describes a "spontaneous quantum creation of the universe."[19] In a *Gedankenexperiment*, Hartle and Hawking consider the Big Bang cosmic expansion in reverse. As one goes back in time, the cosmos contracts. Eventually one reaches the Planck epoch[20] (approximately 10^{-43} seconds after the Big Bang) where it is not clear in what sense, if any, the concept of time retains meaning.[21]

At this point, Hartle and Hawking theorize that particles spontaneously appear and disappear as space becomes separated from time. Hawking offers an image from everyday life as an analogy, stating that it "would be a bit like the formation of bubbles of steam in boiling water."[22] Prior to the Planck epoch, the theorized "Hartle–Hawking state" has no "beginning" because it has no initial boundaries in time and space. In *The Grand Design*, Hawking writes that "the universe can and will *create* itself from nothing ... Spontaneous *creation* is the reason there is something rather than nothing, why the universe exists, why we exist. It is not necessary to invoke God to light the blue touch paper and set the universe going."[23] (emphasis added) A Catholic may ask, What is the relationship between the "creation" described by Hawking (whether or not the physical theory has merit), and the teaching of the Fourth Lateran Council which solemnly declared that God created the material and spiritual order *de nihil condidit et ab initio temporis*?[24] In order to

19 See Stephen Hawking, "Origins of the Universe" (J. Robert Oppenheimer Lecture in Physics, University of California, Berkeley, March 13, 2007), accessed December 7, 2017, http://www.berkeley.edu/news/media/releases/2007/03/16_hawking_text.shtml. A significant concern for Hawking is to deal with the problem of singularities (i.e., infinities) in cosmological models. For example, most Big Bang models involve an initial singularity in (ordinary) time. Hawking speculates that "imaginary time" (real time coordinates multiplied by i where $i^2 = -1$) is more fundamental than "real time." By incorporating imaginary time in his cosmological models (which are solutions of the equations of general relativity), he removes the singularity. According to Hawking, "'The boundary condition of the universe is that it has no boundary.' The universe would be completely self-contained and not affected by anything outside itself. It would neither be created nor destroyed. It would just BE." Stephen Hawking, *A Brief History of Time*, 10th ed. (New York: Bantam, 1998), 141.

20 Max Planck, "On Irreversible Radiation Processes," in *Physikalische Abhandlungen Und Vorträge*, vol. 1 (Braunschweig: Friedr. Wieweg & Sohn, 1958), 597.

21 James Hartle and Stephen Hawking, "Wave Function of the Universe," *Physical Review D 28*, no. 12 (December 15, 1983): 2960–2975.

22 Hawking, "Origins of the Universe."

23 Leonard Mlodinow and Stephen Hawking, *The Grand Design* (New York: Bantam, 2012), 180.

24 "*Deus ... creator omnium visibilium et invisibilium, spiritualium et corporalium: qui sua omnipotenti virtute simul ab initio temporis utramque de nihilo condidit creaturam, spiritualem et corporalem, angelicam videlicet et mundanam: ac deinde humanam, quasi communem ex spiritu et corpore constitutam.*" Lateran IV, *Constitutions*, 1215, chap. 1 "Confession of Faith" in Peter Hünermann,

answer that question, and the more general question of relating Catholic belief in creation with the natural sciences, we present the fundamentals of the doctrine in the next section.

2. Fundamentals of the Catholic Doctrine of Creation

Joseph Cardinal Ratzinger states that in our contemporary era, the doctrine of creation[25] has an "unprecedented topicality."[26] He laments the obscuring and in some cases the suppression of faith in creation in modern thought. Ratzinger identifies three principal instigators of the present situation. First, the divinization of the universe in Giordano Bruno's pantheistic cosmology was detrimental to the Christian view of creation during the Renaissance and in the years following. His 1584 book, *Spaccio de la Besta Trionfante*, is filled with Greek mythology, Egyptian religion (especially the worship of Isis[27]), Hermeticism,[28] magic, and astrology.[29] Bruno imagines that the cosmos was God and God was the cosmos. In the aforementioned book, he writes, "Nature ... is none other than God in things ... Whence all of God is in all things."[30]

ed., *Heinrich Denzinger—Enchiridion Symbolorum: A Compendium of Creeds, Definitions, and Declarations of the Catholic Church*, 43rd ed. (San Francisco: Ignatius Press, 2012), DS 428.

25 Ratzinger suggests a fascinating connection between the doctrine of creation and theological reflection on the Blessed Virgin Mary. He writes, "Mariology demonstrates that the doctrine of grace does not revoke creation, but is the definitive Yes to creation. In this way, Mariology guarantees the ontological independence [*Eigenständigkeit*] of creation, undergirds faith in creation, and crowns the doctrine of creation, rightly understood." Joseph Ratzinger, *Mary: The Church at the Source* (San Francisco: Ignatius Press, 2005), 31.

26 Joseph Ratzinger, *In the Beginning: A Catholic Understanding of the Story of Creation and the Fall*, trans. Boniface Ramsey (Grand Rapids, MI: Eerdmans, 1995), 81.

27 Isis is the ancient Egyptian goddess believed to help the dead enter the afterlife.

28 Hermeticism is a religious, philosophical, and esoteric tradition based on the Egyptian-Greek wisdom texts from the second century AD and later attributed to Hermes Trismegistus. Hermes Trismegistus may be associated with the Greek deity, Hermes, and the Egyptian deity, Thoth. See Ernest Alfred Thompson Wallis Budge, *The Gods of the Egyptians*, vol. 1 (London: Methuen & Co, 1904), 414–415.

29 See Giordano Bruno, *The Expulsion of the Triumphant Beast*, trans. Arthur D. Imerti, 2nd ed. (Lincoln, NE: Bison Books, 2004).

30 Cited in Mary Ellen Barrett, *Encyclopedia of Catholic Social Thought, Social Science, and Social Policy: Supplement*, ed. Michael L. Coulter, Richard S. Myers, and Joseph A. Varacalli, vol. 3 (Lanham, UK: Scarecrow Press, 2012), 239.

Second, in the following decades, Ratzinger identifies Galileo Galilei's emphasis on the mathematical aspect of Platonism as a contributor to stifling faith in creation. Ratzinger regrets that Galileo's stress on "God the geometer" led some modern thinkers to believe that the knowledge of God was *simply* the knowledge of the mathematical structures of nature. Ratzinger writes, "The concept of nature, in the sense of the object of science, takes the place of the concept of creation."[31] As a consequence, the personal God of Sacred Scripture is reduced to the First Cause of deism.

Finally, Ratzinger posits that the obscuring or abnegation of faith in creation can be traced back to Martin Luther and his quest to de-Hellenize Christianity. He points out that for Luther, "the cosmos, or more correctly, being as such, is an expression of everything that is proper to human beings, the burden of their past, their shackles and chains, their damnation: Law."[32] Luther envisions grace in essential opposition to creation which is brought low by sin. Man's redemption lies in rejecting fallen creation and making an act of faith in Christ, thereby receiving imputed justification.[33]

As far back as the post-Apostolic period, there is written testimony that Catholic Christians professed faith in the doctrine that

(1) God is the *creator mundi*,
(2) God created *ex nihilo*,
3) God created directly, *sine causis secundariis*, and
4) God created the universe *cum tempore*.[34]

This belief was unambiguously articulated as early as the ante-Nicene Fathers. Belief in the Creator is a clear indicator throughout the second century in distinguishing orthodox Christian belief from Gnostic error, especially in the writings

---

31 Ratzinger, *In the Beginning*, 84.

32 Ibid., 87.

33 For example, consider this excerpt from Martin Luther's *Exegetica Opera Latina: Operationes in Psalmos* which concisely summarizes the spiritual aspect of his theology of creation: "*Homo enim homo est, donec fiat deus, qui solus est verax, cuius participatione et ipse verax efficitur, dum illi vera fide et spe adheret, redactus hoc excessu in nihilum. Quo enim perveniat, qui sperat in deum, nisi in sui nihilum? Quo autem abeat, qui abit in nihilum, nisi eo, unde venit? Venit autem ex deo et suo nihilo, quare in deum redit, qui redit in nihilum.*" Cited in Wilfried Joest, *Ontologie der Person bei Luther* (Göttingen: Vandenhoeck & Ruprecht, 1967), 246. In Luther's theology of faith, man must make a concrete, personal decision and commitment of trust in God and abandon hope in what Luther considers man's nothingness (*sui nihilum*). See Wilhelp Pauck, *The Heritage of the Reformation* (New York: The Free Press of Glencoe, Inc., 1961), 22–27.

34 Thomas Aquinas, *Aquinas on Creation*, trans. Steven Baldner and William E. Carroll (Toronto: Pontifical Institute of Mediaeval Studies, 1997), 22.

of Irenæus.[35] A lucid, developed doctrine is seen in the writings of Hippolytus of Rome. Around the year 230, he writes,

> The first and only (one God), both Creator and Lord of all, had nothing coeval with Himself; not infinite chaos, nor measureless water, nor solid earth, nor dense air, not warm fire, nor refined spirit, nor the azure canopy of the stupendous firmament. But He was One, alone in Himself. By an exercise of His will He created things that are, which antecedently had no existence, except that He willed to make them.[36]

Confronting the errors of the Albigensians who had revived some heresies of Manicheism, the Profession of Faith of Innocent III proclaims,

> By the heart we believe and by the mouth we confess that the Father also and the Son and the Holy Spirit, one God, concerning whom we are speaking, is the creator, the maker, the ruler, and the dispenser of all things corporal and spiritual, visible and invisible. We believe that God is the one and same author of the Old and the New Testament, who existing in the Trinity, as it is said, created all things from nothing.[37]

The Fourth Lateran Council reaffirms this dogma in the face of continued errors from the Albigensians as well as the Waldesians.[38] The Council of Florence's "Instruction of Faith for the Jacobites," *Cantate Domino*, echoes this essential element of the Catholic faith.[39]

In the modern era, the First Vatican Council's Dogmatic Constitution, *Dei Filius*, concisely states the doctrine *De Deo Rerum Omnium Creatore*:

> The holy, Catholic, Apostolic, Roman Church believes and confesses that there is one, true, living God, Creator and Lord of heaven and earth, omnipotent, eternal, immense, incomprehensible, infinite in intellect and will, and in every perfection; who, although He is one, singular, altogether simple and unchangeable spiritual substance, must be proclaimed distinct in reality and essence from the world; most blessed in Himself and of Himself, and ineffably most high above all things which are or can be conceived outside Himself. This sole true God by His goodness and omnipotent power, not to increase His own beatitude, and not to add to, but to manifest His perfection by the blessings which He bestows on creatures, with most free volition, immediately from

---

35 See Irenaeus of Lyons, *Against Heresies*, ed. Alexander Roberts, James Donaldson, and A. Cleveland Coxe (Ex Fontibus, 2015), II, 9.

36 Hippolytus, "Refutation of All Heresies," in *Ante-Nicene Fathers*, ed. Alexander Roberts, James Donaldson, and Arthur Cleveland Coxe, trans. John Henry MacMahon, vol. 5 (Buffalo, NY: Christian Literature Publishing Co., 1886), bk. X, chap. 28, accessed May 21, 2018, http://www.newadvent.org/fathers/050110.htm.

37 Profession of Faith of Innocent III cited in DS 790.

38 See DS 800.

39 See DS 1333.

the beginning of time fashioned each creature out of nothing, spiritual and corporeal, namely angelic and mundane; and then the human creation, common as it were, composed of both spirit and body [Lateran Council IV, can. 2 and 5] But God protects and governs by His providence all things which He created, reaching from end to end mightily and ordering all things sweetly [cf. Wis 8:1]. For all things are naked and open to His eyes [Heb 4:13], even those which by the free action of creatures are in the future.[40]

A key aspect of this chapter of *Dei Filius* is the dogmatic teaching on the perfection of God. A syllogistic argument is typically offered in support of this belief. In Thomistic thought, a thing is perfect in proportion to its actuality. God is actual *in toto* and has no potential—"I am Who am."[41] Therefore, God is absolutely perfect.

According to the British theologian and priest, Paul Haffner, "creation theology is one area where the interface between human thought and Christian belief stands out in bold relief. Through reason, man studies creation in search of its Creator. Through revelation, God enters His own creation in search of man."[42] Catholic Christians profess that God is the origin, foundation, and end (i.e., τέλος [télos]) of the universe. According to the American theologian, Anne M. Clifford, CSJ, "creation is a fundamental belief from which flows much of what Christians profess about God, about the cosmos we inhabit, and about our destiny and hope."[43] A correct understanding of creation is essential for a Christian because, as Clifford wisely states, "creation itself is the self-revelation of God."[44]

A German *peritus* of the Second Vatican Council, Michael Schmaus,[45] points out that "only through a true doctrine of creation can we understand grace, the supernatural, [and] the promise of the ultimate consummation of all things."[46] In Catholic thought, there is real continuity between the creation, redemption, and

---

40 First Vatican Council, "Dei Filius," in *Decrees of the Ecumenical Councils*, ed. Norman P. Tanner, vol. 2 (Washington, DC: Georgetown University Press, 1990), chap. 1.

41 Exodus 3:14 (RSV).

42 Paul Haffner, *Mystery of Creation* (Leominster, UK: Gracewing Publishing, 1995), 6.

43 Clifford, "Creation," 195.

44 Ibid., 196. Although this analogy implies similarity with greater dissimilarity.

45 Michael Schmaus is well-known for his role on the *Habilitationsschrift* committee of Joseph Ratzinger at the University of Munich. Schmaus initially rejected Ratzinger's thesis because he thought it could lead to the subjectivization of the concept of Divine revelation. Ratzinger edited the thesis and it was eventually accepted and published as *Die Geschichtstheologie des heiligen Bonaventura* in 1957. To this day, Ratzinger maintains the orthodoxy and accuracy of his analysis of Bonaventure's notion of revelation. See Joseph Ratzinger, *Milestones: Memoirs 1927–1977* (San Francisco: Ignatius Press, 2005), 107–112.

46 Michael Schmaus, *God and Creation: The Foundations of Christology*, trans. Ann Laeuchli, William McKenna, and T. Patrick Burke, vol. 2, Dogma (New York: Sheed and ward, 1969), 84.

consummation of the cosmos.[47] Given that theological reflection on creation, as well as the empirical sciences, take the natural world as a primary object of study, it would be of great benefit for a fruitful dialogue, and possibly an integrative approach, to emerge. Perhaps Ian Barbour's approach to relating theology and science, with appropriate modifications in light of Catholic doctrinal commitments, can offer a way forward.

One problematic aspect of Barbour's approach to science and theology that will be addressed is how he often treats the two disciplines as if they were of the same order. Given his reliance on Whiteheadian process metaphysics, Barbour ignores at times the ontological difference between God (*actus purus*) and creation (*actus potestatis Dei*). Creation is in total potency to God. It is pure potentiality in relation to His act and without His act, it is not. Creation is a *dependence* in the order of being.[48] In the Catholic theological tradition, particularly as it has been developed by Saint Thomas Aquinas,[49] a clear need is demonstrated for a metaphysics[50] of God as perfect, unconditioned, eternal act—"I am who am." This principle ensures the transcendence of theology, the ultimate coherence of being as a whole, and causal[51] reason. As a result, there exists the possibility of *dialogue*

---

47 Ibid., 2:78.

48 See Aquinas, *Aquinas on Creation*, 4.

49 G.K. Chesterton pointed out that if Saint Thomas Aquinas were to have a religious name in the Carmelite tradition, e.g., "... of the Child Jesus," it would be *Thomas a Creatore* (Thomas of the Creator). G.K. Chesterton, "Saint Thomas Aquinas," in *Collected Works*, vol. 2 (San Francisco: Ignatius Press, 1986), 129. It is important to note that for Thomas Aquinas and the medieval tradition in general, *scientia est cognitio certa per causas*. Therefore, mathematics, natural philosophy, metaphysics, and revealed theology are all sciences. See Thomas Aquinas, *Summa Contra Gentiles*, ed. Joseph Kenny, trans. James F. Anderson (New York: Hanover House, 1957), I, 94.

50 Metaphysics is the ultimate and most universal science. Its subject is being in general (ontology), substance (first being), and God (first cause). It is concerned with being as being—*ens qua ens*. It is said to have received its names when a scholar was trying to classify the works of Aristotle and he came across research which did not fit into the traditional categories. It was classified beyond (μετά) physics (φυσικά): τὰ μετὰ τὰ φυσικά.

51 Following St. Thomas, we consider a cause to be both a principle of being (*ontological*) and an order of knowledge (*epistemological*). According to Henri Dominique Gardeil, OP, "Primarily, it is a principle of being, of concrete reality. Everything that is, save God, depends on something not only for its being but also for its becoming. This something of whatever sort, is a cause." Henri Dominique Gardeil, *Introduction to the Philosophy of St. Thomas Aquinas: Cosmology*, trans. John A. Otto, vol. 2 (Eugene, OR: Wipf & Stock Publishers, 2009), 61. Gardeil references the words of St. Thomas Aquinas, "*causæ autem dicuntur ex quibus res dependent secundum esse suum vel fieri.*" (I *Phys*, Lect 1, No 10). He also highlights the fact that John of St. Thomas seeks even a more precise definition: "*Causa est principium alicujus per modum influxus seu dervationis, ex qua*

and *integration* for theology and science. Potency[52] must be reduced to act by that which is actually whole and thus "prior" to purely physical causes. Just as being is prior to, and inclusive of, discretely physical parts and processes, so too is metaphysical theology (the study of being as a whole) rationally prior to, and inclusive of, physics.[53]

In addition, a proper realism is particularly crucial for the interaction of the natural sciences with the theology of creation because as Pope Paul VI states,

> It is of the greatest importance to recognize that over and above what is visible, the reality of which we discern through the sciences, God has given us an intellect which can attain to that which is, not merely the subjective content of the "structures" and the developments of human consciousness.[54]

In *Evangelii Gaudium*, Francis echoes Paul VI's call for philosophical realism in light of the problems associated with nominalism and idealism.[55]

---

natum est aliquid consequi secundum dependentiam in esse." (*Cursus Philosophicus*) Causes are the basis of scientific knowledge, hence the medieval expression, attributed to Aristotle, "*scientia est cognitio per causas.*" Martin X. Moleski, *Personal Catholicism: The Theological Epistemologies of John Henry Newman and Michael Polanyi* (Washington, D.C.: CUA Press, 2000), 130.

52 Act is a perfection of a subject while potency is the capacity to have a perfection. In itself, potency is not mere privation of act, but a real capacity for perfection (metaphysical possibility). God does not have potency because it would imply imperfection. He is *esse* without essence and *actus purus*.

53 A key distinction in this area is between God's self-subsistent *esse*, which contains the non-subsistent *esse* of the world, including countless cosmic forms. Within the non-subsistent *esse*, one must distinguish between *esse commune*, which may be understood as an open principle, realizing countless forms, and *ens commune*, which may be taken to signify the complete cosmos in God.

54 Paul VI, *Solemni Hac Liturgia* (Credo of the People of God), 1968, 5, http://w2.vatican.va/content/paul-vi/la/motu_proprio/documents/hf_p-vi_motu-proprio_19680630_credo.html.

55 "Ideas—conceptual elaborations—are at the service of communication, understanding, and praxis. Ideas disconnected from realities give rise to ineffectual forms of idealism and nominalism, capable at most of classifying and defining, but certainly not calling to action. What calls us to action are realities illuminated by reason. Formal nominalism has to give way to harmonious objectivity. Otherwise, the truth is manipulated, cosmetics take the place of real care for our bodies. We have politicians—and even religious leaders—who wonder why people do not understand and follow them, since their proposals are so clear and logical. Perhaps it is because they are stuck in the realm of pure ideas and end up reducing politics or faith to rhetoric. Others have left simplicity behind and have imported a rationality foreign to most people." Francis, *Evangelii Gaudium*, 232.

In Catholic theology, creation is a basic rational axiom: God is perfect act and *ipsum esse*[56] *subsistens*,[57] who freely creates beings *ex nihilo*.[58] This doctrine ensures that beings are not "absorbed" into physical processes. By contrast, the derivation of actuality from potency, as process thought can imply, is irrational and unintelligible in principle: sheer possibility (which is unintelligible and unreal) is granted primacy over intelligible reality, which undermines order from the start.

That being said, Barbour is certainly correct that the natural sciences can enrich the Church's reflection on God, and therefore theology. In fact, Schmaus states, "that a constructive relationship exists between science and theology is implicit in the belief that God created the world."[59] For Catholics, there is indeed no final dualism: God allows "lower" causes to be real, intelligible causes. Indeed, higher, i.e., more real and actual, causes receive contributions from "lower" causes. Analogously, theology can be continually enriched through interaction with science. Pope Francis writes that "science and religion, with their distinctive approaches to understanding reality, can enter into an intense dialogue fruitful for both."[60] A Catholic reception of Barbour's approaches for dialogue and integration will certainly involve some modifications to ensure an epistemologically and metaphysically justified theology of creation. We now review some substantial academic investigations into Barbour's corpus.

3. Status Quæstionis

A number of scholars have already begun to analyze Ian Barbour's thought from the disciplinary perspectives of religious studies,[61] Protestant theology, or philosophy.

---

56 *Esse* is *actus essendi* (to be = the act of being), while essence is *potentia essendi* (potency of being). *Actus essendi* is an act that encompasses all perfections. Additionally, the act of being is different in each individual, so *esse* is given in different degrees. On the other hand, all being exist equally. For example, a person has more *esse* than a plant but they exist equally.

57 Thomas Aquinas, *Summa Theologiæ*, trans. Fathers of the English Dominican Province, 2nd ed. (London, 1920), I, Q 4, A 2.

58 John M. McDermott, SJ wisely observes that "if everything comes out of nothing, nothing can explain nothing, and existence is given as an irrational fact unless, of course, the world is a divine creation, a mystery to which human intelligence is referred." John M. McDermott, "Matter, Modern Science, and God," *Angelicum* 88, no. 2 (2011): 487.

59 Schmaus, *God and Creation: The Foundations of Christology*, 2:84.

60 Francis, *Laudato Si'*, 2015, 62.

61 Religious Studies is a distinct field from theology. Formerly called "comparative religion," this discipline claims to engage the topic of religion from a secular, "impartial" viewpoint. For further reading on some key concepts and theories from the field of religious studies, see Craig Martin, *A Critical Introduction to the Study of Religion*, 2nd ed. (New York: Routledge, 2017).

A brief review of their work is provided in this section. In 1995, at the Southern Baptist Theological Seminary, Elmer Woodson Brewer completed a doctoral dissertation entitled *The Approaches of John Polkinghorne, Arthur Peacocke, and Ian Barbour for the Integration of Natural Science and Christian Theology*.[62] Within an evangelical context, Brewer explores the approaches of the three aforementioned theologians in bringing theology and science into a relationship that is mutually beneficial. In his fourth chapter, he analyzes Barbour's use of process philosophy as a basis for integration. Brewer observes that "Barbour's utilization of process thought has significant difficulties."[63]

Brewer points out that certain aspects of process thought actually exacerbate the divisions between theology and science. For example, the principle of panpsychism[64] is extremely difficult for scientists to accept. Additionally, few Christian theologians would accede to the revisions of the doctrine of God required by process thought. At the end of the dissertation, Brewer compares and contrasts the integrative approaches of Polkinghorne, Peacocke, and Barbour. He concludes that similarities among them provided a credible basis for the integration of science and theology but that no individual approach is clearly superior.

That same year, Walter Reagan White Jr. finished a PhD dissertation in the philosophy of religion at Southwestern Baptist Theological Seminary entitled *The Integration of Science and Religion: Implications of Process Thought's Dependence on the New Physics*.[65] This project examines the process metaphysics developed by Alfred North Whitehead, a major influence on Ian Barbour. White summarizes Ian Barbour's four ways of relating science and religion before explicating how process philosophy exemplifies Barbour's *systematic synthesis* approach, which seeks to unify theology and science within a comprehensive conceptual scheme.

Ultimately, White concludes that the viability of process metaphysics is in question given what he sees as fundamental conflicts with modern science deriving

---

62 Elmer Woodson Brewer, "The Approaches of John Polkinghorne, Arthur Peacocke, and Ian Barbour for the Integration of Natural Science and Christian Theology" (PhD, The Southern Baptist Theological Seminary, 1995), accessed October 10, 2017, https://search.proquest.com/dissertations/docview/304218674/abstract/D0BD7AB8396D4439PQ/1.

63 Ibid., 192.

64 Panpsychism is the belief that everything material, however small, has an element of individual consciousness. It is posited as an alternative to materialism (which denies mental reality) and "dualism." See Godehard Brüntrup and Ludwig Jaskolla, eds., *Panpsychism: Contemporary Perspectives*, Philosophy of Mind (New York: Oxford University Press, 2016).

65 Walter Reagan White, "The Integration of Science and Religion: Implications of Process Thought's Dependence on the New Physics" (PhD, Southwestern Baptist Theological Seminary, 1995), accessed October 10, 2017, https://search.proquest.com/dissertations/docview/304245028/abstract/CDD323051D654D77PQ/4.

from relativity and quantum mechanics. He recommends that process thinkers acknowledge the highly changeable nature of science, and therefore avoid using the science of any era too strictly in developing a metaphysics. Ian Barbour's *dialogue* approach, which encourages theology and science to inform one another by exploring the indirect interactions between the two disciplines, is suggested as a promising approach for relating science and a process metaphysics.

The 1997 doctoral dissertation of Stanley Brian Stratton at Princeton Theology Seminary (Presbyterian Church USA), *Coherence, Consonance, and Conversation: The Interaction of Theology and Natural Science in the Quest for a Unified World-View*,[66] examines a variety of approaches to the positive interaction of theology and the natural sciences. Stratton's analysis concludes that Barbour has many helpful insights especially in using informal criteria to evaluate theology and science, but that his overall quest is not successful. He prefers the approach of Thomas Torrance, a Church of Scotland minister and Reformed theologian who studied under Karl Barth in Basel, Switzerland. Stratton supports the methodology of Torrance which posits that "a harmonization of theology and science [can] take place at certain 'boundary points' where contingent reality points to the transcendent reality of God."[67]

In 2000, Bernard Jerold Angelo defended a dissertation entitled *Conceptual Frameworks: Their Uses and Potential Abuses*,[68] for a PhD in philosophy at the historically Methodist-Episcopal school, Syracuse University. Angelo conducts an analysis of the notion of conceptual frameworks and their use to resolve particular philosophical problems. In the context of this research, Angelo examines Barbour's use of the terms "myth," "model," "metaphor," and "paradigm" from a philosophical perspective. He concludes that "framework thinking" is as philosophically useful as it is potentially problematic. He believes that despite the diversity of frameworks, a unified theory of reality is still a possibility.

A Philosophical Framework within the Science-Theology Dialogue: A Critical Reflection on the Work of Ernan McMullin, completed in 2001 at the University of Ottawa by Paul Allen, examines the philosophical work of the Irish-American philosopher of science and priest, Ernan McMullin. Allen asserts that McMullin's

66   Stanley Brian Stratton, "Coherence, Consonance, and Conversation: The Interaction of Theology and Natural Science in the Quest for a Unified World-View" (PhD, Princeton Theological Seminary, 1997), accessed October 10, 2017, https://search.proquest.com/dissertations/docview/304371222/abstract/CDD323051D654D77PQ/3.

67   Ibid., 6.

68   Bernard Jerold Angelo, "Conceptual Frameworks: Their Uses and Potential Abuses" (PhD, Syracuse University, 2000), accessed October 10, 2017, https://search.proquest.com/dissertations/docview/304649084/astract/CDD323051D654D77PQ/2.

use of critical realism, which is distinct from Barbour's in some important ways, strongly supports the claim that scientific rationality is broadly consistent with and even supportive of theological knowledge claims about God and creation. Allen found much utility in McMullin's theory of retroduction (an alternative to Charles Peirce's theory of abduction, i.e., inference to the "best explanation"). In particular, Allen suggests that McMullin's theory can form the basis for an integrated, critical realist theory of knowledge in the natural sciences.

The German Lutheran theologian and pastor, Hans Schwarz,[69] points out that "in the Anglo-Saxon world there are considerably more theologians dealing with issues of the natural sciences than in the continental world."[70] His fellow Lutheran, Christian Berg, is an exception.[71] Berg produced a dissertation at Heidelberg University which was published in 2002 as *Theologie im technologischen Zeitalter: Das Werk Ian Barbours als Beitrag zu Verhältnisbestimmung von Theologie zu Naturwissenschaft und Technik.*[72] Berg carries out an analysis of Barbour's four-fold typology and then investigates three dimensions of the relationship between science and religion: epistemological and methodological issues, metaphysical issues, and ethical ones.

Berg takes a more critical approach than most commentators of Barbour. He acknowledges Barbour's status as a premier scholar in the space of theology and science in the Anglophonic world, but argues that Barbour's concepts and views often seem inaccurate, that his treatment of certain topics can be superficial, and that his proposed solutions are unsustainable. Berg claims that Barbour's scholarship places a one-sided emphasis on the similarities between science and theology,

69   Like Barbour, Schwarz is very interested in the doctrine of creation. He explores this essential element of Christian faith from Biblical, historical, and scientific perspectives. Schwarz argues that true dialogue between Christianity and the natural sciences provides the fullest and most meaningful picture of the universe. See Hans Schwarz, *Creation* (Grand Rapids, MI: Eerdmans, 2002).

70   Hans Schwarz, *Vying for Truth—Theology and the Natural Sciences: From the 17th Century to the Present* (Göttingen: Vandehoeck & Ruprecht, 2014), 172.

71   Another significant, early twentieth century German scholar in theology and science was Karl Heim (1874–1958). Heim was a professor of dogmatics at Münster and Tübingen. Ian Barbour acknowledges that Heim has been referred to as the "dean of German Protestant theologians." Barbour judges Heim's major contribution concerning "thinking in spaces" to be an "illuminating insight." Ian G. Barbour, "Karl Heim on Christian Faith and Natural Science," *The Christian Scholar* 39, no. 3 (1956): 229. Heim's concept of "space" is always a relational term involving subject and object. Following Kant, he asserts that "space is not an *ens*, a being, a reality, a 'thing in itself.' It is … a relation into which a reality enters with respect to me, the percipient subject." Karl Heim, *Christian Faith and Natural Science* (New York: Harper & Brothers, 1953), 163.

72   Christian Berg, *Theologie Im Technologischen Zeitalter: Das Werk Ian Barbours Als Beitrag Zu Verhältnisbestimmung Zu Theologie Zu Naturwissenschaft Und Technik* (Stuttgart: Kohlhammer, 2002).

while the differences are neglected. Berg believes that in Barbour's approach, theology is overly subjected to the axioms of natural science at the expense of its own foundations.

Sandra B. Auld wrote an MA thesis at the University of Guelph, Canada, in 2002 entitled *Barbour, Whitehead, and Bohm: Can Process Philosophy Reveal a Metaphysical Basis for Both Religion and Science?*[73] Auld investigates pertinent aspects of Alfred North Whitehead's process philosophy which Barbour utilizes to develop a common metaphysical basis for the engagement of religion and science. She draws on David Bohm's application of the concepts of process philosophy to quantum physics to clarify applications of process thought in the philosophy of science. Auld is at times quite critical of Barbour, e.g., asserting that a large part of the difficulty of his discussing the interaction between religion and science is exemplified by his lack of definitional precision.[74] She concludes that while process philosophy can provide a metaphysical foundation for *some* religions and *some* philosophies of science, it cannot provide a basis for all.

In 2007, Raymond K. Meyer defended the dissertation, *An Evangelical Analysis of the Critical Realism and Corollary Hermeneutics of Bernard Lonergan with Application for Evangelical Hermeneutics*,[75] at Southeastern Baptist Theological Seminary. Meyer's quest into various forms of critical realism is oriented toward discovering a suitable *via media* between modernity and postmodernity as well as between objectivity and subjectivity. Meyer is primarily interested in the thought of the Canadian Jesuit philosopher and theologian, Bernard Lonergan. Specifically, he is interested in

> Lonergan's notions of authentic subjectivity and genuine objectivity, his understanding of the "dynamic interdependence and unity" of theological and hermeneutical method, his understanding of understanding itself, and his suggestions related to epistemological foundations, which is a foundation based on human interiority.[76]

---

73 Sandra B. Auld, "Barbour, Whitehead, and Bohm: Can Process Philosophy Reveal a Metaphysical Basis for Both Religion and Science?" (MA, University of Guelph (Canada), 2002), accessed October 10, 2017, https://search.proquest.com/dissertations/docview/305582962/abstract/CDD323051D654D77PQ/5.

74 Ibid., 4–5.

75 Raymond K. Meyer, "An Evangelical Analysis of the Critical Realism and Corollary Hermeneutics of Bernard Lonergan with Application for Evangelical Hermeneutics" (PhD, Southeastern Baptist Theological Seminary, 2007), accessed October 10, 2017, https://search.proquest.com/dissertations/docview/304719979/abstract/CDD323051D654D77PQ/7.

76 Ibid, *xi.*

However, Meyer does briefly explore the work of Roy Bhaskar, Alister McGrath, Ian Barbour, and others who suggest critical realism as a bridge between theology and science. For example, in relating Bhaskar and Barbour, Meyer writes,

> The multi-layered reality of both Bhaskar and Barbour provides a spectrum of being and a spectrum of investigation for science, theology and all other areas of human inquiry. Each level of reality is equally grounded in *being*, each level of inquiry equally seeks to describe this *being* using human terms and symbols.[77]

Robert Kevin Bolger's dissertation in the field of religious studies, *Kneeling at the Altar of Science: Miscues and Mishaps in the Contemporary Dialogue between Science and Religion*,[78] was completed in 2009 at the private, unaffiliated Claremont Graduate University. Bolger's research engages the issue of "religious scientism," i.e., attempting to improve the "legitimacy" of religion by making it look more scientific. Bolger asserts that greater confusion results when one attempts, as Ian Barbour does, to suggest religious models with some sort of parity with scientific models. Bolger argues that it is more desirable to find a form of religious language that does not rely in any way on the principles, methods, or philosophy of science.

Anne M. Clifford, CSJ briefly examines aspects of Barbour's thought as they relate to Catholicism in a 2004 book chapter published in a *Festschrift* dedicated to Barbour.[79] This essay was later republished in 2017 in a special edition of the journal *Theology and Science*.[80] In ten pages, she presents elements of Barbour's writings as they relate to the Galileo affair, Saint John Paul II's positive interventions in the theology-science interaction, and Barbour's theological anthropology as it relates to Catholic interpretations of the theory of evolution. Clifford's article is a helpful start to a Catholic evaluation of Ian Barbour's theology but much work remains.

---

77 Ibid., 99.

78 Robert Kevin Bolger, "Kneeling at the Altar of Science: Miscues and Mishaps in the Contemporary Dialogue between Science and Religion" (PhD, The Claremont Graduate University, 2009), accessed October 10, 2017, https://search.proquest.com/dissertations/docview/304863534/abstract/CDD323051D654D77PQ/6.

79 Anne M. Clifford, "Catholicism and Ian Barbour on Theology and Science," in *Fifty Years in Science and Religion: Ian G. Barbour and His Legacy*, ed. Robert John Russell, Ashgate Science and Religion Series (Burlington, VT: Ashgate Publishing, 2004), 287–300.

80 Anne M. Clifford, "Catholicism and Ian Barbour on Theology and Science," *Theology and Science* 15, no. 1 (January 2, 2017): 88–100.

4. Novitas

This monograph offers a much more in-depth, Catholic investigation of Barbour's thought. We evaluate Barbour's work according to fundamental Catholic theological criteria.[81] A major concern of fundamental theology is the relationship between faith and reason.[82] *Fides quarens intellectum* requires philosophically appropriate foundations, especially in the areas of epistemology and metaphysics. Catholic theology is intimately connected with foundational philosophical concepts, e.g., God as *ipsum esse subsistens*, Jesus as incarnate λόγος (*lógos*)—ὁμοούσιος τῷ Πατρί (*homooúsios tô Patrí*): Divine Word—consubstantial with the Father, and God the Creator as the origin of creation's *actus essendi*. It is established upon a rigorous philosophical realism that acknowledges that the simple actuality of being precedes the knowing of any particular human subject. This realism also supports the *certitudo fidei* and affirms the ability to come to know truth.

The American theologian and priest, Thomas G. Guarino, points out in *Foundations of Systematic Theology* that Catholic fundamental "theology requires certain theoretical exigencies in order to give its doctrinal claims architectonic structure and logical intelligibility."[83] He argues convincingly that

> some kind of metaphysical horizon, some first philosophy, is essential if the character-
> istics attributed to Christian doctrine by both the universal church and a wide range of
> individual theologians—such as its universality, continuity, and material identity—are
> not simply asserted, without philosophical support.[84]

In this light, we thoroughly evaluate Barbour's Whiteheadian process thought. Its implications for the doctrine of God the Creator, the creation of man, the problem of panentheism, and the perfection of God are given particular focus. It will be shown that a metaphysically justified doctrine of God and creation relies on a metaphysical notion of causality and certain ontological concepts, e.g., substance and essence.

---

81 The Australian theologian, Tracey Rowland, notes that "'fundamental theology' is called 'fundamental' because without it one's scholarship is rudderless." Tracey Rowland, *Catholic Theology*, Doing Theology (New York: T&T Clark, 2017), 29.

82 See Salvador Pié-Ninot, *La Teologia Fondamentale*, trans. Pietro Crespi, 3rd ed., Biblioteca di Teologia Contemporanea 121 (Brescia: Queriniana, 2007), 46–59.

83 Thomas Guarino, *Foundations of Systematic Theology* (New York: T&T Clark, 2005), 58.

84 Ibid.

Fundamental theology is also concerned with the Word of God, written and transmitted in the Church.[85] Related to this, it is interested in the notion of religious experience, its relationship to revelation, its interpretation, and its role in theological inquiry.[86] In addition, fundamental theology explores the use of paradigms, analogy, and models. Analogy enjoys a place of particular importance, given its role in the faith-reason interaction; it is a point of contact between natural and supernatural revelation, and therefore influences discourse on the Divine.[87] The foundational concept of *obœdientia fidei* is essential as well. We evaluate Barbour in all these areas.

Throughout this research, substantial reference is made to Saint Thomas Aquinas, as a Catholic "monument" to the doctrine of creation in particular,[88] and more generally, the beneficial interaction of natural philosophy, metaphysics, and revealed theology. At times we cite Aquinas *in extenso* as his eloquence and articulacy is beyond compare in this area. By judging Barbour's work according to the aforementioned fundamental criteria of Catholic theology, we intend to show the ramifications of his approach. Of particular interest is the possibility for his philosophical foundations and theological methodology to enrich *dialogue* and *integration* between the Catholic doctrine of creation and the natural sciences. Throughout this book, we intend to answer questions such as: How can Barbour help Catholics relate the doctrine of creation to the natural sciences? Where are his ideas problematic? How can these problems nevertheless unveil something of the truth? Barbour will not likely be affecting the development of doctrine, but can he aid in deepening our understanding of doctrine?

---

85 See Donath Hercsik, *Elementi di teologia fondamentale: Concetti, contenuti, metodi* (Bologna: EDB, 2006), chap. 1.

86 See Gerald O'Collins, *Rethinking Fundamental Theology* (Oxford: Oxford University Press, 2013), 52–55.

87 See Lawrence Feingold, *Faith Comes from What Is Heard: An Introduction to Fundamental Theology* (Steubenville, OH: Emmaus Academic, 2016), 136.

88 Joseph Ratzinger shows how Saint Thomas' theology of creation is a "complete transformation of Aristotelianism." Ratzinger writes, "Being referred to God, to truth himself, is not, for man, some optional pleasurable diversion for the intellect ... relationship to God can be seen to express the core of his very essence ... it constitutes what is deepest in man's being ... [this relation] is not a product of human achievement. It is given to man; man depends for it on Another. But it is given to man to be his very own possession. That is what is meant by creation, and what Thomas means when he says that immortality belongs to man by nature. The constant background here is Thomas' theology of creation: nature is only possible by virtue of a communication of the Creator's, yet such communication both establishes the creature in its own right and makes it a genuine participator in the being of the One communicated." Joseph Ratzinger, *Eschatology: Death and Eternal Life*, trans. Michael Waldstein, 2nd ed. (Washington, DC: The

5. Structure

The next section of this chapter offers a *précis* of significant biographical information. Subsequently, we present an overview of Barbour's early work as a physicist. Chapter One continues with a presentation of Barbour's four-fold typology for the interaction of theology and science: *conflict, independence, dialogue,* and *integration.* Finally, we describe his influence on some other prominent scholars in the field of theology and science who both further develop his thought at certain points, and in other areas take a contrasting approach.

In Chapter Two, we examine the personal, philosophical, and theological influences that played a substantial role in the development of Barbour's approach to relating theology and science. We identify and explicate Barbour's fundamental axioms and insights. His epistemology (critical realism) and metaphysics (process thought) are creative proposals for the theology-science interaction, so they must be presented clearly and fairly. Barbour's motivations for, and applications of, these philosophies are made manifest.

Chapter Three describes similarities and differences between theology and science according to Barbour. This analysis begins by examining approaches taken in scientific materialism, fundamentalism, neo-orthodoxy, existentialist philosophy, and linguistic analysis that Barbour characterizes as emphasizing *contrasting* perspectives on science and theology. Next, we present approaches that Barbour finds helpful in relating theology and science. Neo-Thomism, mainline Protestant liberal theology, and process thought emphasize conceptual and methodological *parallels* according to Barbour. After that, we explicate Barbour's perspectives on theological and scientific experience and interpretation, the role of religious and scientific communities in paradigm formation, the use of analogy and models in theological and scientific language, and some criteria for evaluating religious beliefs and scientific theories. Similarities between theology and science according to Barbour with regard to data, coherence, and comprehensiveness, as well as differences on the influence of interpretation on experience, criteria of evaluation, and intersubjective testability are also explored.

Chapter Four is dedicated to a thorough evaluation of Barbour's epistemological, metaphysical, and theological principles. This assessment begins with an analysis of Barbour's critical realism in relation to other significant forms of critical realism, as well as "non-critical" realisms utilized in relating Catholic theology and the empirical sciences, e.g., the Hungarian-American priest and philosopher

Catholic University of America Press, 2007), 154–155. On the related and fascinating issue of grace and nature, on which so much has been written, the reader is referred to Nicholas J. Healy, "Henri de Lubac on Nature and Grace: A Note on Some Recent Contributions to the Debate," *Communio* 35, no. 4 (2008): 535–564.

of science, Stanley Jaki, OSB's, moderate (methodical) realism.[89] Next, it is necessary to evaluate Barbour's use of Whiteheadian process metaphysics. Barbour developed these philosophical foundations because he saw them as appropriate for use in the natural sciences as well as theology, and therefore helpful for a fruitful interaction of the two disciplines.

While "the [Catholic] Church has no philosophy of her own nor does she canonize any one particular philosophy in preference to others,"[90] theologians must embark on a journey of discernment around the appropriateness of a particular philosophy for use in Catholic theology. A Catholic theologian should ensure that a philosophy brought to bear in theology is indeed compatible with the Catholic faith and has the possibility of offering "an ever deeper understanding of the Word of God found in the inspired Scriptures and handed on by the living Tradition of the Church."[91] Chapter Four will also critically engage issues that were introduced in Chapter Three such as the role of experience in theology, the notion of paradigms in theology, and the role of analogy. Throughout the chapter, Barbour's positions on key issues in fundamental theology are analyzed.

Based on the evaluation of Barbour's thought offered in Chapter Four, Chapter Five investigates where and how Barbour's approach can facilitate dialogue and integration between the Catholic doctrine of creation and the natural sciences. According to the interaction typology of *dialogue*, we explore two issues: presuppositions and limit questions in theology and science as well as methodological and conceptual parallels. Within the *integration* typology, we investigate the role of natural theology, Barbour's notion of a theology of nature, and the possibility of a systematic synthesis of theology and science through a common metaphysics.

This final chapter also offers some conclusions in the form of summations of the positive and negative aspects of Barbour's thought from the perspective of the Catholic tradition, i.e., where he makes a real contribution as well as where his approach is not helpful. An aspect of this is where Barbour was a "prophet," and where he failed to see difficulties. We then close the monograph by describing possible paths for future Barbour studies. The principal contribution of this book is an evaluation of the implications of Barbour's insights for the Catholic doctrine

---

89 For an analysis of Jaki's scholarly contributions, see Paul Haffner, *Creation and Scientific Creativity: A Study in the Thought of S. L. Jaki*, 2nd ed. (Leominster, UK: Gracewing Publishing, 2009); Paul Haffner, *The Tiara and the Test Tube: The Popes and Science from the Medieval Period to the Present* (Leominster, UK: Gracewing Publishing, 2014), 5–41.

90 John Paul II, *Fides et Ratio*, 49.

91 Congregation for the Doctrine of the Faith, *Donum Veritatis*, 1990, 6.

of creation's interaction with the natural sciences. In the next section, we present relevant biographical details of our scholarly subject.

6. Biography

Ian Graeme Barbour was born on October 5, 1923 in Peking (now Beijing), China to George Brown and Dorothy (née Dickinson) Barbour. The Barbours were Protestant lay missionaries. George was a Scottish Presbyterian and Dorothy was an American Episcopalian. George Brown had accepted a faculty position in the Department of Geology at Yenching University and Dorothy served in the Department of Religious Education. Yenching University was a Protestant institution of higher education created through the merger of four small Christian colleges between 1915 and 1920.[92]

Interestingly, both George Brown's and Dorothy's fathers, Alexander Hugh Freeland Barbour and Robert Latou Dickinson, were physicians specializing in obstetrics and gynecology. The two families met in Dr. Barbour's hometown of Edinburgh, Scotland.[93] Dorothy's father, Dr. Dickinson, was born in Jersey City, New Jersey, USA.[94]

Ian's father, George Brown, was a friend and professional colleague of the French paleontologist and geologist, Pierre Teilhard de Chardin, SJ. The two worked together on the team that discovered the skull of "Peking Man" (*Homo erectus pekinensis*). Subsequent scientific dating sets the age of this particular *homo erectus* to between 680,000 and 780,000 years old.[95] George Brown and Father Teilhard enjoyed a close friendship and were intimate collaborators in research. Over four decades of correspondence between George Brown and Teilhard have been published in a book edited by George Brown.[96]

In 1931, the Barbour family left China due to the poor health of Ian's older brother, Hugh. Hugh made a good recovery and eventually would take a similar career path as Ian, becoming professor of religion at Earlham College, a Quaker school in Richmond, Indiana. Ian's father, George, was able to find term-hire faculty

92 Philip West, *Yenching University and Sino-Western Relations, 1916–1952* (Harvard University Press, 1976), 34–39.
93 Ian G. Barbour, "A Personal Odyssey," *Theology and Science* 15, no. 1 (January 2, 2017): 5.
94 "Dickinson, Robert Latou, 1861–1950," *Harvard University Library: Online Archival Search Information System*, accessed November 14, 2017, http://oasis.lib.harvard.edu/oasis/deliver/~med00073.
95 Guanjun Shen et al., "Age of Zhoukoudian Homo Erectus Determined with 26Al/10Be Burial Dating," *Nature* 458, no. 7235 (March 12, 2009): 198–200.
96 George B. Barbour, *In the Field with Teilhard de Chardin* (New York: Herder, 1965).

positions and support his family through the Great Depression. Unfortunately, these job opportunities required a great deal of moving, e.g., living in Pasadena, Cincinnati, New York, and London.

While living in England, Ian attended a prestigious Quaker boarding school for three years. There, he had the opportunity to study poetry under the famous English-American poet, Wystan Hugh Auden. Barbour continued his secondary education at the prestigious Deerfield Academy in Massachusetts, USA.[97] On Sundays, he enjoyed listening to the radio sermons of the New York multi-denominational Protestant pastor, Harry Emerson Fosdick,[98] well-known for his role in the "Fundamentalist-Modernist Controversy" within American Protestantism at that time.[99]

Ian Barbour began his undergraduate career at Swarthmore College in 1940 as an engineering student. His emerging interests, both theoretical and experimental, led him to switch to the Department of Physics. Barbour earned his Bachelor of Science degree in three years and in light of the Second World War, he attempted to enlist in the American Field Service Ambulance Corps. Unfortunately, his British citizenship excluded him from that American service opportunity. Influenced by a summer work experience during college with the Quakers, Barbour registered as a conscientious objector and joined the Civilian Public Service (CPS) program.[100] His experiences in the CPS ranged from serving as a fire fighter in Oregon to caring for the mentally ill in North Carolina.[101]

The assignment to North Carolina was particularly beneficial for Barbour. He enrolled in Duke University and earned a Master of Science degree in Physics in 1946. Barbour also met an undergraduate in the Department of Religion named Deane Kern, originally from Washington, DC. They fell in love and married in 1947.[102] The Barbours then moved to Illinois where Ian began doctoral work at the

97 Deerfield Academy is one of the oldest secondary schools in the United States, founded in 1797. See Robert K. Moorhead, *Deerfield 1797–1997: A Pictorial History of the Academy* (Deerfield, MA: Deerfield Academy Press, 1997).

98 Pastor Fosdick served at Baptist, Presbyterian, and non-denominational churches throughout his ministerial career. See Robert Moats Miller, *Harry Emerson Fosdick: Preacher, Pastor, Prophet* (New York: Oxford University Press, 1985).

99 Barbour, "A Personal Odyssey," 5.

100 For more information on the CPS program, see John M. Dyck, *Faith under Test: Alternative Service during World War II in the U.S. and Canada* (Gospel Publishers, 1997).

101 Barbour, "A Personal Odyssey," 6.

102 William Yardley, "Ian Barbour, Who Found a Balance between Faith and Science, Dies at 90," *The New York Times*, January 12, 2014, sec. U.S., accessed November 14, 2017, https://www.nytimes.com/2014/01/13/us/ian-barbour-academic-who-resisted-conflicts-of-faith-and-science-dies-at-90.html.

University of Chicago and Deane pursued graduate studies at Chicago Theological Seminary. Ian had the good fortune of receiving a teaching assistantship under the celebrated Italian-American nuclear physicist, Enrico Fermi, the creator of the world's first nuclear reactor. Barbour's course on Quantum Mechanics was offered by the renowned Hungarian-American physicist, Edward Teller. Barbour's own research focused on the use of photographic emulsions to study cosmic-ray mesons. His experimental apparatus included a 70-pound magnet which was brought to high altitude by a helium-filled balloon in order to deflect mesons.[103]

In the summer of 1948, Ian and Deane volunteered as camp counselors for a Congregationalist young adult apostolate to clear rubble from bombed out German cities. The Barbours supervised students from Holland, the USA, and Germany. This experience had a profound impact on Ian. Years later, he wrote, "The presence of the Dutch students was impressive, since many of them had had close relatives imprisoned or killed during the Nazi occupation, and the German students included former soldiers and even a former SS officer."[104]

On August 29, 1949, the Soviet Union detonated its first atomic bomb (American Code Name Joe-1). US President Harry S. Truman responded with the announcement of a research project to develop a hydrogen bomb to maintain American military superiority. This led Barbour's teacher, Edward Teller, to return to Los Alamos National Laboratory where he would eventually earn the title "Father of the H-bomb."[105] Teller was eager to recruit many of his former students, but Barbour had no interest in weapon research. Barbour's hope was to find a physics faculty position in a liberal arts college. He succeeded, and was appointed assistant professor of physics at Kalamazoo College in Michigan.[106]

Barbour flourished during his short time at Kalamazoo. He received external grant funding to continue his cosmic ray research and was named the chairman of the Physics Department. Ian and Deane welcomed their first two children: John and Blair during this period. The couple was also very involved in an inter-denominational campus ministry program serving Kalamazoo College, Western Michigan University, and Bronson School of Nursing, under the pastoral leadership of the Presbyterian minister, John Duley. Of Pastor Duley, Barbour writes, "[He] helped us to seek the meaning of Christian community in an academic context."[107] Duley was very involved in the peace and justice movements of the

---

103 Barbour, "A Personal Odyssey," 6.

104 Ibid.

105 Gregg Herken, *Brotherhood of the Bomb: The Tangled Lives and Loyalties of Robert Oppenheimer, Ernest Lawrence and Edward Teller* (New York: Henry Holt and Co., 2002), 201–210.

106 Barbour, "A Personal Odyssey," 6.

107 Ibid.

mid-twentieth century. He was a collaborator with Martin Luther King, Jr. in promoting racial equality in the United States.[108]

In 1953, a Ford Foundation Fellowship enabled Barbour to apply to Yale Divinity School to pursue a formal theological education. He enjoyed his classes so much that he extended his leave from Kalamazoo College an additional year. With supplementary course work taken over two summers at Union Theological Seminary in New York, Barbour earned the Bachelor of Divinity degree.[109] Ian Barbour's opportunity for a theological education forced him to engage in some soul searching. During his second year at Yale, he began to discern his next career move in academia. Should he return to Kalamazoo to teach physics or start off on a new path more directly related to theology? Barbour even wrote a paper for a class taught by Helmut Richard Niebuhr on this process entitled "A Vocational Decision."[110] He ended up accepting a job offer that supported both his scientific and religious interests. Barbour was given a joint appointment in the Departments of Physics and Philosophy at Carleton College in Northfield, Minnesota.

When the Barbour family moved to Northfield in 1956, they quickly found a spiritual home in what was then the local Congregational Church,[111] which soon joined the United Church of Christ (UCC).[112] Ian and Deane were both regular worshipers at the UCC and all four of their children were confirmed there. Ian's son, John, a professor of religion at St. Olaf College, who is still a member of the church, describes their community this way: "This church has had a succession of

---

108 Dawn Parker, "Lansing-Area Men Played Key Role in Civil Rights Movement," *Lansing State Journal*, March 2, 2015, accessed November 14, 2017, http://www.lansingstatejournal.com/story/news/local/2015/03/02/okemos-man-recalls-civil-rights-work/24253241/.

109 The degree of Bachelor of Divinity (BDiv) was first conferred by Yale Divinity School in 1867. In June 1971, it was replaced by the Master of Divinity (MDiv) degree in common use today as the first graduate professional degree in ministry. See "Mission & History | Yale Divinity School," accessed October 5, 2017, http://divinity.yale.eduabout-yds/mission-history. The BDiv/MDiv degrees are analogous to the first ecclesiastical graduate degree, the *Sacrae Theologiae Baccalaureus* (STB), conferred by Pontifical faculties.

110 John Barbour, "The Life of Ian Barbour: An Interview with His Son, John," interview by Joseph R. Laracy, Email, November 14, 2017.

111 The Congregational churches in North America were constituted when the Puritan Pilgrims of Plymouth Plantation (1620) and the Puritans of the Massachusetts Bay Colony (1629) arrived in the New World. See Joseph Dillaway Sawyer, *History of the Pilgrims and Puritans: Their Ancestry and Descendants; Basis of Americanization*, 3 vols. (New York: Century History Company, 1922); James Fenimore Cooper, *Tenacious of Their Liberties: The Congregationalists in Colonial Massachusetts* (Oxford: Oxford University Press, 2002).

112 The UCC was formed when the Evangelical and Reformed Church and the General Council of the Congregational Christian Churches merged in 1957. See Johnson and Hambrick-Stowe, *Theology and Identity*, 44.

very lively and thoughtful ministers, and a very strong commitment to social justice activities of various kinds."[113] The church's current pastor, Todd Lippert, said
of Ian: "He was a humble, remarkable man, deeply formed in the best ways the
church can shape a person's life."[114]

John Barbour sheds further light on the personal, religious life of Ian:

> My parents were also involved with the Quakers, and often participated in that style
> of worship when they were traveling. Ian had gone to Swarthmore College (with
> Quaker roots) and had known many Friends when he was doing alternative service as
> a conscientious objector during WWII. Deane had worked for the American Friends
> Service Committee after she graduated from college. They were great advocates of
> work camps, especially those organized by the Friends. Ian's older brother Hugh was
> also a professor of religion at Earlham College (another Quaker institution) and an
> eminent historian of the Quakers. And there were other connections. Ian and Deane
> went on many spiritual retreats at a variety of places, including some Catholic centers
> in the Twin Cities. Especially dear to them was Iona Abbey in Scotland, where they
> several times spent a week. I think the wild natural setting and Celtic theme of God's
> presence in nature appealed a lot to Ian.[115]

The early years at Carleton were extremely busy for Ian, and in "A Personal
Odyssey," he expresses regret that he did not spend more time with his family, especially his two youngest children, David and Heather. The situation became more
manageable in 1960 when Carleton College created a free-standing Department
of Religion. Ian left the Departments of Physics and Philosophy, and assumed the
chair of the new Religion Department. This move allowed him to focus his scholarly efforts, while still supporting interdisciplinary work.[116]

In 1961, Harold K. Schilling, professor of physics and dean of the Graduate
School at Pennsylvania State University, invited Barbour to join a study group
of scientists, philosophers, and theologians. The group met two weekends a year
for about ten years. It was in the context of this group that Daniel Day Williams
introduced Barbour to process theology. Upon receiving a fellowship to do research at Harvard University in 1963, Barbour attended a seminar on the English
mathematician and philosopher, Alfred North Whitehead. It was offered by the
Mennonite minister and professor of divinity, Gordon D. Kaufman. This experience prompted a personal quest into process thought and Barbour began to read

113 Barbour, "The Life of Ian Barbour: An Interview with His Son, John."
114 Todd Lippert, "Interview of Ian Barbour's Pastor, Rev. Todd Lippert," interview by Joseph
R. Laracy, Email, October 31, 2017.
115 Barbour, "The Life of Ian Barbour: An Interview with His Son, John."
116 Barbour, "A Personal Odyssey," 7.

extensively the works of process philosophers and theologians such as Charles Hartshorne, John B. Cobb, and David Ray Griffin.[117]

When Barbour returned to Carleton College, he began to further synthesize and implement his approach to science and religion in the classroom. Revised versions of his lectures led to the publication of perhaps his most famous book, *Issues in Science and Religion*, in 1966.[118] This important work may be justly designated as the nonpareil of its kind in the Protestant world. In the coming years, Barbour would receive Guggenheim and Fulbright Fellowships that enabled him to move with his family to Cambridge, England and further explore his scholarly interests. This research led to the 1973 book, *Myths, Models, and Paradigms*.[119] Upon returning to Carleton College, Barbour began to explore more intentionally his interests in ethics and science. He and a colleague in the Department of Political Science secured grant funding from the National Science Foundation and the National Endowment for the Humanities to develop an interdisciplinary undergraduate program in Science, Technology, and Public Policy (STPP).[120]

Barbour then split his time teaching in the Department of Religion and the new STPP program. Once again, he further developed his class lectures into a book and published *Technology, Environment, and Human Values* in 1980.[121] Carleton then honored Barbour with an endowed chair, the Winifred and Atherton Bean Professor of Science, Technology, and Society. Barbour's next stops were as a visiting professor at Purdue University in West Lafayette, Indiana and as a visiting scholar at the National Humanities Center in North Carolina. It was at the later location that he co-authored the book *Energy and American Values*.[122] He eventually took emeritus status at Carleton in 1986.

Barbour received an invitation to give the Gifford Lectures during the years 1989–1991, one of the most prestigious honors in Scottish academia. He saw this as an opportunity to bring together his theological and ethical interests. According to the will of the nineteenth century Scottish advocate and judge, Adam Lord Gifford, the lecture series is offered annually at one of four prominent Scottish universities: the University of Saint Andrews, the University of Glasgow, the University of Aberdeen, or the University of Edinburgh. The lecture series was

---

117 Ibid.

118 Ian G. Barbour, *Issues in Science and Religion* (Upper Saddle River, NJ: Prentice-Hall, 1966).

119 Ian G. Barbour, *Myths, Models, and Paradigms* (New York: HarperCollins College Division, 1974).

120 Barbour, "A Personal Odyssey," 7–8.

121 Ian G. Barbour, *Technology, Environment, and Human Values* (New York: Praeger, 1980).

122 Ian G. Barbour, Sanford Lakoff, and John Opie, *Energy and American Values* (New York: Praeger, 1982).

established to "promote and diffuse the study of natural theology in the widest sense of the term—in other words, the knowledge of God."[123]

Barbour's lectures were not the first to make a major contribution to the study of the relationship between theology and science. For example, Stanley L. Jaki, OSB's celebrated lectures from 1974 to 1976 were published as *The Road of Science and the Ways to God*.[124] Barbour's first lecture series led to the book *Religion in An Age of Science*.[125] This work investigates the impact of science and its relationship to religious life. Great attention is paid to the compatibility of theology and science.

The second lecture series was published as *Ethics in An Age of Technology*.[126] It explores the ethical implications of modern engineering accomplishments, reflecting on the value of these achievements in relation to potential environmental and human detriments. *Religion in an Age of Science* would later be revised, expanded, and re-released under the title: *Religion and Science: Historical and Contemporary Issues* in 1997.[127]

After the Gifford Lectures, Barbour's interests shifted toward the relationship of theological anthropology with genetics, evolutionary theory, artificial intelligence, and robotics.[128] In 1999, Barbour received the Templeton Prize for Progress in Religion. Established in 1972 by American-born British investment fund manager, Sir John Templeton, "the Templeton Prize honors a living person who has made an exceptional contribution to affirming life's spiritual dimension, whether through insight, discovery, or practical works."[129]

In the statement nominating Barbour for the award, John B. Cobb, then emeritus professor at the School of Theology at Claremont College in California and founder and co-director of the Center for Process Studies, wrote, "No contemporary has made a more original, deep and lasting contribution toward the needed integration of scientific and religious knowledge and values than Ian G. Barbour. With respect to the breadth of topics and fields brought into this integration, Barbour has no equal."[130] Barbour donated most of the prize money ($1 million) to

---

123 "The Gifford Lectures," *The Gifford Lectures*, accessed November 20, 2017, https://www.giffordlectures.org/.

124 Stanley L. Jaki, *The Road of Science and the Ways to God*, 3rd ed. (Real View Books, 2005).

125 Ian G. Barbour, *Religion in an Age of Science* (San Francisco: Harper Collins, 1990).

126 Ian G. Barbour, *Ethics in an Age of Technology* (San Francisco: Harper Collins, 1992).

127 Ian G. Barbour, *Religion and Science: Historical and Contemporary Issues* (San Francisco: Harper, 1997).

128 Barbour, "A Personal Odyssey," 9.

129 "Templeton Prize - Purpose," *Templeton Foundation*, accessed November 20, 2017, http://www.templetonprize.org/purpose.html.

130 Donald Lehr, "Templeton Prize Laureate Ian Barbour, Pioneer in Science and Religion, Dies at 90," *Templeton Foundation*, last modified 2014, accessed November 15, 2017, http://www.templetonprize.org/news_barbour.html.

support the Center for Theology and the Natural Sciences in Berkeley, California. In 2000, Barbour published *When Science Meets Religion*.[131] For this book, he used the four-fold typology proposed in *Religion in an Age of Science* as the organizing structure to address topics in astronomy and creation; the implications of quantum physics; evolution and continuing creation; genetics, neuroscience, and human nature; and God and nature.

Mrs. Deane Barbour died in 2011. Ian would follow his wife on Christmas Eve, 2013 at the age of 90. At that time, he had four children, three grandchildren, and one great-grandson.[132] He is regarded by many Protestants as the *ne plus ultra* of twentieth century scholars in theology and science. At this point, having offered a concise biography of Ian Barbour, we now examine in greater detail his accomplishments as a physicist. His scientific reputation helped to establish his credibility as a promoter of dialogue and integration between science and theology.

7. Barbour's Scientific Achievements

While the primary focus of this book is to analyze Ian Barbour's approach to relating science and theology from a Catholic perspective, particularly as it relates to the doctrine of creation, a lacuna would be present if a brief discussion of his early scientific work in instrumentation (bioengineering) and nuclear physics were omitted. A salient aspect of Barbour's credibility in the theology-science field comes from his early career work as an experimental physicist. As a master's student in physics at Duke University, Barbour had the unique opportunity to work under the direction of Hans Löwenbach, MD, professor of neurology and psychiatry. Löwenbach was interested in instrumentation to advance the quantitative analysis of electroencephalograms (EEGs), i.e., the recording of the brain's electrical activity over a period of time. At that time, the analysis of EEGs was limited to qualitative methods.[133]

More than a century prior, the French mathematician and physicist, Jean-Baptiste Joseph Fourier, showed how any periodic function could be decomposed into an infinite sum of sines and cosines, i.e., the Fourier series. The Fourier transform converts a function with respect to time, $f(t)$, into a sum of sine waves of different frequencies. Each of these represents a frequency component, typically

131 Ian G. Barbour, *When Science Meets Religion: Enemies, Strangers, or Partners?* (San Francisco: HarperOne, 2000).

132 Yardley, "Ian Barbour, Who Found a Balance between Faith and Science, Dies at 90."

133 Carl M. York, "Ian Barbour's Contributions as a Scientist," *Theology and Science* 15, no. 1 (January 2, 2017): 19.

denoted by $F(\omega)$.[134] Barbour was charged with sampling an EEG signal and analyzing its component sine waves. Electronic devices existed which would perform such an analysis on higher frequency signals such as radio waves, but EEG signals are very low frequency, e.g., 2–25 Hz. Barbour designed and implemented an instrument to graphically display a curve of the amplitude of each component sine wave against its frequency. To do this he had to invent a stable, low-frequency oscillator, as none existed at that time.[135]

The resulting system allowed a physician to monitor a patient's brain wave pattern as well as the amplitudes of the various frequencies in the EEG. Patients with healthy brains typically display most brain waves around a narrow band of frequencies close to 11 Hz. Particular brain disorders were found to have distinct patterns when analyzed in the frequency domain. Barbour's device enabled neurologists to make quick diagnoses in potentially life threatening situations, e.g., encephalitis, an acute inflammation of the brain caused by an infection (bacterial, viral, or fungal) or autoimmune response.[136] Barbour published two papers on his novel device entitled "An Automatic Low Frequency Analyzer,"[137] and "An Automatic Device for Continuous Frequency Analysis of Electroencephalograms."[138]

As mentioned earlier, Ian Barbour did his doctoral studies in physics at the University of Chicago. He joined the research group on cosmic rays[139] led by the Slovak-American scientist, Marcel Schein. As a doctoral student in experimental physics in the 1940s, Barbour worked without the benefit of the high energy particle accelerators that exist today. In the mid-twentieth century, energetic nuclear particles were studied primarily through observations of cosmic radiation. As a doctoral student, Barbour was part of a team that studied the variations in the number and kinds of nuclear particles at different altitudes within Earth's atmosphere. Their work showed that the observed phenomena could not be explained

---

134 See Jean-Baptiste-Joseph Fourier, *Théorie analytique de la chaleur* (Paris: Chez Firmin Didot, 1822). $F(\omega) = \int_{-\infty}^{\infty} f(t)e^{-i\omega t}dt$ where $\omega \in (-\infty, +\infty)$.

135 York, "Ian Barbour's Contributions as a Scientist," 19.

136 Ibid.

137 Ian G. Barbour, "An Automatic Low Frequency Analyzer," *Review of Scientific Instruments* 18, no. 7 (July 1, 1947): 516–522.

138 Hans Löwenbach and Ian G. Barbour, "An Automatic Device for Continuous Frequency Analysis of Electroencephalograms," *Federation Proceedings* 5, no. 1 (1946): Part II, 65.

139 Interestingly, another major figure in the field of theology and science, Stanley Jaki, OSB, also did research in the field of cosmic rays. Jaki did his PhD in physics under the Nobel Prize winner, Victor F. Hess, the discoverer of cosmic rays. An extract of Jaki's thesis was published in the June 1958 issue of *Journal of Geophysical Research* with the title, "A Study of the Distribution of Radon, Thoron, and Their Decay Products Above and Below the Ground."

with the existing understanding of nuclear processes and their fundamental particles.[140]

Barbour's research focused on studying some of the properties of the particles produced in the nuclear reactions associated with cosmic rays. By the end of the Second World War, Allied film companies were creating photographic emulsions for the detection of nuclear particles. The initial motivation for the emulsions was to build radiation monitors needed for nuclear energy research. Barbour designed a brilliant experimental apparatus in which two emulsions were mounted with an air gap between them in a magnetic field generated by a very strong magnet from a World War II inspired klystron.[141] The device was then brought to high altitude, around 90,000 feet, by balloon. The concept was that by measuring the deflection of the path of a charged particle in the field, as well as the distance it traveled, one could compute the electric charge and mass.[142]

Where research teams at the University of Bristol and the University of California, Berkeley had failed, Barbour's experimental setup successfully measured the mass and electric charge of a newly discovered particle, the pion, as well its decay product, the muon.[143] Commenting on this discovery, Carl M. York writes, "Not only did these measurements yield corroborating evidence of the properties of these particles, but they verified that pions are produced by the cosmic rays in equal numbers of positive and negative charges in the atmosphere."[144]

As assistant professor of physics at Kalamazoo College, Barbour continued his work performing cosmic ray measurements using particle tracks through emulsion plates. He focused on measuring nuclear interactions at high energies in various elements. At that time, before modern particle accelerators, Barbour's cosmic ray research provided a great deal of data on a significant number of different elements that had never been available previously. After his move to Carleton College, Barbour chose to participate in the International Geophysical Year 1958. The overall goal was to gather data on various geophysical qualities over the entire globe in the course of the year. Barbour volunteered to measure the neutrons produced by cosmic rays in the atmosphere, setting up a "Northfield Station."[145]

---

140 York, "Ian Barbour's Contributions as a Scientist," 17.

141 A klystron is specialized linear-beam vacuum tube used as an amplifier for high radio frequencies. It was invented by two brothers, Russell and Sigurd Varian. See Russell H. Varian and Sigurd F. Varian, "A High Frequency Oscillator and Amplifier," *Journal of Applied Physics* 10, no. 5 (May 1939): 321–327.

142 York, "Ian Barbour's Contributions as a Scientist," 21.

143 Ian G. Barbour, "Magnetic Deflection of Cosmic-Ray Mesons Using Nuclear Plates" (PhD, University of Chicago, 1950).

144 York, "Ian Barbour's Contributions as a Scientist," 21.

145 Ibid., 22–24.

Barbour was also very passionate about pedagogy. He wanted to break out of the "cookbook" approach to undergraduate science education, e.g., students show up for their laboratory class with detailed instructions and all the equipment and materials prepared. To inspire creativity and a research mentality, Barbour would give the students a problem and require that they select the necessary equipment, and learn how to operate them, to gather the desired data. One particularly interesting laboratory assignment presented the problem of measuring the temperature of a mixture of dry ice (solid carbon dioxide) and alcohol. At the beginning, Barbour showed how a "non-creative method" would fail, e.g., a standard mercury thermometer plunged into the mixture freezes solid and sometimes shatters. Carl York describes Barbour's approach:

> The class was divided into teams of two persons each and a laboratory assistant was on hand to help them find any equipment they might need and even do some glass blowing or make other equipment as needed. The first lab period was devoted to choosing a method and selecting and assembling their equipment. During the second period the students made their measurements and calculated their results complete with estimates of the errors in their answers. At the end of the second period the students came together, presented their results and discussed which method gave the most accurate values for the temperature of the solution. Over several semesters the students came up with 11 different ways to measure the temperature of the dry ice, alcohol mixture. With each method they were able to explore and compare the problems of assembling and calibrating equipment, the reliability of standards used in the calibration, the accuracy of the measured values, and the limits of extrapolating calibrations to heretofore unknown regions of the temperature scale. The students had a very positive response to this "real life" approach to laboratory problems. Most were strongly motivated by the challenge of selecting a method and pursuing it.[146]

As an educator, Barbour was also very concerned with the problems of compartmentalization (e.g., academic silos) and reductionism. In a paper for the *American Journal of Physics*, Barbour describes four ways that science can be integrated with other academic disciplines. First, he suggests a "practical approach" in which a student identifies an everyday object, e.g., perhaps now one might think of a mobile phone. The student then proceeds to identify the scientific principles that underlie its operation. A second approach could remain in the "realm of ideas" and examine how various scientific fields interact with each other. A third way involves a "case history approach" to explore how a scientific concept emerged. The fourth way is an extension of the third, taking a "history of science" approach.[147]

---

146 Ibid., 24–25.
147 Ian G. Barbour, "Integration as an Objective in the Physical Sciences," *American Journal of Physics* 20 (1952): 565.

In Barbour's scientific teaching and writing, certain themes are recurring. First, Barbour was very interested in the relationship of science and society. For example, he insisted that nuclear physics should not be dismissed by disinterested undergraduates as an arcane subject. When discussing nuclear energy with his students, Barbour would bring up the then recent events of the atomic bombings of Hiroshima and Nagasaki. Second, Barbour was attentive to the similarities and differences between the physical and social sciences. His attention to "method" arises again in a stronger way in his later research in theology and science. Finally, Barbour was concerned with the impact of science on man's thinking. Many of his students had some level of implicit "scientism" in their working epistemology.[148]

Barbour's scientific research from 1944 to 1960 was certainly prolific and of high quality. It is of great benefit to the discipline of theology that Barbour channeled his intellectual gifts toward theological questions with the establishment of the Department of Religion at Carleton College. One of Barbour's most significant achievements, discussed in the next section, is the development of his four typologies of interaction for theology and science.

8. Typologies of Interaction for Theology and Science

The first series of Gifford Lectures offered by Barbour, and published as *Religion in an Age of Science*, proposed a four-fold typology (conflict, independence, dialogue, and integration) to characterize the relationship of science and religion since the emergence of modern science in the medieval period. The *conflict* hypothesis may be embraced by both Christian and atheist alike. It often emerges in the modern period around interpretations of the theory of evolution. Scientific materialists posit unavoidable conflict between religious faith and their understanding of evolutionary biology and its philosophical implications. In a similar way, Christian fundamentalists may suggest a relationship of conflict due to their particular form of Biblical literalism. Barbour notes that these opposing groups get the majority of popular media attention as the relationship of conflict makes "more exciting news stories."[149]

The *independence* hypothesis offers an alternative perspective in which science and religion can peacefully coexist. One form of the independence hypothesis suggests that religion and science occupy separate domains, or aspects of reality.

---

148 York, "Ian Barbour's Contributions as a Scientist," 25.
149 Barbour, *When Science Meets Religion*, 2.

The language of theology is different from that of experimental science. These distinct languages serve dissimilar functions for mankind, and therefore there should be no conflict. Another form of the independence hypothesis is inspired by the complementarity perspective of Niels Bohr on wave-particle duality in quantum phenomena.[150] From this standpoint, both theology and science can make non-mutually exclusive and objective statements about the world because their fields of inquiry are complementary.

According to Barbour, "compartmentalization avoids conflict, but at the price of preventing any constructive interaction."[151] He is also cautious about the application of the notion of complementarity outside of the natural sciences, stating that the "use of the Complementarity Principle outside physics is *analogical not inferential.*"[152] Barbour concludes, however, that the "idea" of complementarity inspired by physics, but adapted for theology, is helpful as it "underscores the abstractive and symbolic character of concepts, the indirectness of their relation to observable phenomenon, the limitations of models, and the inadequacy of attempts to visualize reality in terms of the categories of everyday experience."[153]

A better form of interaction between science and theology according to Barbour is *dialogue.* Based on similarities in principles and methods for theology and natural science, an exchange of ideas is possible in some cases. One area where similarities are found, for example, is the use of conceptual models and the role of analogy in both disciplines. Another opportunity for dialogue arises when science reaches "limit questions." According to Barbour, these are "ontological questions raised by the scientific enterprise as a whole but not answered by the methods of science,"[154] e.g., Why is there a universe? or Why is it intelligible? A third form of dialogue occurs when concepts from the sciences are used as analogies in theology, e.g., Can information theory[155] or bioinformatics[156] contribute to models of Divine revelation? or If the universe is indeed radically indeterminate according

---

150 See Niels Bohr, "The Quantum Postulate and the Recent Development of Atomic Theory," *Nature* 121 (April 14, 1928): 580–590.

151 Barbour, *When Science Meets Religion,* 2.

152 Barbour, *Issues in Science and Religion,* 292.

153 Ibid., 294.

154 Barbour, *Religion and Science,* 90.

155 Information theory is a science concerned with the quantification, storage, and communication of data. See Claude Shannon, "A Mathematical Theory of Communication," *The Bell System Technical Journal* 27, no. 3 (July 1948): 379–423.

156 Bioinformatics is an interdisciplinary field that integrates ideas from biology, computer science, mathematics, and statistics to analyze and interpret biological data. See Paulien Hogeweg, "The Roots of Bioinformatics in Theoretical Biology," ed. David B. Searls, *PLoS Computational Biology* 7, no. 3 (March 31, 2011), https://doi.org/10.1371/journal.pcbi.1002021.

to some interpretations[157] of quantum theory, is it appropriate to speak of God as the determiner?[158]

For Barbour, the interaction model of *integration* offers the most "systematic and extensive kind of partnership."[159] A traditional example of integration is found in natural theology, i.e., the development of arguments for the existence of God without supernatural revelation, based solely on reason and one's experience of nature. In the Catholic tradition, one thinks immediately of Saint Thomas Aquinas' *quinque viæ*:

(1) The argument from motion,
(2) The argument from causation,
(3) The argument from contingency,
(4) The argument from degree, and
(5) The teleological argument ("the argument from design").[160]

Modern science, e.g., Big Bang cosmology, has added another level of sophistication to these classical arguments for the rationality of belief in the existence of God. These often take the form of "fine-tuning" arguments, i.e., lines of reasoning that acknowledge the fact that various universal dimensionless physical constants[161] must lie within an incredibly small range for matter to emerge, galaxies to form, and the initial conditions for life to occur, thus making their precise values very special, perhaps pointing to some greater Reason.

One example of a fine-tuning of an initial conditional is found in the critical density of the universe. In order for the cosmos to progress in a way that would ultimately be supportive of life, it must have preserved an *extremely* precise overall density. The precision must have been so critical that a variation of one part in 10^{15} (i.e., 0.0000000000001%) would have resulted in a collapse, or "big crunch," occurring far too early for life to have arisen, or there would have been an expansion so fast that no stars, no galaxies, and therefore no life would have emerged.[162]

---

157 See Hermann Wimmel, *Quantum Physics & Observed Reality: A Critical Interpretation of Quantum Mechanics* (River Edge: World Scientific Publishing Company Inc., 1992).
158 Barbour, *When Science Meets Religion*, 3.
159 Ibid.
160 Aquinas, *Summa Theologiæ*, I, Q 2, A 3.
161 Fundamental physical constants are physical quantities that are believed to be both universal in nature and have constant values in time, e.g., the fine-structure constant, $\alpha \approx 1/137.036$.
162 John Polkinghorne and Nicholas Beale, *Questions of Truth: Fifty-One Responses to Questions About God, Science, and Belief* (Louisville: Westminster John Knox, 2009), Appendix A.

According to the BioLogos Foundation,[163] "this degree of precision would be like a blindfolded man choosing a single lucky penny in a pile large enough to pay off the United States' national debt."[164]

Another of Barbour's approaches to integration is in developing a "theology of nature," rather than a "natural theology." In his thought, a theology of nature should begin in a particular religious tradition, rather than from empirical science. While theology and science are considered relatively independent sources of knowledge, though with some overlap with regard to shared concerns, Barbour suggests that certain theological doctrines must be reformulated in light of mature science. As examples, he proposes the doctrines of creation, providence, and human nature. The goal of developing a theology of nature is to bring theological positions into greater harmony with the best scientific knowledge.[165] Barbour regards the scholarship of Pierre Teilhard de Chardin, SJ, in his book, *The Phenomenon of Man*,[166] to be an example of a theology of nature. Teilhard develops his concept of God based on his work as a paleontologist and geologist, e.g., Teilhard writes about a God immanent in creation and develops a novel eschatology around his principle of the "Omega Point."[167]

Another way that Barbour advances the integration mode of interaction is to suggest a metaphysics that is compatible with theology *and* science. The inclusive metaphysical system that Barbour favors is the process metaphysics of Alfred North Whitehead.[168] Whitehead wanted to develop a metaphysics for science and religion that was both "applicable to experience," and "coherent," i.e., concepts are not merely logically consistent, but should be part of a unified system. Some of the basic ideas that Barbour extracts from Whitehead's system is the primacy of time, the interfusion of events, viewing reality as an organic process, and the self-creation of each event.[169] Barbour's process thought will be examined in much greater detail in the subsequent chapters.

Barbour was not alone in his quest for typologies of interaction for theology and science. The American Catholic theologian, John Haught, offers a modification

---

163 The BioLogos Foundation is a non-profit educational organization founded by the physician-geneticist, Francis Collins, whose focus is to show the compatibility of Biblical faith with modern science.

164 "What Do 'Fine-Tuning' and the 'Multiverse' Say about God?," *BioLogos Foundation*, accessed November 20, 2017, https://biologos.org/common-questions/gods-relationship-to-creation/fine-tuning.

165 Barbour, *Religion and Science*, 100–101.

166 Pierre Teilhard de Chardin, *The Phenomenon of Man* (New York: Harper & Row, 1961).

167 Barbour, *Religion and Science*, 102.

168 See Alfred North Whitehead, *Process and Reality* (New York: Free Press, 1969).

169 Barbour, *Issues in Science and Religion*, 129–130.

of Barbour's system.[170] Haught suggests that the interaction categories should be *conflict, contrast, contact,* and *confirmation.* Conflict and contrast are consistent with Barbour's first two categories. Contact is a synthesis of Barbour's categories of dialogue and integration. Confirmation refers to a scientific justification of fundamental assumptions that are rooted in theological doctrines, e.g., the belief in the rationality of the universe.[171]

The American Lutheran theologian, Ted Peters, suggests a more complex classification based on eight categories.[172] Barbour's category of conflict is divided into *scientism, scientific creationism,* and *ecclesiastical authoritarianism.* Peters adds a new category called *ethical overlap* to address moral issues arising from technology. Other categories include *scientific imperialism, the two-language theory, hypothetical consonance,* and *New Age spirituality.*

The Dutch religious naturalist, Willem B. Drees, defines nine modes of interaction for theology and science. It is presented as a 3 × 3 table in which the horizontal headings correspond to what Drees classifies as defining the character of religion: *cognitive, experiential,* and *traditional* elements. The left-hand, vertical column presents three challenges posed by science: *new knowledge, new views of knowledge,* and *appreciation of the world.*[173]

The Swedish philosopher and theologian, Mikael Stenmark, develops Barbour's schema by focusing on the diverse ways in which the practice of the natural sciences interacts with theology. Stenmark argues that the relationship varies depending on whether the particular science is in the development, justification, or application phases.[174] Some other theology-science scholars who have adopted and applied Barbour's approach to interaction typologies are the Anglican biochemist and theologian, Christopher Southgate, and the Anglican cleric and theologian, Graham Buxton.[175]

Engaging the interaction of physical cosmology and the theology of creation, Barbour identifies two common forms of *conflict.* One emerges among those cosmologists who want to avoid a "creation event" and the implications of the

170 John Haught, *Science & Religion: From Conflict to Conversation* (New York: Paulist Press, 1995).

171 Barbour, *When Science Meets Religion,* 4.

172 Ted Peters, "Theology and Natural Science," in *The Modern Theologians,* ed. David Ford, 2nd ed. (Oxford: Blackwell, 1997), 649–668.

173 Willem B. Drees, *Religion, Science and Naturalism* (Cambridge: Cambridge University Press, 1998), 45.

174 Mikael Stenmark, *How to Relate Science and Religion: A Multidimensional Model* (Grand Rapids, MI: Wm. B. Eerdmans Publishing, 2004), 209–250.

175 Christopher Southgate, ed., *God, Humanity and the Cosmos: A Textbook in Science and Religion,* 3rd ed. (London: T&T Clark, 2011), 6–7; Graham Buxton, *The Trinity, Creation and Pastoral Ministry: Imaging the Perichoretic God* (Eugene, OR: Wipf & Stock Publishers, 2007), 16–41.

fine-tuning arguments. Their presuppositions lead them to seek a universe that exists "by chance." These schemes often fall within the category of the "many-worlds" interpretations, e.g., successive cycles of an oscillating universe, multiple isolated domains created by a single Big Bang, many-worlds quantum theory (i.e., the universe splitting into branches for every quantum indeterminacy), and quantum vacuum fluctuations (i.e., creation of particle-antiparticle pairs of virtual particles in a vacuum).[176]

An inappropriate harmonizing of Big Bang cosmology and the Book of Genesis can also create a relationship of conflict between theology and science through Biblical concordance. The most popular example of concordism was the 1650 chronology of the history of the world developed from a literalist reading of the Old Testament by the Anglican Archbishop, James Ussher. In *Annales Veteris Testamenti, a prima mundi origine deducti*, Ussher placed the moment of creation as nightfall on October 22, 4004 BC.[177] Attempts at Biblical concordance take many forms. In the twentieth century, after the Belgian priest and cosmologist, Georges Lemaître's, formulation of the Big Bang hypothesis,[178] some well-meaning Christians tried to associate the "primeval fireworks" with the event of creation. Well aware of tentative character of scientific theories and trained in classical Thomism, Lemaître himself never made that mistake.

The *independence* mode of interaction asserts that theology and science are "autonomous enterprises, each asking a distinctive type of question, employing distinctive methods, and serving distinct functions in human life."[179] Barbour identifies Saint Augustine's theological hermeneutic for the beginning of the Book of Genesis as one example.[180] Augustine recognized that the literary genre of the first chapters of Genesis is not natural philosophy. Rather, God is teaching mankind profound religious lessons about who He is and about our relationship to Him. Augustine had harsh words for those Christian who imagined that they were interpreting Sacred Scripture while only promoting erroneous physical theories.[181]

---

176 Barbour, *When Science Meets Religion*, 42–44.

177 James Ussher, *The Annals of the World*, ed. Larry Pierce and Marion Pierce (Green Forest, AR: Master Books, 2007), 9.

178 See Georges Lemaître, "Un Univers Homogène de Masse Constante et de Rayon Croissant Rendant Compte de La Vitesse Radiale des Nébuleuses Extragalactiques," *Annales de la Société Scientifique de Bruxelles* 47 (1927): 49–59.

179 Barbour, *When Science Meets Religion*, 47.

180 Ibid., 49.

181 Augustine writes, "There is knowledge to be had, after all, about the earth, about the sky, about the other elements of this world, about the movements and revolutions or even the magnitude and distances of the constellations, about the predictable eclipses of moon and sun, about the cycles of years and seasons, about the nature of animals, fruits, stones, and everything else of this kind. And it frequently happens that even non-Christians will have knowledge of this sort in

Even outside the Judæo-Christian tradition, the major pre-Christian civilizations of antiquity had creation stories or cosmogonies that served an important cultural function expressing their sense of wonder before the world and recognition of their interdependence with nature.[182]

Barbour's approach to *dialogue* between physical cosmology and creation theology identifies the intelligibility and the contingency of the universe as topics of interest. Scientists working in the field of physical cosmology cannot help but ask themselves why the cosmos that they are studying is rationally intelligible. Given the nature of the question, the formal and natural sciences cannot offer an answer. Barbour identifies four types of contingency that characterize the universe: contingent existence (e.g., Why is there anything at all?), contingent boundary conditions (e.g., a true singularity at the beginning would be inaccessible to the methods of science), contingent laws (e.g., a universe could exist with different laws), and contingent events ("The cosmos is a unique and irreversible sequence of events.").[183] All four contingencies offer profound areas for the dialogue of the Catholic doctrine of creation with the natural sciences and will be explored later in Chapter Five.

According to Barbour, opportunities for *integration* between creation and cosmology arise in the context of the Anthropic Principle,[184] models of God as creator, and acknowledging the significance of humanity. Fine-tuned phenomena

---

a way that they can substantiate with scientific arguments or experiments. Now it is quite disgraceful and disastrous, something to be on one's guard against at all costs, that they should ever hear Christians spouting what they claim our Christian literature has to say on these topics, and talking such nonsense that they can scarcely contain their laughter when they see them to be *toto caelo*, as the saying goes, wide of the mark. And what is so vexing is not that misguided people should be laughed at, as that our authors should be assumed by outsiders to have held such views and, to the great detriment of those about whose salvation we are so concerned, should be written off and consigned to the waste paper basket as so many ignoramuses." Augustine, *On Genesis*, ed. John E. Rotelle, trans. Edmund Hill, vol. 13, The Works of St. Augustine 1 (Hyde Park, NY: New City Press, 2002), bk. I, chap. 19, 39.

182 Jaki, *Science and Creation*.

183 Barbour, *When Science Meets Religion*, 54–56.

184 The Anthropic Principle acknowledges that the laws of physics and key parameters of the cosmos take on values that are consistent with conditions for life as we know it, including human life. The universe could be conceivably have been defined by a different set of values and fundamental laws that would have been inconsistent with life on Earth. See John D. Barrow and Frank J. Tipler, *The Anthropic Cosmological Principle*, Revised. (Oxford: Oxford University Press, 1988). A common objection to the Anthropic Principle is the possibility of a multiverse. If multiple universes exist, having all possible combinations of characteristics, it could be considered unremarkable that man finds himself within a universe that allows him to exist. However, by definition, a multiverse cannot be observed so its existence cannot be proven.

such as an expansion rate of the universe that allows galaxies to form, the relative strength of the strong nuclear force that enables the formation of elements larger than hydrogen, and the asymmetry of the particle/antiparticle[185] ratio that allows for ordinary matter, can all contribute to a modern natural theology rooted in cosmology.[186] Theological models of God as Creator "updated" in light of modern cosmology would fit into Barbour's notion of a theology of nature. In Chapter Five, the applicability of these prospects for integration will be evaluated to assess their ability to contribute to a more profound understanding of God's act of creation.

In his reflection on opportunities for integration, Barbour also asks, "What are the implications of current cosmology for our self-understanding? Can they be reconciled with the Biblical view of man?"[187] Despite the immensity of time and space, a higher level of complexity is present in the human person than in the physical phenomena of distant universes. In addition, when cosmology is considered in relation to evolutionary biology, molecular biology, and ecology, the interdependence of all creation is made manifest.[188] Nonetheless, human beings are the most advanced form of life that we have encountered. The "Great Filter" argument offers a compelling case against ever encountering alien life.[189]

---

185 According to contemporary particle physics, every type of particle has an associated antiparticle with the same mass but with opposite physical charges, e.g., an electron's antiparticle is the positron. Although some neutral particles are their own antiparticles, e.g., photons and neutral pions. Particle–antiparticle pairs annihilate each other and produce photons. Antiparticles are produced naturally via beta decay, or the collision of cosmic rays with Earth's atmosphere. See Richard P. Feynman, "The Reason for Antiparticles," in *Elementary Particles and the Laws of Physics: The 1986 Dirac Memorial Lectures*, by Steven Weinberg and Richard P. Feynman (Cambridge, UK: Cambridge University Press, 1999), 1–60.

186 Barbour, *When Science Meets Religion*, 57–58.

187 Ibid., 61.

188 Ibid., 62.

189 The Swedish philosopher, Nick Bostrom, writes, "The observable universe contains approximately 10^{22} stars. The universe might well extend infinitely far beyond the part that is observable by us, and it may contain infinitely many stars. If so, then it is virtually certain that an infinite number of intelligent extraterrestrial species exist, no matter how improbable their evolution on any given planet. However, cosmological theory implies that because the universe is expanding, any living creatures outside the observable universe are and will forever remain causally disconnected from us: they can never visit us, communicate with us, or be seen by us or our descendants ... Our galaxy is about 100,000 light-years across. If a probe were capable of traveling at one-tenth the speed of light, every planet in the galaxy could thus be colonized within a couple of million years (allowing some time for each probe that lands on a resource site to set up the necessary infrastructure and produce daughter probes). If travel speed were limited to 1 percent of light speed, colonization might take 20 million years instead." Nick Bostrom, "Where Are They?," *MIT Technology Review*, April 22, 2008, accessed November 21, 2017,

In our discussion of Ian Barbour's life and works, we have attempted to show his significance as scholar of theology and science. The impact of any scholar is surely seen in his influence on colleagues and students. This last section of Chapter One examines Barbour's impact on three highly prominent theology-science researchers.

9. Influence on other Theology-Science Scholars

Ian Barbour's influence on the field of theology and science is considerable. He is no dilettante! For example, the German Lutheran theologian, Hans Schwarz, refers to Barbour as the "Grand Senior of the Dialogue" between theology and science.[190] One way to demonstrate Barbour's significant impact is to explore his influence on other major scholars. This section will concisely examine his relationship with Arthur Peacocke, John Polkinghorne, and Robert John Russell. Each scholar builds on Barbour's work, citing his substantial influence on their own research. At the same time, each one diverges in unique ways from Barbour.[191] Points of divergence are particularly helpful to clarify Barbour's own positions.

9.1 Arthur Peacocke

Arthur Robert Peacocke was born in Watford, in the county of Hertfordshire, England. He attended Exeter College, Oxford and earned a BA degree in physics with honors and therefore, after the prescribed time, received the Oxford "rank" of Master of Arts.[192] Peacocke then began postgraduate studies. He earned the

---

https://www.technologyreview.com/s/409936/where-are-they/. Current spacecraft have a maximum velocity around 0.00005 times the speed of light.

190 Schwarz, *Vying for Truth - Theology and the Natural Sciences*, 108.

191 Barbour's severest critics have come from the postmodern feminist, womanist, and mujerista movements. For example, see: Sallie McFague, "Ian Barbour: Theologian's Friend, Scientist's Interpreter," *Zygon* 31, no. 1 (March 1, 1996): 21–28. Barbour appreciates their critical engagement with his thought, but ultimately states that he "cannot agree with those postmodern feminists who recommend that we should reject objectivity and accept relativism. Western thought has indeed been dualistic, and men have perhaps been particularly prone to dichotomize experience. But the answer surely is to try to avoid dichotomies, not merely relativize them." Barbour, *Religion and Science*, 149.

192 In most British universities, the MA degree is a free-standing graduate degree awarded by examination. At Oxford and Cambridge, the status of "Master of Arts" is a designation of seniority. It may be conferred 21 terms after initial matriculation. In the "Oxbridge" context, it indicates a higher status within the University. It is neither an upgrade of the BA, nor an additional qualification. See "Graduation," *Oriel College, University of Oxford*, last modified June 7, 2016, accessed November 22, 2017, http://www.oriel.ox.ac.uk/life-oriel/graduation.

graduate degree of BSc in 1947 and the DPhil in 1948 in physical biochemistry under the direction of Sir Cyril Hinshelwood. Hinshelwood later received the Nobel Prize in Chemistry in 1956 for his work on the mechanism of chemical reactions. Peacocke's research focused on the kinetics of bacterial growth.[193] The newly minted Dr. Peacocke then took a faculty position at the University of Birmingham.[194]

While at Birmingham, a colleague in the Department of Theology, Geoffrey William Hugo Lampe, encouraged Peacocke to study theology. Peacocke earned a diploma in theology in 1960 and was licensed as a Lay Reader for the Anglican Diocese of Oxford, allowing him to lead the Divine Office, preach, and teach in the absence of an ordained member of the clergy. Meanwhile, in 1959, Peacocke took a position as a lecturer in the Department of Biochemistry at the University of Oxford and was named a Fellow and Tutor of Saint Peter's College. Oxford bestowed the higher doctorate of Doctor of Science (ScD) on Peacocke in 1962. In 1971, he earned the Bachelor of Divinity (BD) post-graduate credential from the University of Birmingham. Peacocke was then ordained a priest in the Church of England by Kenneth Woolcombe, Bishop of Oxford. Two years later, he was appointed Fellow and Dean of Clare College, Cambridge where he taught biochemistry as well as theology.[195]

In 1982, Oxford conferred the higher doctorate of Doctor of Divinity (DD) on Peacocke for distinction in theological research. At that time, Peacocke was the only living recipient of both the Oxford Doctor of Science and Doctor of Divinity degrees.[196] In 1984, Oxford recruited him to return to the campus as the Director of the newly founded Ian Ramsey Centre for Science and Religion. Peacocke retired at Oxford and was named an honorary canon of Christ Church Cathedral in 1995. In 2001, like Ian Barbour, Peacocke was awarded the Templeton Prize. Canon Peacocke died at Oxford on October 21, 2006.[197]

In the preface to his first book on theology and science, *Science and the Christian Experiment*, Peacocke expresses his gratitude for Barbour's early scholarship in the field:

---

193 Donald Lehr, "Templeton Prize Laureate Arthur Peacocke Dies," *Templeton Foundation*, last modified October 25, 2006, accessed November 24, 2017, http://www.templetonprize.org/tplapd.html.

194 John Polkinghorne, "Canon Arthur Peacocke," *The Independent* (London, November 6, 2006), sec. Obituaries, accessed November 22, 2017, http://www.independent.co.uk/news/obituaries/canon-arthur-peacocke-423175.html.

195 Ibid.

196 Lehr, "Templeton Prize Laureate Arthur Peacocke Dies."

197 Polkinghorne, "Canon Arthur Peacocke."

An attempt of this kind cannot hope to deal at all fairly and comprehensively with the many issues on which there should be at least a dialogue between those involved in the scientific and theological enterprises. These have been magisterially surveyed by I.G. Barbour in his *Issues in Science and Religion* and I willingly refer the reader to that systematic and documented account.[198]

In Peacocke's next two books, *Creation and the World of Science*[199] (the 1979 Bampton Lectures) and *Intimations of Reality: Critical Realism in Science and Religion*[200] (the 1983 Mendenhall Lectures), he endorses Barbour's critical realism in science and theology as well as builds upon a number of other ideas from Barbour's book *Myths, Models, and Paradigms*. With the publication of *When Science Meets Religion* by Barbour in 2000, Peacocke wrote, "No surer and fairer guide to the proliferating literature on the relation of science and religion can be found than Ian Barbour."[201]

The exchange between Barbour and Peacocke was certainly not unidirectional. Peacocke also had an influence on Barbour and they shared much in common in their approach to theology and science. In an article published after Peacocke's death, Barbour writes,

> Despite our differences I felt more commonality with his viewpoint than with any other contemporary writer. We agreed in pursuing a theology of nature that starts from religious experience and a historical tradition and reinterprets them in the light of science, rather than seeking a natural theology that relies on scientific evidence alone. We both defended a view of the world as an open-ended process whose future cannot be known even by God. We both portrayed a role for chance as well as law and divine purpose in the unfolding of events, which we referred to as continuing creation. We defended a dipolar concept of God as temporal in some respects and eternal in others. The presence of suffering and human freedom, as well as the Christian understanding of the cross, led us to argue that God participates in the world's suffering. We spoke of the self-limitation of divine power (*kenosis*) and of God's empowerment of creation from within rather than power over creation by intervention from without.[202]

Barbour notes much compatibility in their views on evolution, emergence, top-down causality, and continuing creation. He also identifies four areas where their

---

198 Arthur R. Peacocke, *Science and the Christian Experiment* (London: Oxford University Press, 1971), *vi*.

199 Arthur Peacocke, *Creation and the World of Science: The Re-Shaping of Belief*, 2nd ed. (Oxford: Oxford University Press, 2004).

200 Arthur Peacocke, *Intimations of Reality: Critical Realism in Science and Religion* (Notre Dame: University of Notre Dame Press, 1984).

201 Barbour, *When Science Meets Religion*.

202 Ian G. Barbour, "Remembering Arthur Peacocke: A Personal Reflection," *Zygon* 43, no. 1 (March 1, 2008): 91.

approaches diverge: the notion of subjectivity in emergent monism, the label of panentheism,[203] the meaning of creation *ex nihilo*, and understanding the limitations of God's power.[204]

Barbour's approach to process metaphysics, built on the foundations of Alfred North Whitehead and Charles Hartshorne, posits that the basic constituents of reality are not two classes of enduring beings (e.g., immaterial and material) or one class of enduring being (e.g., as found in idealism or materialism), but rather one type of *event* with two distinct aspects. Explicating his position, Barbour writes,

> It is postulated that every momentary entity has an objective phase in which it is receptive from the past and a subjective phase in which it is at least minimally creative toward the future. This philosophy is monistic in portraying the common character of all events, but it recognizes that events can be organized in diverse ways, leading to an organizational pluralism of many levels.[205]

Peacocke's metaphysics is based on a notion of *emergent monism*, another attempt at the rejection of all forms of "dualism" (e.g., mind and brain). In his understanding of ontological emergence, higher-level events can be causally effectual by placing constraints on lower level events.[206] But, according to Barbour, Peacocke diverges from a classical process approach "in insisting that entities at lower levels are totally devoid of anything resembling the subjectivity, interiority, or experience found at higher levels."[207]

Barbour sees Peacocke's "restriction" on the subjectivity of lower level entities as a limitation on Divine causality. He asserts that emergent monism reduces the realm of God's action in lower life forms, e.g., plants, to "providing built-in propensities and maintaining lawful regularities."[208] Barbour views this position as straying from the Scriptural teaching that provides a much broader range of action of the Holy Spirit in creation, e.g., "When thou sendest forth thy Spirit, they are created; and thou renewest the face of the ground."[209]

Both Barbour and Peacocke depart from traditional theism and its emphasis on God's transcendence. However, they do so in distinct ways. According to Barbour's process approach, God is active at all levels of reality as *one* factor

---

203 Panentheism is an alternative to classical theism and pantheism in which the world is in God and God is in the world.

204 Barbour, "Remembering Arthur Peacocke," 89.

205 Ibid., 93.

206 Arthur Peacocke and Philip Clayton, eds., *All That Is: A Naturalistic Faith for the Twenty-First Century* (Minneapolis: Fortress Press, 2007), 12–16.

207 Barbour, "Remembering Arthur Peacocke," 92.

208 Ibid., 94.

209 Psalm 104:30 (RSV).

among many in the realization of every event. Divine causality is not simply "top-down" or "whole-part." Barbour describes every new event as "a present response (self-cause) to past events (efficient cause) in terms of potentialities grasped (final cause)."[210] God is "the primordial ground of order structures, the potential forms of relationships before they are actualized … and the ground of novelty in presenting new possibilities among which alternatives are left open."[211]

Like Barbour, Peacocke seeks to emphasize Divine immanence but his theology of God is more explicitly *panentheistic*. Peacocke defines his form of panentheism as "the belief that the Being of God includes and penetrates the whole universe, so that every part of it exists in God, and (as against pantheism) that God's being is more than, and is not exhausted by, the universe."[212] He does not adopt the traditional panentheistic analogy that God is to the world as the mind is to the body. His panentheism attributes to God the concept of whole-part constraints. Peacocke asserts that the Divine, as "the most inclusive whole," acts on "the world-as-a-whole," which is "a system-of-systems," in order to affect events without violating any natural laws.[213] Barbour is more comfortable with his own process approach[214] for a number of reasons, one of which is the opportunity it provides for special, providential action in the process that leads to the emergence of the human person.[215]

With regard to God's role as *creator cæli et terræ*, Peacocke and Barbour are similar in their rejection of the traditional doctrine of creation *ex nihilo*. They both favor an emphasis on God's ongoing work in "continuing creation" in their theologies of creation. Peacocke addresses the traditional understanding of creation *ex nihilo* by completely restating the belief. For Peacocke, *ex nihilo* simply affirms the creativity of God and the contingency of the cosmos. It is therefore an ontological statement and not a historical one, as he does not associate it with the beginning of time. Consequently, it cannot be associated with any particular physical cosmology. Barbour claims that Peacocke emphasizes God's transcendence

---

210 Barbour, "Remembering Arthur Peacocke," 95.

211 Ibid.

212 Arthur Peacocke, "Articulating God's Presence in and to the World Unveiled by the Science," in *In Whom We Live and Move and Have Our Being: Panentheistic Reflections on God's Presence in a Scientific World*, ed. Philip Clayton and Arthur Peacocke (Grand Rapids: William B. Eerdmans, 2004), 145.

213 Peacocke and Clayton, *All That Is: A Naturalistic Faith for the Twenty-First Century*, 45.

214 Barbour's process metaphysics is implicitly panentheistic. However, he avoids using the term "panentheism" and at times distances himself from those who assume that label. Barbour's panentheism is critiqued in Chapter Four.

215 Barbour, "Remembering Arthur Peacocke," 96.

more than he and Whitehead by employing the notion of *ex nihilo* to characterize the ontological distance between God and the world.[216]

Barbour follows Whitehead who asserts that God "is not *before* all creation but *with* all creation."[217] Contrary to the belief of Creedal Christians that places God *ante omnia sæcula*, Whitehead posits that both God and the world always coexisted, and that God "created" with preexisting matter.[218] Whitehead asserts an infinite temporal past consistent with steady-state theories of the universe. However, these physical models are completely contradictory with the vast experimental evidence in support of big bang cosmology. Theories of an oscillating universe could be compatible with an infinite past. But, as Barbour points out, recent observations indicate that the universe is expanding too quickly for it to slow down and eventually contract.[219]

Multiverse theories resulting from quantum fluctuations might be compatible with Whitehead's theology. However, these theories are not subject to scientific falsification. A multiverse, as usually defined, cannot be observed. Therefore, it cannot be confirmed.[220]

Barbour and Peacocke are alike in their rejection of the Christian belief in *unum Deum omnipotentem*. According to Barbour, Peacocke follows Charles Hartshorne[221] in rejecting God's omniscience and omnipotence in light of the problem of suffering and other issues. They advocate "a dipolar concept of God as temporal and changing in interaction with the world, but eternal and unchanging in character and purpose."[222]

Barbour and Peacocke differ in whether the limitations they attribute to God are voluntary or necessary. Peacocke posits that God, in a supreme act of self-emptying love (*kenosis*), imposes on Himself limitations to His omnipotence and omniscience. This self-limitation leaves God vulnerable to the very processes He himself created.[223] Conversely, in Barbour's process thought, the limits on God's power derive from metaphysical necessity. Barbour insists that "every being has

---

216 Ibid., 96–97.

217 Whitehead, *Process and Reality*, 343.

218 Ibid., 91.

219 Ian G. Barbour, *Nature, Human Nature, and God* (Minneapolis: Fortress Press, 2002), 114–115.

220 For a contemporary critique of multiverse theories by the South African mathematician and theoretical physicist, George Ellis, see George F.R. Ellis, "Does the Multiverse Really Exist?," *Scientific American* 305, no. 2 (August 2011): 38–43.

221 Charles Hartshorne, *The Divine Relativity: A Social Conception of God* (New Haven, CT: Yale University Press, 1948).

222 Barbour, "Remembering Arthur Peacocke," 98.

223 Arthur Peacocke, *Theology for a Scientific Age: Being and Becoming–Natural, Divine and Human*, 2nd ed. (Minneapolis: Augsburg Fortress Publishers, 1993), 123.

passive and receptive capabilities as well as active and causally effective ones. No being can have a monopoly of power or effect unilateral control."[224]

9.2 John Polkinghorne

Another major scholar of theology and science influenced by Ian Barbour is John Charlton Polkinghorne. Polkinghorne was born in Weston-super-mare in the County of Somerset, England in 1930. As an adolescent, he attended the prestigious Perse School in Cambridge. Upon graduation in 1948, Polkinghorne fulfilled his national service obligation as a sergeant-instructor in the Royal Army Education Corps. Polkinghorne was awarded a major scholarship to Trinity College, Cambridge and earned a BA in mathematics in 1952. Afterward, he began doctoral studies in theoretical physics and joined a particle physics research group led by Paul Adrien Maurice Dirac.[225] Dirac and Erwin Schrödinger won the 1933 Nobel Prize in Physics for their discovery of "new productive forms of atomic theory."[226] Ultimately, Polkinghorne's dissertation director was the Pakistani Nobel laureate, Abdus Salam.[227] Polkinghorne successfully defended his dissertation entitled *Contributions to Quantum Field Theory* in 1955.[228]

Dr. Polkinghorne went to the California Institute of Technology on a postdoctoral Harkness Fellowship. While at Cal Tech, he had the good fortune of working with Murray Gell-Mann who would go on to receive the Nobel Prize in Physics in 1969 for his work on the quark structure of matter. After two years teaching at the University of Edinburgh, Polkinghorne returned to Cambridge. He was named professor of mathematical physics in 1968. Polkinghorne's work in physics led to substantial results in scattering matrix theory[229] and the properties of Feynman integrals.[230] In 1974, he was elected

224 Barbour, "Remembering Arthur Peacocke," 100.
225 John Polkinghorne, *From Physicist to Priest: An Autobiography* (Eugene: Wipf & Stock Publishers, 2008), 3–31.
226 "The Nobel Prize in Physics 1933," *NobelPrize.org*, accessed November 27, 2017, https://www.nobelprize.org/nobel_prizes/physics/laureates/1933/.
227 Polkinghorne, *From Physicist to Priest*, 34.
228 John Polkinghorne, "Contributions to Quantum Field Theory" (PhD, University of Cambridge, 1955).
229 A scattering matrix relates the initial and final states of a physical system subject to a scattering process. See Asim Orhan Barut, *The Theory of the Scattering Matrix for the Interactions of Fundamental Particles* (New York: Macmillan, 1967).
230 Feynman path integrals refer to representations in the form of a path integral, or integral over trajectories, of the transition functions of some dynamical system. See Sergio Albeverio,

a Fellow of the Royal Society and received the higher doctorate, ScD, from Cambridge.[231]

In 1979, Polkinghorne resigned his professorship to enter the Anglican seminary at Westcott House. Reflecting on the decision in his autobiography, he wrote, "The most fundamental reason for thinking about such an unconventional move was simply that Christianity has always been central to my life. Therefore, becoming a minister of Word and Sacrament would be a privileged vocation that held out the possibility of deep satisfaction."[232] John A.T. Robinson ordained Polkinghorne an Anglican priest at Trinity Chapel, Cambridge in 1982. Polkinghorne served in a variety of parochial and higher education ministries, eventually accepting the post of President of Queens' College, Cambridge from 1986 to 1996 when he retired.[233] He was invited to give the Gifford Lectures, 1993–1994 (published in the UK as *Science and Christian Belief*[234] and in the USA as *The Faith of a Physicist*[235]). Further honors came in 1997 when he was named a Knight Commander of the Order of the British Empire (KBE), and in 2002 when Polkinghorne received the Templeton Prize.[236]

John Polkinghorne described Ian Barbour as the "*doyen* of contemporary writers on science and theology."[237] According to Polkinghorne, "there is no doubt that [the publication of Barbour's 1966 book, *Issues in Science and Religion*,] was indeed a seminal event in terms of its wide influence in the academic world."[238] That being said, Polkinghorne also asserts that many of the philosophical issues that Barbour discusses were anticipated by the Anglican clergyman and existential Thomist,[239] Eric Lionel Mascall.[240] Polkinghorne follows Barbour in adopting

---

Rafael Høegh-Krohn, and Sonia Mazzucchi, *Mathematical Theory of Feynman Path Integrals: An Introduction*, 2nd ed. (Berlin: Springer-Verlag, 2008).

231 Polkinghorne, *From Physicist to Priest*, 40–70.

232 Ibid., 73.

233 Ibid., 81–130.

234 John Polkinghorne, *Science and Christian Belief: Theological Reflections of a Bottom-up Thinker* (London: SPCK Publishing, 1994).

235 John Polkinghorne, *The Faith of a Physicist: Reflections of a Bottom-Up Thinker* (Princeton: Princeton University Press, 2014).

236 "The Templeton Prize: Rev. Dr. John C. Polkinghorne (2002)," *Templeton Foundation*, accessed November 28, 2017, http://www.templetonprize.org/previouswinners/polkinghorne.html.

237 Barbour, *When Science Meets Religion*.

238 See John Polkinghorne, *Science and the Trinity: The Christian Encounter with Reality* (New Haven, CT: Yale University Press, 2004), 4.

239 Mascall widely promoted existential Thomism in his 1970–1971 Gifford Lectures, see Eric L. Mascall, *Openness of Being: Natural Theology Today* (London: Darton, Longman & Todd Ltd., 1971).

240 See Eric L. Mascall, *Christian Theology and Natural Science: Some Questions in Their Relations* (London: Longmans Green and Co., 1957).

a critical realist epistemology for science and theology. He justifies this position with a "bottom-up" approach, arguing from particular circumstances in science and theology, rather than as an *a priori* general principle imposed "from above."[241]

Polkinghorne further develops Barbour's critical realism by stressing its "realism" through what he calls "verisimilitude" in both scientific and theological inquiry. Reflecting on both the tentative character of scientific theories and the development of religious doctrines in *Belief in God in an Age of Science*, Polkinghorne writes, "Our attainment is verisimilitude, not absolute truth. Our method is the creative interpretation of experience, not rigorous deduction from it. Thus I am a critical realist."[242] It should be noted that Polkinghorne's critical realism is also influenced by Bernard Lonergan, SJ.[243] Lonergan's epistemology will be briefly explicated in the next chapter.

Both Polkinghorne and Barbour advocate ontological theories of dipolar or dual-aspect monism. Polkinghorne writes, "there is only one stuff in the world (not two—the material and the mental) but it can occur in two contrasting states (material and mental phases, a physicist might say) which explain our perception of the difference between mind and matter."[244] Barbour's variety of dipolar monism, panexperientialism, however, posits that every actual, integrated event, no matter how small, includes the capacity for experience. This subjective aspect can be described as mind or consciousness in higher-level organisms.[245]

Polkinghorne labels Barbour's approach to the study of science and religion as theistic, in contrast to the deistic approach of the British physicist and 1995 Templeton Prize winner, Paul Davies. Nonetheless, Polkinghorne believes that Barbour's scholarship does not give sufficient attention to the fundamental dogmatic commitments shared by most Christians and summarized in the Nicene-Constantinopolitan Creed, especially *expecto resurrectionem mortuorum*.[246] In his reformulation of Christology, Barbour identifies *history* and *relationship* as the central categories for theological investigation, rather than *substance*. Barbour states that "what was unique about Christ ... was his relationship to God, not his metaphysical 'substance.'"[247] Barbour acknowledges that this implies that what makes Christ unique compared to us is simply a matter degree—Jesus is better at being

241 Polkinghorne, *From Physicist to Priest*, 150.
242 John Polkinghorne, *Belief in God in an Age of Science* (New Haven, CT: Yale University Press, 1998), 104.
243 John C. Polkinghorne, *Reason and Reality: The Relationship between Science and Theology* (Philadelphia: Trinity Press International, 1991), 5, 17.
244 Polkinghorne, *Science and Christian Belief*, 21.
245 Barbour, *Nature, Human Nature, and God*, 112.
246 Polkinghorne, *From Physicist to Priest*, 155.
247 Barbour, *Religion in an Age of Science*, 210.

authentically human.[248] In light of the resonating witness of the New Testament and the Patristic tradition, Polkinghorne critiques Barbour for not acknowledging the Divine nature of Christ and His role as *salvator et redemptor mundi*.[249]

One area in which Polkinghorne diverges significantly from Barbour is in his use of process philosophy. From a scientific perspective, Polkinghorne posits that process metaphysics is not compatible with the theoretical foundations of modern quantum mechanics, "which assigns at least as important a role in physical process to continuous development as it does to discontinuous change."[250] From the point of view of theology, Polkinghorne characterizes the God of process theology as too limited in power. The deity of Whiteheadian metaphysics that Barbour endorses acts through "persuasion" alone. Again, turning to soteriology, Polkinghorne recognizes that it is hard to understand the resurrection of Jesus Christ and the salvation of the just with a deity whose power is limited to "influence."[251]

While Barbour distinguishes his own theology of God from the clear panentheism of Arthur Peacocke, Polkinghorne characterizes both of them as "inclined to panentheistic views."[252] Polkinghorne views process theology in general as a "very qualified form of panentheism."[253] In his own scholarship, Polkinghorne has been very intentional about maintaining the orthodox Christian doctrine of God that maintains a clear distinction between creation and Creator. He believes that in diminishing God's transcendence and over-emphasizing His immanence, thus blurring the line between Creator and creature, the problem of evil (both natural and supernatural) intensifies.[254] Interestingly, Barbour himself acknowledges that "process theology does call into question the traditional expectation of an *absolute victory over evil*."[255]

9.3 Robert John Russell

Back in the United States, the theologian and physicist, Robert John Russell, is another leading scholar influenced by Ian Barbour. Born in 1946 in Los Angeles, California, Russell would go on to study at Stanford University, majoring in physics and minoring in music and religion. During his sophomore year, he read Barbour's

248 Ibid., 213.
249 Polkinghorne, *Science and the Trinity*, 18.
250 Ibid., 19.
251 Ibid.
252 Polkinghorne, *From Physicist to Priest*, 149.
253 John Polkinghorne, *Scientists as Theologians* (London: SPCK, 1996), 33.
254 Polkinghorne, *From Physicist to Priest*, 149.
255 Barbour, *Religion in an Age of Science*, 264.

seminal work, *Issues in Science and Religion*, which had a profound effect on him. In particular, it opened up for him the possibility of the theology-science interaction moving behind the conflict or independence paradigms. After graduating from Stanford in 1968, Russell earned an MS in physics from the University of California at Los Angeles in 1970. Russell then began to discern a vocation to ordained ministry and entered the Pacific School of Religion at Berkeley. He earned the BDiv and MA in theology degrees.[256]

Russell later went on to the University California at Santa Cruz and studied experimental condensed matter and material physics. He earned a PhD with the dissertation *The Paraelectric Resonance of Lithium-Doped Potassium Bromide* in 1978.[257] Russell was ordained a UCC minister that same year.[258]

Dr. Russell then took a faculty position in physics at Carleton College, where he met Ian Barbour. He remained at Carleton until 1981, when he moved back to California to teach at the Jesuit School of Theology at Berkeley and found a non-profit organization, the Center for Theology and the Natural Sciences. The Center[259] has since become a unit at the Graduate Theological Union (GTU), presently a consortium of eight private, independent theological schools and 11 centers and affiliates.[260] Russell himself joined the GTU faculty and is currently the Ian G. Barbour Professor of Theology and Science.[261] Russell is well-known for his role as an editor in the five-volume *Scientific Perspectives on Divine Action* series that covers topics in neuroscience, chaos theory, quantum mechanics, evolutionary biology, and cosmology.[262] *Scientific Perspectives on Divine Action* was the fruit of more than a decade of scholarly conferences co-sponsored by the Vatican Observatory and the Center for Theology and the Natural Sciences.

256 Robert John Russell, "Life and Significance of Ian Barbour," interview by Joseph R. Laracy, Email, December 23, 2017.

257 Robert John Russell, "The Paraelectric Resonance of Lithium-Doped Potassium Bromide" (PhD, University of California at Santa Cruz, 1978).

258 Robert John Russell, "Curriculum Vitæ," last modified 2009, accessed December 6, 2017, http://www.ctns.org/BOBCV%209%2009.pdf.

259 In 2017, the Center was renamed the Francisco J. Ayala Center for Theology and the Natural Sciences following Professor Ayala's $2 million gift.

260 David Stiver, "History of the Graduate Theological Union," *Graduate Theological Union*, last modified July 5, 2017, accessed December 6, 2017, https://www.gtu.edu/about/history.

261 Russell, "Curriculum Vitæ."

262 As an example, see: Robert John Russell, Nancey Murphy, and Arthur R. Peacocke, eds., *Chaos Complexity: Scientific Perspectives On Divine Action*, 2nd ed., vol. 2 (Vatican City State: University of Notre Dame Press, 1997).

As the name of his endowed professorship implies, Russell is a great admirer of the life and work of Ian Barbour. In 2004, Russell edited the first *Festschrift*[263] for a contemporary scholar of theology and science entitled *Fifty Years in Science and Religion: Ian G. Barbour and His Legacy*.[264] This volume brought together 19 prominent academics to present a largely positive, yet also critical assessment of Barbour's scholarship. More recently, in a special edition of the journal, *Theology and Science*, Russell paid tribute to the remarkable influence of Ian Barbour on that interdisciplinary field. He described Barbour's 1966 book, *Issues in Science and Religion*, as a "turning point in the constructive relations between science and religion."[265]

For Russell, a fundamental issue for the field of theology and science is the methodological question of how to relate two, seemingly disparate fields. He sees Barbour's critical realism as *the methodology* for a bridge[266] between the two areas of inquiry, permitting "traffic" in both directions.[267] Russell concurs with Barbour in his rejection of what Barbour calls *naïve* realism,[268] as well as instrumentalism and idealism. They both agree that metaphors and models, the linguistic expressions of scientific theories and religious beliefs, are to "be taken seriously, but not literally"[269]—*cum grano salis*. Russell believes that despite fifty years of critique and development, Barbour's notion of critical realism continues to be "defended, deployed, and diversified widely in theology and science, and continues to be presupposed by most working scientists, by many theologians, and in much of the public discourse about both science and religion."[270] He goes on to write, "I believe it be of enduring importance, both for its crucial role in the historical development of the past decades and as a point of departure for future research."[271]

Russell follows Barbour's approach, seeking an *integration* of science and theology through a "theology of nature," in which, according to Barbour,

---

263 Interestingly, the second *Festschrift* was for Russell himself: Nathan Hallanger and Ted Peters, eds., *God's Action in Nature's World: Essays in Honour of Robert John Russell* (Burlington: Routledge, 2006).

264 Robert John Russell, ed., *Fifty Years in Science and Religion: Ian G. Barbour and His Legacy*, Ashgate Science and Religion Series (Burlington, VT: Ashgate Publishing, 2004).

265 Robert John Russell, "Assessing Ian G. Barbour's Contributions to Theology and Science," *Theology and Science* 15, no. 1 (January 2, 2017): 1.

266 Robert John Russell, "Bridging Theology and Science: The CTNS Logo," *Theology and Science* 1, no. 1 (April 2003): 1–3.

267 Robert John Russell, "Ian Barbour's Methodological Breakthrough: Creating the 'Bridge' Between Science and Theology," *Theology and Science* 15, no. 1 (January 2, 2017): 28.

268 True *naïve* realism posits that human perceptions are *direct* registers of reality.

269 Barbour, *Myths, Models, and Paradigms*, 50.

270 Russell, "Ian Barbour's Methodological Breakthrough," 36.

271 Ibid.

"scientific theories may affect the reformulation of certain doctrines, particularly the doctrines of creation and human nature."[272] Russell attempts to take the latest scientific theories and bring them into "creative mutual interaction" with Christian doctrines.[273] In many instances, this integration is a "one-way street." Contemporary scientific developments are invoked either to strengthen a doctrinal position, or to force theologians to reformulate it.

Russell differs from Barbour in his ontological commitments and utilizes non-foundationalist[274] epistemologies in his work in theology and science.[275] In his effort to avoid both monism (e.g., reductive materialism or idealism) and dualism (e.g., vitalism[276] or Cartesianism[277]), Barbour adopts Whitehead's approach of organicism (referred to as *panexperientialism* by David Griffin[278]) that "attributes *experience* in progressively more attenuated forms to persons, animals, lower organisms, and cells (and even, in principle, to atoms, though at that level it is effectively negligible), but not to stones or plants or other unintegrated entities."[279] Russell, on the other hand, favors a theory of ontological emergence in which

272 Barbour, *Religion and Science*, 98.

273 Robert John Russell, *Cosmology: From Alpha to Omega* (Minneapolis: Fortress Press, 2008).

274 It must be noted that there are variety of forms of foundationalism and non-foundationalism. Foundationalism can refer to a Cartesian epistemic standard requiring "clear and distinct ideas" to provide a solid base for inquiry. A foundationalist may also insist that rational justification for knowledge requires evidential certainty in a Humean sense. In addition, foundationalism can refer to the use of a "first philosophy" to provide metaphysical underpinnings for theological or scientific claims. According to Guarino, non-foundationalists often assert that the use of metaphysics "calcifies reality and betrays the encompassing horizons of historicity and cultural-linguistic determinacy." See footnote 30 in Guarino, *Foundations of Systematic Theology*, 30–31.

275 Robert John Russell and Kirk Wegter-McNelly, "Science," in *The Blackwell Companion to Modern Theology*, ed. Gareth Jones (Malden: Wiley-Blackwell, 2007), 517.

276 The philosophy of vitalism posits that a non-material, i.e., spiritual, "force" or "principle" is necessary to bring organic matter to life.

277 Cartesian dualism posits that the ontologically distinct immaterial mind and the material body causally interact, perhaps through the pineal gland (*glandula pinealis*)—a small endocrine gland in the brain that produces melatonin. See Gert-Jan Lokhorst, "Descartes and the Pineal Gland," in *The Stanford Encyclopedia of Philosophy*, ed. Edward N. Zalta, Winter 2017. (Stanford: Metaphysics Research Lab, Stanford University, 2013), accessed May 9, 2018, https://plato.stanford.edu/archive/win2017/entries/pineal-gland/. See Werner Korf, Christof Schomerus, and Jörg H. Stehle, *The Pineal Organ, Its Hormone Melatonin, and the Photoneuroendocrine System*, vol. 146, Advances in Anatomy, Embryology and Cell Biology (New York: Springer, 1998).

278 David Ray Griffin, "Some Whiteheadian Comments," in *Mind in Nature: Essays on the Interface of Science and Philosophy*, ed. John B. Cobb and David Ray Griffin (Washington, D.C.: University Press of America, 1977), 97–100.

279 Barbour, *Nature, Human Nature, and God*, 95.

the new properties and processes that emerge at higher levels of organization indicate that the ontology of the world, though monistic, cannot be reduced to that described by physics alone. The ontological unity or monism of complex phenomena is thus intrinsically differentiated (as suggested by the term "dipolarity").[280]

While Russell's research certainly engages issues in the philosophy of physics, he does not work with one fundamental metaphysical system, e.g., process metaphysics or a particular Neo-Thomist metaphysics.

Notwithstanding the aforementioned differences with Peacocke, Polkinghorne, Russell, and other scholars working in the area of theology and science, Barbour's impact on the field in the late twentieth century and into the twenty-first century is enduring. His typologies of interaction continue to be applied and adapted. Barbour's attempt to develop common epistemological and metaphysical principles for both theology and science still inspire philosophical reflection on fundamental issues in the field. In the next chapter, Barbour's fundamental principles for relating theology and science will be examined. Without shifting fields into the discipline of intellectual biography, we must present some essential historical information on his major scholarly influences that clearly contribute to his theological presuppositions, epistemology, and metaphysics. Barbour's critical realism and process metaphysics will be a major focus of the next chapter.

280 Russell and Wegter-McNelly, "Science," 517.

CHAPTER TWO

Barbour's Fundamental Principles: Theological Presuppositions, Epistemology, and Metaphysics

1. Sources of Barbour's Theological Presuppositions

In order to investigate Ian Barbour's classification of the similarities and differences between theology and natural science (Chapter Three), and eventually critically examine his approach for relating the two fields (Chapter Four), it is necessary to elucidate his fundamental principles—*finis origine pendet*. These principles clearly emerge from some of the significant personal influences on his development as a scholar. Salient historical details are included as they relate to Barbour's intellectual formation and his significance in the history of ideas, e.g., advancing a realist epistemology in theology and science.[1]

Ian's father, George Brown Barbour, his father's close friend, Pierre Teilhard de Chardin, SJ, the philosophers Albert North Whitehead and Charles Hartshorne, as well as his professors at Yale Divinity School, especially H. Richard Niebuhr, Roland Bainton, and Robert Calhoun, all played a significant role in Ian Barbour's

---

1 Albert Einstein maintained that "epistemology without contact with science becomes an empty scheme. Science without epistemology is—insofar as it is thinkable at all—primitive and muddled." Albert Einstein, "Remarks Concerning the Essays Brought Together in This Co-Operative Volume," in *Albert Einstein: Philosopher-Scientist*, ed. Paul Arthur Schilpp, Library of Living Philosophers 7 (Evanston, IL: Northwestern University Press, 1949), 683.

development as a theology-science scholar. Many of his theological and philosophical commitments can be traced back to these individuals. Later in the chapter, Barbour's epistemological and metaphysical principles will be explored in depth. While the inspiration for his critical realism and process metaphysics comes from the natural sciences, he determines that these philosophical approaches are applicable in the religious sphere as well. We begin now identifying some central theological presuppositions that are inspired by his major personal influences.

1.1 George Brown Barbour

Ian Barbour's father, George Brown, was born in Edinburgh, Scotland in 1890, the son of an accomplished professor of obstetrics and gynecology, Alexander Hugh Freeland Barbour, and his wife, Margaret Nelson (née Brown). He was named after Margaret's father, the late George Brown, who was one of the Fathers of Confederation of Canada and later one of its prime ministers. When George Brown was a young child, Alexander Barbour took him and the rest of the family on a medical mission to China. As a husband and father, George Brown would do similarly decades later.[2]

Young George Brown attended a Montessori school, Merchiston Castle, in Edinburgh. In 1904, he had the opportunity for an academic year at Marburg University. There, George Brown studied organ performance and the German language. Afterward, he returned to Scotland and attended the University of Edinburgh, earning the MA degree with honors in classics. Alexander Barbour's graduation gift to his son was a trip around the world. George Brown decided to visit China to discern a possible vocation as a medical missionary. While he ultimately ruled out a career as a physician, he did become convinced of a vocation to bring Christ to the Chinese people. His son Hugh writes, "His travels and his later wartime experience convinced [George Brown] Barbour that the only hope for humanity lay in the practical application in everyday life of the principles and spirit of Christ."[3] George Brown also discerned that a science-based profession would benefit the Chinese people. Therefore, at the conclusion of his trip, George Brown enrolled in Saint John's College, Cambridge, to pursue a BA in geology.[4]

The start of World War I interrupted George Brown's scientific studies. He enlisted in the Friends' Ambulance Unit, serving from September 1914 until January 1919. Outside of Ypres, Belgium, George Brown treated casualties of German

---

2   Hugh S. Barbour, "Memorial to George Brown Barbour," *Geological Society of America* 9 (1979): 1.
3   Roger Mark Selya, "George Brown Barbour," *Geographers Biobibliographical Studies* 23 (2004): 14–33.
4   Barbour, "Memorial to George Brown Barbour," 1.

chemical warfare. As a budding scientist, he assisted with the chemical analysis of the poison gas.[5] George Brown also distinguished himself by managing the typhoid[6] epidemic in the area. For his valor, the British Red Cross enrolled him in the Order of Saint John. After the war, George Brown decided to continue his studies in geology at Columbia University in New York. There he met and married Dorothy Dickinson, a Columbia alumna with a passion for religious education.[7]

Upon the completion of his graduate coursework in 1920, George Brown began his mission to China, accepting a position as professor of applied geology at Yenching University in Peking. Dorothy continued her work in religious education, both teaching children and forming catechists. The couple welcomed three children of their own during their time in China: Hugh, Ian, and Robert Freeland. In August 1924, George Brown met the Jesuit paleontologist and philosopher, Pierre Teilhard de Chardin. Father Teilhard would prove to be a life-long professional colleague and personal friend.[8] In 1927, the Barbour family moved back to New York for George Brown to conclude his doctoral studies in geology. He earned his PhD in 1929.[9]

The Barbour family returned to China, but their second tour of duty proved to be short-lived. George Brown's field work during this time was mainly in Shansi and Shensi, endeavoring to analyze the Pliocene (5.333 to 2.58 million years ago) and Pleistocene (2.58 million to 11,700 years ago, also known as "The Ice Age") geological epochs of Yellow River basin. This work was essential for dating the "Peking Man."[10] With Teilhard, he also did important work at sites

5   The first large scale use by Germany of poison gas on the Western Front took place at the Second Battle of Ypres using chlorine gas. Chlorine gas reacts with water to form hypochlorous acid ($HClO$) which destroys moist tissue such as the eyes and lungs. The French lost over 5,000 men that day at Gravenstafel Ridge. For more information, see Ronald A. Greenfield et al., "Microbiological, Biological, and Chemical Weapons of Warfare and Terrorism," *The American Journal of the Medical Sciences* 323, no. 6 (June 2002): 326–340; Ulf Schmidt, *Secret Science: A Century of Poison Warfare and Human Experiments* (New York: Oxford University Press, 2015), 20–21.

6   Typhoid is often confused with typhus. Typhoid fever is a food-borne illness transmitted through contaminated food or water. It is a bacterial infection due to *Salmonella typhi*. Typhus fever is also caused by pathogenic bacteria, e.g., *Rickettsia prowazekii*, but transmitted by lice, ticks, and chiggers. Both diseases are potentially deadly. For more information, see Estée Török, Ed Moran, and Fiona Cooke, *Oxford Handbook of Infectious Diseases and Microbiology*, 2nd ed. (New York: Oxford University Press, 2017).

7   Selya, "George Brown Barbour."

8   Barbour, "Memorial to George Brown Barbour," 2.

9   Selya, "George Brown Barbour."

10 George B. Barbour, "The Geological Background of Peking Man (Sinanthropus)," *Science* 72, no. 1877 (December 19, 1930): 635–636; Shen et al., "Age of Zhoukoudian Homo Erectus Determined with 26Al/10Be Burial Dating."

in Niangtzekuan and Sangkanho.[11] Sadly, George Brown's sons came down with "Peking Fever," what is now known to be Histoplasmosis, a serious fungal infection caused by breathing in spores found in bat and bird excrement.[12]

The Barbours moved to California in 1931 due to the beneficial climate for respiratory diseases and the access to superior medical care. The rise of Maoist Communism prevented the family from returning.[13] In 1932, George Brown received a faculty position at the University of Cincinnati where he taught for two semesters. The Rockefeller Foundation then enabled him to enjoy a two-year stint at the University of London. George Brown would eventually return to Cincinnati for the bulk of his academic career, retiring as emeritus professor of geology and dean emeritus of the College of Arts and Sciences in 1960. He died peacefully in 1977 at age 86.[14]

Growing up as the son of George Brown Barbour, Ian surely received his passion for the natural sciences.[15] Along with his wife, Dorothy, George Brown also instilled in Ian and his siblings an active Christian faith. Despite the "conflict hypothesis" environment into which George Brown was born in the late nineteenth century, he lived his life as dedicated disciple of Jesus and a serious scientist. The seeds for Ian's development of the "alternative" modes of interaction for science and theology, e.g., dialogue and integration, no doubt were first planted in China by this missionary professor of geology. Ian Barbour learned at a young age that Christianity and natural science are not inherently in conflict.

1.2 Pierre Teilhard de Chardin, SJ

The influence of Pierre Teilhard de Chardin on Ian Barbour was due to the close friendship of the French priest with Ian's father mentioned in the previous section. Teilhard arrived in China three years after George Brown and family. Born in 1881 in the Château of Sarcenat at Orcines, France, Teilhard grew up in a home where his father, an amateur naturalist, taught him to appreciate the splendor of

---

11 Barbour, "Memorial to George Brown Barbour," 2–3.

12 "Histoplasmosis - Symptoms and Causes," *Mayo Clinic*, accessed January 10, 2018, http://www.mayoclinic.org/diseases-conditions/histoplasmosis/symptoms-causes/syc-20373495.

13 The Chinese Soviet Republic (CSR) was established in November 1931 by the future Communist Party of China leader, Mao Zedong, and others. After the Second World War and the successful Communist takeover of mainland China, Chairman Mao proclaimed the establishment of the People's Republic of China (PRC) in September 1949. For more information on twentieth century Chinese history, see Sun Shuyun, *The Long March: The True History of Communist China's Founding Myth* (New York: Anchor, 2008).

14 Selya, "George Brown Barbour."

15 Ian Barbour dedicated his ground-breaking text, *Issues in Science and Religion*, to his father.

creation; his mother, a very devout woman, instilled in him a deep spirituality. Teilhard attended the Jesuit College of Mongré, in Villefranche-sur-Saône, where he completed undergraduate degrees in mathematics and philosophy. He began the Jesuit novitiate at Aix-en-Provence in 1899.[16] Teilhard continued his education, earning a licentiate in literature in Caen, France in 1902. As a Scholastic, he taught physical sciences in Cairo, Egypt at the Jesuit College of the Holy Family. Teilhard was assigned to the theologate in Hastings, England, and was ordained a Catholic priest in 1911.[17]

Father Teilhard's first assignment was to the research staff of the Paleontology Laboratory of the *Muséum National d'Histoire Naturelle* in Paris.[18] The outbreak of World War I cut short his work at the museum. Teilhard was offered an officer's commission as a Catholic chaplain, but he chose to work as an enlisted stretcher-bearer instead. He served bravely in major battles including Champaign, Verdun, and the second Battle of the Marne. Teilhard was awarded the *Croix de Guerre* and the *Chevalier de la Legion d'Honneur*. Following the Allied victory over the Central Powers in 1918, Teilhard went to the Sorbonne in Paris for doctoral studies in geology. He earned his PhD in 1922 and proceeded to China for fieldwork in 1923.[19] According to American theologian and Teilhard scholar, Thomas King, SJ, over most of the next 23 years, Teilhard's "expeditions took him to difficult areas where he endured blistering heat, icy blizzards, poor food, sandstorms, snakes, flash floods, marauding bandits, civil war, political intrigue, bribery, and maddening policy changes leveled by unstable governments."[20] It was in this context that a life-long friendship emerged with a Scottish colleague, George Brown Barbour.[21]

In a letter to his sons following Teilhard's death, George Brown Barbour wrote,

> This afternoon came sad news, Père Teilhard had a brain hemorrhage yesterday after a joyous Easter ... he was gone within four minutes ... I am glad that you two boys, and

16 Editors of Encyclopædia Britannica, "Pierre Teilhard de Chardin," *Encyclopedia Britannica*, April 26, 2013, accessed January 10, 2018, https://www.britannica.com/biography/Pierre-Teilhard-de-Chardin.

17 "Pierre Teilhard de Chardin, SJ (1881–1955)," *Ignatian Spirituality*, accessed January 10, 2018, https://www.ignatianspirituality.com/ignatian-voices/20th-century-ignatian-voices/pierre-teilhard-de-chardin-sj.

18 Frank Frost Productions, "Accessing Teilhard's Past," *The Teilhard de Chardin Project*, November 19, 2017, accessed January 10, 2018, http://www.teilhardproject.com/accessing-teilhards/.

19 "Pierre Teilhard de Chardin, SJ (1881–1955)."

20 Pierre Teilhard de Chardin, *The Divine Milieu*, trans. Sion Cowell (Brighton, England: Sussex Academic Press, 2003), xvii.

21 Barbour, *In the Field with Teilhard de Chardin*.

Freeland also, knew him ... He was the most God-like man I have known—the only close friend among men I have loved after we were married.[22]

Toward the end of the letter, George Brown states, "He lived as he prayed, and with such deep humility that he was without the intellectual arrogance and assurance that spoils what so many men do. He was intensely interested in Ian's plans, and when I saw him ... asked that I keep him informed of how things were working out."[23] It was during this time that Ian Barbour was on sabbatical from his physics position at Kalamazoo College and pursuing a divinity degree at Yale.

According to Ian Barbour, one of Teilhard's great contributions is his development of a theology of nature, an approach for relating theology and science that Barbour places within the *integration* classification. A representative example of Teilhard's theology of nature is *Le Phénomène Humain*. It was written in the 1930s, published posthumously in 1955, and later translated into English in many editions as *The Phenomenon of Man*.[24] Barbour states that this book is most appropriately "viewed as a synthesis of scientific ideas with religious ideas derived from Christian tradition and experience."[25] While aspects of Teilhard's Roman Catholic theological and spiritual heritage are clearly present in this text, Barbour highlights how Teilhard's

> concept of God was modified by evolutionary ideas ... Teilhard speaks of continuing creation and a God immanent in an incomplete world. His vision of final convergence to an "Omega Point" is both a speculative extrapolation of evolutionary directionality and a distinctive interpretation of Christian eschatology.[26]

The Phenomenon of Man, and related works, have received a good deal of stricture, both from scientists and from theologians. Barbour acknowledges that many scientists challenge Teilhard's metaphorical extension of scientific terms without offering explanation or justification, e.g., "radial energy" and "psychic temperature."[27] Teilhard also at times fails to distinguish between well-established scientific theories and abstract philosophical concepts. From a Catholic theological perspective, objections have been raised that Teilhard's theology of nature at times contains ambiguities and errors related to panpsychism, pantheism, the doctrine of original sin, the doctrine of the incarnation, and the immutability of God.

22   George B. Barbour, "Letter to His Sons," April 11, 1955.
23   Ibid.
24   Chardin, *The Phenomenon of Man*.
25   Barbour, *Religion and Science*, 101.
26   Ibid., 101–102.
27   Ibid., 248.

For example, like Barbour, Teilhard does not maintain the traditional distinction between matter and spirit. Spiritual realities, such as intellective processes, are attributed to the simplest material entities, i.e., panpsychism. For example, in *The Phenomenon of Man*, Teilhard writes, "We are logically forced to assume the existence in rudimentary form of some sort of psyche in every corpuscle, even in those whose complexity is of such a low or modest order as to render it imperceptible."[28] Teilhard then takes the next step, like Barbour, in no longer maintaining a well-defined distinction between Creator and creature. He describes his view of the cosmos and God as a "superior form of pantheism,"[29] and in a letter admits to being "essentially pantheist."[30]

In discussions on drafts of *Gaudium et Spes*, Joseph Ratzinger, Karl Rahner, Hans Urs von Balthasar, and others critically engaged what they perceived to be an uncritical assessment of scientific and technological progress, a position personally associated with Teilhard.[31] Ratzinger's principal critique of the content of Schema XIII addressed the Church's relationship to the world of science and technology. The American priest and theologian, Joseph A. Komonchak, observes that "Joseph Ratzinger echoed many of Rahner's criticisms and added others to his own. He saw the text as approaching a Teilhardian identification of Christian hope with modern confidence in progress."[32]

Teilhard's optimism aside, in light of his ambiguities and errors related to panpsychism, pantheism, the doctrine of original sin, the doctrine of the incarnation, and the immutability of God, on June 30, 1962, the Congregation of the Holy Office issued a *monitum* (warning) for the writings of Teilhard de Chardin.[33] The

---

28 Chardin, *The Phenomenon of Man*, 301.

29 Ibid., 294.

30 Philippe de la Trinité, *Rome et Teilhard de Chardin* (Paris: Arthème Fayard, 1964), 168.

31 For example, see Hans Urs von Balthasar, *Theo-Drama: The Last Act*, trans. Graham Harrison, vol. 5, 5 vols. (San Francisco: Ignatius Press, 2003), I, B; Joseph Ratzinger, *Theological Highlights of Vatican II*, trans. Henry Traub, Gerard C. Thormann, and Werner Barzel (New York: Paulist Press, 1966), 100; Brandon Peterson, "Critical Voices: The Reactions of Rahner and Ratzinger to 'Schema XIII' (Gaudium et Spes)," *Modern Theology* 31, no. 1 (January 1, 2015): 1–26; Giovanni Turbanti, *Un Concilio per Il Mondo Moderno: La Redazione della Costituzione Pastorale "Gaudium et Spes" del Vaticano II* (Bologna: Il Mulino, 2000).

32 Joseph A. Komonchak, "Augustine, Aquinas, or the Gospel *sine glossa*? Divisions over *Gaudium et Spes*," in *Unfinished Journey: The Church 40 Years after Vatican II*, ed. Austen Ivereigh (New York: Continuum, 2004), 105.

33 "Several works of Fr. Pierre Teilhard de Chardin, some of which were posthumously published, are being edited and are gaining a good deal of success. Prescinding from a judgement about those points that concern the positive sciences, it is sufficiently clear that the above-mentioned works abound in such ambiguities and indeed even serious errors, as to offend Catholic doctrine. For this reason, the most eminent and most revered Fathers of the Holy Office exhort all Ordinaries

Congregation for the Doctrine of the Faith reiterated this concern in 1981 in light of reports that the 1962 warning no longer applied.[34] Teilhard's fellow Frenchman, the noted theologian and Church historian, Jean Cardinal Daniélou, SJ writes,

> Certainly the work of Père Teilhard, if studied in itself, presents many problems which should be progressively elucidated. It admits of serious lacunae, which could lead one astray from the true thought of the author. A not always rigorous language can lend itself to dangerous ambiguities. And so its usage is not without risks. It may possibly confuse Christians in their faith and only attract non-Christians to a vague "Christism."[35]

Barbour notes that Teilhard's writings do not "simply draw on inherited beliefs, for he proposes extensive doctrinal reformulation in the light of the idea of evolution."[36]

The aforementioned doctrinal concerns do not mean that Teilhard's thought should be dismissed. He is clearly a very significant intellectual of the twentieth century. Like Ian Barbour, his writings must be critically evaluated. No less a theologian than Benedict XVI has identified some positive aspects of Teilhard's thought. For example, in a 2009 homily, Pope Benedict referred to the "great vision" of Teilhard with his notion of the "cosmic liturgy":

> The role of the priesthood is to consecrate the world so that it may become a living host, a liturgy: so that the liturgy may not be something alongside the reality of the world, but that the world itself shall become a living host, a liturgy. This is also the great vision of Teilhard de Chardin: in the end we shall achieve a true cosmic liturgy, where the cosmos becomes a living host. And let us pray the Lord to help us become priests in this sense, to aid in the transformation of the world, in adoration of God, beginning with ourselves. That our lives may speak of God, that our lives may be a true liturgy, an announcement of God, a door through which the distant God may become the present God, and a true giving of ourselves to God.[37]

as well as the superiors of Religious institutes, rectors of seminaries and presidents of universities, effectively to protect the minds, particularly of the youth, against the dangers presented by the works of Fr. Teilhard de Chardin and of his followers." Sacred Congregation of the Holy Office, "Warning Regarding the Writings of Pierre Teilhard de Chardin," last modified June 30, 1962, accessed February 17, 2018, https://www.ewtn.com/library/CURIA/CDFTEILH.HTM.

34 Sacred Congregation for the Doctrine of the Faith, "Communiqué of the Press Office of the Holy See," July 20, 1981, accessed January 15, 2018, https://www.ewtn.com/library/CURIA/CDFTEILH.HTM.

35 Jean Danielou, "The Meaning and Significance of Teilhard de Chardin," trans. John Lyon, *Communio* 15, no. 3 (1988): 350–351.

36 Barbour, *Religion and Science*, 248.

37 Benedict XVI, "Homily at the Vespers in the Cathedral of Aosta," *L'Osservatore Romano*, July 24, 2009, accessed February 17, 2018, https://w2.vatican.va/content/benedict-xvi/en/homilies/2009/documents/hf_ben-xvi_hom_20090724_vespri-aosta.html.

More recently, Pope Francis made favorable reference to Teilhard in his encyclical, *Laudato Si'*.[38] Francis' Teilhardian ecological eschatology is consistent with the views of many contemporary Teilhard interpreters. Scholars such as Thomas Berry, John Haught, Ilia Delio, and Mary Evelyn Tucker all seek in various ways to utilize Teilhardian thought for the ecological movement.[39]

Nonetheless, very recent scholarship by the American theologian, John P. Slattery, reveals how from the 1920s until his death in 1955, Teilhard supported artificial contraception, racist eugenic practices, and looked down upon those whom he deemed to be "imperfect" humans.[40] Slattery argues that these ideas explicitly lay the foundation for Teilhard's cosmological theology. He writes, "An implementation of Teilhard's theology poses a serious problem ... as it can be shown to be unequivocally tied to Teilhard's opinions on the inequality of races, the acceptability of violence, and the employment of eugenics to create a more perfect humanity."[41]

Slattery adduces many examples showing how Teilhard's cosmic theology is "unequivocally and undeniably founded upon layers of bias against persons of various ethnicities, patent disregard for limits of science, and apathy in the face of massive suffering."[42] The connections between Teilhard's notions of the Omega Point,[43] the

---

38   Francis, *Laudato Si'*, 2015, 53.

39   John P. Slattery, "Dangerous Tendencies of Cosmic Theology: The Untold Legacy of Teilhard de Chardin," *Philosophy and Theology* 29, no. 1 (January 25, 2017): 72.

40   In a letter to Father Pierre Leroy, SJ, Teilhard expresses anger with the Vatican condemnation of the eugenics movement: "Why is it that in Rome, along with a 'Biblical Commission' there is no 'Scientific Commission' charged with pointing out to authorities the points on which one can be sure Humanity will take a stand tomorrow—points, I repeat, such as: 1) the question of eugenics (aimed at the optimum rather than the maximum in reproduction, and joined to a gradual separation of sexuality from reproduction); and 2) the absolute right (which must, of course, be regulated in its 'timing' and in its conditions!) *to try everything right to the end—even in the matter of human biology* ... And while all this is going on churchmen really think that they can still satisfy the world by promenading a statue of Fatima across the continents!—This kind of thinking manifests itself here in New York too, where Catholic organizations are noisily separating themselves from Trusts or Boards of charitable organizations which have agreed to associate with groups interested in methods of eugenics (even though these groups are just as interested in fecundity as they are in birth prevention)—O Pharisees!" (emphasis added) Pierre Teilhard de Chardin, *Letters from My Friend, Teilhard de Chardin, 1948–1955*, ed. Pierre Leroy, trans. Mary Lukas (New York: Paulist Press, 1980), 172.

41   Slattery, "Dangerous Tendencies of Cosmic Theology," 70.

42   Ibid., 73.

43   Teilhard speculated that all of history was moving toward a point of Divine unification at which there would be a maximum level of complexity and consciousness. See Chardin, *The Phenomenon of Man*, 261.

Noosphere,[44] and the divinization of the human species with biological "purification" and "perfection" are extremely troubling. A twenty-first century reception of Teilhard's thought cannot ignore these serious concerns. Slattery does note that there is no evidence of racist language until the mid-1920s. Therefore, perhaps scholars interested in Teilhard's thought should focus primarily on his early liturgical writings (as Benedict has done), e.g., the "Mass on the World."[45] *Nil desperandum,* there is no evidence of racism or eugenicist ideology in the writings of Ian Barbour.

As mentioned earlier, for Barbour, the highest degree of integration between theology and science is possible when a systematic synthesis is achieved through an inclusive metaphysical system. Barbour sees in Teilhard's research a "partially developed set of evolutionary metaphysical categories."[46] Teilhard rejected the Neo-Scholastic metaphysics of his Jesuit formation in favor of new approach that closely resembles process thought. While not as developed as Whitehead's metaphysics, Teilhard's philosophical foundations contain many similarities, e.g., emphasizing "becoming" and "process" over "being" and "substance," denying the distinction between matter and spirit, and asserting that there is a "mental" quality in all matter.[47]

Given the life and work of Pierre Teilhard de Chardin, it is not surprising that Ian Barbour was unsatisfied with the somewhat common, Protestant Anglophonic opinion that the only modality of interaction between Christian theology and the natural sciences was one of conflict. Here we have a reinforcement of the fundamental principle that he learned from his father. We also see an inspiration for Barbour's notion of *theologies of nature* and the importance of a *comprehensive metaphysics* for theology and science.

1.3 Alfred North Whitehead

During his early years at Carleton College, Ian Barbour was awarded a research fellowship that brought him to Harvard University in 1963. While there, Barbour attended a seminar on the English mathematician and philosopher, Alfred North Whitehead, by divinity professor Gordon D. Kaufman. Whitehead had previously served on the philosophy faculty at Harvard from 1924 until 1937. Born in Ramsgate, Kent, England, in 1861, Alfred was the son of an Anglican clergyman,

---

44 This "sphere of thought" emerges as the result of collective human consciousness and Teilhard considered it the next phase in human evolution. See Ibid., 278.

45 Slattery, "Dangerous Tendencies of Cosmic Theology," 80.

46 Barbour, *Religion and Science,* 249.

47 Ian G. Barbour, "Teilhard's Process Metaphysics," *Journal of Religion* 59 (1969): 136–159.

Alfred Whitehead, and his wife, Maria Sarah (née Buckmaster). He was the youngest of four children. After attending the Sherborne School in Dorset, he enrolled in Trinity College, Cambridge, where he earned the BA in Mathematics in 1884[48] under the direction of the dynamicist, Edward J. Routh.[49]

That same year he completed a dissertation on Maxwell's *Treatise on Electricity and Magnetism*, and was elected a Fellow of Trinity College. He then began his teaching career, lecturing in mathematics and physics. In 1890, he married Evelyn Wade, an Irish Catholic woman who grew up in France. Wade had a significant impact on Alfred. He seriously considered entering into full communion with the Catholic Church for the first seven years after their marriage, although he never "swam the Tiber." Shortly after his wedding, Whitehead also shifted his research emphasis from applied to pure mathematics, focusing on topics in algebra and logic.[50]

Recognizing the originality and significance of his research up to this point,[51] Cambridge conferred the degree of ScD on Whitehead in 1905.[52] His most famous mathematical text, a three-volume work, *Principia Mathematica*,[53] co-written with a former student, Bertrand Russell, was published between 1910 and 1913. Through a rigorous application of mathematical logic, Russell and Whitehead formally developed logical foundations for set theory, cardinal numbers, ordinal numbers, and real numbers.

After *Principia*, Whitehead shifted gears once again and began to explore topics in the philosophy of science, seeking more fundamental foundations than he thought that formal logic could offer. In 1924, he was recruited to join the philosophy faculty of Harvard University. Shortly after, he was invited to offer the 1925 Lowell Lectures. In this context, Whitehead presented his research on the history and philosophy of science as well as its relationship to culture. It was later published in book form as *Science and the Modern World*.[54]

48   John J. O'Connor and Edmund F. Robertson, "Alfred North Whitehead," *MacTutor History of Mathematics* (Scotland: School of Mathematics and Statistics | University of St Andrews, October 2003), accessed January 10, 2018, http://www-groups.dcs.st-and.ac.uk/history/Biographies/Whitehead.html.

49   "Edward Routh - The Mathematics Genealogy Project," accessed January 10, 2018, https://www.genealogy.math.ndsu.nodak.edu/id.php?id=101929.

50   O'Connor and Robertson, "Alfred North Whitehead."

51   Specifically, his research published in *Universal Algebra* (1898) and four *American Journal of Mathematics* papers (1901–1904) led to the ScD degree.

52   Michel Weber, *Whitehead's Pancreativism: The Basics*, Process Thought 7 (New Brunswick: Ontos Verlag, 2006), 3.

53   Alfred North Whitehead and Bertrand Russell, *Principia Mathematica*, 2nd ed., 3 vols. (Cambridge: Cambridge University Press, 1923).

54   Alfred North Whitehead, *Science and the Modern World* (New York: The Macmillan Co., 1931).

Whitehead is less well-known for his philosophical critique of Darwinian ideology.[55] As a logician and metaphysician, Whitehead was able to successfully parse Darwin's science from Darwinian ideology. For example, Whitehead drolly writes, "Scientists animated by the purpose of proving that they are purposeless constitute an interesting subject for study."[56]

Whitehead was invited to deliver the Gifford Lectures at the University of Edinburgh 1927–1928. These were published in 1929 as *Process and Reality: An Essay in Cosmology*,[57] and the book is regarded by many as his *magnum opus*. It endeavors to offer "a coherent, logical, necessary system of general ideas in terms of which every element of our experience can be interpreted."[58] Whitehead's metaphysical system has been analyzed by philosophers throughout the globe, not limited to the Anglophonic world.[59] In Whitehead's process thought, Ian Barbour found a metaphysics that sought to overcome Cartesian dualism. Rather than considering reality as matter *and* spirit (mind), a new event-based ontology promised an alternative that was not only scientifically reasonable to Barbour, but also had potential applicability for theology. Barbour's motivation and application of Whiteheadian metaphysics will be made manifest in detail later in this chapter.

55 The American theologian, Michael Hanby, also offers a compelling critique of Darwinian ideology. Hanby argues that metaphysics and theology are not "optional" in the discipline of science, and that the intractable problems of Darwinian biology are the direct result of its deeply flawed metaphysical and theological foundations. See Michael Hanby, *No God, No Science: Theology, Cosmology, Biology* (Oxford, UK: Wiley-Blackwell, 2016).

56 Alfred North Whitehead, *The Function of Reason* (Princeton: Princeton University Press, 1929), 12.

57 Stanley Jaki observes that although the subtitle indicates that *Process and Reality* will treat the topic of cosmology, it never deals with the cosmos or universe *per se*. Whitehead never acknowledges the important fact that there is a strict totality of things. Jaki writes, "Even the last chapter, 'God and the World,' is far more about a pantheistic God, who co-acts and even co-suffers with the world, than about the world itself. None of the half a dozen references in that book to relativity are to its cosmology ... Whitehead gave away something of his debt to Bergson and revealed much of the self-defeating tactic whereby purpose and humanness are reclaimed through a vitalization of the cosmos." Stanley L. Jaki, *Is There a Universe?* (New York: Wethersfield Institute, 1993), 70.

58 Whitehead, *Process and Reality*, 3.

59 For example, for an analysis in French from Jean-Marie Breuvart (emeritus professor of philosophy at the Catholic University of Lille) using tools borrowed from the French-German, post-Hegelian Kantian, Éric Weil, see Jean-Marie Breuvart, *Le Questionnement métaphysique d'A.N. Whitehead* (Louvain-la-Neuve, Belgium: Chromatika, 2013). In English, Leo A. Foley, SM offers a Neo-Scholastic critique of Whitehead's epistemology, ontology, notion of causality, and philosophy of God. See Leo A. Foley, *A Critique of the Philosophy of Being of Alfred North Whitehead in the Light of Thomistic Philosophy* (Washington, DC: The Catholic University of America Press, 1946).

1.4 Charles Hartshorne

Another major intellectual influence on Ian Barbour was the American philosopher, Charles Hartshorne. Hartshorne was born in Kittanning, Pennsylvania, USA on June 5, 1897 to Francis Cope, a clergyman in the Episcopal Church, and his wife, Marguerite (née Haughton) Hartshorne. Hartshorne entered Haverford College in 1915 but the First World War interrupted his education. Following his service as an Army medic in France, Hartshorne returned to the United States and enrolled in Harvard University. He earned the BA (1921), MA (1922), and PhD (1923) degrees in philosophy in record time. His dissertation, *The Unity of Being*, was supervised by Alfred North Whitehead.[60] Over the next two years, Hartshorne pursued a postdoctoral fellowship in Germany. At the University of Freiburg, he studied under Edmund Husserl. At the University of Marburg, he worked with Martin Heidegger.[61] In 1928, Dr. Hartshorne married Dorothy Eleanore Cooper, a Universalist, whom he had met at Harvard.[62]

Charles Hartshorne eventually found his intellectual home at the University of Chicago, the same place where Ian Barbour earned his PhD in Physics in 1950. Hartshorne served on the philosophy faculty from 1928 until 1955 and was an influential professor in the School of Divinity as well. Hartshorne later received a joint appointment at the Meadville Lombard Theological School, a Unitarian Universalist seminary.[63]

Given his strong interests in the philosophy of religion, Hartshorne is generally credited with transforming Whitehead's process philosophy into a process theology. Although, according to two of his biographers, he considered himself neither a Christian nor a theologian.[64] In 1948, Hartshorne published *The Divine Relativity: A Social Conception of God* in which he clearly identifies his deviation from the classical, Christian conception of God.[65] *Reality as Social Process: Studies*

60 Donald Wayne Viney, "Charles Hartshorne," *American Philosophers Before 1950*, Dictionary of Literary Biography, 2003, accessed January 15, 2018, https://web.archive.org/web/20070420043457/http://www.harvardsquarelbrary.org/Hartshorne/Viney/index.html.

61 Dan Dombrowski, "Charles Hartshorne," in *The Stanford Encyclopedia of Philosophy*, ed. Edward N. Zalta (Stanford: Metaphysics Research Lab, Stanford University, 2017), accessed January 15, 2018, https://plato.stanford.edu/archives/spr2017/entries/hartshorne/.

62 Donald Wayne Viney, "Charles Hartshorne," *Dictionary of Unitarian and Universalist Biography* (Unitarian Universalist History & Heritage Society, July 15, 2002), accessed January 15, 2018, http://uudb.org/articles/charleshartshorne.html.

63 Ibid.

64 Donald Wayne Viney and George W. Shields, "Charles Hartshorne: Dipolar Theism," *Internet Encyclopedia of Philosophy*, accessed January 26, 2018, https://www.iep.utm.edu/hart-d-t/#H1.

65 Hartshorne, *The Divine Relativity*.

in Metaphysics and Religion appeared in 1953, and lays out Hartshorne's intensely social, panpsychist view of creation.[66]

Hartshorne's theology of God, often referred to as "Neo-Classical," diverges significantly from orthodox, Christian theism. For example, Hartshorne's description of God involves potentiality (God is not *actus purus*). God creates *ex materia* (instead of *ex nihilo*), God has corporeality, God is non-omnipotent, and God is associated with temporality, mutability, only relative perfection, and ultimately panentheism.[67] Much of Hartshorne's revisions to traditional Christian doctrine are captured in his term, "dipolar theism," mentioned in Chapter One. Barbour is sympathetic to this perspective and concisely sums up Hartshorne's view expressed in the *Divine Relativity*:

> God is eternal in character and purpose but changing in the content of experience. God's essential nature is not dependent on any particular world. God will always exist and be perfect in love, goodness, and wisdom. God is omniscient in knowing all reality—though not the future, which is undecided and hence inherently unknowable. Even aspects of the divine that change have perfection of their own. God is not merely influenced by the world; God is "infinitely sensitive" and "ideally responsive." Divine love is supremely sympathetic participation in world processes.[68]

While Ian Barbour considers a variety of perspectives in his quest to promote integration between theology and the natural sciences, he ultimately concludes that the process approach of Whitehead and Hartshorne is the most promising. Barbour's use of process concepts and categories will be developed in detail later in this chapter.

1.5 Yale Divinity School

Ian Barbour's formal theological education at Yale Divinity School was a decisive experience in his development as a scholar. The Collegiate School (which would later become Yale College) was founded in 1701 with "the grand errand" of propagating "the blessed reformed Protestant religion in the wilderness."[69] The primary mission was the formation of Congregationalist ministers in what was then the Connecticut River Colony, a British Puritan settlement. In the mid-twentieth century, when Barbour was a student, Yale had become a center of post-liberal,

---

66 Charles Hartshorne, *Reality as Social Process: Studies in Metaphysics and Religion* (New York: Free Press, 1953).

67 Dombrowski, "Charles Hartshorne."

68 Barbour, *Religion and Science*, 294.

69 Roland Herbert Bainton, *Yale and the Ministry: A History of Education for the Christian Ministry at Yale from the Founding in 1701* (New York: Harper & Brothers, 1957), xi.

neo-orthodox Protestant theology. This form of narrative theology, sometimes referred to simply as the "Yale School," was a reaction to modernist theological liberalism in American and European academia.

Barbour's Yale theology professors discovered new foundations in the thought of Swiss Reformed theologian and pastor, Karl Barth. They also cautiously (re)examined Catholic thinkers such as Thomas Aquinas and Henri de Lubac, SJ.[70] Many of Barbour's Yale professors sought to take the Word of God—the Scriptures, and the Word Himself—Jesus, more seriously than their colleagues who had altered Christian doctrine and morals according to *Aufklärung* principles.

A constitutive aspect of Karl Barth's fundamental theology is the assertion of the ἀναλογίαν τῆς πίστεως[71] (*analogían tes písteos*)—*analogia fidei*, in opposition to the *analogia entis*. The analogy of faith has always been associated with the Church's *depositum fidei*. Some Protestant Christians define *analogia fidei* as the principle that *Scripturam ex Scriptura explicandam esse*. The analogy of faith also delineates Christian faith and praxis.[72] For *sola Scriptura* Protestants, the *analogia fidei* is identical with the *analogia Scripturæ*.

The German-Polish theologian, Erich Przywara, SJ, defines the analogy of being as the "the metaphysical insight that everything mutable or *in fieri* (and hence everything finite) can exist and act only by virtue of the fact that the ultimate ground of its existence and action is a being (*ein Seiendes*) that exists absolutely (and, as such, is infinite)."[73] Catholic theologians have always regarded the *analogia entis* as a fundamental metaphysical principle. It supports the natural knowledge of God, and therefore Catholics take a "both/and" approach to the two analogies (*entis et fidei*). Saint Bonaventure describes the *analogia entis* in his *Itinerarium mentis ad Deum*, 2.11:

> All created things of the sensible world lead the mind of the contemplator and wise man to eternal God ... They are the shades, the resonances, the pictures of that efficient, exemplifying, and ordering art; they are the tracks, simulacra, and spectacles; they are divinely given signs set before us for the purpose of seeing God. They are exemplifications set before our still unrefined and sense-oriented minds, so that by the sensible things which they see they might be transferred to the intelligible which they cannot see, as if by signs to the signified.[74]

---

70 William C. Placher, "Postliberal Theology," in *An Introduction to Christian Theology in the Twentieth Century*, ed. David F. Ford (Malden: Blackwell Publishers Ltd., 1997), 343–356.

71 Romans 12:6.

72 Charles Hodge, *Systematic Theology*, vol. 1 (Peabody, MA: Hendrickson Publishers, Inc., 1999), chap. 6.

73 Erich Przywara, *Schriften*, vol. 2 (Einsiedeln: Johannes Verlag, 1962), 7 cited in Thomas Joseph White, ed., *The Analogy of Being: Invention of the Antichrist or Wisdom of God?* (Grand Rapids: Eerdmans, 2010), 50.

74 Bonaventura, *The Mind's Road to God*, trans. George Boas (New York: Macmillan, 1953), 20.

Given the complexity of the issues involved in the mid-twentieth century Barthian debate around the use of analogy in theology, and the detail of his treatment of issues in his 14-volume *magnum opus, Kirchliche Dogmatik*,[75] there is always a risk of over-simplifying the problems when attempting to treat them succinctly. However, we believe it is fair to concisely state that Karl Barth's primary fear was that in acknowledging the legitimacy of the analogy of being, philosophy would be placed in a position superior to the Word of God. Barth believed that Biblical revelation was the only way by which the God of Jesus Christ, the Holy Trinity, revealed Himself. He insisted that man cannot come to know the one true God by reason alone.[76]

Barth's reaction to the notion of the analogy of being was quite vituperative. He writes, "I regard the *analogia entis* as the invention of Antichrist, and I believe that because of it, it is impossible ever to become a Roman Catholic, all other reasons for not doing so being to my mind shortsighted and trivial."[77] Like his Reformation forefathers, Barth's philippic is rooted in a fear that the unity and beauty of creation might overwhelm the *gloria crucis*.[78]

Catholic theologians such as Hans Urs von Balthasar[79] and Gottlieb Söhngen[80] responded to Barth with a vibrant defense of *analogia entis*. Söhngen and Balthasar both show how Barth gravely misunderstood the traditional Catholic position. Although very much a disciple of Barth, his fellow Swiss Protestant theologian, Emil Brunner, points out that to reject the analogy of being completely "cuts man off so radically from God that ... the end result can be nothing but the most advanced form of Nominalism, in which human words take on divine meanings that are purely arbitrary and are in no way reflected in a reality already existing in the midst of creatures."[81] The American theologian, Thomas Joseph White, OP, argues that Barth as well as Barthians as a group, "frequently adopt Kantian epistemological premises ... not because of a theological understanding derived

75 Karl Barth, *Die Kirchliche Dogmatik*, 14 vols. (Zürich: TVZ Theologischer Verlag, 1993).

76 See Karl Barth, *Church Dogmatics*, trans. Geoffrey W. Bromiley, 2nd ed. (Edinburgh: T&T Clark, 1975), vol. I.

77 Ibid, vol I.1, *xiii*.

78 For a brilliant analysis, comparing Protestant and Catholic approaches to relating the ontological and soteriological orders, see Guarino, *Foundations of Systematic Theology*, 20–25.

79 Hans Urs von Balthasar, *Karl Barth: Darstellung Und Deutung Seiner Theologie* (Köln: Verlag Jakob Hegner, 1951).

80 Gottlieb Söhngen, "Analogia Fidei: Gottähnlichkeit Allein Aus Glauben?," *Catholica* 3, no. 3 (1934): 116–136.

81 John I. Murphy, "Analogy of Faith," ed. Thomas Carson, *New Catholic Encyclopedia* (Farmington Hills: Thompson Gale, 2003), accessed January 29, 2018, http://www.encyclopedia.com/religion/encyclopedias-almanacs-transcripts-and-maps/analogy-faith.

from divine revelation but because they have inherited a set of philosophical commitments and presuppositions from the German Enlightenment and modern liberal Protestantism."[82]

Given the Barthian influence at Yale Divinity School, Ian Barbour's general rejection of natural theologies is not surprising. For example, at the very beginning of *Issues in Science and Religion*, Barbour writes,

> There is little interest today in looking to nature for support for religious beliefs; the once-popular arguments of "natural theology"—such as the claim that evidences of design prove the existence of a Designer—appear dubious logically and, more significantly, reflect a speculative approach very different from the attitudes characteristic of religion itself.[83]

Almost forty years later, Barbour writes, "Even if the argument [of the existence of God from natural theology] is accepted, it leads only to the distant God of deism … not the God of theism actively involved with the world and human life."[84] One can clearly see how the Barthian influence at Yale led Barbour to assert that *theologies of nature* (i.e., ecclesial theology, based on Divine revelation, in which doctrines are reformulated based on the finding mature science) are preferred to *natural theologies* (i.e., knowledge of God from creation, not directly dependent on supernatural revelation).

Barbour particularly appreciated his classes with Helmut Richard Niebuhr (the younger brother of theologian Reinhold Niebuhr), Roland Bainton, and Robert Calhoun.[85] H. Richard Niebuhr was a Reformed/Evangelical Minister who served as a professor of Christian ethics at Yale. An alumnus of Yale (PhD 1924), H. Richard Niebuhr was a clear leader of the "Yale School." He is perhaps most well-known for his 1951 book, *Christ and Culture*, in which he examines Christ's relationship with society. Niebuhr explores scenarios in which Christ is "against," "of," and "above" culture. He also examines the situations of Christ "transforming" culture as well as being in "paradoxical" relation to it.[86] According to Ian Barbour's son, John, Niebuhr's scholarship on the limitations of kataphatic theology due to the role of context and interpretation for the theologian was very influential for Ian. Niebuhr also played a role in Barbour's theological understanding of conscience as

---

82 Thomas Joseph White, *The Incarnate Lord* (Washington, D.C.: CUA Press, 2015), 234–235.
83 Barbour, *Issues in Science and Religion*, 2.
84 Barbour, *Nature, Human Nature, and God*, 3.
85 Barbour, "A Personal Odyssey," 6–7.
86 H. Richard Niebuhr, *Christ and Culture*, 2nd ed. (San Francisco: Harper & Row, 1975).

a state of responsiveness to what God is doing in the world, which always requires interpretation.[87]

Barbour also mentions Roland Bainton as a significant scholar in his theological formation in "A Personal Odyssey."[88] Bainton was a Congregationalist minister with Quaker roots and professor of American Church History. He also specialized in the Reformation and particularly Martin Luther. Like Niebuhr, Bainton was a Yale alumnus (PhD 1921).[89] Bainton is well-known for his book on the history of Yale Divinity School, *Yale and the Ministry*.[90]

Beginning with Barbour's famous work, *Issues in Science and Religion*, and continuing throughout his life of scholarship, one notices a clear historical approach in his theological research, no doubt due to Professor Bainton. In his work to develop credible, contemporary modes of interaction for theology and the natural sciences, he realizes that he must understand deeply the issues of past centuries.[91] This idea comes through strongly in his revision of *Religion in an Age of Science*, published as *Religion and Science: Historical and Contemporary Issues*. Barbour's work shows a deep conviction that in-depth historical analysis of theological issues must precede attempts at new explorations and considerations—*historia est vitæ magistra*.

Finally, Ian Barbour cites Robert L. Calhoun, Yale professor of historical theology, as an important figure in his intellectual life. Calhoun received his PhD from Yale Divinity School and began teaching there in 1920. With the exception of a one-year assignment at Carleton College, Calhoun taught at Yale until 1965. He had strong ecumenical interests and served on significant committees with the World Council of Churches and the Federal Council of Churches. In his *New York Times* obituary, he is credited with helping "the Protestant churches find a unity of ancestry with the Orthodox and Roman Catholic churches."[92]

Barbour certainly absorbed his professor's ecumenical sensibilities. Throughout Barbour's books on theology and science, he looks not only within his mainline Protestant tradition, but also examines approaches taken by existentialist philosophers, linguistic analysts, Roman Catholics, and others. An awareness and

---

87 John Barbour, "The Life of Ian Barbour: An Interview with His Son, John," Email, November 14, 2017.

88 Barbour, "A Personal Odyssey," 6.

89 Walter H. Waggoner, "Dr. Roland H. Bainton Dies; Retired Yale Divinity Teacher," *The New York Times*, February 14, 1984, accessed January 16, 2018, http://www.nytimes.com/1984/02/14/obituaries/dr-roland-h-bainton-dies-retired-yale-divinity-teacher.html.

90 Bainton, *Yale and the Ministry*.

91 Barbour, "A Personal Odyssey," 6.

92 Walter H. Waggoner, "Rev. R.L. Calhoun, a Professor, Dies," *The New York Times*, September 30, 1983, accessed October 18, 2017, http://www.nytimes.com/1983/09/30/obituaries/rev-rl-calhoun-a-professor-dies.html.

appreciation of Neo-Thomism, especially that of Étienne Gilson, is a clear point of contact with the Catholic intellectual tradition.[93] Gilson tried very carefully in his philosophy to be congruent with Catholic doctrine. Consequently, Gilson's thought serves as a legitimate Catholic dialogue partner with Ian Barbour. Barbour unambiguously believed that research in theology and science should explore the approaches of diverse ecclesial communities and philosophical systems.

Having elucidated some of Ian Barbour's presuppositions for theological research and their origins in his major intellectual influences, we now consider his philosophical foundations in more depth. The remainder of Chapter Two will explicate Barbour's epistemology and metaphysics. The next section treats his particular form of philosophical realism—*critical realism*.

2. Critical Realism

2.1 Origins of the Critique of Knowledge

"Critical realism," Ian Barbour's epistemology for the theology-science interaction, is a term used equivocally by many other scholars. Before expounding Barbour's notion of critical realism, it is beneficial to understand the historical antecedents and distinguish other contemporary uses. Kees van Kooten Niekerk's research indicates that the first use of the term was in German philosophy. *Kritischer Realismus* "designates those positions which take account of Kant's critical epistemology but deny that the subjectivity of our experience makes it impossible to acquire valid knowledge of the external world as it is in itself."[94] Immanuel Kant supported an "empirical realism" alongside a "transcendental idealism."[95] In particular, he argued that his transcendental idealism could support a form of realism at the empirical level.

Most forms of critical realism are a consequence of Cartesian doubt. Cartesian doubt must be distinguished from scepticized doubt. For the French mathematician and philosopher, René Descartes, doubt is a *philosophical method* to discover truth. Scepticized doubt is more of a *way of life* and is inimical to seeking truth. Given his intellectual insecurity and the plethora of contradictions in the history of philosophy, Descartes questioned everything in his pursuit of truth. The Spanish

---

93   For example, see Barbour, *Religion and Science*, 309–310.

94   Kees van Kooten Niekerk, "A Critical Realist Perspective," in *Rethinking Theology and Science: Six Models for the Current Dialogue*, ed. Niels Henrik Gregersen and J. Wentzel van Huyssteen (Grand Rapids: Eerdmans, 1998), 51.

95   "… *das Ding an sich besteht zwar, ist aber nicht erkennbar.*" Rudolf Eisler, "Realismus," *Wörterbuch Der Philosophischen Begriffe* (Berlin: Mittler, 1929), 623.

philosopher, Julián Marías, synoptically sums up Descartes' basic axiom: "He must not accept a single 'truth' that is open to doubt."[96] Descartes arrives at his method of doubt for six reasons:

(1) People have championed the most diametrically opposed theses;
(2) Our senses often deceive us;
(3) We are subject to dreams;
(4) We are subject to hallucinations;
(5) We frequently fall into error;
(6) The presence of an "Evil Genius."[97]

Descartes hypothesizes the existence of an evil demon, a personification of deception who is "as clever and deceitful as he is powerful, who has directed his entire effort to misleading me."[98]

Descartes' reflection on doubt leads him to believe that the one thing that he knows for sure is his own existence:

> I noticed that while I thus chose to think that everything was false, it was necessarily true that I, who was thinking this, was something. And observing that this truth *I think, therefore I am* was so firm and so assured that all the most extravagant suppositions of the skeptics were incapable of shaking it, I judged that I could accept it without scruple as the first principle of the philosophy that I was seeking.[99]

Descartes concludes, *"Ego sum res cogitans"*—*"Je ne suis qu'une chose qui pense"*— "I am therefore precisely nothing but a thinking thing; that is, a mind, or intellect, or understanding, or reason."[100] With his *cogito* argument, Descartes has certainty of his own existence. From it, he develops an argument in favor of the existence of God based on the idea of God in his mind as a perfect, infinite, omnipotent, and

96 Julián Marías, *History of Philosophy*, trans. Stanley Appelbaum and Clarence C. Strowbridge, 22nd ed. (New York: Dover Publications, 1967), 213.
97 Ibid.
98 René Descartes, Meditations on First Philosophy in Which the Existence of God and the Distinction of the Soul from the Body Are Demonstrated, trans. Donald A. Cress (Indianapolis: Hackett Publishing Company, Inc., 1979), 16.
99 René Descartes, *Discourse on Method*, ed. Pamela Kraus and Frank Hunt, trans. Richard Kennington (Indianapolis: Hackett Publishing Company, Inc., 2012), 33.
100 Descartes, *Meditations on First Philosophy in Which the Existence of God and the Distinction of the Soul from the Body Are Demonstrated*, 19.

omniscient being. In Descartes' method, the philosophical starting point is not *esse*, but himself. It is both rationalistic[101] and idealistic.[102]

The Prussian Lutheran philosopher, Immanuel Kant, attempts to unite the post-Cartesian schools of Continental rationalism and British empiricism with his own synthesis. He seeks to develop a transcendental theory of knowledge. Commenting on Kant's reasoning, the Spanish philosopher, Julián Marías, writes, "if knowledge were transcendent, it would know external things. If it were immanent, it would know only ideas; that is, what is in me. But knowledge is transcendental: it knows the phenomena, that is, *the things in me.*"[103] This assertion is the basis for Kant's distinction between *noumena* and *phenomena*. Kant distinguishes between the extra-mental thing (i.e., noumenon) and the impression it makes on me (i.e., phenomenon). He posits that *das Ding an sich* is unattainable because one can only know it as it is affected by one's own subjectivity.[104] Kant acknowledges that one cannot envision anything outside of time and space, yet he asserts that the noumena are strangely neither spatial nor temporal.[105] Hence, Kant adopts ontological agnosticism.

2.2 Some Significant Equivocal Uses of the Term "Critical Realism"

The German Lutheran pastor and theologian, Andreas Losch, has done extensive research into the origins of critical realism. His investigation of critical realism(s) suggests that while the term is used by a number of philosophers, the connections between them are surprisingly few. It seems as though various scholars reinvent the term.[106] For example, in 1916, Roy Wood Sellars published the book *Critical Realism: A Study of the Nature and Conditions of Knowledge.*[107] According to Sellars' critical realism, "knowledge of external things and of past events is an

---

101 Philosophical rationalism posits that the criterion of truth is not sensory and empirical but intellectual and deductive. For more information, see Vernon J. Bourke, "Rationalism," ed. Dagobert D. Runes, *Dictionary of Philosophy* (Totowa, NJ: Littlefield, Adams, and Company, 1962), 263.

102 Descartes distinguishes between the *res extensa* (i.e., corporeal substance) and the *res cogitans* (i.e., mental reality). See René Descartes, *Principia Philosophiæ* (Amsterdam: Ludovicum Elzevirium, 1644), 2.002.

103 Marías, *History of Philosophy*, 286.

104 Immanuel Kant, *Critique of Pure Reason, Second Edition*, ed. Gary Banham, trans. Norman K. Smith, 2nd ed. (New York: Macmillan And Company Limited, 2007), part I, bk. II, chap. 3.

105 Ibid., 613.

106 Andreas Losch, "On the Origins of Critical Realism," *Theology and Science* 7, no. 1 (February 1, 2009): 85–106.

107 Roy Wood Sellars, *Critical Realism. A Study of the Nature and Conditions of Knowledge* (New York: Russell & Russell, 1916).

interpretation of these objects in terms of understood predicates and does not involve the literal presence of these objects in the field of consciousness of the knower."[108] Sellars, like Barbour decades later, develops his critical realism in order to avoid the problems he associates with so-called *naïve* realisms.

In 1932, the French Neo-Thomist, Jacques Maritain, published *Distinguer pour unir, ou Les degrés du savoir*. It appeared in English for the first time in 1937 as *Distinguish to Unite, or, The Degrees of Knowledge*. In defining his critical realism, Maritain strongly states that he does not engage in the idealism of Descartes and Kant. He wishes to frame *la critique du savoir* "in a manner quite different from the way idealism states it."[109]

According to the French philosopher and theologian, Réginald Marie Garrigou-Lagrange, OP, "in the strict sense of the word, to criticize is *to judge*, in conformity with the requirements of the object under investigation."[110] Along these lines, Maritain reframes the "critical problem." He maintains that the critical question is not: "How does one pass from *percipi* to *esse*?" Rather, Maritain asks,

> On the different levels of elaborating knowledge, what value must be assigned to *percipere* and what to *iudicare*? Since the mind, from the very start, reveals itself as warranted in its certitude by things and measured by an *esse* independent of itself, how are we to judge if, how, on what conditions, and to what extent it is both in principle and in the various moments of human knowledge?[111]

Maritain's critique focuses on the second act of the intellect: judgment.[112]

According to Maritain's critical realism, being is implicitly apprehended in sense experience. He asserts that being is known reflexively by abstraction from our senses, e.g., When I experience wetness on my feet while walking down the street, I immediately recognize that the object in question, the puddle, is an existent. One may also reach an "intuition of being" through the apprehension of *ens secundum quod est ens*. Maritain insists that

---

108 Roy Wood Sellars, "What Is the Correct Interpretation of Critical Realism?," *The Journal of Philosophy* 24, no. 9 (1927): 238.

109 Jacques Maritain, *Distinguish to Unite, or, The Degrees of Knowledge*, trans. Gerald Phelan, 4th ed. (New York: Charles Scribner's Sons, 1959), 73.

110 Réginald Garrigou-Lagrange, "Le Réalisme Thomiste et Le Mystere de La Connaissance," *Revue de Philosophie* 38, no. 1–2 (1931): 12.

111 Maritain, *Distinguish to Unite, or, The Degrees of Knowledge*, 73.

112 The object of the first act of the intellect, apprehension, is essence. The object of the second act of the intellect, judgment, is existence. Therefore, judgment is dependent on the existence of the entity. The entity may only exist in the mind (a being of reason), e.g., a unicorn.

the intellect embraces at one and the same time, and in its own proper sphere, both the possible real (the object "all being ..." set before the mind and grasped by it and signified in the statement of the principle of identity),[113] and the actual real (the reality of the thinking subject, though as not yet attained in final act [*in actu secundo*]). *Intelligible being* and the self are given to the intellect together and from the very start. But *being* is given in the foreground and up-stage; the *self* is in the background, behind the scenes, as it were. It is only with the mind's second moment, in the reflex intuition that serves as a starting point for critique, that it moves to the front of the stage. An authentic critique of knowledge does not imply a single instant of real or universal doubt.[114]

The American Thomist, John F.X. Knasas, concisely explains that "the heart of Maritain's 'critical realism' is the autonomous 'intellectual perception as such.'"[115]

Another American Thomist, Stephen Chamberlain, classifies Maritain's approach as a *via media* between the post-Kantian Transcendental Thomists[116] and the strict Aristotelians. Unlike some Transcendentalists who begin with the problem of knowing and implicitly place epistemology as first philosophy, Maritain concurs with Gilson and his school that "realism begins with sensation and the immediate apprehension and affirmation of the extra-mental real which cannot be doubted."[117] Maritain's use of the term "critical" for his realism is simply to distinguish the "Aristotelian-Thomistic noetic" from common sense, possibly *naïve* realism. Gilson is more comfortable simply calling this "philosophical realism."[118] For Maritain, "the task of critique is purely and exclusively reflexive and secondary ... it cannot for one single instant dispense with the knowledge of reality."[119] Barbour does not specify his critical realism with the detail and rigor of Maritain. However, one could envision Barbour concurring with Maritain's

---

113 "Every being is what it is."

114 Maritain, *Distinguish to Unite, or, The Degrees of Knowledge*, 78.

115 John F.X. Knasas, "Transcendental Thomist Methodology and Maritain's 'Critical Realism,'" in *Jacques Maritain and the Many Ways of Knowing*, ed. Douglas A. Ollivant (Washington, DC: CUA Press, 2002), 74.

116 As the British theologian, Francesca A. Murphy, describes it, while some critical realists, such as Maritain, sought to respond to Kant, Transcendental Thomists engaged Kant "on his own ground, by making rationality, in Kantian terms, the 'transcendental condition' of knowledge, the criterion of being or reality." Francesca Aran Murphy, *God Is Not a Story: Realism Revisited* (Oxford: Oxford University Press, 2007), 13.

117 Stephen Chamberlain, "The Dispute between Gilson and Maritain over Thomist Realism," *Studia Gilsoniana* 2, no. 2 (2017): 180.

118 Etienne Gilson, *Thomist Realism and the Critique of Knowledge*, trans. Mark A. Wauck (San Francisco: Ignatius Press, 2012), 53.

119 Maritain, *Distinguish to Unite, or, The Degrees of Knowledge*, 75.

approach: affirming a strong realism and also offering some supporting analysis of the process of cognition.

In his 1957 book, *Insight*, the Canadian scholar, Bernard Lonergan, SJ, developed his now popular "generalized empirical method" (GEM).[120] The GEM divides the process of human knowing into four levels: experience, understanding, judgment, and decision. Lonergan refers to the GEM as a *transcendental method* and a *critical realism*.[121] Like Barbour, his realism is inspired by the practice of natural science. He too wants to avoid the errors of *naïve* realism[122] on one hand, and empiricism on the other:

> The naïve realist knows the world mediated by meaning but thinks he knows it by looking. The empiricist restricts objective knowledge to sense experience; for him, understanding and conceiving, judging and believing are merely subjective activities. The idealist insists that human knowing always includes understanding as well as sense; but he retains the empiricist's notion of reality, and so he thinks of the world mediated by meaning as not real but ideal. Only the critical realist can acknowledge the facts of human knowing and pronounce the world mediated by meaning to be the real world; and he can do so only inasmuch as he shows that the process of experiencing, understanding, and judging is a process of self-transcendence.[123]

Following Thomas Aquinas, Lonergan maintains realism by according a priority to being and affirming that man makes true judgments of fact and of

120 Bernard Lonergan, *Insight: A Study of Human Understanding*, ed. Frederick Crowe and Robert Doran, 5th ed., vol. 3, Collected Works of Bernard Lonergan (Toronto: University of Toronto Press, Scholarly Publishing Division, 1992).

121 Andrew Beards, "Generalized Empirical Method," *The Lonergan Review* 3, no. 1 (2011): 33–87.

122 It is worth noting that in his 1966 article, "Metaphysics as Horizon," Lonergan critiques Barbour's favorite Thomist, Étienne Gilson, and accuses of him of "dogmatic," *naïve* realism. Gilson posits an "intuition of being"—an intellectual vision of the notion of *esse* in any sensible datum. For Gilson, the existence of a "bridge" between the mind and external reality is an axiom of Thomas Aquinas' epistemology and one does not "prove" axioms because they are self-evidently true. Lonergan accuses Gilson of not appreciating the conscious dynamics of "coming to know." Lonergan describes knowing as a dynamic structure of experiencing, understanding, and judging. See Bernard Lonergan, "Metaphysics as Horizon," *CrossCurrents* 16, no. 4 (1966): 481–494. Concisely summarizing Lonergan's position, Richard Liddy writes, "In the light of our innate drive toward the infinite horizon of being, the dynamics of our experiencing, understanding, and judging transcends the perceptual realm and, to the extent that we understand correctly, achieves objectivity." Richard Liddy, "Jaki and Lonergan: Confrontation or Encounter?," in *Stanley Jaki International Congress*, ed. Paul Haffner and Joseph R. Laracy (Leominster, UK: Gracewing Publishing, 2020), 87–88.

123 Bernard Lonergan, *Method in Theology*, 2nd ed. (Toronto: University of Toronto Press, Scholarly Publishing Division, 1990), 224.

value.[124] In light of Kant,[125] Lonergan incorporates a "critical aspect" as he sought to establish a theory of cognition in a critique of the operations of the mind. For Lonergan's metaphysics, the axioms are not a "set of propositions, but the dynamic structure of the human mind."[126]

One goal of the GEM is to inspire an "intellectual conversion" by which an individual has *personally* engaged the tasks of a cognitional theory, an epistemology, a metaphysics, and a methodology.[127] This "conversion" involves a "breakthrough" to one's own mind. It is similar to what happened to Saint Augustine in the summer of 386 AD when he read "a few books by the Platonists"[128] which he writes about in *The Confessions*. Lonergan's critical realism emerges from a personal journey of philosophical self-appropriation, using exercises that stimulate insights from mathematics, the natural sciences, and common sense. For Lonergan, What do I say about my *own* mind? is the key question. In *Insight*, Lonergan states,

> The crucial issue is an experimental issue, and the experiment will be performed not publicly but privately. It will consist in one's own rational self-consciousness clearly and distinctly taking possession of itself as rational self-consciousness. Up to that decisive achievement all leads. From it all follows. No one else, no matter what his knowledge or his eloquence, no matter what his logical rigor or his persuasiveness, can do it for you.[129]

124 The American philosopher, Gregory Floyd, points out that Lonergan's critical realism "maintained that in coming to know something through a reasoned and verified judgment we come to know the thing in itself. *Intelligere*—the key term in Lonergan's early study of Aquinas—is precisely the possibility of 'reading the inside of things' (*leger ab intus*)." Gregory P. Floyd, "Review of Transforming Light: Intellectual Conversion for Early Lonergan by Richard M. Liddy," *The Lonergan Review* 9 (2018): 146.

125 Lonergan believed that there was a need for a "second enlightenment" in order to address the philosophical problems created by Descartes and Kant. See Giovanni B. Sala, *Lonergan and Kant: Five Essays on Human Knowledge*, ed. Robert M. Doran, trans. Joseph Spoerl (Buffalo, NY: University of Toronto Press, 1994).

126 Lonergan, *Insight*, 3:532.

127 Echoing Lonergan, the American philosopher and theologian, Thomas Aquinas (Tad) Dunne, writes, "(1) A *cognitional* theory asks, 'What do I do when I know?' It encompasses what occurs in our judgments of fact and value. (2) An *epistemology* asks, 'Why is doing that knowing?' It demonstrates how these occurrences may appropriately be called 'objective.' (3) A *metaphysics* asks 'What do I know when I do it?' It identifies corresponding structures of the realities we know and value. (4) A *methodology* asks, 'What therefore should we do?' It lays out a framework for collaboration, based on the answers to the first three questions." Tad Dunne, "Bernard Lonergan," ed. James Fieser and Bradley Dowden, *Internet Encyclopedia of Philosophy*, 2018, accessed January 19, 2018, http://www.iep.utm.edu/lonergan/.

128 Augustine, *The Confessions*, ed. David Vincent Meconi, trans. Maria Boulding, Ignatius Critical Editions (San Francisco: Ignatius Press, 2012), xv.

129 Lonergan, *Insight*, 3:13.

According to Lonergan, to get the fourth level of the GEM (i.e., decision) correct, one needs the intellectual conversion that consists in getting the first three levels correct.

According to Paul Allen, what is crucial to appreciate from Lonergan's theory of knowing "is that the justification of critical realism as a theological epistemology arises from the success of theological method, not as something presupposed by artificially imposed categories."[130] Losch's research has shown that Lonergan's critical realism includes the medieval sense of the term "realism," *vis-à-vis* the reality of universals. Barbour's critical realism on the other hand is primarily concerned with the question of the existence of the spatio-temporal cosmos in light of Kant.[131] Phillip Thompson points out that Lonergan made a significant contribution with his epistemology as it created a "bridge," or "single perspective," that could be shared by mathematicians, natural scientists, philosophers, and theologians, to promote an authentic dialogue.[132]

Given Barbour's reliance on Alfred North Whitehead's philosophy, it should be noted that Lonergan scholars often strongly emphasize the distinction between Whiteheadian inspired critical realism and that of Lonergan. A common Lonerganian critique of process thought, concisely developed by Andrew Beards, and worth quoting at length, levels the charge of *epistemic perceptualism*:

> [According to] Lonergan's account of cognition and epistemology, a critical realism needs more than dogmatic assertions of the success of perceptual awareness in giving us a true picture of the world. What is required is a distinction between what is proper to human knowing alone and what we share with the animals in our spontaneous reactions to the environment. What is proper to human knowing alone are the intelligent and reasonable processes that, as was argued, can be verified in the data, that are our cognitional acts. Thus, judgments of truth, of what is the case, are a matter of reasonable operations on our part in which we gather and assess evidence and arrive at probable or definite conclusions. Arriving at such conclusions is a matter of exercising one's capacity for reasonableness, not an immediate or subrational staring or looking at reality. The perceptualist myth evident in Whitehead's account of consciousness and knowledge is the breeding ground for the endless variety of skeptical, idealist, and relativist philosophies, that from the dawn of philosophy down to our day, have relied in a parasitic fashion upon the myth of knowing as direct perception for their existence.

130 Paul L. Allen, "Is There Verification in Theology?," *Open Theology* 3, no. 1 (September 2, 2017): 428.

131 Andreas Losch, "Wright's Version of Critical Realism," in *God and the Faithfulness of Paul: A Critical Examination of the Pauline Theology of N. T. Wright*, ed. Christoph Heilig, J. Thomas Hewitt, and Michael F. Bird (Minneapolis: Fortress Press, 2017), 104.

132 Phillip M. Thompson, *Between Science and Religion: The Engagement of Catholic Intellectuals with Science and Technology in the Twentieth Century* (Plymouth, UK: Lexington Books, 2009), xix–xx.

Lonergan's critical realist position is presented not only as an argument for the possibility of a realist metaphysics in general but, in particular, it grounds metaphysical claims concerning the reality known in knowing our own cognitive structure and metaphysical principles operative in achieving that knowledge.[133]

In 1975, Roy Bhaskar completed his doctoral dissertation in philosophy at Oxford entitled *A Realist Theory of Science*.[134] Like Barbour, Bhaskar's early work in the philosophy of science sought to offer a defense of the rationality of scientific inquiry in the face of challenges from positivism and postmodernism. Bhaskar insists that a critical objectivity is possible and his critical realism accentuates the import of differentiating between metaphysical and epistemological issues. Losch's study of critical realism judges Bhaskar's variant to be a "self-contained" epistemology, clearly not reliant on Sellars' or Barbour's critical realism.[135] According to Losch, the origin of Bhaskar's use of the term arises from "a merger between his two basic assumptions of a *critical* naturalism and a transcendental *realism*."[136] While Barbour's philosophy is influenced by Alfred North Whitehead, Bhaskar's later thought is decidedly Marxist.[137] Brad Shipway's research has attempted to relate Bhaskar's critical realism to various forms of theological critical realism.[138]

Writing in the 1980s and responding to the work of Barbour and others, Ernan McMullin also employed the term *critical realism* in his treatment of issues in theology and science.[139] He offers a helpful clarification in the sometimes muddled historical discussion of the varieties of realism: "The realisms that philosophers in the past opposed to nominalism and to idealism are very different doctrines, and neither is connected, in any straightforward way at least, with the realism being referred here."[140] McMullin asserts that critical realism, understood as the concept of "approximating reality" in a cumulative sense, is only directly applicable to sciences like physics and chemistry.

133 Andrew Beards, *Method in Metaphysics: Lonergan and the Future of Analytical Philosophy* (Toronto: University of Toronto Press, 2008), 71–72.

134 Roy Bhaskar, "A Realist Theory of Science" (DPhil, University of Oxford, 1975).

135 Losch, "On the Origins of Critical Realism," 96.

136 Andreas Losch, "On the Relationship of Ian Barbour's and Roy Bhaskar's Critical Realism," *Journal of Critical Realism* 16, no. 1 (February 2017): 77.

137 Hans G. Ehrbar, "Marxism and Critical Realism" (Presented at the Meeting of the Heterodox Economics Students Association, University of Utah, Salt Lake City, 1998).

138 Brad Shipway, "Critical Realism and Theological Critical Realism: Opportunities for Dialogue?," *Alethia* 3, no. 2 (2000): 29–33.

139 Paul L. Allen, *Ernan McMullin and Critical Realism in the Science-Theology Dialogue* (Burlington: Routledge, 2006), 53.

140 Ernan McMullin, "A Case for Scientific Realism," in *Scientific Realism*, ed. Jarrett Leplin (Berkeley: University of California Press, 1984), 26.

In a 1985 article, responding to Arthur Peacocke, who follows Ian Barbour's critical realism very closely, McMullin describes where he differs with Peacocke (and consequently Barbour). McMullin does not believe that one epistemology (of critical realism) can apply in a similar way to both science and theology because the two disciplines do not deal with reality in an identical way. He avers that

> theology and science deal for the most part with different domains of the same reality. Science has no access to God in its explanations; theology has nothing to say about the specifics of the natural world. Where the two, however, may overlap and thus interact is in the *human domain*: each has things to say about the nature of the human reality.[141]

While acknowledging that the objects of study in both theology and science can never be described in an exhaustive, literal way, he cautions that "it would be unwise to push the parallels any further, or suggest that what enables the realism of science to be self-critical and progressive may somehow be transferred to the domain of religious belief."[142]

Compared to Barbour, McMullin emphasizes the *distinctive* cognitive processes involved in science and theology. In his elucidation of critical realism *in science*, he employs the theory of retroduction (i.e., inference to the best explanation). Retroductive (abductive) inference in science succeeded the inductive method of the Renaissance, which succeeded the earlier deductive method of Aristotle (e.g., reasoning syllogistically). McMullin writes,

> The principal way in which natural science enlarges our world is … through retroductive inference to structures, process, and entities postulated to be causally responsible for the regularities established by the experimental scientist or for the individual "traces" with which historical sciences like geology and evolutionary biology are concerned.[143]

James Pambrun describes McMullin's theory of retroduction as a "method of inquiry which incorporates distinct processes and operations (observation, theory, affirmation). It is a refined way of asking questions, identifying theories, and validating these theories."[144] For McMullin, this scientific method is not suitable for Catholic theology.

---

141 Ernan McMullin, "Realism in Theology and Science: A Response to Peacocke," *Religion and Intellectual Life* 2, no. 4 (1985): 39.

142 Ibid., 47.

143 Ernan McMullin, "Enlarging the World," in *Physics and Our View of the World*, ed. Jan Hildevoord (Cambridge: Cambridge University Press, 1994), 101.

144 James R. Pambrun, "Creation Ex Nihilo and Dual Causality," in *Creation and the God of Abraham*, ed. David B. Burrell et al. (Cambridge: Cambridge University Press, 2010), 196.

The Anglican bishop and Biblical scholar, N.T. Wright, authored a four-book series entitled *Christian Origins and the Question of God*. It includes *The New Testament and the People of God*,[145] *Jesus and the Victory of God*,[146] *The Resurrection of the Son of God*,[147] and *Paul and the Faithfulness of God*.[148] Wright's scholarship manifests at least two forms of critical realism. The critical realism expounded in his early work for the methodological Part II of *The New Testament and the People of God* is clearly inspired by Ian Barbour. Following the publication of Ben F. Meyer's, *Critical Realism and the New Testament*,[149] Wright claims that he adopted elements of Meyer's realism, which in turn comes from Bernard Lonergan.[150]

Wright defines critical realism as

> a way of describing the process of "knowing" that acknowledges the reality of the thing known, as something other than the knower (hence "realism"), while also fully acknowledging that the only access we have to this reality lies along the spiraling path of appropriate dialogue or conversation between the knower and the thing known (hence "critical").[151]

Wright's fundamental theological concern is that "where positivism cannot utter its shrill certainties, all that is left is subjectivity or relativity. The much-discussed contemporary phenomenon of cultural and theological relativism is itself in this sense simply the dark side of positivism."[152] He notes that

> in the New Testament field, some critics have made a great song and dance about the fact that the details of Jesus' life, or the fact of his resurrection, cannot be proved "scientifically"; philosophical rigor should compel them to admit that the same problem pertains to the vast range of ordinary human knowledge, including the implicit claim that knowledge requires empirical verification.

As a Biblical scholar, Wright posits the notion of *stories* as an analogue for the role of scientific hypotheses in Barbour's critical realism (which will be developed later in this chapter). Wright points out that in general, man perceives reality according to a worldview, which itself is characterized by key stories. He adapts Barbour's notion of the theory-ladenness of data, suggesting a "story-ladenness"

145 N.T. Wright, *The New Testament and the People of God* (Minneapolis: Fortress Press, 1992).

146 N.T. Wright, *Jesus and the Victory of God*, 6th ed. (Minneapolis: Fortress Press, 1997).

147 N.T. Wright, *The Resurrection of the Son of God*, 2nd ed. (London: SPCK Publishing, 2017).

148 N.T. Wright, *Paul and the Faithfulness of God* (Minneapolis: Fortress Press, 2013).

149 Ben F. Meyer, *Critical Realism and the New Testament*, Princeton Theological Monograph Series 17 (Allison Park: Pickwick, 1989).

150 Wright, *The New Testament and the People of God*, 32 note 3.

151 Ibid., 35.

152 Ibid., 33.

of objects. Wright concludes that the absolute extremes of the "objective" (e.g., *naïve* realism) and "subjective" (e.g., relativism) in exegesis must be discarded as nugatory.[153]

The Dutch Reformed minister and theologian, Jacobus Wentzel van Huyssteen, is another significant scholar associated with critical realism. His general quest is to develop a nonfoundationalist epistemology for theology and science in light of the challenges of postmodernism. He considers *foundationalism* a pejorative term, defined as "the view that systems of knowledge, in content or method, always require first principles."[154]

Van Huyssteen sees postmodern nonfoundationalism as the solution to modernity's reductivist rationality that has been largely hostile to religion. He writes,

> On a postfoundationalist view no generic, universal claims for realism (or even critical realism) can be made for the domains of our intellectual inquiry in general. For specifically theology I would still claim a mild form of critical realism as we try to understand the specific nature and standards of rationality of this specific mode of knowing. The form of modest critical realism I am arguing for sees exactly our experience as a transaction or relation between the rational agent and the world.[155]

Van Huyssteen therefore advocates a "pragmatic" or "weak" form of critical realism.[156] He believes that his postfoundationalist approach to rationality "transcends pitfalls like the kind of dualism that sets up a false dichotomy between 'natural' and 'supernatural.'"[157] In this area, one sees congruence with Barbour who also denies the distinction between the natural and spiritual. Through a perplexing combination of ontological realism and epistemological relativism,[158] Van Huyssteen tries to create "a safe place where our different discourses and actions are seen at times to link up with one another, and at times to contrast or conflict with one another."[159]

---

153 Ibid., 43–44.
154 J. Wentzel Van Huyssteen, *The Shaping of Rationality: Toward Interdisciplinarity in Theology and Science* (Grand Rapids, MI: Wm. B. Eerdmans Publishing Co., 1999), 61–62.
155 Ibid., 213.
156 Ibid., 218.
157 Ibid., 219.
158 Brad Shipway asserts that in this form of critical realism "the existence of an external reality is not a position to be argued towards, but a position from which argument proceeds. Instead of being a matter of discovery or the result of argument, it is seen as a pragmatic presupposition of inquiry." Shipway, "Critical Realism and Theological Critical Realism: Opportunities for Dialogue?," 31. This approach supports the "fallibilist" epistemology of van Huysteen and others.
159 Huyssteen, *The Shaping of Rationality*, 250.

He ultimately contends that this "transversal" or postfoundationalist approach to rationality can facilitate a fruitful interaction between theology and the natural sciences. Throughout *The Shaping of Rationality*, Huyssteen respectfully refers to Barbour's contributions to the theology-science interaction, including his form of critical realism. Huyssteen differs principally with Barbour in his strong embrace of postmodernism and nonfoundationalism.

The Evangelical Anglican clergyman and theologian, Alister McGrath, is known for his three-book series, *A Scientific Theology*, which investigates similarities and differences between the presuppositions and methodologies of theology and the natural sciences. He adopts a critical realism in order to navigate the epistemological issues associated with modern and postmodern thought; McGrath wishes to maintain objective truth but also incorporate the personal nature of all knowledge. In Book One of the series, entitled *Nature*, McGrath seeks to maintain a traditional concept of nature. He attempts to give it a proper foundation in the doctrine of creation.[160]

In Book Two, *Reality*, McGrath makes a strong argument in favor of realism, in the face of modern and postmodern criticism. He attempts to refute the claim that an acceptance of non-foundationalist ontologies implies the rejection of realist epistemologies. McGrath employs the critical realism of Roy Bhaskar.[161]

Book Three, *Theory*, explores how reality is represented in theology and the natural sciences. He defines theory quite generally as a "communal beholding of reality." McGrath concurs with Barbour on the importance of metaphysics in theology, although he does not adopt process thought. His analysis shows the postmodern objections to foundationalism to be incoherent. According to McGrath, theory serves as a bridge between experience (e.g., in science: empirical observation, in theology: revelation) and metaphysics.[162]

2.3 Origins in the Natural Sciences

Coming from a scientific background as an experimental physicist, Ian Barbour views theories as representations of the world; he was always a philosophical realist. In the inaugural issue of *Zygon: Journal of Religion & Science* in 1966, Barbour

---

160 Alister E. McGrath, *Nature*, A Scientific Theology 1 (Grand Rapids, MI: William B. Eerdmans Publishing Company, 2001).

161 Alister E. McGrath, *Reality*, A Scientific Theology 2 (Grand Rapids, MI: William B. Eerdmans Publishing Company, 2002).

162 Alister E. McGrath, *Theory*, A Scientific Theology 3 (Grand Rapids, MI: William B. Eerdmans Publishing Company, 2003).

first introduced his notion of critical realism.[163] The idea was popularized that same year when Barbour published his now classic work, *Issues in Science and Religion*. Critical realism is a theory of knowledge that Barbour uses throughout his scholarly works, although he never specifies it in the way that a "professional" philosopher would. His descriptions and definitions remain somewhat informal compared to other epistemologies.

According to Barbour, "*scientists usually assume realism* in their work."[164] Barbour rejects the positivist position that views theories as merely summaries of data, the instrumentalist position that sees theories as simply useful tools, and the idealist position that reduces theories to mental structures. In *Issues in Science and Religion*, Barbour writes,

> Against the positivist, the realist asserts that the real is not the observable. Against the instrumentalist, he affirms that valid concepts are true as well as useful. Against the idealist, he maintains that concepts represent the structure of events in the world. The patterns in the data are not imposed by us, but originate at least in part in *objective relationships in nature*. The object, not the subject, makes the predominant contribution to knowledge. Hence science is discovery and exploration, not just construction and invention.[165]

Although they represent a great diversity of viewpoints, Barbour mentions Max Planck, Albert Einstein, Norman Robert Campbell, William Henry Werkmeister, Alfred North Whitehead, Thomas Nagel, and of course, the Neo-Thomists, as significant thinkers (or schools of thinkers) who support some form of philosophical realism.

In order to justify his starting point in realism, which he ultimately hopes to apply both in the natural sciences as well as theology, he confronts the other common epistemologies present in the mid-twentieth century. The philosophy of science known as *positivism* is a variant of the broader school of *empiricism*. When speaking of empiricism, it is necessary to distinguish between the strict empiricism of the seventeenth and eighteenth century British empiricists (e.g., Francis Bacon and David Hume) and ancient skeptics (e.g., Pyrrho of Elis and his school), with the mitigated, metaphysical empiricism of Aristotle—the "Father of Western Science"—and Thomas Aquinas. While sense experience is the common starting point for both epistemologies, a metaphysical empiricist would assert that

---

163 Ian G. Barbour, "Commentary on Theological Resources from the Physical Sciences," *Zygon* 1, no. 1 (March 1966): 29.
164 Barbour, *Issues in Science and Religion*, 171.
165 Ibid., 168–169.

knowledge *begins* with sense experience, while a strict empiricist would claim that knowledge can be *reduced* to sense experience.[166]

The twentieth century positivists followed the strict empiricists in declaring that data obtained directly from sense experience, and filtered through human logic, constitutes the sole font of all (certain) knowledge. When Barbour was a young student of physics, the philosophies of Ernst Mach, Karl Pearson, and Percy Bridgman were very influential. As positivists, they reduced, each in his own way, scientific theories to "mental devices for classifying observations."[167]

Observability is often identified with reality for positivists. For example, in his famous book, *The Grammar of Science*, Karl Pearson writes,

> Either the atom is real, that is, capable of being a direct sense impression, or else it is ideal, that is, a purely mental conception by the aid of which we are enabled to formulate natural laws ... To no concept, however invaluable it may be as a means of describing the routine of perceptions, ought phenomenal existence to be ascribed until its perceptual equivalent has actually been disclosed.[168]

During Barbour's early research, two main variants of positivism existed: phenomenalism (advocated by Bertrand Russell[169]) and physicalism (advocated by Otto Neurath[170]). For a phenomenalist, the only valid data is sense-data. The only valid propositions are those which are simply statements of sense impressions.[171] The physicalist, on the other hand, insists that every proposition must be equivalent in meaning with some physical statement arising from direct experimental results.[172]

Positivism would eventually develop into "logical" positivism, emphasizing a verification principle, and more explicitly reject the rationality of theology, ethics, and even metaphysics. Citing Carl Gustav Hempel's article, "Problems and Changes in the Empiricist Criterion of Meaning,"[173] Barbour notes that "even

---

166 Richard De Brasi and Joseph R. Laracy, "An Empirical Critique of Empiricism," *Logos: A Journal of Catholic Thought and Culture* 16, no. 4 (October 3, 2013): 124.

167 Barbour, *Issues in Science and Religion*, 162.

168 Karl Pearson, *The Grammar of Science*, 3rd ed. (New York: The Macmillan Co., 1911), 96.

169 Bertrand Russell, *Our Knowledge of the External World* (London: The Open Court Publishing Company, 1914).

170 Otto Neurath, "Physicalism," *The Monist* 41, no. 4 (1931): 618–623.

171 Jack Lyons, "Epistemological Problems of Perception," in *The Stanford Encyclopedia of Philosophy*, ed. Edward N. Zalta (Stanford: Metaphysics Research Lab, Stanford University, 2016), accessed January 17, 2018, https://plato.stanford.edu/archives/spr2017/entries/perception-episprob/.

172 Daniel Stoljar, "Physicalism," in *The Stanford Encyclopedia of Philosophy*, ed. Edward N. Zalta (Stanford: Metaphysics Research Lab, Stanford University, 2015), accessed January 17, 2018, https://plato.stanford.edu/archives/win2017/entries/physicalism/.

173 Carl Gustav Hempel, "Problems and Changes in the Empiricist Criterion of Meaning," *Revue Internationale de Philosophie* 11 (1950), 41–63.

the attempt to translate all scientific sentences into *sense-data language* was never successfully carried out, and partial attempts produced unmanageable systems."[174] Barbour confidently rejects positivism for its manifest failure to acknowledge the essential role of theories and concepts in the history of the natural sciences.[175]

Logical positivism eventually gave birth to the school of linguistic analysis, which, when applied to the natural sciences, established the school of *instrumentalism*. In the 1950s and 1960s, when Barbour was a young scholar, he believed that instrumentalism was the most popular perspective among philosophers of science. It is certainly still with us today. Stephen Toulmin's 1953 book, *The Philosophy of Science*, was a representative work from the instrumentalism school. Toulmin and his colleagues reduced scientific laws to "instructions" for guiding a researcher. Theories were seen as simply procedures for making inferences.[176]

Barbour points out that, for the instrumentalist, theories are "fictions in the sense of being human inventions for coordinating or generating observation-statements."[177] As instrumentalists do not require real correspondence of theories to observable data, and in fact do not assert that there are real objects corresponding to theories, they cannot resolve the conflict between two contradictory theories that both explain the observed data. For a practicing scientist, such as Ian Barbour, this is a "game stopper."

The British scientists, Arthur Stanley Eddington, James Jeans, and Edward Arthur Milne, coming from the position of philosophical *idealism*, emphasized the role of the knowing subject even more than the instrumentalists. In the presence of sense-data, any theory that a scientist develops is merely an imposition of structure originating in the human mind. Eddington took this philosophy of science so far as to attempt to derive the fundamental constants of nature and the laws of physics from *a priori* principles without the benefit of experimental data. For him, scientific laws are really just the fruit of subjective selection:

> The fundamental laws and constants of physics are wholly subjective ... for we could not have this kind of *a priori* knowledge of laws governing an objective universe. The subjective laws are a consequence of the conceptual frame of thought into which our observational knowledge is forced by our method of formulating it.[178]

---

174 Barbour, *Issues in Science and Religion*, 163.

175 In Barbour's opposition to positivism in science, one notices parallels with the Hungarian physician and chemist, Michael Polanyi's, thought on the role of personal commitments in the actual practice of science. See Michael Polanyi, *Science, Faith, and Society* (Chicago: University Of Chicago Press, 1964).

176 Stephen Edelston Toulmin, *Philosophy of Science* (New York: Harper Collins, 2000).

177 Barbour, *Issues in Science and Religion*, 165.

178 Arthur Eddington, *The Philosophy of Physical Science* (Cambridge: Cambridge University Press, 1949), 105.

Barbour wisely points out that the views of Eddington neglect the experimental aspect of science in a manner similar to how the positivists, mentioned earlier, neglected the theoretical aspect.[179] Experimental results are indispensable for practicing scientists who need to reject one theory in order to accept another.

Barbour also engages idealists who developed a modified form of Neo-Kantianism such as Ernst Cassirer, Henry Margenau, and Carl Friedrich von Weizsäcker. Even for these philosophers of science, the mental construct (e.g., scientific theory) *is* the reality. For example, in his book, *The Nature of Physical Reality*, Margenau writes, "I am perfectly willing to admit that reality does change as discovery proceeds. I can see nothing basically wrong with a real world which undergoes modifications along with the flux of experience."[180] Barbour illustrates the absurdity of this position recognizing how Margenau asserted that the neutron did not exist until it was "invented" in 1932.[181]

According to Barbour, "realism insists that *being is prior to knowing*."[182] In light of the issues associated with studying atomic and sub-atomic phenomena, he suggests that direct perceptibility cannot be the definition of that which is real, given that these phenomena are often not directly apprehensible. Instead of observability, intelligibility may be considered the fundamental characteristic of what is real. Barbour writes that "it is precisely the organizing power of theoretical structures which shows that they correspond to the structure of the world."[183]

In Whitehead's philosophy, which Barbour largely adopts, while the object is given priority over the subject, the role of the subject is not neglected because

1) reality consists not of things but of events occurring in networks of relations which included both the knower and the known;
2) knowledge arises not from either subject or object alone but from a situation of mutual interaction; and
3) scientific language is symbolic, deriving from the subject's selective abstraction from the total situation.[184]

Barbour is very clear that he intends to avoid what he refers to as a *naïve realism*—a way of knowing that ignores human subjectivity all together and is often associated with a reductionistic view of reality. Reductionism in modern science is often traced back to the French mathematician and physicist, Pierre-Simon,

179 Barbour, *Issues in Science and Religion*, 167.
180 Henry Margenau, *The Nature of Physical Reality*, 2nd ed. (New York: McGraw-Hill Book Company, 1950), 295.
181 Barbour, *Issues in Science and Religion*, 168.
182 Ibid., 169.
183 Ibid., 170.
184 Ibid., 171.

Marquis de Laplace. While a truly brilliant scientist, Laplace's celestial mechanics, and physics in general, were explicitly deterministic. He writes,

> We ought then to regard the present state of the universe as the effect of its anterior state and as the cause of the one which is to follow. Given for one instant an intelligence which could comprehend all the forces by which nature is animated and the respective situation of the beings who compose it—an intelligence sufficiently vast to submit these data to analysis—it would embrace in the same formula the movements of the greatest bodies of the universe and those of the lightest atom; for it, nothing would be uncertain and the future, as the past, would be present to its eyes.[185]

Laplace's eighteenth century science could not foresee the significant role of "the observer" in many interpretations of quantum mechanics. There was also a strong sense in Laplacian (and more generally Newtonian) mechanics that differential equations written to model physical phenomena were literal descriptions of reality. Barbour identifies how *epistemological* reductionism was present in Laplace's belief that all phenomena would one day be explained exclusively with the laws of physics. *Metaphysical* reductionism arose from Laplace's conviction that reality is nothing more than matter-in-motion.[186] Although Laplace died in 1827, various forms of reductionism continue to emerge in the philosophy of science.

The creativity of the human imagination and the presence of mental constructs certainly influences the interpretation of experiences, including scientific ones. Therefore, Barbour advocates a *critical realism* that acknowledges the creativity of the human mind as well as the true presence of patterns in events that are not the product of mental operations. This realism must also recognize the indirectness of reference and the realistic intent of scientific language. According to Barbour, critical realism supports both the highly abstract nature of theoretical physics, as well as the requirement for corresponding experimental investigation.[187]

Barbour's critical realism posits that scientific theories are *representations* of the objective world. A theory is said to be valid for a scientist if it is both true and useful. Always careful to avoid *naïveté*, Barbour also recognizes that all scientific theories are *incomplete* and *selective*, i.e., they describe particular aspects of the natural world for specific purposes. His epistemology strives to avoid both the errors of literalism and fictionalism in theoretical models.[188] A critical realism approach takes these models *seriously but not literally*. Objects of study, e.g., gas molecules,

---

185 Pierre Simon Laplace, *A Philosophical Essay on Probabilities*, trans. Frederick Wilson Truscott and Frederick Lincoln Emory (New York: Dover, 1961), 4.
186 Barbour, *Issues in Science and Religion*, 59.
187 Ibid., 172.
188 Barbour, *Myths, Models, and Paradigms*, 37.

are acknowledged as often two stages removed from the well-known systems on which a model may be established. Barbour offers a helpful analogy from the kinetic theory of gases:

1) gas molecules are *not* the 'tiny elastic spheres' of the model (if we are not naïve realists), and
2) 'tiny elastic spheres' are *not* billiard balls (if we have kept negative analogy in mind).[189]

Ultimately, Barbour's critical realism posits that being (as *event*) precedes knowing. His emphasis on the fundamental metaphysical category of event will be explicated in section three of this chapter on process philosophy. At this point in the analysis, it is sufficient to point out the potential metaphysical problem of *esse* "dissolved" into event.[190] In the next section, we examine two applications of Barbour's critical realism. These application areas are chosen to further clarify his epistemology.

2.4 Applications: Quantum Indeterminacy and Human Freedom

Barbour propounds a variety of applications of the critical realist theory of knowing in the practice of science. One interesting example is motivated by the question of quantum indeterminacy, i.e., the apparent necessary incompleteness in the description of an atom or subatomic particle. Acknowledging that Laplace's mechanistic, deterministic description of the world is very inadequate, how is one to interpret Werner Heisenberg's uncertainty principle?[191]

(1) Is "uncertainty" a result of temporary human ignorance, e.g., exact laws for the atomic and subatomic realm remain to be discovered?
(2) Is "uncertainty" an intrinsic conceptual or experimental limitation, e.g., an observer necessarily disturbs any system that he studies?
(3) Is the "uncertainty" observed at the micro-scale an indication of true indeterminacy in nature, e.g., alternative potentialities?

Barbour characterizes the first proposal as *realistic* in epistemology and *deterministic* in metaphysics. He describes the second as *positivistic* in epistemology and

---

189 Ibid., 47.
190 This hazard can be resolved metaphysically by reference to the manner in which God's perfect actuality interiorly retains the flux of beings as distinct from itself.
191 Werner Heisenberg, "Über den Anschaulichen Inhalt der Quantentheoretischen Kinematik und Mechanik," *Zeitschrift für Physik* 43, no. 3–4 (1927): 172–198.

agnostic in metaphysics. The final solution, which he supports, is classified as *realistic* in epistemology and *indeterministic* in metaphysics.[192]

The realistic, deterministic solution was supported by Albert Einstein, Max Planck, Louis de Broglie, and David Bohm (known for his theory of "hidden variables"). In a letter to Max Born, Einstein states, "The great initial success of quantum theory cannot convert me to believe in that fundamental game of dice ... I am absolutely convinced that one will eventually arrive at a theory in which the objects connected by laws are not probabilities but conceived facts." He further avers, "I, at any rate, am convinced that [God] does not throw dice."[193]

While Bohr and Heisenberg are often grouped together as fathers of the Copenhagen interpretation of quantum mechanics, their actual interpretations of quantum theory differ in significant ways. Niels Bohr was the most well-known advocate of the interpretation that uncertainty arises from *experimental* (i.e., the process of observation) or *conceptual limitations* (i.e., a fundamental limitation of the human intellect).[194] Werner Heisenberg himself maintained the third position, i.e., that indeterminacy is an *objective feature of nature*. He believed that "the transition from the 'possible' to the 'actual' takes place during the act of observation."[195] Heisenberg's interpretation seems to enjoy the support of thousands of experiments, and many scientists today would accept it as a trustworthy description of nature. Barbour concludes that "such a viewpoint would accord with the critical realism we have advocated in which scientific theories are held to be representations of nature, albeit limited and imperfect ones."[196]

The implications of indeterminacy for human freedom is another area in which Ian Barbour applies his critical realism in an illustrative way. A starting point for this discussion is the claim that quantum indeterminacy provides for human freedom, whereas determinism in physics would exclude the possibility.

---

192 Barbour, *Issues in Science and Religion*, 298–299. It should be noted that Barbour's reading of Heisenberg's uncertainty principle seems to imply that one is observing indeterminacy (i.e., potency as such) somehow prior to its actualization. This is incoherent for a classical metaphysics of creation. To say that potency ever exists prior to act is to make act into an irrational, emergent phenomenon. *Esse* actualizes the potency of a thing's essence. Act brings potency into existence.

193 Albert Einstein, "Letter to Max Bohm," in *Natural Philosophy of Cause and Chance*, by Max Bohm (London: Oxford University Press, 1949), 122.

194 Niels Bohr, "Discussions with Einstein on Epistemological Problems in Atomic Physics," in *Albert Einstein: Philosopher-Scientist*, by Albert Einstein (Cambridge: Cambridge University Press, 1949).

195 Werner Heisenberg, *Physics and Philosophy: The Revolution in Modern Science* (New York: Harper & Brothers, 1958), 54.

196 Barbour, *Issues in Science and Religion*, 303.

"Hard determinism" is a well-known phenomenon. Barbour concisely summarizes it this way:

1) all events are determined,
2) freedom is the absence of determinism, and thus
3) freedom is illusory.[197]

Some behavioral psychologists, such as Burrhus Frederic Skinner, subscribe to a form of hard determinism and reduce the human person to a complex stimulus-response machine. Skinner writes,

> If we are to use the methods of science in the field of human affairs, we must assume that behavior is lawful and determined. We must expect to discover that what a man does is the result of specifiable conditions and that once these conditions have been discovered, we can anticipate and to some extent determine his actions … The self is most commonly used as a hypothetical cause of action. So long as external variables go unnoticed or are ignored, their function is assigned to an originating agent within the organism.[198]

Barbour describes "soft determinism" in the following way:

1) all events are determined,
2) freedom is not the absence of determinism, but a particular kind, namely *self-determination*, and thus
3) freedom so defined is compatible with determinism.[199]

"Motives" are the key principle in soft determinism and self-determination. While the definition of motives varies from "tendencies" to physical forces, for a soft determinist, "acts are determined by motives, and *motives are determined by earlier events.*"[200]

The development of quantum mechanics in the early twentieth century instigated some philosophers of science, such as Charles Sanders Peirce, to reflect on the implications for the brain and mind. Could minute, probabilistic fluctuations in physical causality explain the apparent spontaneity of the natural world and behavior of the human mind?[201] Arthur Stanley Eddington speculated that "at some brain center the course of behavior of certain atoms or elements of

---

197 Ibid., 305.
198 Burrhus Frederic Skinner, *Science and Human Behavior* (New York: The Macmillan Co., 1956), 6, 283.
199 Barbour, *Issues in Science and Religion*, 306.
200 Ibid., 307.
201 Charles Peirce, *Chance, Love, and Logic* (New York: Harcourt, 1923).

the physical world is directly determined for them by mental decision."[202] Debates arose, that continue to this day, about the possibility of single quantum event affecting the behavior of an organ, such as the brain. Further questions have been asked if the presence of randomness arising from a stochastic process[203] in nature necessarily implies "freedom" in the philosophical (moral) sense. Having investigated the matter thoroughly, Barbour concludes that a satisfactory understanding of human freedom will not be resolved through a further exploration of quantum indeterminacy.

Barbour posits that the phenomenon of human freedom can only be understood through an analysis of man's experience of "deliberation, decision, and the initiation of action."[204] He writes,

> Man's creativity is unpredictable in principle as well as in practice. To have predicted a Beethoven symphony would have required writing it before Beethoven did; to have foreseen Newton's laws would have meant discovering them before Newton. For a person to predict his own decision before it is made would require that he made it already.[205]

Barbour identifies a potential solution to the question of human freedom in René Descartes' anthropology (i.e., mind-body dualism). Descartes viewed the mind as a non-material entity that controls the body, free from the constraints of physical laws.[206] Barbour employs the approach of linguistic analysis to apply "complementary language" to resolve the dilemma, i.e., first person "actor language" is used when referring to human freedom and third person "spectator language" is employed when doing scientific observation.[207] In a surprising alliance between behaviorist and humanistic psychologists, Carl Rogers and Burrhus Frederic Skinner apply this approach in an article for *Science*:

202 Arthur Eddington, *The Nature of the Physical World* (Cambridge: Cambridge University Press, 1928), 332.
203 A stochastic process is a collection of random variables from some probability space. See Ionut Florescu, *Probability and Stochastic Processes* (Hoboken, NJ: John Wiley & Sons, 2014), 293. In the field of physics, a representative stochastic process is radioactive decay. Unstable nuclei emit radiation at unpredictable rate. According to quantum theory, it is impossible to predict when a particular nucleus will decay by emitting radiation, such as an alpha particle, beta particle, or gamma ray. See Brian R. Martin, *Nuclear and Particle Physics: An Introduction*, 2nd ed. (Chichester, UK: John Wiley & Sons, 2009), 53–55.
204 Barbour, *Issues in Science and Religion*, 310.
205 Ibid.
206 René Descartes, *The Passions of the Soul: Les Passions De l'Âme*, trans. Stephen Voss (Indianapolis: Hackett Publishing Company, Inc., 1989).
207 Barbour, *Issues in Science and Religion*, 310–311.

Behavior, when it is examined scientifically, is surely best understood as determined by prior causation. This is one great fact of science. But responsible personal choice, which is the core experience of psychotherapy, and which exists prior to any scientific endeavor, is an equally prominent fact in our lives. To deny the experience of responsible choice is, to me, as restricted a view as to deny the possibility of behavioral science. That these two important elements in our experience appear to be in contradiction has perhaps the same significance as the contradiction between the wave theory and the corpuscular theory of light, both of which can be shown to be true though incompatible.[208]

While determinist, indeterminist, dualist, and two-language perspectives can engage the concept of human freedom in a variety of interesting ways, Barbour is not convinced that any of them provide an adequate model of the human person. He believes that "the critical realist must seek *a coherent picture* while recognizing that all language-systems are selective and abstractive."[209] Barbour works toward a solution by starting with two fundamental propositions that few people would dismiss. First, he posits that it must be acknowledged that events in the past do condition the activity of a person. These influences could vary from clear memories to unconscious motives. Second, Barbour suggests that human decisions are influenced in some way by intellectual and moral principles.

Every person has values and ideals, some more noble than others, which influence his choices. Man is both *free from* total constraint (i.e., absolute compulsion) and *free to* achieve certain goals.[210] Although he does not cite the existential psychology of the Austrian neurologist and psychiatrist, Viktor Frankl, popularized in his 1946 book, … *trotzdem Ja zum Leben sagen: Ein Psychologe erlebt das Konzentrationslager*, and introduced in English in the United States in 1959 as *Man's Search for Meaning*, one notices a striking similarity in their understanding of human freedom.[211]

In rejecting the reductionist claim that human behavior can be directly derived from "physico-chemical" principles and the Cartesian dualist position that posits a realm of the person completely independent from the laws of physics, Barbour introduces his "theory of levels."[212] From his reading of the systems theorists, Karl

---

208 Carl Rogers and Burrhus Frederic Skinner, "Some Issues Concerning the Control of Human Behavior," *Science* 124, no. 3231 (November 30, 1956): 1057.

209 Barbour, *Issues in Science and Religion*, 312.

210 Ibid., 312–313.

211 Both Frankl and Barbour affirm the *fact* of human freedom. Frankl writes, "Everything can be taken from a man but one thing: the last of the human freedoms—to choose one's attitude in any given set of circumstances, to choose one's own way." Viktor E. Frankl, *Man's Search for Meaning*, trans. Ilse Lasch (Boston: Beacon Press, 2006), 66.

212 Barbour, *Issues in Science and Religion*, 313.

Ludwig von Bertalanffy and Norbert Wiener, Barbour seeks a system-level perspective that allows for a "whole" to be greater than the sum of its "parts" due to emergent properties. The resultant theory of levels includes *levels of analysis, levels of organization,* and *levels of activity.* Barbour's critical realism conceives scientific "symbols" as both *abstractive* and *selective.* Therefore, it is possible to utilize theories at different methodological levels simultaneously. Moving from higher to lower levels of analysis, one can speak coherently of psychological theories of major depressive disorder, neuro-scientific theories of brain function, and quantum theory of atoms that are contained in the human cranium. A notion of "weak causality" does not constrain higher levels to absolute dependence on the lower ones, as would be the case if there were no emergent properties.[213]

Barbour's critical realism also assumes that *levels of analysis* reflect objective *levels of organization* in nature, i.e., *levels of being.* Here one encounters not simply a methodological concept, but an ontological one. Drawing on his commitment to process thought that will be developed later in this chapter, Barbour rejects the "one-level" metaphysics of philosophical *materialism* and the "two-level" metaphysics of *vitalism*[214] inspired by Cartesian dualism, in favor of a multi-level *organicism* that more resembles a spectrum than discrete strata. Barbour writes, "To the critical realist, the concept of level is indeed an abstraction, and is relative to the concept of inquiry, but it reflects in a limited, partial fashion the real structure of the world."[215]

Process metaphysics leads Barbour to further consider *levels of activity* in contrast to *levels of substance.* He makes the point that the "types of events" that occur at varying levels in the human person do not occur in isolated atomic particles. Absolute dichotomies are avoided so that low-level events can be interpreted in terms of higher-level categories and vice-versa. For example, basing himself on Whitehead, Barbour asserts that the categories of "animate" and "inanimate" are present at all levels of nature, but in varying degrees.[216]

As the next chapter on the similarities and differences between theology and science according to Ian Barbour will make clear,

> science is not as objective, nor religion as subjective, as these two opposing schools of thought both assumed. Despite the presence of distinctive functions and attitudes in

---

213 Ibid., 335–336.
214 William Bechtel and Robert C. Williamson, "Vitalism," ed. Edward Craig, *Routledge Encyclopedia of Philosophy* (New York: Routledge, 1998), accessed January 19, 2018, https://www.rep.routledge.com/articles/thematic/vitalism/v-1.
215 Barbour, *Issues in Science and Religion*, 336.
216 Ibid., 336–337.

religion which have no parallels in science, there are also functions and attitudes in common, wherein I see differences of degree rather than an absolute dichotomy.[217]

Both science and theology make cognitive truth claims, i.e., they are knowledge-seeking enterprises. As the philosopher, Fabio Gironi, points out, if postmodernism pursues an amicable relationship between theology and science by weakening both fields' quest for knowledge, "(proclaiming the death of both God *and* reason), critical realist theology seeks to reconcile them by putting emphasis on different yet connatural rational abilities to know the world."[218] Having explored Ian Barbour's epistemology, the next section will offer an investigation of his metaphysics for theology and science: process philosophy.

3. Process Philosophy

3.1 Origins in Ancient Greece and the Thought of A.N. Whitehead

The beginning of process thought can be traced back to the sixth century before Christ with the pre-Socratic Greek philosopher, Heraclitus of Ephesus. Heraclitus' theory of a "ubiquitous dynamicity" posits a cosmic fire as the source of all change in the cosmos. His fundamental teaching is often concisely summarized with the maxim: πάντα ῥεῖ (*pánta rhei*)—everything flows. It is frequently presented with the expression: "No man ever steps in the same river twice." With the later development of the theories of atomism of Leucippus, Democritus, and Epicurus, a "counter-model" emerged that would prevail in Western thought for many centuries to come.[219] The fourth century BC substance metaphysics of Aristotle would eventually become a dominant paradigm, not seriously challenged until a twentieth century English-American philosopher of science explored an alternative.

In his Lowell Lecture of 1925, Whitehead stated that "nature is a structure of evolving processes. The reality is the process."[220] In the next years, Whitehead developed this view into an entirely new metaphysics. Originally presented at the Gifford Lectures, it would take its published form in the 1929 book *Process and Reality*. Whitehead begins his quest stating that his goal is to develop a *speculative*

217 Barbour, *Myths, Models, and Paradigms*, 5–6.

218 Fabio Gironi, "The Theological Hijacking of Realism: Critical Realism in 'Science and Religion,'" *Journal of Critical Realism* 11, no. 1 (2012): 50.

219 Johanna Seibt, "Process Philosophy," ed. Edward N. Zalta, *The Stanford Encyclopedia of Philosophy* (Stanford: Metaphysics Research Lab, Stanford University, October 26, 2017), accessed January 23, 2018, https://plato.stanford.edu/archives/win2017/entries/process-philosophy/.

220 Whitehead, *Science and the Modern World*, 106.

philosophy, "a coherent, logical, necessary system of general ideas in terms of which every element of our experience can be interpreted."[221] For Whitehead, such a philosophy must have a *rational* side (expressed by the terms "coherent" and "logical") and an *empirical* side (expressed by the terms "applicable" and "adequate"). The philosophy is "necessary" because it bears "in itself its own warrant of universality throughout all experience."[222]

Looking back to the seventeenth century, Whitehead judges Descartes' theory of two types of substance, corporeal and mental, as a source of *incoherence* in Western thought. He sees a positive development in Benedict de Spinoza's metaphysics which posits one thing, substance, and its modifications (or modes).[223] Whitehead's own metaphysics, which he often refers to as a *philosophy of organism*, differs from Spinoza's in that the "substance-quality" concept is not present. "Dynamic processes" are emphasized over "morphological descriptions."[224]

According to Whitehead, all philosophical systems include

> an ultimate which is actual in virtue of its accidents. It is only then capable of characterization through its accidental embodiments, and apart from these accidents is devoid of actuality. In the philosophy of organism this ultimate is termed "creativity;" and God is its primordial, non-temporal accident.[225]

In order to avoid the "taint of ineffectiveness,"[226] Whitehead suggests that philosophy always remain in dialogue with the natural sciences and religion. In fact, he states that philosophy "attains its chief importance by fusing the two ... into one rational scheme of thought."[227] This fusion does not imply a denial of the distinctiveness of either discipline. In Whitehead's thought, which bears echoes of Friedrich Schleiermacher, "religion is centered upon the harmony of rational thought with the sensitive reaction to the percepta from which experience originates [while] science is concerned with the harmony of rational thought with the percepta themselves."[228]

---

221 Whitehead, *Process and Reality*, 5.

222 Ibid., 6.

223 Spinoza's metaphysics are quite pantheistic. He asserts that there is only one substance, which is absolutely infinite, self-caused, and eternal, i.e., God or "Nature." For a systematic interpretation of the core of Spinoza's metaphysics, see Yitzhak Y. Melamed, *Spinoza's Metaphysics: Substance and Thought* (Oxford, UK: Oxford University Press, 2015), 3–138.

224 Whitehead, *Process and Reality*, 9.

225 Ibid., 10.

226 Ibid., 19.

227 Ibid.

228 Ibid., 19–20.

The philosophy of organism is based on four fundamental notions: *actual entity, prehension, nexus*, and the *ontological principle*. Whitehead's actual entities, also referred to as *actual occasions*, are spatiotemporally extended processes. They "are the final real things of which the world is made up. There is no going behind actual entities to find anything more real,"[229] writes Whitehead. In this system, actual entities vary from an undiscovered exocomet to God Himself.

The notion of prehension has origins in *Science and the Modern World*. Because of man's "pre-epistemic grasp of the world,"[230] he can begin a journey to know the world, and even carryout the activities of science. Whitehead asserts that prehension serves as a referent to the external world and includes emotion, purpose, valuation, and causation. Furthermore, "any characteristic of an actual entity is reproduced in a prehension."[231]

Because actual entities interact with each other through their mutual prehensions, nexūs arise. (Whitehead designates nexūs as the plural of nexus.) Every "particular fact of togetherness"[232] among actual entities is a nexus. Finally, having rejected the notion of substance in favor of actual entities, and having asserted that "the reasons for things are always to be found in the composite nature of definite actual entities," Whitehead encapsulates an ontological principle with the expression: "no actual entity, then no reason."[233]

The American priest and philosopher, Leo Foley, SM, makes the penetrating observation about how significant Whitehead's philosophy of God is for the rest of his metaphysics. Foley writes,

> We might say that Whitehead's notions of the "primordial" and "consequent" natures of God are a concise summary of his entire philosophy. Each actual entity acts according to its active nature, causes itself, tends towards its subjective aim. This subjective aim is the value phase for each entity, and each entity tending toward its value does so as an individual and as a member of an organic totum which is the world. The value phases is [*sic*] the "primordial" nature of God. God's "primordial" nature exists conceptually as the "lure for feeling." The achievement of perfection in the ordered activity constitutes the "consequent" nature of God, which is his function as the kingdom of heaven.[234]

---

229 Ibid., 23.
230 Gary L. Herstein, "Alfred North Whitehead," *Internet Encyclopedia of Philosophy*, accessed January 23, 2018, https://www.iep.utm.edu/whitehed/.
231 Whitehead, *Process and Reality*, 23.
232 Ibid., 24.
233 Ibid., 23.
234 Foley, *A Critique of the Philosophy of Being of Alfred North Whitehead in the Light of Thomistic Philosophy*, 82.

Whitehead's metaphysics is also rooted in a variety of categories. He posits that

> every entity should be a specific instance of one category of existence, every explanation should be a specific instance of categories of explanation, and every obligation should be a specific instance of categoreal obligations. The category of the Ultimate expresses the general principle presupposed in the three more special categories.[235]

The notions of "one," "many," and "creativity" define the category of the *Ultimate* and are assumed in the other categories. For Whitehead, creativity[236] is the principle of novelty and "the universal of universals, characterizing ultimate matters of fact."[237] He also develops eight categories of existence, 27 categories of explanation, and 9 categoreal obligations.[238] The aforementioned 44 classifications will not be treated in this work as they are not utilized by Barbour.

3.2 Barbour's Implementation of Whiteheadian Philosophical Principles

Ian Barbour adopts, adapts, and in many ways simplifies Whitehead's exceptionally detailed and complex metaphysics. He identifies four aspects of Whitehead's system that he sees as particularly consistent with twentieth century science and its evolutionary, many-leveled view of nature:

(1) the primacy of time,
(2) the interconnection of events,
(3) reality as an organic process, and
(4) the self-creation of every entity.

The primacy of time[239] encapsulates the process view that "becoming" is more significant than "being." According to Barbour, Whitehead is quite right in his

---

235 Whitehead, *Process and Reality*, 25.
236 A compelling critique of Whitehead's notion of "creativity" in light of Christian faith in creation is offered by Langdon Gilkey, *Reaping the Whirlwind* (New York: Seabury Press, 1981), 110–114. He is highly critical of panentheists who posit that the power of God is limited by the world.
237 Whitehead, *Process and Reality*, 25.
238 Ibid., 26–33.
239 One may notice parallels between Whitehead's notion of the primacy of time with one of Pope Francis' fundamental principles for building a people, "time is greater than space." For example, Francis writes, "A constant tension exists between fullness and limitation. Fullness evokes the desire for complete possession, while limitation is a wall set before us. Broadly speaking, 'time' has to do with fullness as an expression of the horizon which constantly opens before us, while each individual moment has to do with limitation as an expression of enclosure. People live poised between each individual moment and the greater, brighter horizon of the utopian future as the final cause which draws us to itself. Here we see a first principle for progress in building a people: time

assertion that "transition and activity are more fundamental than permanence and substance."[240] Barbour sees support for this perspective in the contemporary quantum perspective on subatomic particles as patterns of vibration,[241] as well as in the synthesis of Charles Darwin and Gregor Mendel's ideas which undergirds the modern evolutionary framework.

The Whiteheadian emphasis on the *interaction of events* is also consistent with modern science according to Barbour. He concurs with Whitehead that every entity is defined by its relationship to others. Events necessarily influence other events. In physics (e.g., the role of dynamic, interpenetrating fields) and in biology (e.g., the web of mutual dependencies that characterizes ecosystems), one finds support for an emphasis on the *interaction* of events. Directly related to interaction is the Whiteheadian view of *reality as organic process*. Components influence and are influenced by wholes. Barbour offers the multi-level example of mutual influence when considering the complex interaction of atoms, molecules, cells, organs, organisms, and communities. He sees creation "as a community of events."[242]

Whitehead posits that all entities, at any level of complexity, should be considered as experiencing subjects.[243] Events are not merely instantiations of potential interactions, but entities themselves with their own "individuality." Barbour avers that the *self-creation of every entity* occurs as a result of the "unique synthesis of the influences upon it, a new unity formed from an initial diversity."[244]

is greater than space." Francis, *Evangelii Gaudium*, 222. The Argentinian Jesuit and former professor of Jorge Bergoglio, Juan Carlos Scannone, SJ, traces the principle, "*tiempo sobre el espacio*," to the writings of General Juan Manuel de Rosas (1793–1877). Specifically, Scannone discovers the apparent origin of the principle in an 1834 letter from de Rosas to General Facundo Quiroga (1788–1835). See Juan Carlos Scannone, "El Papa Francisco y La Teología del Pueblo," *Razón y Fe*, no. 1395 (2014): 42.

240 Barbour, *Religion and Science*, 285.
241 According to quantum field theory, particles are viewed as "quanta," or "excitations," i.e., "vibrations," of a specific quantum field. These excitations or quanta in the field are often manifested to us as what one commonly thinks of as particles. For example, in the case of the electromagnetic field, photons are considered as quanta, or excitations, of that field. Each mode of vibration of the electromagnetic field corresponds to certain properties that we perceive in them, like momentum (of the photon). The key point to understand is that a particle is not a localized vibration in a quantum field; it is itself a localized vibration of the field with which it is associated. Mathematically, this can be understood with the idea of the harmonic oscillator and its corresponding solutions. It is essentially the solution to the wave equation, but quantized. For a more detailed explanation, see Steven Weinberg, *The Quantum Theory of Fields*, 3 vols. (Cambridge, UK: Cambridge University Press, 2005).
242 Barbour, *Religion and Science*, 285.
243 Whitehead, *Process and Reality*, 23.
244 Barbour, *Religion and Science*, 285.

In brief, Barbour's process view of reality is a dynamic network of particular "moments of experience," corresponding to Whitehead's "actual entities" or "actual occasions." Barbour modifies the terminology slightly by referring to them as "entities" (to highlight their integration) or "events" (to highlight their temporality). Whitehead's very detailed treatment of the complex process of causality is elegantly simplified by Barbour in three steps:

1) Every new entity is in part the product of *efficient causation*, which refers to the influence of previous entities on it. Objective "data" from the past are given to each present entity, to which it must conform, but it can do so in alternative ways.

2) There is thus an element of *self-causation* or self-creation, for an entity unifies its "data" in its own manner from its unique perspective on the universe. Every entity contributes something of its own in the way it appropriates its past, relates itself to various possibilities, and produces a novel synthesis that is not strictly deducible from its antecedents.

3) Thus a creative selection occurs from among alternative possibilities in terms of goals and aims, which is *final causation*.[245]

Concisely, Barbour believes that each novel occurrence in the universe is to be understood as a "present response (self-cause) to past entities (efficient cause) in terms of potentialities grasped (final cause)."[246] A metaphysical problem should be noted right away; Barbour considers final causes as *potential, not actual*.

There are certainly logical and useful aspects to Barbour's process thought, but a major issue is that he does not account for *esse simplex*[247]—the simple *to be*, the act of existing. His metaphysics does not acknowledge God as completely perfect actuality. Also, in Barbour's ontology, there is a fraught elevation of activity over substance. *Esse simplex*, properly understood, involves total stability in God. In creatures, it is the foundational stability of a nature/essence with the possibility of the actuality of potencies. These issues will be discussed in greater detail in Chapter Four.

Despite his falling away from the fundamental tenets of the Christian faith that he received from his parents, God remains a necessary feature of Whitehead's metaphysics.[248] He attributes to the Divine the "ground of novelty" as well as the

---

245 Ibid., 286.

246 Ibid.

247 According to James Doig, "physics must suppose that there is a mobile body, and mathematics that there is quantified or discrete continuum; metaphysics precisely by studying the *esse simplex* of everything, gives to the other two sciences their objects and their principles." James C. Doig, *Aquinas on Metaphysics: A Historico-Doctrinal Study of the Commentary on the Metaphysics* (The Hague: Martinus Nijhoff, 1972), 78.

248 Whitehead, *Process and Reality*, 286.

"ground of order." This perspective, which Barbour adopts as well, depicts God as another entity that exerts "influence" on the universe—God is not pure and perfect act. Barbour asserts that "God never determines the outcome of events or violates the self-creation of each being. Every entity is the joint product of past causes, divine purposes, and the new entity's own activity."[249] Barbour's process view of God will be discussed in greater detail in the next section.

Another aspect of Whitehead's metaphysics that Barbour adopts is his notion of "experience" attributed to all entities, no matter the simplicity. One can explore "levels of experience" that begin at the level of the subatomic particle and increase toward the atom, the cell, the mammal, and the human person. At each "level," a greater degree of "integration" is present and new opportunities for novelty arise. Downward causation is possible in more complex "organisms" as emergent properties influence constitutive entities. While subjective experience is attributed by Whitehead to organisms that range in complexity from *homo sapiens* to *salmonella enterica*, and even in a very minimal way to atomic particles, he does not ascribe it to inanimate aggregates such as rocks. Whitehead views "consciousness" as an emergent property that is only present in higher level organisms, e.g., with a central nervous system.[250] Because he does not acknowledge a "mind" in the lower levels of experience, as the description *panpsychism* might imply,[251] the term *panexperientialism* is suggested as a more accurate label.[252] It is interesting to note the lack of reference to the classical theological position that the intellect is a power of the human soul.[253]

Barbour identifies that Whitehead attributes basic experience to unified entities at all levels of complexity for three reasons. First, Whitehead insists on the *generality of all metaphysical categories*. He does not wish to admit a metaphysical category that is not universally applicable. The "experience" of a proton is postulated for ontological consistency, and experience at higher levels, e.g., the cell, is accounted for through emergence. A second reason for maintaining the general metaphysical category of experience is for *evolutionary and ontological consistency*. Whitehead and Barbour, do not want to make certain classical, fundamental distinctions between the status of an amœba and a human being. Arguing from the perspective of evolutionary history, Barbour states the "universe is continuous and interrelated."[254] In order to avoid what he perceives as any form of dualism—the

249 Barbour, *Religion and Science*, 287.
250 Whitehead, *Process and Reality*, 310–326.
251 Barbour, *Religion and Science*, 287–288.
252 Griffin, "Some Whiteheadian Comments."
253 Aquinas, *Summa Theologiæ*, I, Q 79, A 1.
254 Barbour, *Religion and Science*, 289.

summum malum in his view—Barbour casually rejects distinctions such as living vs non-living, human vs non-human, mind vs matter. He believes that mind cannot arise from matter unless there are "some intermediate stages or levels in between, and unless mind and matter share at least some characteristics in common."[255]

A third reason for applying the category of experience so broadly is the fact of *immediate access to human experience. Scio quod cogito.* Process metaphysics posits that human experience is an "edge case" of all experience in general. Therefore, it suggests that some degree of "interiority," perhaps imperceptible, is present in all organisms, broadly understood. Whitehead's categories of "self-creation" and "subjective aim" are applied to even the lowest level events, albeit in a diminished way. While Barbour follows Whitehead closely in the aforementioned areas, he does suggest modifications which he believes do not disturb the coherence of the system. One concern deals with the issue of treating the ends of the experience spectrum. On the lower end, dealing with the inanimate world, Barbour asks,

> Does process philosophy allow adequately for the radical diversity among levels of activity in the world and the emergence of genuine novelty at all stages of evolutionary history? Could greater emphasis be given to emergence and the contrasts between events at various levels, while preserving the basic postulate of metaphysical continuity?[256]

On the upper end, Barbour suggests that Whitehead's approach inadequately treats *the continuing identity of the human self.* Based on insights from quantum theory, Whitehead wants to characterize interactions as transitory and discrete. In light of Einstein's theories of relativity, he wishes to affirm that a finite time interval is necessary for the transmission of effects. Whitehead's metaphysics permits persisting characteristics through the repetition of patterns, rather than an enduring substance as found in the Aristotelian-Thomistic ontology. In Whitehead's thought, the *self* arises at the conclusion of a moment of unification, by which time it is already passing away. Barbour is not satisfied with this description and expresses his critique in this way:

> I would question whether human experience has such a fragmentary and episodic character. Perhaps reality at higher levels is more like a continually flowing process, from which temporal moments are abstractions. This might allow for a continuing self-identity without reverting to static or substantive or dualistic categories.[257]

---

255 Ibid.
256 Ibid., 290.
257 Ibid.

Overall, Ian Barbour finds process metaphysics to be an amiable first philosophy for the natural sciences. Both process thought and modern science rely on concepts of temporality, indeterminacy, and holism. In common with evolutionary biology, process metaphysics emphasizes historical continuity, e.g., panexperientialism. Barbour also appreciates the parallels with the general systems theory of Ludwig von Bertalanffy,[258] the systems philosophy of Ervin Laszlo,[259] and the theory of cybernetics of Norbert Wiener,[260] which emphasize concepts such as hierarchy, constraints, emergence, communication, and feedback.[261]

Barbour acknowledges that the notion of "subjective experience" in process metaphysics is a problem for some scientists. At least since the beginning of the seventeenth century, and due to the influence of Francis Bacon in particular,[262] empirical science has, at times, limited its scope to explore material and efficient causality. Formal and final causality have been deemed by some as "un-scientific."[263] In addition, referring to "experience" and "mind" in non-humans provokes the charge from some scientists of anthropomorphism. Despite these unresolved issues, Barbour states that "on balance ... process philosophy seems to be a promising attempt to provide a coherent system of concepts for interpreting a wide variety of phenomena in the world."[264]

3.3 Barbour's Appropriation of Process Theology

Ian Barbour's investigation into Whitehead's process thought was not simply for the purpose of adopting a metaphysics inspired by the discoveries of twentieth century physics, chemistry, and biology. Barbour, like Whitehead, desires a first philosophy that can handle the *data* of both scientific and religious experience.[265] In addition to Whitehead himself, Barbour identifies Charles Hartshorne as a

---

258 See Ludwig von Bertalanffy, *General System Theory: Foundations, Development, Applications,* Revised. (New York: George Braziller Inc., 2015); Mark Davidson, *Uncommon Sense: The Life and Thought of Ludwig von Bertalanffy, Father of General Systems Theory* (Los Angeles: J.P. Tarcher, 1983).

259 See Ervin Laszlo, *An Introduction to Systems Philosophy* (New York: Gordon & Breach, 1972).

260 See Norbert Wiener, *Cybernetics, or Control and Communication in the Animal and the Machine,* 2nd ed. (Cambridge: The MIT Press, 1965).

261 Barbour, *Religion and Science,* 291–292.

262 See Francis Bacon, *The Advancement of Learning* (London: Cassell & Company, 1893), accessed January 25, 2018, http://www.gutenberg.org/files/5500/5500-h/5500-h.htm.

263 There have certainlty been scientists throughout the ages that see finality and purpose in nature. It is also interesting to note that modern physics places a great emphasis on "mathematical form."

264 Barbour, *Religion and Science,* 293.

265 Barbour, *Issues in Science and Religion,* 129.

highly "influential exponent" of process thought who further develops the religious dimension of Whitehead's philosophy.[266] Barbour's theologies of God, creation, and man, all have clear foundations in Whitehead and/or Hartshorne.

Every *event* in the Whiteheadian system attributes a threefold role to God. First, God is *the primordial ground of order*. Due to God's knowledge and responsiveness to the world, He "selects possibilities for the 'initial subjective aims' of particular entities."[267] Second, Whitehead posits that God is *the ground of novelty*. To God is attributed the role of presenting new possibilities in the cosmos, e.g., the evolution of life. According to Whitehead, "apart from the intervention of God, there could be nothing new in the world, and no order in the world."[268] Third, God is *influenced by events in the world*. He is not an un-moved Mover, but highly protean. God is both *primordial* and *consequent*.[269]

Whitehead applies his general metaphysical categories of temporality, interaction, and mutual relatedness to God. Concisely summarizing Whitehead, Barbour writes,

> God's purposes and character are eternal, but God's knowledge of events changes as those events occur. God influences the creatures by being part of the data to which they respond. God is supremely sensitive to the world, supplementing its accomplishments by seeing them in relation to the infinite resources of potential forms and reflecting back to the world a specific and relevant influence.[270]

Further developing Whitehead's doctrine of God, Hartshorne uses the term *dipolar theism*. For example, God is described as *both* temporal and eternal, but in diverse ways. Like Whitehead, Hartshorne does not follow the traditional Christian doctrine on God's perfection. He sees the classical teaching as one-sided, "exalting permanence over change, being over becoming, eternity over temporality, necessity over contingency, [and] self-sufficiency over relatedness."[271] His conception of God is neither theistic, nor pantheistic, but rather *panentheistic*.[272]

The process view of Divine action suggested by Whitehead also differs significantly from orthodox Christian tradition. Because God is *in* the world, He is affected by it. God is not impassible. He cannot determine the outcome of events, i.e., interfere with their *self-creation*. Whitehead's God works through *persuasion*

---

266 Barbour, *Religion and Science*, 293.
267 Ibid.
268 Whitehead, *Process and Reality*, 288.
269 Ibid., 406.
270 Barbour, *Religion and Science*, 294.
271 Ibid.
272 Hartshorne, *The Divine Relativity*, 90.

and *the evocation of response.*[273] God's action is just one factor among others. He does not create *ex nihilo* and was never without a universe. All temporal, actual entities come into being through God in a form of *creatio continua.*[274]

Barbour highlights the fact that the process God cannot be accused of being a "God of the gaps," intervening at special moments in time. God is always at work *influencing* events in the same way as natural causes. His influence on aggregate entities is extremely minimal. Barbour writes, "God cannot stop the bullet speeding toward your head, because a bullet is an aggregate and not a unified occasion of experience susceptible to God's persuasion."[275] According to the process theologian, Daniel Day Williams,

> God's causality is exercised in, through, and with all other causes operating. There is no demand here to factor out what God is adding to the stream of events apart from those events. But there is the assignment of specific functions to God's causality ... Every "act of God" is presented to us in, through, and with the complex of human nature and life in which we are. When we say God elected Israel, or that he sends his rain on the just and the unjust, we must not ignore the complex analysis of assignable causes and factors in Israel's history or in the cosmic record of rainfall. We have no way of extricating the acts of God from their involvement in the activities of the world. To assign any particular historical event to God's specific action in the world is to risk ultimate judgment on our assertions. Faith leads us to take the risk.[276]

Aware of the ways that Whitehead and Hartshorne diverge from Biblical descriptions of God, Barbour also investigates process thinkers who attempt to adhere closer to Creedal Christianity. Barbour supports the concept of *creative-responsive love* articulated by David R. Griffin and John B. Cobb. According to Cobb and Griffin, God's *creativity*, manifest in a process paradigm by providing order and novelty, is seen as an expression of the Divine *logos*. God's *responsiveness* can be understood through the action of the Holy Spirit in the world, answering the prayers of the people of God. For Griffin and Cobb, Jesus Christ is *God's supreme act.*[277] Barbour highlights that in this process view, *particular Divine initiatives* are admissible.[278]

273 Barbour, *Religion and Science*, 295.

274 Whitehead, *Process and Reality*, 263.

275 Barbour, *Religion and Science*, 303.

276 Daniel Day Williams, "How Does God Act?: An Essay in Whitehead's Metaphysics," in *Process and Divinity: The Hartshorne Festschrift*, ed. William L. Reese and Eugene Freeman (LaSalle: Open Court Pub. Co., 1964), 180.

277 John B. Cobb and David Ray Griffin, *Process Theology: An Introduction* (Philadelphia: Westminster Press, 1976), chap. 3.

278 Barbour, *Religion and Science*, 297.

Cobb also develops a process model of prayer. In this scheme, the Divine call should elicit a stance of openness and responsiveness from the believer. God moves those who are open to His promptings to realize His goal of all-inclusive love. Cobb advocates a stance of radical "openness" in prayer, as he believes that God could require believers to question the leaders and official teachings of an ecclesial community or Church.[279]

Although Barbour does not concur with the anti-foundationalism often associated with postmodern feminism, he does agree with elements of feminism that align with process thought, as articulated by Marjorie Hewitt Suchocki for example.[280] In his quest to avoid all dualisms (e.g., man vs woman, mind vs body, humanity vs nature), Barbour aligns himself with some feminist thinkers. He writes,

> Feminists usually agree with process thinkers, not only in rejecting these dualisms, but in replacing them with a holistic rationality and an inclusive mutuality. They also agree in insisting on openness and creativity in human self-determination and in seeking freedom from the hierarchical roles of the past.[281]

Barbour's view of creation and the fall deviates from his Presbyterian roots. He believes that "neither a primeval state of perfection nor a historical fall are credible today."[282] He asserts that our postlapsarian experience of sin, suffering, and death is simply a "mystery that we do not understand but that we should accept in faith and submission to God."[283] In process thought, God not only endures with us in our suffering (*cum passio*) as most Christians believe, but Whitehead's possible God suffers Himself. On the subject of the immortality of the human person, Barbour indicates that there is some diversity among process thinkers. Whitehead himself posited an *objective immortality* in which a person lives on through participation in God's consequent nature. Other process theologians believe in a *subjective immortality* in which a person continues to live on as a unique center of experience.[284]

Barbour's adoption of process theism is a response to his negative judgment on what he classifies as the "monarchical model" of God. While he does acknowledge some Biblical basis for the description of God as an omnipotent and omniscient

---

279 John B. Cobb, "Spiritual Discernment in a Whiteheadian Perspective," in *Religious Experience and Process Theology*, ed. Harry J. Cargas and Bernard J. Lee (New York: Paulist Press, 1976), 349–368.

280 Marjorie Hewitt Suchocki, "Openness and Mutuality in Process Thought and Feminine Action," in *Feminism and Process Thought*, ed. Sheila Greeve Davaney (New York: Edwin Mellen Press, 1981), 62–82.

281 Barbour, *Religion and Science*, 300.

282 Ibid., 301.

283 Ibid.

284 Ibid., 304.

king, he is critical of the "formal theological doctrines" developed by the Church around these Biblical themes, e.g., as articulated by Thomas Aquinas. His understanding of the classical teaching is that God's omniscience involves "not only foreknowledge, but also the predetermination of every event."[285] Barbour also struggles with Thomas Aquinas' argument for the impassibility of God. He summarizes his concerns with the so-called "monarchical model" of God with six problems: *human freedom, evil and suffering, patriarchy, religious intolerance, an evolutionary world,* and *law and chance in nature.*

For Barbour, the doctrines of Divine omnipotence and predestination are incompatible with human choice (freedom), responsibility, and maturity. He also sees a contradiction in an all-powerful God permitting evil and suffering. According to Barbour, the claims of the monarchical model would seem to imply that God Himself is responsible for evils, both natural and moral. In addition, Barbour believes that a monarchical model of God fosters an "exclusivist" belief with regard to Divine revelation. Such a view can lead to religious intolerance and violence. He sees little room for dynamicity in creation in his description of the monarchical model, and therefore judges the theory of biological evolution to be a challenge to the "static" world preordained by God's sovereign power. Finally, Barbour struggles to reconcile the existence of stochastic processes in nature with an all-knowing God.[286]

Barbour's quest leads him to explore a variety of alternatives to classical theism. He classifies them in the following way: *God as determiner of indeterminacies* (e.g., that arise in quantum mechanics and chaos theory), *God as communicator of information* (e.g., God influencing natural processes, such as biological evolution, through the non-energetic input of information), *a self-limited God* (e.g., dialectical theism), *God as agent* (e.g., God is an agent among agents expressing his intentions), *the world as God's body* (e.g., as found in certain forms of panentheism), and *God as creative participant* (e.g., process theism). Acknowledging that there is a certain degree of similarity and overlap between the different alternatives, Barbour maintains that process theism offers the best response to the six aforementioned difficulties with the monarchical approach.[287]

While process theism is not a uniform doctrine, the various forms all envision God as a "creative participant" in the universe. In Whitehead's "social" view of nature, all entities are interdependent, including God. While God is not described as a "monarch" in the process perspective, He is envisioned as a "leader of a cosmic community."[288] Barbour maintains that the process model incorporates

285 Ibid., 306.
286 Ibid., 308–309.
287 Ibid., 312–322.
288 Ibid., 322.

key aspects of some of the aforementioned perspectives, e.g., *God as a determiner of indeterminacies, God as a communicator of information,* and *a self-limited God.* Some process thinkers, such as Hartshorne, adopt the analogy of *the world as God's body.* God influences processes in nature with his "infinitely sympathetic" intentions from within, analogous to the way that the human mind influences the body in a multi-level description of reality.[289] While Barbour avers that Hartshorne's approach is helpful, he believes that *interpersonal social models* best characterize the relationships that entities have with each other and with the Divine.[290]

On the topic of *human freedom,* Barbour contends that process theism offers a reasonable *via media* that supports man's responsibility to work creatively to advance the Divine plan, while also acknowledging human frailty and limits— biological, psychological, and social. The problem of *evil and suffering* is treated by process thought by accepting the limits of God's power, thereby avoiding the error of blaming God for sin and pain. *Patriarchy* is avoided in process theism by ascribing to God "feminine virtues" such as nurturance, sensitivity, interdependence, responsiveness, tenderness, patience, participation, and cooperation. Barbour posits that process theism also avoids the problem of *religious intolerance.* The God of process philosophy is not identified with any exclusive religion or experience of Divine revelation. God is "permitted" to be present to different people in diverse ways at various times in history. Thus, Barbour believes that the "militancy of absolutism and the vagueness of relativism"[291] are avoided.

The *evolutionary world view* is strongly supported by process metaphysics as reality is characterized by a situation of constant change and development. Finally, with regard to *law and chance in nature,* Barbour states the process God permits both stability and openness. God is a ground of order but also supports and participates in a dynamic, ever changing world.[292] Having presented Barbour's appropriation of process thought, we now focus our analysis on his evaluation of it from a distinctly Christian perspective.

3.4 Barbour's Christian Evaluation of Process Thought

While manifesting great *élan* about the possibilities of applying process thought to theology, and Divine revelation in particular, Barbour does acknowledge three criticisms of process theology. Influenced by the post-liberal, neo-orthodox

---

289 Charles Hartshorne, *Man's Vision of God* (Chicago: Willet Clark, 1941), chap. 5. and Charles Hartshorne, *The Logic of Perfection* (LaSalle: Open Court, 1962), chap. 7.

290 Barbour, *Religion and Science,* 323.

291 Ibid., 324.

292 Ibid., 324–325.

Protestant theology of his Yale days, Barbour is aware of the concern of some theologians that metaphysical approaches to Christian faith are inherently problematic. He is also cognizant of the difficulties that can arise within the realm of natural science when a metaphysical system is applied rigidly, and without sophistication, to describe reality. For example, Barbour judges the Aristotelian framework to have been detrimental to both science and theology from the thirteenth to the seventeenth centuries. As passionate as he is about process metaphysics, Barbour admits that "Christianity cannot be identified with any metaphysical systems. The theologian must adapt, not adopt, a metaphysics"[293]

Another major critique admitted by Barbour is of Whitehead's process God. Barbour notes the dissimilarity with the God of the Bible who is characterized by his power and transcendence. Colin Gunton suggests that the process God might be more worthy of sympathy than adoration.[294] Barbour ascribes to the process God not power in the Biblical sense, but the "evocative power of love and inspiration."[295] He draws a parallel between the κένωσις (*kénosis*) of Jesus Christ and the metaphysical, self-limitation of Whitehead's God. Barbour writes, "Process theology reiterates on a cosmic scale the motif of the cross, a love that accepts suffering."[296] By denying His omnipotence, God is not personally responsible for evil in the world according to Barbour. Ultimately, Barbour is comfortable identifying Whitehead's process deity with the God of the Bible.

Traditional Christian theology, firmly established on Sacred Scripture, anticipates a τέλος (*télos*) of the κόσμος (*cósmos*), the ἔσχατον (*éschaton*), in which Jesus, the ἔσχατος (*éschatos*), will return in glory, *iudicare vivos et mortuos*, and accomplish an absolute victory over evil.[297] Process theology does not foresee such any end. According to Barbour, it foresees "a continued journey toward greater harmony and enrichment."[298] Whether one adopts the aforementioned objective or subjective process views of immortality, personal, perfect communion with the Holy Trinity in heaven as envisioned by the New Testament seems distant in process theology.

Barbour recognizes another incongruity between process thought and Christian theology with regard to God's sovereignty over creation. Throughout the Bible, God's power over nature knows no limits, e.g., the Great Flood (Genesis

---

293 Ibid., 325.
294 Colin Gunton, *Becoming and Being: The Doctrine of God in Charles Hartshorne and Karl Barth* (Oxford: Oxford University Press, 1978).
295 Barbour, *Religion and Science*, 326.
296 Ibid.
297 For example, see Matthew 24.
298 Barbour, *Religion and Science*, 326.

6–9) and the parting of the Red Sea (Exodus 13:17–14:29). The God of Sacred Scripture also has power over the natural reality of death, e.g., the raising of Lazarus (John 11:1–46). The deity of *Process and Reality* interacts with nature through "influence"; the greatest influence possible occurs with his interactions with humans.[299]

How are these departures from classic theism on the part of process theology to be adjudicated? Barbour suggests four criteria that could justify a reformulation of Christian doctrines: *agreement with data, coherence, scope,* and *fertility.* Like Thomas Kuhn,[300] Barbour acknowledges that because "all data are theory-laden, and religious experience is influenced by theological interpretation,"[301] the *agreement with data* criterion cannot offer a definitive resolution on its own. Nonetheless, Barbour suggests that the data of religious stories, rituals, and mystical experiences, both Christian and Eastern, e.g., East Asian, Indian, and animistic indigenous, often can be reconciled with the process perspective.

On the criterion of *coherence*, Barbour recognizes that the reformulation of Christian doctrines cannot be inconsistent with the core of the Christian Tradition. He opportunely defines the "core" to be belief in God as "creative love revealed in Christ."[302] God's omnipotence, for example, is then classified as an "auxiliary hypothesis." Barbour asserts that auxiliary hypotheses can be modified by "new" data on human freedom and suffering, the experience of evil, and our evolutionary understanding of the universe. He also believes that Whiteheadian theology merits "high marks for internal coherence."[303] Barbour evaluates it to be logical and self-consistent.

Barbour identifies the broad *scope* of process theology also to be in its favor. This scope is wide enough to engage all religious traditions, including Christianity—an important feature in a pluralistic world, according to Barbour. Process theology's scope is also comprehensive enough to engage not only dogmatic questions but also moral, aesthetic, and scientific issues. Barbour highlights the notions of *levels of experience* and *evolutionary emergence* as particularly important foundations for process thought.[304]

---

299 Ibid., 327.
300 Thomas S. Kuhn, *The Structure of Scientific Revolutions*, 4th ed. (Chicago: University Of Chicago Press, 2012). Barbour's assessment of Kuhn's book can be found in Ian G. Barbour, "Paradigms in Science and Religion," in *Paradigms & Revolutions: Applications and Appraisals of Thomas Kuhn's Philosophy of Science*, ed. Gary Gutting (Notre Dame, IN: University of Notre Dame Press, 1980), 223–245.
301 Barbour, *Religion and Science*, 327.
302 Ibid., 328.
303 Ibid.
304 Ibid.

Fertility is the last criterion that Barbour offers for evaluating the appropriateness of doctrinal reformulation. On this subject, he is influenced by the Hungarian philosopher of mathematics and science, Imre Lakatos', notion of "progressive research programmes,"[305] i.e., groups of diverse theories that share some common idea and contribute to the discovery of novel facts. Barbour points out that Whitehead and Hartshorne's process view has stimulated vast, inventive theological speculation. He also believes that it has the potential to encourage religious experience and facilitate personal transformation. Therefore, Barbour deems the process reformulation of theology to be fertile.[306]

In the end, based on all four criteria, Barbour judges that there are sufficient grounds for doctrinal reformulation. In modesty, he does invoke his *critical realism* to affirm that "all models [including process theism] are limited and partial, and none gives a complete or adequate picture of reality."[307] Barbour concludes that "only in worship can we acknowledge the mystery of God and the pretensions of any system of thought claiming to have mapped out God's ways."[308] *Lex orandi, lex credendi.* Having explored in detail Ian Barbour's theological presuppositions, epistemology, and metaphysics, we can now investigate his classification of the similarities and differences between theology and natural science, particularly as they relate to the doctrine of creation.

305 Imre Lakatos, "Falsification and the Methodology of Scientific Research Programmes," in *Criticism and the Growth of Knowledge*, ed. Imre Lakatos and Alan Musgrave (Cambridge: Cambridge University Press, 1970), 91–195.

306 Barbour, *Religion and Science*, 328.

307 Ibid., 332.

308 Ibid.

Theology and Science: Similarities and Differences According to Barbour

1. Relating Theology and Science

In Chapter Two we examined Ian Barbour's fundamental principles, both philosophical and theological. Now in Chapter Three, we are in a position to explicate Barbour's reasoning about the similarities and differences between the natural sciences and theology. His analysis about similarities and differences directly impacts how he relates the two disciplines, and therefore his interaction typologies of *dialogue* and *integration*. In Chapter Four, Barbour's foundations will be assessed and his particular approach evaluated in light of fundamental Catholic theological principles and the Church's doctrine of creation.

A starting point for identifying similarities and differences between theology and science is in methodology. Barbour acknowledges the complexity in entering into this space. The key question is: Are the methods of theology and science radically different? One's answer is heavily dependent on one's philosophical and theological perspective. For those who emphasize *contrasting* perspectives in method and/or ignore the differences between theology and science, the typology of *conflict* arises. In this situation, according to Barbour, the *independence* typology can sometimes be prescribed as an alternative. In the independence typology, both theology and science's subject matter and content, as well as their ways of knowing, are recognized as so dissimilar "that there are no points of fruitful comparison or analogy."[1]

Barbour explores a vast array of contrasting and parallel twentieth century perspectives.[2] He ultimately employs aspects of those parallel perspectives that he finds most beneficial for relating theology and science. These allow him to engage fruitfully scientific and religious experience and interpretation, the roles of religious and scientific communities and their paradigms, the use of analogies and models in science and religion, and the criteria for evaluating religious beliefs and scientific theories. We find that he generally understands well the perspectives that he critiques. One exception, however, is his understanding of the relationship of form and matter, e.g., soul and body, in the Thomistic tradition. We engage his criticism of the alleged dualism in Roman Catholic Neo-Thomism in the next chapter. Problematic aspects of his process thought will also be elucidated—*mali principii malus finis.*

2. Identifying Contrasting Perspectives

2.1 Scientific Materialism

One contrasting perspective for relating theology and science that Barbour identifies is scientific materialism. Materialism is a multivalent term. In the area of ethics, it refers to the penchant for material possessions and physical comforts over spiritual values. Barbour's interest is in the epistemological and metaphysical theory that nothing (knowable) exists except matter and its interactions. Despite their diverse meanings, those who subscribe to one materialist philosophy often subscribe to the other. The "scientific" materialism that Barbour critically engages is the intellectual heir of French Enlightenment materialism,[3] David Hume's empiricism,[4]

---

1 Barbour, *Issues in Science and Religion*, 115–116.
2 The influence of Robert Calhoun and Roland Bainton is seen in Barbour's historical *and* ecumenical quest.
3 A famous analysis of this philosophical school is found in Karl Marx, "French Materialism," in *Selected Writings*, trans. Henry James Stenning (New York: Classic Books International, 2010), 99–107. According to Marx, French materialism was not only a struggle against existing political structures, but also against theology and all forms of metaphysics.
4 See David Hume, *An Enquiry Concerning Human Understanding* (Hollywood, FL: Simon & Brown, 2011). Hume was willing to grant mathematics and logic a particular exception both to philosophical materialism and to inductive uncertainty.

and nineteenth century Darwinian evolutionary naturalism.[5] Barbour summarizes the doctrine of scientific materialism in two statements:

1) the scientific method is the only reliable path to knowledge;
2) matter (or matter and energy) is the fundamental reality in the universe.[6]

Laplacian reductionism, mentioned earlier, is present in both statements—epistemological in the first and ontological in the second. Scientific materialists believe that ultimately all phenomena can and will be explained by the causality and laws of physics. They often assert that only the scientific method is capable of unveiling reality. Barbour concisely summarizes the materialist position: "Science alone is objective, open-minded, universal, cumulative, and progressive. Religious traditions, by contrast are said to be subjective, close-minded, parochial, uncritical, and resistant to change."[7]

Scientific materialism is often presented alongside of actual science. Barbour points out how the American physicist and science popularizer, Carl Sagan,[8] would often inject his own philosophical commentary in his writings and TV show, *Cosmos*. For example, Sagan writes, "The Cosmos is all that is, or ever was, or ever will be."[9] On the matter of creation, Sagan asserts that the universe is eternal, and if it has an "origin," it is unknowable. Barbour describes Sagan as "a new kind of high priest" that reverences nature over God. According to Barbour, Sagan has "unlimited confidence in the scientific method" to bring about world peace and universal justice.[10]

Another influential example of scientific materialism is found in the book, *Chance and Necessity*, by the French biochemist, Jacques Monod. Monod makes the incredible claim that biology has proven that there is no purpose in nature. Monod writes, "Man knows at last that he is alone in the universe's unfeeling immensity, out of which he emerged only by chance."[11] He avers that "chance alone is the source of all novelty, all creation, in the biosphere."[12] Joseph Ratzinger pithily

---

5   For contemporary perspectives in this area, see Michael Ruse, ed., *Evolutionary Naturalism: Selected Essays* (New York: Routledge, 2014).

6   Barbour, *Religion and Science*, 78.

7   Ibid.

8   Thomas Ross has further researched some of Sagan's philosophical and theological foundations. See Thomas W. Ross, "The Implicit Theology of Carl Sagan," *Pacific Theological Review* 18 (Spring 1985): 24–32.

9   Carl Sagan, *Cosmos* (New York: Random House, 1980), 4.

10 Barbour, *Religion and Science*, 79.

11 Jacques Monod, *Chance and Necessity: An Essay on the Natural Philosophy of Modern Biology*, trans. Austryn Wainhouse (New York: Vintage Books, 1972), 180.

12 Ibid., 112.

summarizes Monod's position writing, "In place of God's will Monod postulates chance—the lottery—as having produced us."[13] In a BBC lecture, Monod stated that "anything can be reduced to simple, obvious mechanical interactions. The cell is a machine. The animal is machine. Man is a machine."[14] For Monod, consciousness is an illusion and human behavior is predetermined by genetics. The American biochemist, Jeffrey Wicken, describes *Chance and Necessity* as a "manifesto of materialist biology in the most reductivist sense."[15] Barbour finds Monod's reductionism to be utterly inadequate in science and his opprobrium of theism entirely unconvincing.[16]

A very strong materialist position is advanced by the American biologist, Edward Osborne Wilson. Wilson is a radical reductionist and claims that all human behavior is reducible to genetics. He writes, "It may not be too much to say that sociology and the other social sciences, as well as the humanities, are the last branches of biology to be included in the Modern Synthesis."[17] Wilson hopes that one day religion will be explained away as a product of evolution and that scientific materialism will replace it.[18] In an interview published in *New Scientist*, Wilson states, "Religion is dragging us down and must be eliminated for the sake of human progress ... So I would say that for the sake of human progress, the best thing we could possibly do would be to diminish, to the point of eliminating, religious faiths."[19] Barbour believes that Wilson tends to over-generalize and over-extend

---

13 Ratzinger, *In the Beginning*, 53. Later, Ratzinger offers a compelling critique: "But we must have the audacity to say that the great projects of the living creation are not the products of chance and error. Nor are they the products of a selective process to which divine predicates can be attributed in illogical, unscientific, and even mythic fashion. The great projects of the living creation point to a creating Reason and show us a creating Intelligence and they do so more luminously and radiantly today than ever before. Thus we can say today with anew certitude and joyousness that the human being is indeed a divine project, which only the creating Intelligence was strong and great and audacious enough to conceive of Human beings are not a mistake but something willed; they are the fruit of love. They can disclose in themselves, in the bold project that they are, the language of the creating Intelligence that speaks to them and that moves them to say: Yes, Father, you have willed me." Ibid., 56–57.

14 Jacques Monod, BBC Lecture, cited in John Lewis, ed., *Beyond Chance and Necessity* (London: Garnstone Press, 1974), ix.

15 Jeffrey S. Wicken, "The Cosmic Breath: Reflections on the Thermodynamics of Creation," *Zygon* 19, no. 4 (December 1984): 487–505.

16 Barbour, *Religion and Science*, 80.

17 Edward O. Wilson, *Sociobiology: The New Synthesis* (Cambridge: Harvard University Press, 1975), 4.

18 Edward O. Wilson, *On Human Nature* (Cambridge: Harvard University Press, 1978), chaps. 8–9.

19 Edward O. Wilson, "E. O. Wilson: Religious Faith Is Dragging Us Down," interview by Penny Sarchet, New Scientist, January 21, 2015, accessed February 28, 2018, https://www.newscientist.com/article/mg22530050-400-e-o-wilson-religious-faith-is-dragging-us-down/.

his arguments based on genetics in an attempt to develop an all-encompassing explanation of human behavior, ignoring the "causal efficacy of other facets of human life and experience."[20]

The philosopher, Daniel Clement Dennett III, advocates a form of Neo-Darwinism that views evolution as an absolutely purposeless process. He utilizes concepts from computer science, cognitive science, and probability theory in an attempt to strengthen his argument. Barbour notes that Dennett self-identifies as a "good reductionist," as opposed to the "greedy" variety who "tries to explain higher-level phenomena by direct appeal to the laws of the lowest level."[21] Dennett insists that "the mind is the brain."[22] He believes that all mental phenomena can be explained with physical laws and that consciousness is a *trompe-l'œil*.[23]

Barbour also engages the scientific materialism of the biologist, Richard Dawkins,[24] and the physicist, Steven Weinberg.[25] He finds that all the scientific materialists tend in one way or another to blend scientific and philosophical questions. They all advance some form of the epistemology of *scientism*—assuming that the scientific method is the only source of knowledge. Ontologically, they over-extend scientific concepts beyond their scope to define a materialist metaphysics. Hence, materialists reduce mind, purpose, and human love to "matter in motion." Barbour concludes that "theism, in short, is not inherently in conflict with science, but it does conflict with a metaphysics of materialism."[26] Scientific materialism offers such a contrasting view of reason and reality that the only possible modality of interaction with theology is one of conflict.

2.2 Fundamentalism

Contrasting perspectives on science and theology are also emphasized by those who assume a fundamentalist perspective toward Christianity, according to Barbour. While the origins of Biblical fundamentalism can be traced to Reformation principles, e.g., the doctrine of *sola Scriptura*, the actual movement did not arise until the nineteenth century.[27] At that time, a group of British and

20 Barbour, *Religion and Science*, 81.
21 Ibid.
22 Daniel C. Dennett, *Consciousness Explained* (New York: Little Brown, 1991), 33.
23 See Daniel C. Dennett, *Darwin's Dangerous Idea: Evolution and the Meanings of Life* (New York: Simon & Schuster, 1996).
24 See Richard Dawkins, *The God Delusion* (Boston: Mariner Books, 2008).
25 See Steven Weinberg, "A Designer Universe?," *PhysLink: Physics and Astronomy Online*, 1999, accessed February 28, 2018, http://www.physlink.com/Education/essay_weinberg.cfm.
26 Barbour, *Religion and Science*, 82.
27 Some scholars believe that the sociological impact of the First (c. 1730–1755) and Second (c. 1790–1840) Great Awakenings created the conditions in which Fundamentalism was a logical

American Protestant pastors and theologians felt compelled to propose a radically different form of Christianity than what was emerging as a result of modernist Christians embracing the philosophy and theology of the German pastor and exegete, Friedrich Schleiermacher.

In the late eighteenth and early nineteenth centuries, some German, post-Kantian philosophers such as Johann Gottfried Herder, Friedrich Heinrich Jacobi, and Jakob Friedrich Fries advanced the theory that the human person possesses a religious sense, or faculty, *distinct* from the rational. This philosophical idea contributed to the Protestant theological notion that Divine revelation does not reach man by way of an "exterior promulgation," but consists instead in man's personal "adaptation" towards God. This idea ultimately found strong expression in the thought of Schleiermacher. Schleiermacher ignored the classical Christian distinction between natural and supernatural revelation and faith, and taught that "religion is to be found neither in knowledge nor in action, but in a peculiar attitude of mind which consists in the consciousness of absolute dependence upon God."[28]

Schleiermacher's quest was to unite Enlightenment values with Protestant principles. His approach was a rigorous application of hermeneutical analysis and literary criticism to the Bible. Schleiermacher's work emphasized the role of human techniques in the formation of the Biblical texts. He also challenged the sixteenth century Reformers' understanding of inspiration and inerrancy. As a result of significant historical events in the Bible, e.g., the miracles of Christ, being reclassified as "myth" or "symbol," and the accompanying doctrinal consequences, Schleiermacher offered a radically novel religious perspective. He imagined that *religious feeling*, e.g., the *sensus divinitatis*, especially the sense of man's radical dependence on God experienced by introspection, was the most authentic expression of Christianity.[29]

The American fundamentalist response was conceived and funded by the Stewart brothers, Lyman and Milton. With their vast financial resources from Union Oil, they commissioned a set of 90 essays (written by 64 different theologians) published between 1910 and 1915. The collection was entitled *The Fundamentals: A Testimony to the Truth*.[30] The Scottish Presbyterian minister and scholar, James Orr,

outcome in the United States. See Joe E. Morris, *Revival of the Gnostic Heresy: Fundamentalism* (New York: Palgrave Macmillan, 2008), 76.

28 Francis Aveling, "Rationalism," *Catholic Encyclopedia* (New York: Robert Appleton Company, 1911), accessed March 2, 2018, http://www.newadvent.org/cathen/12652a.htm.

29 See Friedrich Schleiermacher, *On Religion: Speeches to Its Cultured Despisers*, trans. John Oman (New York: Harper & Brothers, 1958).

30 Reuben Arche Torrey and Amzi Clarence Dixon, eds., *The Fundamentals: A Testimony to the Truth* (Grand Rapids: Baker Books, 2003).

composed the article entitled "Science and Christian Faith." In it, he endorsed a form of "progressive creationism."[31] While most fundamentalists simply desired a return to sixteenth century Reformation doctrines, Barbour points out that "the most extreme adherents attacked not only evolution but modern science and education in general, because of their materialistic and atheistic influence."[32] Not surprisingly, Barbour critically engages this approach and does not adhere to fundamentalist principles in his own attempt to relate theology and science.

2.3 Neo-Orthodoxy

Despite his intellectual formation in a neo-orthodox seminary, Barbour classifies the neo-orthodox approach to theology and science as emphasizing contrasting perspectives. Barbour acknowledges Karl Barth as *the* prominent example of a neo-orthodox theologian. As mentioned in the last chapter, Karl Barth and his disciples at Yale Divinity School wanted, like the fundamentalists, to develop an alternative to modern, liberal Protestantism and return to what they viewed as authentic Reformation faith and values. Barth and his fellow neo-orthodox Protestants sought to emphasize the uniqueness of Divine revelation and distinguish Christian theology from other forms of human inquiry. Barbour concisely summarizes the Barthian critique of the liberal project:

> God had become an immanent force within the cosmic process, Christ was reduced to an example of human goodness, man's sinfulness was ignored in the assumption of inevitable progress and—most important of all—divine revelation had been replaced by human attempts to discover God through philosophical reflection, moral conscience, or religious experience.[33]

Barth's theology emphasizes God's *alterität*. God is holy, transcendent, and sovereign. Like the Danish philosopher Søren Kierkegaard, Barth suggests an

---

31 "Young Earth Creationists" follow the general approach of Archbishop Ussher and posit that the planet is between 5,700 and 10,000 years old. "Old Earth Creationists" are sometimes referred to as "progressive Creationists." They accept the geological age of the Earth (~4.5 billion years old) and acknowledge micro-evolution—small evolutionary changes, e.g., changes in gene frequencies in a population. Old Earth Creationists still reject macro-evolution, i.e., speciation. See Ronald L. Numbers, *The Creationists: From Scientific Creationism to Intelligent Design* (Cambridge: Harvard University Press, 2006), 11. It should be noted that Big Bang models date the universe to be ~14 billion years old. See P. a. R. Ade et al., "Planck 2015 Results - XIII. Cosmological Parameters," *Astronomy & Astrophysics* 594 (October 2016), 1–63.

32 Barbour, *Issues in Science and Religion*, 100.

33 Ibid., 117.

"infinite qualitative difference" (*unendliche qualitative Unterschied*)[34] between man and God. God can only be known through *His* self-communication in supernatural revelation, particularly in the person of Jesus Christ. Barth's soteriology emphasizes human depravity, the power of grace, and Divine election.[35]

In areas where some liberal Christians see continuity and similarity between theology and science, Barth conjectures the opposite. According to Barbour, Karl Barth "found *discontinuity* and *dissimilarity* predominant: discontinuity between revelation and natural reason, between God and the world, between Christ and other men, between Christianity and other religions."[36] However, unlike fundamentalists, neo-orthodox theologians accept some use of historical-critical methods in the study of Sacred Scripture.

For neo-orthodox theologians, such as Walter Whitehouse[37] and Aldert van der Ziel,[38] the methods and objects of theology and science are completely unrelated. Theology's main focus is the doctrine of God, who is totally other, and can only be known through His self-revelation. As mentioned in Chapter Two, the neo-orthodox reject natural theologies. The true God cannot be known through reason alone because of the infinite gap between Creator and creature, as well as the weakening of man's intellect after the fall. Science's object is the natural world, and the discipline is carried out entirely using human reason. Because supernatural revelation in Christ is not lacking in any way, reason and science cannot enhance Biblical faith.

Barbour summarizes the neo-orthodox position by stating that "science can thus *neither contribute to nor conflict with* theology."[39] While fundamentalism creates the possibility for the conflict mode of interaction between theology and science, neo-orthodoxy insists that the Bible does not offer a literal, scientific description of creation or nature in general. For the neo-orthodox, the beginning of the Book of Genesis describes a substantial and enduring *relationship* between the Creator and His creation. It is not viewed primarily as a poetic description of cosmic origins.[40]

For Barbour, Reinhold Niebuhr exemplifies neo-orthodoxy when he claims that the Bible should be taken "seriously, but not literally."[41] With regard to the

---

34 Søren Kierkegaard, *Journals of Søren Kierkegaard*, trans. Alexander Dru (Oxford: Oxford University Press, 1948), Entry for November 20, 1847.

35 See Barth, *Church Dogmatics*, vol. 4.

36 Barbour, *Issues in Science and Religion*, 117.

37 Walter A. Whitehouse, *Christian Faith and Scientific Attitude* (New York: Philosophical Library, 1952).

38 Aldert van der Ziel, *The Natural Sciences and the Christian Message* (Minneapolis: Denison, 1960).

39 Barbour, *Issues in Science and Religion*, 118.

40 Barbour, *When Science Meets Religion*, 48.

41 Daniel F. Rice, *Reinhold Niebuhr and John Dewey: An American Odyssey* (Albany: SUNY Press, 1993), 162.

doctrine of creation, the American philosopher and theologian, Derek Michaud, describes Karl Barth's dialectical theology as one that "oscillates back and forth from the radical discontinuity between God and creation ... and the equally radical love of God for creation."[42] Barbour is ultimately not satisfied with this approach to relating science and theology.

2.4 Existentialism

Existentialism is another perspective that Ian Barbour associates with proposing a contrasting perspective for theology and science. He views existentialism's dichotomy between impersonal objects and personal selfhood—existence—as the basis for the dissimilarity. Existentialism is not a "school" or "system," but rather a general "orientation." Søren Kierkegaard is regarded by most scholars as the first existentialist thinker. The broad label of *existentialist* includes atheists as well as theists, Nazis as well as those whom they persecuted, philosophers, novelists, playwrights, psychologists, and theologians. Existentialists propose that the starting point of philosophical reflection must be the acting, feeling, living human subject who is characterized by his response to a world that may seem devoid of meaning,[43] and perhaps absurd.[44] Although some scholars rejected the label, Friedrich Nietzsche, Jean-Paul Sartre, Albert Camus, Martin Heidegger, Karl Jaspers, Martin Buber, Rudolf Bultmann, Gabriel Marcel, Paul Tillich, and Viktor Frankl are all associated with existentialist thought.

While existentialism engages topics associated with anxiety and despair, guilt and sin, life and death, freedom and creativity, values and decisions, Barbour's main interest is the existentialist *subject-centered epistemology*.[45] Existentialists posit an antithesis between *impersonal objectivity* and *personal subjectivity*. The Jewish philosopher, Martin Buber, expresses this view succinctly in his notion of *I-It* vs *I-Thou* relationships. *I-It* relationships are between a human subject and an impersonal object, e.g., a physicist doing research on the quasi-periodic oscillations seen in the emission from bright galactic X-ray sources. The *I-Thou* relationship, on the other hand, is only possible between two existential subjects, man-man or man-God. *I-Thou* relationships imply mutual availability, participation, awareness, sensitivity, involvement, and the possibility of love.[46] This philosophical distinction is also

---

42 Derek Michaud, "Karl Barth (1886–1968)," ed. Wesley Wildman, *Boston Collaborative Encyclopedia of Western Theology* (Boston, 1994), accessed February 5, 2018, http://people.bu.edu/wwildman/bce/barth.htm.

43 E.g., the problem of *ennui*.

44 John Macquarrie, *Existentialism* (Philadelphia: Westminster Press, 1972), 14–15.

45 Barbour, *Issues in Science and Religion*, 120.

46 See Martin Buber, *I and Thou*, trans. Ronald G. Smith (Edinburgh: T&T Clark, 1937).

an important one in the Catholic intellectual tradition, as the encyclical *Lumen Fidei* reminds us: "Theology is more than simply an effort of human reason to analyze and understand, along the lines of the experimental sciences. God cannot be reduced to an object. He is a subject who makes himself known and perceived in an interpersonal relationship."[47]

The German Lutheran New Testament scholar, Rudolf Bultmann, developed his own form of Christian existentialism. He posited two forms of knowing, similar to Buber. For Bultmann, the natural world must be understood through the scientific paradigm applied to spatio-temporal events. God and the supernatural realm are known only through *relational* experience. In his analysis of Sacred Scripture, Bultmann applied the term "myth" to refer to any application of "objective terminology" to refer to God and his action, which, according to him, necessarily transcends spatio-temporal constraints.[48]

According to Barbour, Bultmann's fundamental exegetical question is: "What does the mythical imagery say about *my personal existence* and about *my relationship to God?*"[49] For example, according to Bultmann, the resurrection of Christ is a cosmic, mythical event,[50] experienced by the first disciples. It does not belong to the realm of history:

> The real Easter faith is faith in the word of preaching which brings illumination. If the event of Easter Day is in any sense an historical event additional to the event of the cross, it is nothing else than the rise of faith in the risen Lord, since it was this faith which led to the apostolic preaching. The resurrection itself is not an event of past history.[51]

Barbour highlights the fact that for most Christian existentialists, the doctrine of creation is not a declaration about a cosmological beginning, but rather one of absolute dependence on God the creator.[52] One sees this clearly in the thought of Bultmann:

> God's creation is a creation out of nothing; and to be God's creature means absolutely and in every present to have one's source in him, in such a way that were he to

---

47 Francis, *Lumen Fidei*, 2013, 36.
48 See Rudolf Bultmann, *Jesus Christ and Mythology* (London: Hymns Ancient & Modern Ltd, 2012).
49 Barbour, *Issues in Science and Religion*, 121.
50 Rudolf Bultmann, "New Testament and Mythology," in *Philosophy, Religious Studies, and Myth*, ed. Robert A. Segal (New York: Garland Publishing Inc., 1996), 38.
51 Ibid., 42.
52 Barbour, *Issues in Science and Religion*, 121.

withhold his creative will the creature would fall back into nothing. Thus to be God's creature means to be constantly encompassed and threatened by nothingness.[53]

In his exegesis of the beginning of John's Gospel, Bultmann finds Biblical support for a doctrine of *creatio ex nihilo* in the declaration that "all things were made through him, and without him was not anything made that was made."[54] Later, in John 17:24,[55] Bultmann finds further validation for *creatio ex nihilo* (as opposed to a *formation* from pre-existing matter) in the words: "πρὸ καταβολῆς κόσμου" (*pro kataboles kósmou*)—before the foundation of the world.[56] American Protestant pastor and New Testament scholar, Robert Kysar, although nonplussed at one level at Bultmann's Biblical affirmation of a traditional Christian doctrine, attributes his interpretation of the aforementioned pericopes to two recurring themes in his theology. First, Bultmann tends to interpret doctrines anthropocentrically—man's self-understanding involves "creatureliness." Second, one finds a general emphasis on the absolute dependence of man on God in Bultmann's existential theology—man's existence is a gift from the Creator.[57]

Despite the Christian existentialist affirmation of creation, Barbour concludes that this perspective is not conducive to a rich interaction with the natural sciences: "[Existential] theology, dealing with the realms of selfhood and transcendence, has no points of contact with science, which investigates impersonal objects in the external world without personal involvement of the subject."[58] On this point, Barbour is in agreement with the German theologian, Walter Cardinal Kasper. Kasper writes,

> It would be utterly mistaken to deduce a lack of mutual relation from the distinction between natural-scientific and theological statements. Such an indifference would make faith in God a luxury without inner-worldly consequences. Liberal and existential Protestant theology drew this false conclusion ... A reason emancipated from the theology of creation is on the verge of becoming irrational.[59]

---

53 Rudolf K. Bultmann, "Faith in God the Creator," in *Existence and Faith: Shorter Writings of Rudolf Bultmann*, trans. Schubert M. Ogden (New York: Meridian Books, 1960), 207.

54 John 1:3 (RSV).

55 "Father, I desire that they also, whom thou hast given me, may be with me where I am, to behold my glory which thou hast given me in thy love for me before the foundation of the world." John 17:24 (RSV).

56 Rudolf Bultmann, *The Gospel of John: A Commentary*, ed. Paul N. Anderson, trans. G. R. Beasley-Murray (Eugene: Wipf & Stock, 2014), 38.

57 Robert Kysar, *Voyages with John: Charting the Fourth Gospel* (Waco: Baylor University Press, 2005), 15.

58 Barbour, *Issues in Science and Religion*, 121.

59 Walter Kasper, "The Logos Character of Reality," trans. Stephen Wentworth Arndt, *Communio* 15, no. 3 (Fall 1988): 279–280.

Having expounded Barbour's analysis of the existentialist understanding relating theology and science, we now turn to one final approach that emphasizes a contrasting perspective.

2.5 Linguistic Analysis

Another twentieth century movement that Ian Barbour considers to have contributed to a strong differentiation of science from theology is linguistic analysis. As mentioned in the previous chapter, the philosophy of linguistic analysis is an outgrowth of the logical positivist school. In the 1920s, positivists in Europe began to seriously study the logical structure of language. An assembly of mathematicians, physical scientists, and philosophers met from 1924 to 1936 at the University of Vienna. They constituted the informal group referred to as the "Vienna Circle." It promoted a *Logischer Empirismus* (logical empiricism) perspective to spread a "scientific" *Weltanschauung* (world-view). Their method was the rigorous application of symbolic logical analysis to clarify linguistic statements.[60]

The Vienna School was very hostile to any form of metaphysics, as evidenced by one of its significant member's 1932 article title: *Überwindung der Metaphysik durch Logische Analyse der Sprache* (*The Elimination of Metaphysics through Logical Analysis of Language*).[61] The rise of *Nationalsozialismus* was very detrimental to the Vienna Circle (which included many Jewish members), and led to its dissolution in 1936. The British philosopher, Sir Alfred Jules "A.J." Ayer, published the book, *Language, Truth, and Logic*, that same year. Ayer greatly popularized the principles of logical analysis in the English-speaking world.[62]

A fundamental tenet of logical analysis is the so-called "verification principle." According to *verificationism*, statements associated with aesthetics, ethics, ontology, theology, and spirituality are "cognitively meaningless" and therefore otiose. While they can affect human feelings and behaviors, they contain no information content and are classified as pseudo-statements.[63] Barbour emphasizes that for linguistic analysts, theological assertions are categorized in the same way as the act of human laughter, i.e., they serve an *expressive* function, but not a *referential* one. He

---

60 Thomas Uebel, "Vienna Circle," ed. Edward N. Zalta, *The Stanford Encyclopedia of Philosophy* (Stanford: Metaphysics Research Lab, Stanford University, February 17, 2016), accessed February 6, 2018, https://plato.stanford.edu/archives/spr2016/entries/vienna-circle/.

61 Rudolf Carnap, "The Elimination of Metaphysics through Logical Analysis of Language," in *Logical Empiricism at Its Peak: Schlick, Carnap, and Neurath*, ed. Sahotra Sarkar (New York: Garland Publishing Inc., 1996), 10–31.

62 See Alfred J. Ayer, *Language, Truth and Logic*, 2nd ed. (New York: Dover Publications, 1952).

63 "Verifiability Principle," *Encyclopædia Britannica*, last modified 2018, accessed February 6, 2018, https://www.britannica.com/topic/verifiability-principle.

astutely observes that because the verification principle itself is "neither verifiable nor simply a definition," it must be classified as "an emotive statement, an expression of taste, or [a] feeling."[64] In essence, for the linguistic analyst, philosophy is not about seeking "truth," but simply the clarification of language and concepts.

While Barbour affirms aspects of linguistic analysis, e.g., the acknowledgment of the diverse uses of language, he judges it to be detrimental to natural science, theology, and their interaction. Barbour laments that the so-called verification principle *"eliminates from serious discussion* whole areas of human experience, thought, and language."[65] He also criticizes the tendency of linguistic analysis to reject the truth claims of science and theology, and focus exclusively on the "usefulness" of the respective statements to accomplish their "functions." Many linguistic analysts maintain an *instrumentalist* view of natural science that focuses on prediction and manipulation. They also believe that theological statements are neither true nor false. Their only function is to make recommendations for a way of life (like the *existentialists*), or express and evoke adoration.[66]

Ultimately, linguistic analysis suggests that theology and science offer contrasting perspectives on the world. As Barbour describes it, "Scientific language is used primarily for prediction and control ... [while] religious language [serves] to recommend a way of life, to elicit a set of attitudes, and to encourage allegiance to particular moral principles."[67] Dialogue and integration between the two fields are ruled out *prima facie*. A unified view of God's creation will not be achieved through linguistics. At this point in our study of how Barbour relates theology and science, we shift to analyzing approaches that Barbour believes offer parallel perspectives on theology and science.

3. Identifying Parallel Perspectives

While scientific materialism, fundamentalism, neo-orthodoxy, existentialism, and linguistic analysis formulate and emphasize contrasts between science and theology according to Barbour, other approaches offer a more promising perspective to promote a beneficial interaction. Barbour's thorough research identifies movements that he believes permit and sometimes highlight *methodological and conceptual parallels* between theology and science. These include Roman Catholic Neo-Thomism, Protestant liberalism, and process theology. While he himself

64 Barbour, *Issues in Science and Religion*, 240–241.
65 Ibid., 243.
66 Ibid., 244–245.
67 Barbour, *When Science Meets Religion*, 19–20.

ultimately adopts elements of liberal Protestant and process theology, the fruitful application of twentieth century Neo-Thomism, as Barbour understood it, will provide a bridge to a Catholic adaption of his thought. "The genius of Thomas Aquinas,"[68] as Pope Francis puts it, has perennial relevance for Catholic theology. The concinnity of Aquinas' theology of creation is truly marvelous.

3.1 Neo-Thomism

Barbour's knowledge of some of the fundamentals of the Thomistic tradition is a *lagniappe* for Catholic readers. G.K. Chesterton wrote that "the nineteenth century left everything in chaos; and the importance of Thomism to the twentieth century is that it may give us back the cosmos."[69] The Australian theologian, Tracey Rowland, notes that the intellectual tradition of Saint Thomas is "arguably one of the most significant of all such traditions for the study of Catholic theology."[70] She also observes that "the term 'Neo-Thomism' is the most nebulous of labels."[71] This label can include Neo-Scholasticism, Transcendental Thomism, Existential Thomism, Lublin Thomism, Whig Thomism, New Natural Law Thomism, River Forest Thomism, Analytical Thomism, Augustinian Thomism, Fribourg Thomism, Toulouse Thomism, and other forms. Rowland introduces a helpful categorization by defining three "streams" that are dominant in contemporary Catholic theology.

"Stream One" is the Neo-Scholastic Thomism specifically encouraged by Pope Leo XIII[72] and was embodied in the work of Réginald Marie Garrigou-Lagrange, OP. "Stream Two" includes the transcendentalists who attempt to respond to the epistemological issues brought to a head by Kant.[73] "Stream Three," Existentialist

---

68 Francis, "A Big Heart Open to God," interview by Antonio Spadaro, America Magazine, September 30, 2013, accessed May 14, 2018, https://www.americamagazine.org/faith/2013/09/30/big-heart-open-god-interview-pope-francis.

69 Chesterton, "Saint Thomas Aquinas," 528.

70 Rowland, *Catholic Theology*, 43.

71 Ibid., 53.

72 Leo XIII, *Aeterni Patris*, 1879.

73 Alan Vincelette offers a very clear description of Transcendental Thomism and distinguishes the two major forms. He states, "The central conclusion of Transcendental Thomism is that the dynamism of a knowing subject toward Infinite and Absolute Being (i.e., God) is … an a priori condition of knowledge. That is to say, God is in some ways always present as a horizon and necessarily co-affirmed with every act of human knowledge. There are two distinct schools of thought, however, in regard to just how this occurs. According to some proponents of Transcendental Thomism, an a priori *desire* for knowledge of the Absolute Being of God is the transcendental condition for all acts of knowledge (Rousselot, Lonergan); others argue that what allows for knowledge is that to some degree humans have an a priori *apprehension* of God as Absolute Being (by the light of the agent intellect) (Maréchal, Rahner). The world is intelligible

Thomism, is concerned with the study of Thomistic principles in their historical context and focuses on the interpretation of *esse*.[74] Marie-Dominique Chenu, OP, a student of Garrigou-Lagrange, helped establish the historical-contextualist reading[75] of Thomas Aquinas based on preliminary work by Étienne Gilson in the 1940s.[76] The American priest and philosopher, Richard Liddy, writes, "In many ways Gilson's commitment to the historical method [and] a detailed study of historical sources in their original languages symbolized the new historically conscious culture."[77] For Chenu (and other "Stream Three"Thomists), the key contribution of Aquinas was his "'body of master intuitions' rather than adhering to a rigidly defined system of propositions."[78]

Barbour applauds Thomists in general for their efforts to "defend divine omnipotence and the lawful world of science without accepting the inactive God of deism."[79] Following the Renaissance scholar, Thomas Cardinal Cajetan, OP, many Thomists consider natural science (or the philosophy of nature), mathematics, and metaphysics as varying degrees, or levels, of abstraction.[80] The third degree of abstraction, metaphysics, is also the foundation of Thomistic theology. Therefore, given this common level of abstraction, the possibility for interaction between science and theology is implicit in this system.

Barbour is very familiar with two of the aforementioned prominent, twentieth century French Thomists, Réginald Marie Garrigou-Lagrange, OP and Étienne Gilson.[81] His understanding of their thought derives primarily from their books, *God: His Existence and Nature*[82] and *The Christian Philosophy of Thomas Aquinas*.[83]

then to Transcendental Thomists because we either seek or actually ascend to God (perfectly intelligible being) in every act of knowing." Alan Vincelette, *Recent Catholic Philosophy: The Twentieth Century*, Marquette Studies in Philosophy 71 (Milwaukee: Marquette University Press, 2011), 82.

74 Rowland, *Catholic Theology*, 54.

75 For an analysis of the "Stream One" reaction to the historical, "Stream Three" approach to the *Corpus Thomisticum*, see Serge-Thomas Bonino, "To Be a Thomist," *Nova et Vetera* 8, no. 4 (2010): 770.

76 Fergus Kerr, "A Different World: Neoscholasticism and Its Discontents," *International Journal of Systematic Theology* 8, no. 2 (April 2006): 128–148.

77 Liddy, "Jaki and Lonergan: Confrontation or Encounter?," 80–81.

78 Christophe F. Potworowski, *Contemplation and Incarnation: The Theology of Marie-Dominique Chenu* (London: McGill-Queen's Press, 2001), 107.

79 Barbour, *Religion and Science*, 309.

80 Benedict M. Ashley, *The Way Toward Wisdom: An Interdisciplinary and Intercultural Introduction to Metaphysics* (Notre Dame: University of Notre Dame Press, 2006), 46.

81 Barbour, *Issues in Science and Religion*, 425.

82 Réginald Garrigou-Lagrange, *God: His Existence and His Nature*, 2 vols. (New York: Charter Press, 2016).

83 Etienne Gilson, *The Christian Philosophy of Thomas Aquinas* (New York: Random House, 1956).

Garrigou-Lagrange was a leader of the Neo-Scholastic form of Thomism, sometimes referred to as "Thomism of the Strict Observance" (colloquially) or "Essentialist / Conceptualist Thomism" (by existentialist critics). This school attempted to "purify" Thomism from the influence of the seventeenth century philosopher and theologian, Francisco Suárez, SJ, and return to the original method and principles of Aquinas. Garrigou-Lagrange was highly respected, not only as a theologian, but also as a preacher and retreat master. Some biographers state that the influential French theologian, Yves Congar, OP, was inspired to join the Order of Preachers as a result of a retreat led by Garrigou-Lagrange. Garrigou-Lagrange also supervised the doctoral dissertation of Karol Wojtyła on the theological virtue of faith in Saint John of the Cross.[84]

Étienne Gilson is a father of the school of "Existentialist Thomism." His historical research led him to be critical of attempts to incorporate Cartesian or Kantian elements into Thomistic thought. He was also concerned by the failure of some philosophers to distinguish the ways that Thomas Aquinas further developed Aristotle's metaphysics. Aristotle's first philosophy was based on being as *substance actualized through a substantial form*. Gilson showed how Thomas conceived of metaphysics as a philosophy of being as *esse—actus essendi* (existential act). God is pure act and His creation participates in that *esse*.[85]

Gilson, like Barbour, desires to confront the mid-twentieth century positivistic vitiation of metaphysics. As a Thomist, Gilson suggests that the only rational explanation for why anything exists is *ipsum esse per se subsistens*. Gilson further suggests that this "Being-act," from which all else comes to be, is creative. Creativity implies freedom, and authentic freedom implies thought. Gilson is very clear that this "first cause" is not a being among beings, but "To-be-act."[86] Gilson works from the very common Catholic translation of the name of God from Exodus 3:14, "אֶהְיֶה אֲשֶׁר אֶהְיֶה" (*'ehyeh 'ăšer 'ehyeh*),[87] based on the primary Biblical text of the Apostles and the early Church, the Septuagint. The Koine Greek, "ἐγώ εἰμι ὁ ὤν," (*egó eimi ho ón*)[88] came into the Latin Vulgate directly as *"Ego sum qui sum,"* literally "I am who am." In this light, Gilson states, "There is but one God and this God is

---

84 Rowland, *Catholic Theology*, 58.

85 Ashley, *The Way Toward Wisdom*, 49–50.

86 Daniel Guerrière, "Continental Theistic Philosophers," ed. Richard Popkin, *The Columbia History of Western Philosophy* (New York: Columbia University Press, January 15, 1999), 712.

87 Karl Elliger and Willhelm Rudulph, eds., *Biblia Hebraica Stuttgartensia* (Stuttgart: German Bible Society, 1997), 89.

88 Alfred Rahlfs and Robert Hanhart, eds., *Septuaginta* (Stuttgart: Deutsche Bibelgesellschaft, 2006), 90.

Being, that is the corner-stone of all Christian philosophy, and it was not Plato, it was not even Aristotle, it was Moses who put it in position."[89]

As is the case with almost every verse in the Bible, alternative translations have been proposed. In the twentieth century, the Jewish philosophers, Martin Buber and Franz Rosenzweig, produced a German translation of the Hebrew Bible. At times, the translation is clearly influenced by Buber's philosophy of mutuality. In K.J. Cronin's analysis of Exodus 3:14, he points out how Buber and Rosenzweig "explicitly reject all philosophical interpretations of Exodus 3:14, maintaining instead that the verse is simply a statement of God's abiding presence with and providence towards Israel."[90] We observe however that every interpretation implies some underlying philosophy.

The Jewish scholar, Everitt Fox's, English translation of the pericope, inspired by the Buber-Rosenzweig German translation of the Hebrew, is: "God said to Moshe: I will be-there howsoever I will be-there. And He said: Thus shall you say to the Sons of Israel: I-Will-Be-There sends me to you."[91] Hence, we have a translation of the name of God that emphasizes Divine accompaniment rather than God as self-subsistent Being. Of course, a plurality of meanings for the Divine name presents no problem for Catholic theology. Therefore, this diversity of interpretation does not challenge the legitimacy of the LXX. Thus, the Thomistic interpretation still enjoys credibility. "To-be-act" can be credibly identified with יהוה (YHWH).

Barbour is particularly attracted to the Thomistic notion of Divine causality, which he describes as "rich and multi-faceted, far from any simple mechanical coercion."[92] He appreciates the distinction between *primary* and *secondary* causes. Thomists acknowledge that God has a continuing role in creation (primary causality), while at the same time accept that the natural sciences are most often apt to describe secondary causes in the cosmos. Though aware of the limits of analogy, Barbour is fond of Gilson's model of a worker using a tool: "In God's hand creatures are like a tool in the hands of the workman."[93]

Barbour also values the Thomistic notions of Divine *conservation* and *concurrence*. The principle of Divine conservation states that all of creation, natural and supernatural, remains in existence by Divine act. In addition, the "powers" of

89 Etienne Gilson, *The Spirit of Mediaeval Philosophy* (Notre Dame: University of Notre Dame Press, 1991), 51.

90 K.J. Cronin, *The Name of God as Revealed in Exodus 3:14* (Exodus-314.com, December 16, 2017), 7, accessed January 24, 2018, http://exodus-314.com/images/banners/the_name.pdf.

91 Everett Fox, *The Five Books of Moses: The Schocken Bible*, vol. 1 (New York: Schocken, 2000), 273.

92 Barbour, *Religion and Science*, 310.

93 Ibid., 309.

creatures, e.g., animals, are only potentialities moved to actuality by God. Theories of concurrence attempt to explain God's influence upon the actions of His creatures. According to Arnold J. Benedetto, SJ, Divine concurrence "though immediately affecting the created cause itself, also carries over into the action and effect, and in that sense partakes of the nature of a 'simultaneous concursus' as well."[94]

Gilson insists on the reality of secondary causes in which God "delegates" causal efficacy to creatures.[95] According to Barbour, the certainty of the stability of such cause-effect relationships provides a basis for natural science. Gilson also argues that the *whole effect* is a result of both natural and Divine causes under different aspects. Barbour summarizes his philosophy this way: "God is primary cause, in a different order from all instrumental secondary causes. God sometimes produces effects directly, as in the case of miracles, but usually works through natural causes."[96]

An ongoing concern for Barbour is to maintain contingency and freedom in any metaphysical system. He shows great interest in Garrigou-Lagrange's treatment of the efficacy of Divine grace and the reality of human freedom. In his book, *Commentary on the Summa Theologica of St. Thomas, Ia IIae, q. 109–14*, Garrigou-Lagrange states,

> Under efficacious grace a man can resist, but he does not do so in fact; grace would then no longer be efficacious. Moreover, we hold that by grace efficacious in itself God infallibly moves the will to determine itself freely in the direction of the commandment; this motion is thus a causal predetermination distinct from the formal determination of the act to which it is ordained. God determines to one object in the sense that He determines us to obey rather than not to obey.[97]

Barbour further elaborates this approach, very relevant to the doctrine of creation, following Garrigou-Lagrange:[98]

> A contingent event is defined as one that is not uniquely determined by its natural causes. If God were merely to calculate the future from the present, as we would have to, God could not know the future. Since God is eternal, however, the future is present

---

94 Arnold J. Benedetto, "Divine Concurrence," ed. Thomas Carson, *New Catholic Encyclopedia* (Farmington Hills: Thompson Gale, 2003), accessed February 7, 2018, http://www.encyclopedia.com/religion/encyclopedias-almanacs-transcripts-and-maps/concurrence-divine.

95 Gilson, *The Christian Philosophy of Thomas Aquinas*, 183.

96 Barbour, *Religion and Science*, 310.

97 Réginald Garrigou-Lagrange, *Grace: Commentary on the Summa Theologica of St. Thomas, Ia IIae, q. 109–14*, trans. The Dominican Nuns of Corpus Christi Monastery (New York: B. Herder Book Co., 1952), chap. 12, accessed February 7, 2018, http://www.ewtn.com/library/theology/gracepref.htm.

98 Garrigou-Lagrange, *God: His Existence and His Nature*.

to God as it will actually be, a single definite outcome. God, being above time and having unchanging knowledge, does not know the future as potentially and indeterminately contained in its worldly causes, but determinately as specified in the eternal divine decree. Within the world, an act is uncertain before it takes place. But for God there is no "before"; for God it has taken place.[99]

Neo-Thomists acknowledge that God, the origin of *materia et forma*, also works through *causæ finales*. God gives each creature a nature that implies *natural* inclinations to accomplish His purposes. For example, man, made in the image and likeness of God, is endowed with a natural attraction to the *bonum, verum, unum, et pulchrum*. Barbour very much likes this aspect of Divine causality and describes God's action as "the power of love."[100] He notes the parallel with process metaphysics' concept of Divine influence referenced in Chapter Two. Barbour writes, "To the present author, this later aspect of Thomistic thought is particularly significant."[101] Barbour comes close to a rapprochement between Catholic Neo-Thomism and some of his best insights into the theology-science interaction.

Nonetheless, due to the traditional Thomistic distinctions of matter and spirit, mind and body, and time and eternity, Barbour does not adopt a Thomistic approach in his quest to bring theology and science into a mutually beneficial interaction. Because he interprets the classical Aristotelian-Thomistic distinctions through a Cartesian lens, Barbour classifies these distinctions as unhelpful dualisms.[102] He also struggles with how an omnipotent and omniscient God could allow evil. Consequently, Barbour is more inclined toward *liberal* and *process* approaches to relating theology and science as will be discussed in the next two sections.

3.2 Liberalism

Another perspective that Barbour classifies as emphasizing similarities between the attitudes of inquiry and methodologies of theology and natural science is liberalism, or more precisely, liberal theology.[103] He distinguishes the "more traditional" liberal theology from the "modernist" movement, which Barbour describes as having "lost all sense of identification with historic Christianity."[104]

---

99   Barbour, *Religion and Science*, 310.
100 Ibid.
101 Barbour, *Issues in Science and Religion*, 427.
102 Barbour, *When Science Meets Religion*, 34.
103 It is important to distinguish liberal theology from liberal political philosophies or economic theories. Although all modern liberalism can be traced to Enlightenment influences, liberal theology should not be reduced to a religious expression of politics.
104 Barbour, *Issues in Science and Religion*, 126.

On a theological spectrum, Barbour places liberal theology to the "right" of pan-theism and the "left" of neo-orthodoxy.[105] He identifies Lotan Harold DeWolf, a Methodist minister and theologian who supervised the doctoral studies of Martin Luther King Jr., as an articulate expositor of liberal theology.[106]

Concisely summarizing the liberal project, Barbour states that liberal theologians emphasize God's immanence over his transcendence,[107] Jesus' way of life over His atoning death, and the possibility of ethical living over man's sinful, fallen nature. In comparison with the aforementioned neo-orthodox perspective, Barbour claims that liberalism finds *continuity* instead of *discontinuity*: "continuity between revelation and reason, between faith and human experience, between God and the world, between Christ and other men, between Christianity and other religions. There are no radical gaps here—there are differences in degree, but not in kind."[108] Relevant to the relationship of theology with the natural sciences, Barbour asserts that for "most liberals, *attitudes similar to those of the scientist are appropriate in religious inquiry.*"[109]

Liberals emphasize a tentativeness to all doctrinal formulations and therefore an openness to reformulation. They also take an atypical approach to Divine revelation. According to Barbour, liberal theologians tend to minimize the distinctiveness of Biblical revelation. They also emphasize that Scripture must constantly be received anew by each generation, reinterpreting it according to the contemporary situation. No Biblical interpretation is ever final or absolutely true, due to the limits of the human intellect. Rather than a record of infallible teachings, in the words of Barbour, the Bible should be viewed as "the record of a people's progressive search for God and response to him."[110]

In addition to DeWolf, Barbour identifies Charles Earle Raven, an English theologian and professor of divinity at Cambridge, as a significant liberal theologian, particularly in the science-theology area. Raven emphasizes the similarities in the methods of inquiry for the physical, life, and social sciences with theology. All sciences are *data-driven*; for theology, according to Raven, "the primary data are the lives and experiences of the saints through whom God fully reveals Himself to us."[111] Like Barbour, Raven seeks to avoid what they both classify as Cartesian

---

105 Barbour, *When Science Meets Religion*, 10–11.

106 See Harold DeWolf, *A Theology of the Living Church* (New York: Harper & Brothers, 1953).

107 See Jürgen Moltmann, *God in Creation: A New Theology of Creation and the Spirit of God*, trans. Margaret Kohl (San Francisco: Harper & Row, 1985) for an "ecological" theology of creation that stresses Divine immanence.

108 Barbour, *Issues in Science and Religion*, 126.

109 Ibid.

110 Ibid.

111 Charles Earle Raven, *Natural Religion and Christian Theology*, vol. 2 (Cambridge: Cambridge University Press, 1953), 12.

dualism by denying the distinction between body and mind. Raven wants science and theology to "tell a single tale which shall treat the whole universe as one and indivisible."[112]

Barbour also considers the thought of Charles Coulson to be beneficial for identifying parallel perspectives in the methods of theology and science from a liberal perspective. Coulson was a British applied mathematician, theoretical chemist, and physicist who taught at King's College London and the University of Oxford. He was also a lay speaker in the Methodist Church.[113] Coulson emphasizes that scientists are human beings, not robots. Like all people, they have the capacity for awe and reverence in the presence of the mystery of creation. In light of his scientific work, a scientist is often struck by the harmony of natural laws and the unity of nature.[114] Coulson realizes that God can be known partially through diverse fields, including the natural sciences:

> For we live among our fellows, and we can make sense of our relationship to them, and of their human needs, only in terms of a God—partly seen in science, and in art and history and philosophy, partly expressed in wholly personal terms in the "living present" and verified in the power of a transformed life.[115]

Coulson also argues that science, like theology, always involves moral commitments and presuppositions. For example, the scientist does (and must) assume that the natural world is intelligible and follows fixed laws. In a real sense, the scientist must have "faith" in these premises. Coulson also suggests that the practice of science requires certain "moral attitudes" similar to religious virtues. Barbour summarizes these attitudes as humility, cooperation, universality, and integrity. He appreciates how this perspective contrasts with the positivistic view of science. Barbour, like Coulson, affirms the importance of "human factors in science, such as the scientist's personal judgment, commitment to truth, and participation in a community of inquiry."[116] Barbour's understanding of the importance

---

112 Ibid., 2:13.

113 A lay speaker is a formal member of a local parish who is knowledgeable of Sacred Scripture and committed to the "doctrine, heritage, organization, and life of the United Methodist Church." A candidate must complete a program of formation and be approved by a conference committee on lay speaking. A lay speaker may conduct worship services, deliver sermons, and lead Bible studies with the authorization of their pastor or the district superintendent. See "Glossary: Lay Speaker," *The United Methodist Church*, accessed February 15, 2018, http://www.umc.org/what-we-believe/glossary-lay-speaker.

114 Barbour, *Issues in Science and Religion*, 127.

115 Charles Alfred Coulson, *Science and Christian Belief* (Chapel Hill: University of North Carolina Press, 1955), 117.

116 Barbour, *Issues in Science and Religion*, 128.

of the "human element" in science is also informed by the scholarship of Michael Polanyi[117] and Harold Schilling.[118]

3.3 Process Theology

Despite his affinity for aspects of Roman Catholic Neo-Thomism and non-modernist (to use his classification) Protestant liberal theology, ultimately Barbour decides that the most "impressive attempt to include science and religion within a unified view of reality is the 'process philosophy' of Alfred North Whitehead."[119] The strongest form of Barbour's *integration* modality of interaction, the *systematic synthesis*,[120] can only take place with a comprehensive metaphysics.[121] Given what Barbour judges to be the strong compatibility of Whitehead's first philosophy with twentieth century science, Barbour's "flexibility" with regard to Christian doctrine, and his desire to eliminate all forms of dualism, he effectively commits himself to that paradigm.[122]

As mentioned in the last chapter, Ian Barbour adopts, adapts, and simplifies, Whitehead's highly specified metaphysics. He concurs with Whitehead on emphasizing *the primacy of time, the interconnection of events, reality as an organic process, and the self-creation of every entity*. Barbour believes that "becoming" is more significant than "being" because "transition and activity are more fundamental than permanence and substance."[123] He finds "scientific support" for this perspective in the quantum mechanical perspective on subatomic particles as patterns of vibration, as well as in contemporary Neo-Darwinism. It must be mentioned that the process view and Protestant liberal theology mentioned in the last section are not mutually exclusive approaches. Barbour's process thought can be classified as a particular school of Protestant liberal theology. According to Robert J. Russell, within

---

117 See Michael Polanyi, *Personal Knowledge* (Chicago: University Of Chicago Press, 1958).

118 See Harold K. Schilling, *Science and Religion* (New York: Charles Scribner's Sons, 1962).

119 Barbour, *Issues in Science and Religion*, 128.

120 Barbour's quest for a systematic synthesis bears many similarities to Teilhard's own efforts at integration.

121 Barbour's process metaphysics is treated in some depth in Chapter 2.

122 It should be noted that the Magisterium has always rejected all forms of ontological dualism, e.g., the good God created the spiritual realm and the "evil principle" is responsible for the material realm. For example, at the Council of Braga II in 561, the following anathema was issued: "If anyone says that the creation of all flesh is not the work of God, but belongs to the wicked angels, just as Priscillian has said, let him be anathema." DS 463 The teaching on the goodness of all creation was reaffirmed in the Profession of Innocent III in 1208, again refuting the error that matter is evil and created by Satan. See DS 790.

123 Barbour, *Religion and Science*, 285.

the field of science and religion, Ian Barbour was a widely recognized leader of the "liberal Anglo-American theological perspective."[124] Having explicated Barbour's assessment of contrasting and parallel perspectives on theology and science, we can now analyze salient methodological aspects of his work to relate theology and science.

4. Theological and Scientific Methodology

The aforementioned approaches that were classified as offering *contrasting perspectives* on theology and science maintained that the methodologies of the two fields are profoundly dissimilar. As a consequence, scientific breakthroughs can have no theological implications, and scientific inquiry cannot be enriched by engagement with theology. Conversely, the Neo-Thomist, liberal, and process approaches were judged by Barbour to offer *parallel perspectives* on the two fields. Neo-Thomism and process thought both offer a metaphysical system applicable to scientific and religious issues. According to Barbour, liberal (Anglophonic) theology adopts attitudes and practices for theological research that are similar to those used in scientific inquiry.

Barbour also identifies a particular "group" that seeks to develop theological conclusions quite directly from observation of the natural world, and science in particular. This group includes those who wish to develop a *natural theology*. Such a theology would infer the existence of God as well as certain aspects of the Divine from the "general features of nature, such as design and order, or from specific findings, such as the directedness of evolution, the increase of entropy, or the mathematical character of modern physics."[125]

This particular community also includes those who, like Barbour, seek to develop a *theology of nature*, in which religious doctrines within a particular community are re-examined in light of the findings of mature science. It should be noted that both scholars who engage in natural theology, as well as the theology of nature, often fit into one of the aforementioned parallel perspectives, e.g., Neo-Thomists developing a natural theology or process theologians developing a theology of nature. The rest of this chapter will explore Barbour's understanding of experience and interpretation in theology and science, the role of religious and

---

124 Robert John Russell, "Ian Barbour's Methodology in Science and Religion," ed. Andreas Losch, *Dialog Theologie & Naturwissenschaften* (Bonn: Evangelischen Akademie im Rheinland, June 2014), accessed February 16, 2018, https://www.theologie-naturwissenschaften.de/startseite/leitartikelarchiv/barbours-methodology.html.

125 Barbour, *Issues in Science and Religion*, 131–132.

scientific communities and their respective paradigms, models and analogies in theology and science, and evaluative criteria for scientific theories and religious beliefs.

4.1 Theological and Scientific Experience and Interpretation

Having clarified the nature and relative strengths of the aforementioned perspectives according to Barbour, we can now examine the notions of *experience* and *interpretation* in the realms of science and theology in order to classify similarities and differences. Experience is never purely subjective, nor purely objective, in Barbour's view. A key issue is that language always influences the structure of human experience. In addition, for Barbour, the distinction between interpretation and experience is not absolute. He believes that their relationship is always context dependent.[126]

Whether one considers the work of Galileo, Newton, or Darwin, it is evident that all influential scientists combine some aspects of the *experimental* and *theoretical* components of scientific research. The experimental component includes the activity of making observations and collecting data. The theoretical component is the interpretative element that formulates concepts, laws, and theories.[127]

Given his education and experience in experimental physics, Ian Barbour is well acquainted with the actual practice of science, as opposed to the "idealized" description that non-scientists sometimes adopt, e.g., the belief that a researcher discovers "pure facts" that lead to "indubitable knowledge" of nature. Barbour acknowledges that in science, there are no *un-interpreted facts*:

> We organize our experience in the light of particular interests, and we attend to selected features ... Significant experimentation requires a selection of relevant variables and a purposeful experimental design dependent on the questions that are considered fruitful and the problems that have been formulated. "Observations" are always abstractions from our total experience, and they are expressed in terms of conceptual structures. The processes of measurement, as well as the language in which results are reported, are influenced by prior theories.[128]

Barbour gives the following illustrative example:

> A doctor sees an X-ray plate differently from someone without medical training. Galileo saw a pendulum as an object with inertia which almost repeats its oscillating

---

126 Barbour, *Myths, Models, and Paradigms*, 120–121.
127 Barbour, *Issues in Science and Religion*, 138.
128 Ibid., 139.

motion, whereas his predecessors had seen it as a constrained falling object which slowly attains its rest. The line between "observation" and "theory," then, is not sharp.[129]

Accordingly, Barbour concurs with the American philosophers of science, Norwood Hanson[130] and Thomas Kuhn,[131] in asserting that all data is *theory-laden.* The important connection between experimental observations and theoretical concepts has been given various terms by different authors, e.g., "rules of correspondence,"[132] "epistemic correlations,"[133] and "coordinative definitions."[134] Barbour points out that for some concepts, the link with observation is quite direct, e.g., the concept of "length" and the measurement of an object with a ruler. Often in modern physics, the link is not so obvious, e.g., the concept of a wave function in a quantum mechanical system. Barbour defines scientific *laws* as the "correlations between two or more concepts that are closely related to observables … *Laws* may or may not imply relationships which could be spoken of as *causal.*"[135] He defines *theories* as "unified and generalized conceptual schemes from which laws can be derived," e.g., Kepler's Laws of Planetary Motion can be developed from Newton's Theory of Gravitation.[136]

In the history of science, there are diverse views about the process of theory formation. The *inductive method* is an idealized process through which a scientist obtains generalized information based on particular experiments.[137] The *deductive method* is similarly idealized and suggests that scientists derive verifiable observation statements from general theories.[138] According to Barbour, both idealized processes omit the critical step of *creative imagination.* He writes, "There is a logic for testing theories but no logic for creating them; there are no recipes for making original discoveries."[139]

Here, Barbour concurs with Albert Einstein who wrote,

129 Ibid.
130 See Norwood R. Hanson, *Patterns of Discovery* (Cambridge: Cambridge University Press, 1958), chap. 1.
131 See Kuhn, *The Structure of Scientific Revolutions.*
132 Margenau, *The Nature of Physical Reality,* 78.
133 Filmer Stuart Cuckow Northrop, *The Logic of the Sciences and Humanities* (New York: The Macmillan Co., 1947), 119.
134 Hans Reichenbach, *The Rise of Scientific Philosophy* (Berkeley: University of California Press, 1951), 132.
135 Barbour, *Issues in Science and Religion,* 140.
136 Ibid., 141.
137 See John Stuart Mill, *A System of Logic, Ratiocinative and Inductive,* 2 vols. (London: John W. Parker, 1843).
138 See Karl R. Popper, *The Logic of Scientific Discovery* (Eastford: Martino Fine Books, 2014).
139 Barbour, *Issues in Science and Religion,* 142–143.

> I have learned something else from the theory of gravitation: no collection of empirical facts however comprehensive can ever lead to the setting up of such complicated equations. A theory can be tested by experience, but there is no way from experience to the construction of a theory.[140]

A realistic assessment of the process of science must acknowledge that there is a diversity of mental operations.

Just as Barbour concludes that there are no un-interpreted facts in the natural sciences, he posits that there are no un-interpreted experiences in matters of religion. All religious experience requires some theological interpretation. Not surprisingly, Barbour looks to Whitehead here:

> The dogmas of religion are the attempts to formulate in precise terms the truths disclosed in the religious experience of mankind. In exactly the same way the dogmas of physical science are the attempts to formulate in precise terms the truths disclosed in the sense-perception of mankind.[141]

Barbour also agrees with the following description by the Church of Scotland minister and theologian, John Baillie:

> The witness of all true religion is that there is no reality which more directly confronts us than the reality of God. No other reality is nearer to us than he. The realities of the senses are more obvious, but his is the more intimate, touching us as it does so much nearer to the core of our being.[142]

Barbour identifies four fundamental aspects of religious experience in the Judæo-Christian tradition:

1) awe and reverence,
2) humility and guilt,
3) acceptance of forgiveness, and
4) responsibility for action in society.[143]

These aspects can be found throughout the Old and New Testaments. For example, one notices all four elements in Isaiah 6:3–9.[144] Religious experience is

140 Albert Einstein, *Albert Einstein: Autobiographical Notes*, trans. Paul Arthur Schlipp (La Salle, IL: Open Court, 1979), 31.

141 Alfred North Whitehead, *Religion in the Making*, 2nd ed. (New York: Fordham University Press, 1996), 47.

142 John Baillie, *Our Knowledge of God* (New York: Charles Scribner's Sons, 1939), 155.

143 Barbour, *Issues in Science and Religion*, 209.

144 "And one called to another and said: 'Holy, holy, holy is the LORD of hosts; the whole earth is full of his glory.' And the foundations of the thresholds shook at the voice of him who called, and the house was filled with smoke. And I said: 'Woe is me! For I am lost; for I am a man of

interpreted systematically within the discipline of theology. Barbour identifies a significant feedback mechanism. He posits that theological concepts affect religious communities from which the "data of religion" arises: "[Theological] beliefs have implications for worship, ethics, and all aspects of corporate and individual life, and thereby influence the data."[145]

Because Barbour believes that all religious experience is interpreted by subjective, fallible beings, he rules out the possibility of "immediate and certain" knowledge in theological questions:

> For when human interpretation is present, there is always the possibility of misinterpretation, especially through wishful thinking, which reads into experience more than is warranted. Moreover, any verbal communication requires the use of symbolic language and conceptual structures that are culturally conditioned.[146]

Barbour's view is a radicalization of his Protestant heritage which does not embrace an authoritative Magisterium, *sensu stricto*, but avouches the self-interpretation of the Bible in faith and morals. However, as the American Catholic bishop and theologian, John Whealon, points out, most Christian communities do posit some final ecclesial authority under Christ: "for the Presbyterians the presbytery; for the Congregationalists the individual congregation; and for the Baptists, no authority exists above the individual Christian."[147]

The Catholic Church recognizes the necessary role of theological hermeneutics, the benefits of Biblical criticism, and the limitations of human language. It also professes doctrines of inspiration and inerrancy with regard to Sacred Scripture[148] as well as the presence of a Magisterium that can teach infallibly on matters of

---

unclean lips, and I dwell in the midst of a people of unclean lips; for my eyes have seen the King, the LORD of hosts!' Then flew one of the seraphim to me, having in his hand a burning coal which he had taken with tongs from the altar. And he touched my mouth, and said: 'Behold, this has touched your lips; your guilt is taken away, and your sin forgiven.' And I heard the voice of the Lord saying, 'Whom shall I send, and who will go for us?' Then I said, 'Here am I! Send me.' And he said, 'Go, and say to this people: "Hear and hear, but do not understand; see and see, but do not perceive."'" Isaiah 6:3–9 (RSV).

145 Barbour, *Issues in Science and Religion*, 210.

146 Ibid., 210–211.

147 John F. Whealon, "The Magisterium: Biblical and Pastoral Aspects," *L'Osservatore Romano* (Vatican City State, April 13, 1978), 7, accessed February 21, 2018, https://www.ewtn.com/library/BISHOPS/MAGPAST.HTM.

148 "*Cum ergo omne id, quod auctores inspirati seu hagiographi asserunt, retineri debeat assertum a Spiritu Sancto, inde Scripturæ libri veritatem, quam Deus nostræ salutis causa Litteris Sacris consignari voluit, firmiter, fideliter et sine errore docere profitendi sunt.*" Second Vatican Council, *Dei Verbum*, 1965, 11.

faith and morals.[149] In addition, the Church acknowledges the historical condi-
tioning of Catholic terminology—although not meaning:

> The transmission of divine Revelation by the Church encounters difficulties of various
> kinds. These arise from the fact that the hidden mysteries of God "by their nature so
> far transcend the human intellect that even if they are revealed to us and accepted by
> faith, they remain concealed by the veil of faith itself and are as it were wrapped in
> darkness."[150] Difficulties arise also from the historical condition that affects the ex-
> pression of Revelation … It must be stated that the dogmatic formulas of the Church's
> Magisterium were from the beginning suitable for communicating revealed truth, and
> that as they are they remain forever suitable for communicating this truth to those
> who interpret them correctly … As for the meaning of dogmatic formulas, this re-
> mains ever true and constant in the Church, even when it is expressed with greater
> clarity or more developed.[151]

In summary, regardless of one's ecclesiology, in Barbour's view, when the scientist studies the natural world and the theologian reflects on creation, both should
be aware that their "data" is theory-laden. As such, it is in need of interpretation according to the norms and criteria of the respective disciplines. However, experience
and interpretation are not the isolated activities of individuals. They are influenced
by communities and their paradigms.

4.2 The Roles of Religious and Scientific Communities and their Paradigms

Barbour's study of science and theology acknowledges the importance of
communities and their *paradigms*. For scientists, the "corporate character of inquiry" is present at many levels. Barbour offers the examples of "the dependence
of each scientist on his predecessors, the necessity of having one's results checked
by others, the reliance of experimentalists on theoreticians and *vice versa*, and the

---

149 "*Haec autem infallibilitas, qua Divinus Redemptor Ecclesiam suam in definienda doctrina de fide
     vel moribus instructam esse voluit, tantum patet quantum divinae Revelationis patet depositum,
     sancte custodiendum et fideliter exponendum. Qua quidem infallibilitate Romanus Pontifex, Collegii
     Episcoporum Caput, vi muneris sui gaudet, quando, ut supremus omnium christifidelium pastor et
     doctor, qui fratres suos in fide confirmat (cf. Lc 22,32), doctrinam de fide vel moribus definitivo actu
     proclamat.*" Second Vatican Council, *Lumen Gentium*, 1964, 25.
150 First Vatican Council, "Dei Filius," 4.
151 Congregation for the Doctrine of the Faith, "Declaration in Defense of the Catholic Doctrine
     on the Church Against Certain Errors of the Present Day," June 24, 1973, sec. 5, accessed April
     17, 2018, http://www.vatican.va/roman_curia/congregations/cfaith/documents/rc_con_cfaith_
     doc_19730705_mysterium-ecclesiae_en.html.

value of knowledge from other fields."[152] Communicability is thus a key aspect of scientific knowledge.

Scientific communities, similar to society at large, have certain attitudes that, in a sense, define the group. Unorthodox views are typically *rejected* (e.g., creationism by most evolutionary biologists), *ignored* (e.g., telekinesis by most experimental psychologists), or simply *tolerated* (e.g., traditional Chinese medicine by most licensed physicians in the United States). Scientists with a particular specialization share "patterns of expectation" and "conceptions of regularity and intelligibility." According to Barbour, explanatory paradigms typically "determine what we take to be 'problems,' what we see as 'facts,' and what we consider to be satisfactory explanations."[153]

Barbour largely adopts Thomas Kuhn's notion of *paradigms* in science.[154] Barbour defines them as "'standard examples' of past scientific work which are accepted by a given group of scientists at a given time."[155] Paradigms both dictate the types of examples given in high school textbooks as well as guide the scope of university research laboratories. According to Kuhn, major changes in paradigms are rare in science. However, when an epistemological *paradigm shift* occurs, Kuhn classifies it as a *scientific revolution*.

Paradigm shifts are very disruptive, and most scientists resist such upheavals. They typically come about not simply from logical argument, but rather from a form of intellectual conversion.[156] Modern examples include the discovery of the

---

152 Barbour, *Issues in Science and Religion*, 151.

153 Ibid., 153.

154 See Kuhn, *The Structure of Scientific Revolutions*. Giorgio Agamben concisely summarizes the heart of Kuhn's concept of paradigm: "Kuhn acknowledges having used the term 'paradigm' in two different meanings. In the first one, 'paradigm' designates what the members of a certain scientific community have in common, that is to say, the whole of techniques, patents and values shared by the members of the community. In the second sense, the paradigm is a single element of a whole, say for instance Newton's *Principia*, which, acting as a common model or an example ... stands for the explicit rules and thus defines a coherent tradition of investigation. Thus the question is for Kuhn to investigate by means of the paradigm what makes possible the constitution of what he calls 'normal science.' That is to say, the science which can decide if a certain problem will be considered scientific or not. Normal science does not mean at all a science guided by a coherent system of rules, on the contrary, the rules can be derived from the paradigms, but the paradigms can guide the investigation also in the absence of rules. This is precisely the second meaning of the term 'paradigm,' which Kuhn considered the most new and profound, though it is in truth the oldest." Giorgio Agamben, "What Is a Paradigm?" (Lecture presented at the European Graduate School, Saas-Fee, Switzerland, October 1, 2002), accessed March 6, 2018, https://www.youtube.com/watch?v=G9Wxn1L9Er0.

155 Barbour, *Issues in Science and Religion*, 154.

156 Barbour, *Myths, Models, and Paradigms*, 93.

molecular structure of DNA for biology, the development of non-linear dynamics and chaos theory in applied mathematics, and the emergence of the theories of special and general relativity in physics.[157]

Ultimately, Barbour is supportive of Kuhn's approach. He judges it to be a "salutary reaction" against positivism but also believes that at times it over emphasizes the "subjective, relativistic, and communal features" of scientific activity.[158] Barbour also believes that it corrects an error common to diverse forms of empiricism that posit the existence of "fixed observational data" not affected by theoretical interpretations. Again, in this context, he emphasizes that "there are *no bare uninterpreted data*."[159]

A certain "social character of knowledge" is also present in religious communities, according to Barbour. He concurs with Harold Schilling who points out that just as there is no "one-man physics," there is likewise no "one-man religion."[160] Theological inquiry takes place in the context of a religious community. Its members typically share common "purposes, attitudes, hope, and loyalties ... [and] a social fabric of mutual interaction, trust, aid, and criticism."[161] For example, the Catholic Church, emphasizes the ecclesial nature of the theologian's vocation.[162] There is also a special *conspiratio* that exists between the faithful and the hierarchy.[163]

Barbour points out that religious communities, like scientific ones, have their own symbolic language that facilitates communication within the community, e.g., just as a scientist uses Newton-Leibniz notation to succinctly communicate a mathematical model of a physical process in nature, a Catholic may use the Niceno–Constantinopolitan Creed to concisely share his Christian faith. Those outside of a scientific or religious community often find this language difficult to comprehend without some intellectual formation, e.g., non-scientists may have no clue how to interpret a second order non-linear differential equation and

---

157 On the other hand, the acceptance of the work in logic of Kurt Friedrich Gödel and Alan Turing came relatively quickly from philosophers and mathematicians. This was partly due to the unsettled nature of the foundations of logic and mathematics at that time.
158 Barbour, *Issues in Science and Religion*, 156.
159 Barbour, *Myths, Models, and Paradigms*, 95.
160 Schilling, *Science and Religion*, chap. 4.
161 Barbour, *Issues in Science and Religion*, 214.
162 See Congregation for the Doctrine of the Faith, *Donum Veritatis*.
163 "*Sacra Traditio et Sacra Scriptura unum verbi Dei sacrum depositum constituunt Ecclesiae commissum cui inhaerens tota plebs sancta Pastoribus suis adunata in doctrina Apostolorum et communione, fractione panis et orationibus iugiter perseverat (cf. Act 2,42 gr.), ita ut in tradita fide tenenda, exercenda profitendaque singularis fiat Antistitum et fidelium conspiratio.*" Second Vatican Council, *Lumen Gentium*, 10.

non-Christians will likely not know what Catholics mean when they profess Jesus to be ὁμοούσιος (*homooúsios*), or in Latin: *consubstantialis*—consubstantial with the Father.

Barbour's notion of *symbol* is informed by the American philosopher of science, Abram Cornelius Benjamin. Benjamin writes,

> Every symbol aims to represent its referent … but no symbol is able to portray *all* of the features of the referent; hence, it is obliged to omit one or more of them. Given any symbol, therefore, one may infer the referent, since the symbol resembles it, but not all of the referent, since the symbol is an abstraction … Since the human mind is incapable of grasping any event in all of its configurations, certain of its relations are more or less arbitrarily neglected and are not included in the resulting symbol. As a consequence, every symbol is abstract in its representations of nature; it *loses some of nature* and hence is not strictly adequate as a representative.[164]

Barbour concludes that "the language of every community of inquiry [scientific or religious] is *abstractive and selective* and replaces complex experiences by symbolic constructs."[165]

This "Kantian view" of symbol is consistent with Thomas Kuhn's position. It defines symbol as strictly partial and incomplete.[166] The symbolic appearance is incomplete and so it points beyond itself to reality—one that the symbol does not reliably communicate.[167] This contrasts with a more Catholic view that would see symbol as a whole form itself, one with the simplicity of the act to be, which therefore communicates God's perfection analogously. In the Catholic metaphysical tradition, e.g., Pseudo-Dionysius,[168] any symbol of Divine reality is always, in some

---

164 Abram Cornelius Benjamin, *Introduction to the Philosophy of Science* (New York: The Macmillan Co., 1937), 449, 70.

165 Barbour, *Issues in Science and Religion*, 157.

166 The philosophy and theology of symbol is a rich area of inquiry with a great diversity of perspectives. For example, a completely different perspective, of interest to theologians, is Paul Ricoeur's notion of symbols as entities with a "surplus of meaning." See Paul Ricoeur, *Interpretation Theory: Discourse and the Surplus of Meaning* (Fort Worth, TX: Texas Christian University Press, 1976).

167 The Swiss theologian, Charles Cardinal Journet, highlights a fundamental distinction between Catholics and Protestants on the issue of Christ's presence. Protestants tend to emphasize Christ's *mnemic* presence in time with signs, tokens, and promises. Catholics on the other hand believe that Christ is *really and truly* present in time under the appearance of signs, tokens, and promises in the Sacraments. See Charles Journet, *The Primacy of Peter*, trans. John Chapin (Westminster, MD: Newman Press, 1954). Barbour's weak notion of symbol comes out of this heritage.

168 According to Andrew Louth, Dionysius "vision is remarkable because, on the one hand, his understanding of hierarchy makes possible a rich symbolic system in terms of which we can understand God and the cosmos and our place within it, and, on the other, he finds room within

sense, a whole in itself. Only as such can it be an authentic communication of the whole that exceeds it. In God's act of creation, He is properly communicated by wholes in relation. The inner essence is communicated through a form that extends that essence, so to speak, rather than simply hiding it. The symbol communicates an infinite mystery that it is super-intelligible. In other words, the symbol *participates* in the fuller reality it signifies, and in this way enacts that reality.[169]

Barbour recognizes that in addition to a common symbolic language, participation in a "corporate history" is a striking feature of both Judaism and Christianity. For the Jews, זָכַר (*zākar*)—to remember—is a very important concept. The question, "Why is this night different from all the other nights?,"[170] asked in song by the youngest capable child attending the Passover Seder, is highly significant. In the Book of Exodus, it is written,

> And you shall tell your son on that day, "It is because of what the Lord did for me when I came out of Egypt." And it shall be to you as a sign on your hand and as a memorial between your eyes, that the law of the Lord may be in your mouth; for with a strong hand the Lord has brought you out of Egypt.[171]

In the present-day, ritual remembrance of the Passover Seder, the Jews enter profoundly into the mystery of God saving the sons and daughters of Abraham from the slavery of Egypt and leading them to a temporal salvation in the Promised Land.[172] The use of the first person ("when *I* came out of Egypt") by generations successive to those whom the Lord brought out of Egypt more than a millennium before Christ reinforces and perpetuates the participation in "corporate history"—a participation that is so active and alive that it continues to be personal.

Likewise in the celebration of the Eucharist, through the ἀνάμνησις (*anámnesis*)—remembrance,[173] Christians recall Jesus' saving work and so truly

this strictly hierarchical society for an escape from it, beyond it, by transcending symbols and realizing directly one's relationship with God as his creature, the creature of his love." Andrew Louth, *Denys the Areopagite* (New York: Continuum, 1989), 134. The reader is also referred to Pseudo-Dionysius, *Pseudo-Dionysius: The Complete Works*, trans. Paul Rorem, The Classics of Western Spirituality (Mahwah, NJ: Paulist Press, 1988).

169 Of course, one must acknowledge that even when a symbol is perfect, any individual's comprehension of it is less than perfect.

170 "מַה נִּשְׁתַּנָּה, הַלַּיְלָה הַזֶּה מִכָּל הַלֵּילוֹת" *Mishna*, Pesachim 10:4, accessed March 6, 2018, https://www.sefaria.org/Mishnah_Pesachim.10.4?lang=bi.

171 Exodus 13:8–9(RSV).

172 See Exodus 12.

173 The following quotation comes from the Roman Canon precisely after recalling the *Mysterium Fidei*. "*Unde et memores, Domine, nos servi tui, sed et plebs tua sancta, eiusdem Christi, Filii tui, Domini nostri, tam beatæ passionis, necnon et ab inferis resurrectionis, sed et in cælos gloriosæ ascensionis: offerimus præclaræ maiestati tuæ de tuis donis ac datis hostiam puram, hostiam sanctam,*

enter into the Paschal Mystery. The merits of Christ's passion, death, and resurrection are actualized. In other words, Catholics are not mere spectators at the Mass; rather, they play an active part, interiorly and exteriorly.[174] Not only in the anamnesis, but throughout the Sacred Liturgy, the prayers recall the key events of salvation history. For example, in the Fourth Eucharist Prayer of the Mass, the Catholic priest prays,

> And you so loved the world, Father most holy, that in the fullness of time you sent your Only Begotten Son to be our Savior. Made incarnate by the Holy Spirit and born of the Virgin Mary, he shared our human nature in all things but sin. To the poor he proclaimed the good news of salvation, to prisoners, freedom, and to the sorrowful of heart, joy. To accomplish your plan, he gave himself up to death, and, rising from the dead, he destroyed death and restored life.[175]

Christian theology, properly speaking, is always done in an ecclesial context and to this end, Barbour states that "the church as a living community is always the context of Christian life and thought."[176] While religious communities have paradigms, they are *different* than scientific paradigms. Barbour describes religious community paradigms as "key examples from the past that influence all its activities."[177] We can rightly speak of a Galilean or Newtonian paradigm *replacing* the Aristotelian paradigm in classical mechanics, e.g., Aristotle incorrectly believed that the velocity at which two identically shaped masses fell was directly proportional to their weights and inversely proportional to the density of the medium through which they fell.[178] In theology, it would seem that the "key examples" from history should include what Barbour refers to elsewhere as the "core" of a Christian tradition.[179] Therefore, these data of revelation, or formalized doctrines, would be outside the realm of substantive revision. According to Barbour's notion of a theology of nature, only "auxiliary hypotheses" may be revised in light of broadly accepted scientific discoveries.

The paradigms of religious and scientific communities often make use of analogy. They also frequently employ models. In the next section, we investigate Barbour's understanding of analogy and diverse types of models in theology and science.

hostiam immaculatam, Panem sanctum vitæ æternæ et Calicem salutis perpetuæ." Missale Romanum, 3rd ed. (2002).

174 Second Vatican Council, *Sacrosanctum Concilium,* 1963, 41; Pius XII, *Mediator Dei,* 1947, 23–24.

175 Excerpt from Eucharistic Prayer IV, *Roman Missal,* 3rd ed. (2011).

176 Barbour, *Issues in Science and Religion,* 216.

177 Ibid., 214.

178 Simon Gindikin, *Tales of Physicists and Mathematicians* (Boston: Birkhäuser, 1988), 29.

179 Barbour, *Religion and Science,* 328.

4.3 Use of Analogies and Models in Theological and Scientific Language

Ian Barbour defines an *analogy* as "an observed or postulated similarity between two situations" and a *model* as "a systematic analogy postulated between a phenomenon whose laws are already known and one under investigation."[180] Mary Hesse's research has shown that analogies and models have played an essential role in the development of scientific theories and Barbour concurs that they are unquestionably fruitful.[181] However, like any tool, there are risks in using analogies and models. Barbour acknowledges historical situations in which scientists forgot that

1) analogies are only similarities in some but not all characteristics,
2) models only suggest possible hypotheses, which must then be tested experimentally, and
3) theories are symbolic and selective representations.[182]

Barbour identifies four different types of models in science, each serving a distinct function. First, there are *experimental* models. These are usually constructed in laboratories to simulate larger-scale systems, e.g., a wind tunnel can be used to study the aerodynamics of a prototype, model rocket before the full-size rocket is constructed. Sometimes an *analogue* model is constructed. For example, engineering students are often introduced to the isomorphism between a mechanical harmonic oscillator and an electrical circuit containing an inductor.[183] A second type of model is *logical*. Pure mathematicians, operating exclusively in the realm of ideas, can define a set of entities that satisfy the axioms and theorems of a formal deductive system, e.g., a set of points and lines can be a logical model for Euclid's formal axioms.

The third type of model that Barbour identifies is *mathematical*. He sees mathematical models as a *via media* between experimental and logical ones. Mathematical models are symbolic representations of quantitative variables that describe systems. Such systems are often physical, biological, engineering, social, economic, or some combination of the aforementioned types, e.g., socio-technical.[184]

---

180 Barbour, *Issues in Science and Religion*, 158.
181 Mary B. Hesse, "Models in Physics," *British Journal for the Philosophy of Science* 4, no. 15 (1953): 198–214.
182 Barbour, *Issues in Science and Religion*, 159.
183 The second order differential equations can be found in Anatol Rapoport, "General Systems Theory," in *Systems Science and Cybernetics*, ed. Francisco Parra-Luna, vol. 1 (Oxford: Eolss Publications, 2009), 120.
184 For an introduction to modeling socio-technical systems, see Joseph R. Laracy, "Addressing System Boundary Issues in Complex Socio-Technical Systems," *Systems Research Forum* 2, no. 1 (2007): 19–26.

For example, the Kermack and McKendrick SIR[185] model is an epidemiological model that computes the theoretical number of people infected with a contagious illness in a closed population over time. It is a system of three, coupled, non-linear ordinary differential equations.[186]

Barbour's fourth type of model is *theoretical*. He describes these models as "imaginative mental constructions invented to account for observed phenomena."[187] A theoretical model can contribute to a theory, and theories describe patterns in experimental observations. For example, the "billiard ball" model of gases contributed to the Kinetic Theory of Gases. This theory explains observable properties of gases, e.g., pressure, temperature, viscosity, thermal conductivity, and volume. Theoretical models are Barbour's main interest in his theology-science research.[188]

Some scientists view models as temporary psychological aids in the process of forming theories. For example, the French physicist and philosopher of science, Pierre Duhem, held that the ideal theory was simply a mathematical formalism (un-interpreted by a model).[189] Barbour supports the careful use of models and agrees more with the perspective of the British physicist, Norman Campbell. Campbell's research has shown how models exceed mere *formulæ* in offering useful interpretations and implying novel means by which a theory might be extended.[190] Barbour ultimately concludes that models should not be discarded, "but that they *must not be interpreted literally* ... An analogy is never a total identity or a comprehensive description, but only a simplified comparison of limited aspects."[191]

Barbour's approach to theoretical models follows directly from his critical realist epistemology. He rejects the *literalist* view of models that can come from *naïve* realism on one hand, and the *fictionalist* view from instrumentalism on the other. Barbour also rebuffs the positivist claim that theories can be inferred directly from observations through induction. As with the Bible, Barbour advocates that models be taken *seriously but not literally*.[192] A critical realist view of models recognizes

185 SIR stands for number of Susceptible people, number of people infected I, and number of people who have Recovered.

186 William Ogilvy Kermack and Anderson Gray McKendrick, "A Contribution to the Mathematical Theory of Epidemics," *Proceedings of the Royal Society A: Mathematical, Physical and Engineering Sciences* 115, no. 772 (August 1, 1927): 700–721.

187 Barbour, *Myths, Models, and Paradigms*, 30.

188 Ibid., 31.

189 Pierre Duhem, *The Aim and Structure of Physical Theory*, trans. Philip P. Wigner (Princeton: Princeton University Press, 1954), 55–106.

190 Norman R. Campbell, *Physics: The Elements* (Cambridge: Cambridge University Press, 1920), chap. 4.

191 Barbour, *Issues in Science and Religion*, 161.

192 Barbour, *Myths, Models, and Paradigms*, 36–38.

their selective character. Any given model can only give insights into a "restricted aspect of events."[193]

Barbour points out that religious language is often metaphorical. He acknowledges that while "a metaphor is *not literally true* ... [it] is not a useful fiction, a mere pretense, a game of make-believe with no relation to reality; it asserts that there are significant analogies between the things compared."[194] In "everyday" language, analogy connotes a correspondence or partial similarity between things. Barbour's notion is more precise. He maintains that analogies are *a font of interpretive symbols* in religion as well as science. Christians who accept the deuterocanonical books of the Old Testament find explicit Biblical warrant for the use of analogy in theology. The Book of Wisdom tells us: "For from the greatness and beauty of created things comes a corresponding perception of their Creator."[195]

Barbour acknowledges that his understanding of the role of analogy as a source of interpretive symbols in theology is influenced by the writings of a Thomist, Eric Lionel Mascall.[196] Yet, Barbour's own discussion of the issue does not patently utilize traditional Thomistic language and concepts. Mascall's approach to the doctrine of analogy builds on the philosophy of Aristotle and the "stimulus of the Judæo-Christian belief in a fully transcendent and yet genuinely creative God," especially as it has been articulated by Thomas Aquinas, Thomas Cajetan,[197] and John of Saint Thomas (who closely follows Cajetan's interpretation of Aquinas).[198]

It must be stated that disagreement exists among Thomists about how being is analogous when attempting to relate Creator and creation. Cajetan argued that there is an *analogy of proportionality* (*plurium ad plura*)[199] between God and creation, not an *analogy of proportion or attribution*.[200] The American priest and philosopher, George Sauvage, CSC, succinctly explains this position:

---

193 Ibid., 47.

194 Ibid., 13.

195 Wisdom 13:5 (RSV).

196 Barbour, *Issues in Science and Religion*, 216.

197 Cajetan is well-known for proposing a three-fold division of analogy: analogy of equality, analogy of attribution, and analogy of proportionality. See Joshua P. Hochschild, *The Semantics of Analogy: Rereading Cajetan's De Nominum Analogia* (Notre Dame: University of Notre Dame Press, 2010).

198 Eric L. Mascall, *Existence and Analogy* (London: Darton, Longman & Todd Ltd., 1966), 94.

199 Two subject-predicate relations are not the same, but similar—there is no proportion but rather a likeness of two proportions to each other, i.e., the proportion of proportion. A is to B as C is to D. See Thomas Aquinas, *De Veritate*, Q 2, A 11.

200 There is a particular agreement between things having a direct proportion to each other because of some relation to each other.

We can conceive and express these perfections only by an analogy; not by an analogy of proportion, for this analogy rests on a participation in a common concept, and, as already said, there is no element common to the finite and the Infinite; but by an analogy of proportionality. These perfections are really in God, and they are in Him in the same relation to His infinite essence that they are in creatures in relation to their finite nature.[201]

With an analogy of *proper* proportionality, the idea indicated by the analogous term "occurs intrinsically and formally in each of the analogates."[202] In the related case of an analogy of *metaphorical* (i.e., improper) proportionality, "the analogated nature exists intrinsically and formally in one analogate, intrinsically but improperly or figuratively in the others."[203]

However, many contemporary Thomists[204] argue that Aquinas' most developed theory of analogy replaces the analogy of proper proportionality in metaphysics and natural theology with a form of analogy of proportion or attribution.[205] In this view, God and creation are designated analogously because of a relation "one thing to another" (*attributio unius ad alterum*).[206] God and creation cannot be subsumed

201 George Sauvage, "Analogy," *The Catholic Encyclopedia* (New York: Robert Appleton Company, 1907), accessed April 4, 2018, http://www.newadvent.org/cathen/01449a.htm.

202 Henri Dominique Gardeil, *Introduction to the Philosophy of St. Thomas Aquinas: Metaphysics*, trans. John A. Otto, vol. 4 (Eugene, OR: Wipf & Stock Publishers, 2012), 54.

203 Ibid., 4:56.

204 See John F. Wippel, *The Metaphysical Thought of Thomas Aquinas: From Finite Being to Uncreated Being*, Monographs of the Society for Medieval and Renaissance Philosophy (Washington, D.C.: The Catholic University of America Press, 2000).

205 For example, consider the following passage from the *Summa*: "And in this way some things are said of God and creatures analogically, and not in a purely equivocal nor in a purely univocal sense. For we can name God only from creatures. Thus whatever is said of God and creatures, is said according to the relation of a creature to God as its principle and cause, wherein all perfections of things pre-exist excellently. Now this mode of community of idea is a mean between pure equivocation and simple univocation. For in analogies the idea is not, as it is in univocals, one and the same, yet it is not totally diverse as in equivocals; but a term which is thus used in a multiple sense signifies various proportions to some one thing; thus 'healthy' applied to urine signifies the sign of animal health, and applied to medicine signifies the cause of the same health." Aquinas, *Summa Theologiæ*, I, Q 13, A 5. An example of the analogy of attribution would be: The carbonara is good. The chef is good. The word "good" has similar, but not the same, meanings in the two sentences. Of course, God is the *summum bonum*. When speaking of an analogy of attribution, there is always a primary analogate, e.g., God. The idea communicated with the analogous term is *intrinsically realized* in the primary analogate. As Gardeil points out, "secondary analogates have this formality (idea) predicated of them by mere extrinsic denomination." Gardeil, *Introduction to the Philosophy of St. Thomas Aquinas, Volume 4*, 4:53.

206 Ralph M. McInerny, *The Logic of Analogy: An Interpretation of St Thomas* (The Hague: Martinus Nijhoff, 1971), 28.

under a "higher category."[207] For example, one can attribute "love" to both God and mankind. If the analogical attribution is *unius ad alterum*, there must be a direct relationship between mankind and God. Furthermore, the description is according to priority and posteriority (*per prius et posterius*). The perfection of love is primarily associated with God (the principal analogate) and only secondarily (derivatively) with His creatures.[208] As the French philosopher, Henri-Dominique Gardeil, OP, puts it, "the analogated nature exists intrinsically and formally in the primary analogate; it is attributed to secondary analogates by extrinsic denomination only."[209]

Mascall's position is that both forms of analogy, *attributio et proportionalitas*,[210] must be used together when discussing the relationship of creature and Creator:

> The conclusion would thus seem to be that, in order to make the doctrine of analogy really satisfactory, we must see the analogical relation between God and the world as combining in a tightly interlocked union both analogy of attribution and analogy of proportionality. Without analogy of proportionality it is very doubtful whether the attributes which we predicate of God can be ascribed to him in more than a merely virtual sense;[211] without analogy of attribution it hardly seems possible to avoid agnosticism.[212]

Despite his admission of adopting Mascall's insights in analogy, Barbour himself does not explicitly enter this intra-Thomism debate.

207 The analogical ascription of a perfection, e.g., wisdom, to God is never *duorum ad tertium*. McInerny notes that "there is no third thing to which God and creature could be referred in receiving a common name, for whatever is not a creature is God and whatever is not God is a creature." Ralph M. McInerny, *Aquinas and Analogy* (Washington, DC: The Catholic University of America Press, 1996), 111.
208 Allan J. Torrance, "Is Love the Essence of God?," in *Nothing Greater, Nothing Better: Theological Essays on the Love of God*, ed. Kevin J. Vanhoozer (Grand Rapids, MI: Wm. B. Eerdmans Publishing, 2001), 120.
209 Gardeil, *Introduction to the Philosophy of St. Thomas Aquinas, Volume 4*, 4:56.
210 Gardeil concurs with Mascall on this point: "In the case of being, then—as for that matter with other transcendental notions: the one, the true, the good—we are confronted with a sort of mixed analogy which includes both proportionality and attribution. Analogy of proportionality is, however, generally admitted by Thomists to be more primary and fundamental, at least from the standpoint of our experience of being. This granted, we shall say with John of St. Thomas that *being is analogous by an analogy of proportionality which includes, virtually, and analogy of attribution.*" Ibid., 4:66.
211 By *virtual*, Mascall means God is able to produce the attributes in creatures but it does not necessarily follow that God possesses them formally Himself.
212 Mascall, *Existence and Analogy*, 113.

Next, we turn our attention to parables. Joseph Ratzinger observes that one of the principal functions of parables is to "transcend the realm of creation, in order, by this transcendence, to draw it above itself to the Creator."[213] The Biblical literary genre of *parable* is an example of a narrative form of analogy according to Barbour. He makes three observations about parables. First, all parables call for a decision. They provoke the reader (or hearer) to engage in self-reflection, apply the story to one's own life, and make a judgment. According to the Anglican clergyman and theologian, Peter Slater,

> The analogies developed in parables are not just any analogies. They are those which help us to develop our policies for living and decide on their adoption. The central analogies are ones which suggest roles and rules in life, such as the role of sonship and the rule of neighborly love. They are rarely analogies to impersonal features of the universe, designed to aid in speculating about anything as abstruse as "being as such."[214]

Barbour states that some parables are "useful fictions."[215] For example, in the Parable of the Good Samaritan,[216] Jesus' story about a man going down from Jerusalem to Jericho who fell victim among robbers, who stripped him and beat him, and departed, leaving him half dead, was not intended to be a recounting of an historical event. Rather, the story is supposed to teach the hearer the Christian mandate to show mercy and compassion to all, particularly those who are suffering.

Barbour also notes the open-ended, multi-faceted character of parables. He concurs with the Welsh Biblical scholar, Charles Harold Dodd, that "at its simplest, the parable is a metaphor or simile, drawn from nature or common life, arresting the hearer by its vividness or strangeness, and leaving the mind in sufficient doubt about its precise application to tease it into active thought."[217] Barbour's third observation about Biblical parables is that they convey vivid images. For example, unlike an academic presentation of abstract concepts in moral theology, the striking scenes of the parables communicate clear ethical teachings that the reader or hearer will not forget.[218]

Barbour notes that religious images and symbols are often integrated into narratives that are classified as *myth*. This genre, like the parables, is unique to religion and not utilized in natural science. Barbour distinguishes religious myths

213 Joseph Ratzinger, *Principles of Catholic Theology: Building Stones for a Fundamental Theology*, trans. Mary Frances McCarthy (San Francisco: Ignatius Press, 1989), 344.

214 Peter Slater, "Parables, Analogues and Symbols," *Religious Studies* 4, no. 1 (1968): 27.

215 Barbour, *Myths, Models, and Paradigms*, 17.

216 Luke 10:25–37.

217 Charles Harold Dodd, *The Parables of the Kingdom* (London: James Nisbet and Co., 1935), 16.

218 Barbour, *Myths, Models, and Paradigms*, 17–18.

from fairy tales in that myths are very significant in peoples' lives, both individually and as a religious community. They also given structure and direction to life. Barbour makes five general observations about religious myths.[219]

First, myths provide a vision of reality that orders human experience. According to the American religion scholar, Frederick Streng, through myths, "the essential structure of reality manifests itself in particular moments that are remembered and repeated from generation to generation."[220] Second, Barbour states that myths help man to realize his self-identity. He points out that "creation myths usually manifest in dramatic form basic convictions about human nature and destiny."[221] Third, myths can express a salvific reality that moves man from his fallen state of ignorance and sin toward his goal of peace, integration, and the fullness of life. Fourth, myths encourage particular forms of behavior. They guide human action in all aspects of life, from conduct at communal meals to ethical expressions of sexuality.

Finally, myths are often enacted in ritual form. Barbour agrees with the stance of the Dutch philosopher of religion, Gerard van der Leeuw, who asserts that myths sometimes justify rituals, while the ritual perpetuates the myth and allows people to enter into it by symbolic means.[222] Barbour points out that in the Judæo-Christian tradition, myths are connected with historical events, unlike most pre-Christian religions that have formulated myths around natural phenomena. Barbour's divinity school professor, H. Richard Niebuhr, explains that "such events help us understand ourselves and what has happened to us."[223] Reflecting on his own Christian tradition, Barbour states that the "liturgy, ritual, and sacraments of the Christian community have, of course, centered its memory on the life of Christ."[224]

Interestingly, Barbour does not enter into the question of the veracity of myths. This is obviously an important issue in Christianity. How are the great stories of the Bible related to the pre-Christian tales of Ancient Greece, for example? The American literature scholar and theologian, Ralph C. Wood, offers an interesting story from an encounter of J.R.R. Tolkien and C.S. Lewis on this very subject. In

---

219 Ibid., 20.

220 Frederick J. Streng, *Understanding Religious Man* (Encino: Dickenson Publishing Company, 1969), 56.

221 Barbour, *Myths, Models, and Paradigms*, 20.

222 Gerardus van der Leeuw, *Religion in Essence and Manifestation*, trans. Ninian Smart and John Evan Turner (Princeton: Princeton University Press, 2014), chap. 60.

223 Cited in Barbour, *Myths, Models, and Paradigms*, 55.

224 Ibid., 22.

the context of helping Lewis find his way back to Christian faith, Tolkien shares a compelling view on the relationship of myth, creation, and truth:

> In a late-night conversation during the spring of 1929, as they walked up and down in the deer park of Magdalen College, Tolkien explained to Lewis that myths are not the dream-wishes that lonely men project onto an empty universe to cheer themselves up. The great mythic repetitions of dying and rising gods, of heroes battling the forces of evil despite their own defeat, are signs of something transcendently significant. Our universal myth-making urge is an anthropological indication that we create because we have been created. We are thus re-enacting the most fundamental order of the cosmos, discerning the basic pattern of all things: life-through-death. However misguided pagan myths may sometimes be, they point toward the Truth.[225]

According to the British Presbyterian pastor and scholar, Jerram Barrs, myths for Tolkien

> are echoes or memories of the truth that God had originally made known to Adam and Eve, the ancestors of the whole human race. There are in myths, memories of the un-fallen world, memories of paradise when the world was not stained by human rebellion but was characterized only by goodness and joy in all of life; there is a sense of the shame and tragedy of the brokenness of our present life; and there are hints of the promise and hope of redemption, of the setting right of all things … In the Gospel of Christ all the elements of truth in the pagan myths find their fulfillment.[226]

In his analysis of Sacred Scripture, Barbour makes a claim that the primary model for God in the Bible is the human person. God is described as "a sovereign ruler, a just judge, and finally a loving father" but only Christ Himself most fully reveals the mystery of God.[227]

However, as in science, there are dangers in the use of analogies and models in theology. Barbour is often concerned with *literalism* and the error of expecting too much from a model or analogy. Barbour draws an interesting connection between the Old Testament prohibition of depicting God in art[228] and the abandonment of "picturability" in modern atomic physics.[229] Both the most profound natural and supernatural realities are beyond visualization. Barbour's critical realism comes

---

225 Ralph Wood, "Biography of J.R.R. Tolkien (1892–1973)," *Leadership University*, accessed March 7, 2018, http://www.leaderu.com/humanities/wood-biography.html.

226 Jerram Barrs, "Echoes of Eden," *CS Lewis*, last modified November 10, 2009, accessed March 7, 2018, http://www.cslewis.com/echoes-of-eden/.

227 Barbour, *Issues in Science and Religion*, 217.

228 "You shall not make for yourself a graven image, or any likeness of anything that is in heaven above, or that is in the earth beneath, or that is in the water under the earth; you shall not bow down to them or serve them." Exodus 20:4–5a (RSV)

229 Barbour, *Issues in Science and Religion*, 218.

through when he states that "the man at worship, like the man in the laboratory, uses language with realistic intent, and yet he recognized that his symbols are not a replica of reality."[230]

In science, Barbour asserts that models provide "vividness, immediacy, and unity of mental grasp not found in a multiplicity of abstract formulæ."[231] He believes that religious models offer even greater vividness and influence as they have the ability to give meaning and direction to one's life. Despite the aforementioned issues with visualization, religious models tend to be associated with images that have the power to evoke strong emotional responses. According to Barbour, religious models often contribute to *conceptual* and *propositional* formulations which are typically defined and evaluated by theologians.[232]

Another function that Barbour attributes to religious models is in aiding the formation of metaphysical systems: "The metaphysician takes a '*co-ordinating analogy*' from some relationships he judges to be specifically important and from it derives a model which can order a diversity of kinds of experience."[233] According to the British philosopher, Dorothy Emmet, "such ideas share something of the character of scientific models. But whereas scientific models suggest possible patterns for the co-ordination of data of a homogenous type, the metaphysical model has to suggest a possible pattern of co-ordination between data of different types."[234] Barbour concurs with the American philosopher of religion, Frederick Ferré, that a metaphysical system can be evaluated according to criteria similar to that for scientific theories.[235] Ferré suggests that a metaphysical system must demonstrate *coherence* (e.g., consistency, interconnectedness, and conceptual unity), *inclusiveness* (e.g., scope, generality, and the ability to integrate diverse languages), and *adequacy* (e.g., relevance and applicability).[236]

For example, in the quantum mechanical model of the atom, the Schrödinger Equation wave function is a complex-valued probability amplitude used to describe a system. The wave function is synonymous with the "orbital" of the atom, which provides a description of the size, shape, and orientation of the region in space available to an electron. See Milton Orchin et al., *The Vocabulary and Concepts of Organic Chemistry*, 2nd ed. (Hoboken: Wiley-Interscience, 2005), 7. This perspective replaces the Rutherford–Bohr model that envisioned the atom like the solar system in which an electron orbits the nucleus like the Earth orbits the Sun.

230 Barbour, *Issues in Science and Religion*, 218.
231 Ibid.
232 Ibid.
233 Barbour, *Myths, Models, and Paradigms*, 64.
234 Dorothy M. Emmet, *The Nature of Metaphysical Thinking* (London: Macmillan And Company Limited, 1946), 215.
235 Barbour, *Myths, Models, and Paradigms*, 66.
236 Frederick Ferré, "Metaphors, Models, and Religion," *Soundings* 51, no. 3 (1968): 327–345.

Barbour identifies three significant *similarities* between theoretical models in science and models in religion. First, both types of models are analogical in origin and extensible to novel circumstances. Second, both classes of models are symbolic representations that should be taken seriously but not literally. Third, whereas scientific models are used to order observations of the natural world, religious models provide structure to the experience of individuals and religious communities.[237]

Barbour also recognizes three substantial *differences*. First, some religious models serve non-cognitive functions, e.g., they are expressive. This is not the case in science. Second, religious models elicit greater personal commitment than scientific ones, e.g., trust and loyalty. Third, Barbour follows Ferré in asserting that religious models are often more influential than the formal, theological doctrines derived from them. Conversely, in science, models are "subservient" to theories.[238]

Barbour's understanding of analogy and models in theology and science certainly constitutes one of his foundational "building blocks" for relating the two disciplines. In the next section, we examine Barbour's criteria for evaluating scientific theories and religious beliefs. The chapter concludes with some of Barbour's methodological conclusions.

4.4 Criteria for Evaluating Religious Beliefs and Scientific Theories

The criteria for evaluating theories is an important issue in the philosophy of science. Barbour believes that there are three criteria by which a theory should be evaluated: *its agreement with observations, the internal relations among its concepts*, and *its comprehensiveness*.[239] The first criterion examines a theory's relationship to data. For credibility, a theory must be capable of verification by independent scientists collecting their own data. As an example, the Fleischmann–Pons assertions of nuclear fusion at room temperature have never been accepted by the physics community as the experiments that they claim demonstrate a cold fusion reaction have never been successfully replicated by other scientists.[240]

The second criterion addresses issues of consistency and coherence. Internal consistency requires the absence of logical contradictions. Coherence implies the

---

237 Barbour, *Myths, Models, and Paradigms*, 69.

238 Ibid.

239 Barbour, *Issues in Science and Religion*, 144–145.

240 See Martin Fleischmann and Stanley Pons, "Electrochemically Induced Nuclear Fusion of Deuterium," *Journal of Electroanalytical Chemistry and Interfacial Electrochemistry* 261, no. 2, Part 1 (April 10, 1989): 301–308. For a contemporary reconsideration of low-energy nuclear reactions, see Michael Koziol, "Scientists in the U.S. and Japan Get Serious About Low-Energy Nuclear Reactions," *IEEE Spectrum* 55, no. 12 (November 28, 2018): 10–11.

presence of rational, meaningful connections between propositions in the theory. The third criterion engages the issue of generality in results and the ability to unify diverse phenomena. Barbour emphasizes that the relationship between an experiment and a theory is usually very indirect because a "whole network of ideas" is usually tested simultaneously.[241]

Applying the criteria to Einstein's general theory of relativity, one finds that his theory is logically consistent and provides a unified description of gravity as a geometric property of space-time.[242] When speeds of gravitating bodies are much less than the speed of light and gravitational fields are weak, the predictions of classical mechanics and Newton's theory of gravity come very close to those of Einstein's theory of general relativity. However, the classical approach is not perfectly accurate. Einstein's theory is also much more comprehensive, handling a variety of applications. For example, the theory can explain gravitational lensing, describe black holes, explore the large-scale dynamics of the universe (cosmology), and theoretically investigate time travel scenarios.[243]

Einstein himself states that

> it is possible to exhibit two essentially different bases, each of which in its consequences leads to a large measure of agreement with experience. This indicates that any attempt logically to derive the basic concepts and laws of mechanics from the ultimate data of experience is doomed to failure.[244]

Barbour concurs and insists that *no theory can be proven true*: "The most that can be said for a theory is that it is in better agreement with the known data and is more coherent and comprehensive than alternative theories available at the moment."[245]

Throughout Barbour's writings, he acknowledges that metaphysical presuppositions and other preferences (or biases) play a role in theory formation and selection. The Nobel Prize winning German physicist, Max Planck, shares Barbour's attitude:

---

241 Barbour, *Issues in Science and Religion*, 145–146.

242 See Albert Einstein, "Die Feldgleichungen Der Gravitation," *Sitzungsberichte der Preussischen Akademie der Wissenschaften zu Berlin* (1915): 844–847.

243 The convergence or concordance of evidence is sometimes referred to as the principle of consilience. The fundamental premise is that evidence from independent, unrelated sources can "converge" on strong conclusions. See Edward O. Wilson, *Consilience: The Unity of Knowledge* (New York: Vintage, 1999).

244 Albert Einstein, "On the Method of Theoretical Physics," *Philosophy of Science* 1, no. 2 (April 1934): 166.

245 Barbour, *Issues in Science and Religion*, 147.

Anyone who has taken part in the building up of a branch of science is well aware from personal experience that every endeavor in this direction is guided by an unpretentious but essential principle. This principle is faith—a faith which looks ahead. It is said that science has no preconceived ideas: there is no saying that has been more thoroughly or more disastrously misunderstood.[246]

According to the American engineer, William A. Wilson,

Einstein, acutely sensitive to these issues, was in favor of bringing the oft-unstated pre-scientific beliefs of scientists out into the light and making them explicit. So, in a very similar way, are feminist philosophers of science like Helen Longino, Lynn Nelson, and Elizabeth Anderson. The difference is that where Einstein's non-empirical, metaphysical criteria for selecting between theories tended to be "internal" qualities of a theory, like mathematical simplicity or aesthetic balance, these later critics are willing to bring political and moral considerations to bear in the selection of a science.[247]

For Barbour, science is about understanding the natural world. The empirical confirmation of predictions is only one aspect of theory confirmation. While scientific laws permit prediction, intelligibility arises from the explanatory power of theories. According to Norwood Hanson, "Physics is a search for intelligibility. Only secondarily is it a search for new objects and facts."[248]

Barbour defines religious beliefs as "interpretations of religious experience and revelatory events."[249] However, Barbour does not explicate a distinction between "religious experience" and "revelatory events." Religious beliefs are often articulated by theologians in propositional form. Because of the parallels that he sees in theology and science, he determines that religious beliefs may be evaluated according to the same criteria as scientific theories: *relation to data, coherence*, and *comprehensiveness*. As mentioned earlier in this section, scientific theories are tested with public sense-data. Religious beliefs on the other hand are formulated based on historical events (e.g., the Last Supper) and interpreted by a particular faith community (e.g., the Apostles) according to a specific tradition (e.g., Catholicism).

Evaluating religious beliefs based on data is certainly not impossible (e.g., much historical data supports the liturgical celebration of the Lord's Supper[250]), but the method is not as straightforward and the results less difficult to reject compared to the natural sciences. Coherence in religious beliefs is very similar to

246 Max Planck, "Science and Faith," in *The Philosophy of Physics*, trans. W.H. Johnston (London: George Allen & Unden Ltd., 1936), 112.

247 William A. Wilson, "The Myth of Scientific Objectivity," *First Things* (November 2017): 33.

248 Hanson, *Patterns of Discovery*, 18.

249 Barbour, *Issues in Science and Religion*, 252.

250 For example, see Hippolytus, *The Apostolic Tradition of Hippolytus*, trans. Burton Scott Easton (Cambridge, UK: Cambridge University Press, 2014), chap. 4.

coherence in science. A theological proposition should not contradict other beliefs in a religious community. Finally, like scientific theories, religious beliefs should have sufficient generality, fruitfulness, and extensibility. Unlike scientific theories, theological propositions often contribute to a *Weltanschauung* and must be capable of not only interpreting exclusively religious matters, but the drama of human life in general.[251]

According to Barbour, scientific research is not principally a quest to gather facts, but rather a search for patterns. Well-formulated scientific theories have the ability to order sense experience comprehensibly. Similarly, religious beliefs should clearly and logically order personal experience, guiding an individual in his relationship with God, his faith community, broader society, and the natural world. Just like in science, paradoxes arise in theological inquiry. Barbour gives an example from Scripture: "For whoever would save his life will lose it, and whoever loses his life for my sake will find it."[252] This statement by Jesus does not contain any contradictions, but theological analysis is required to understand what Jesus means by "save," "life," and "lose."[253] With regard to an over-all evaluation, Barbour states that "if one is to subscribe to a Christian world-view, it must make more sense of all the available evidence than any other world-view."[254]

While the evaluation process of scientific theories and religious beliefs contains some significant similarities in Barbour's approach, there are some important differences. He identifies three areas where theology and science diverge in their criteria of evaluation: *the influence of interpretation on experience, the criteria of evaluation are themselves influenced by religious beliefs,* and *the fact that intersubjective testability occurs only within particular religious communities.* Barbour acknowledges that the influence of interpretation on experience is much greater in theology compared to science. All scientific facts are theory-laden, but in theology, Barbour asserts that the "feedback" from interpretative to experiential aspects is much more significant. For example, when a person becomes a Christian, he interprets reality in a new way and experiences the world differently.[255]

In the natural sciences, the criteria for the evaluation of theories can be influenced by existing theories and other values such as simplicity and beauty. However, in theology, the effect is much more noticeable. According to Barbour, pragmatic concerns can also factor in. For example, does a proposed religious

---

251 Barbour, *Issues in Science and Religion*, 253.
252 Matthew 16:25 (RSV).
253 Barbour, *Issues in Science and Religion*, 253–254.
254 Ibid., 255.
255 Ibid., 258.

belief, e.g., God is the creator of the universe, contribute to personal integration, moral conduct, and social harmony?[256]

In summary, the criteria for evaluation express norms that are themselves influenced by theological doctrines. Barbour offers an example from the German-American existentialist philosopher and theologian, Paul Tillich. Tillich defines idolatry as having ultimate faith in something that is not ultimate. He believes that while man has many concerns, "in true faith the ultimate concern is a concern about the truly ultimate; while in idolatrous faith preliminary, finite realities are elevated to the rank of ultimacy."[257] Barbour points out that this claim already presupposes value-judgments.[258]

Because religion is not a private affair, it is fairly obvious to state that inter-subjective testability occurs only within particular religious communities. Barbour points out that at one level, this is not too different from the situation in science where a community of scientists with common goals, standards, and procedures evaluate new theories. Barbour mentions that while the Christian community is global and ideally universal, it exists alongside other religions. In the world of science, this type of diversity generally does not exist. Barbour cites H. Richard Niebuhr on the prospects and limits of inter-subjectivity:

> Furthermore, historic faith, directed toward a reality which appears in our history and which is apprehended by historic being, is not private and subjective and without possibility of verification. Every view of the universal from the finite standpoint of the individual in such a society is subject to the test of experience on the part of companions who look from the same standpoint in the same direction, as well as to the test of consistency with the principles and concepts that have grown out of past experience in the same community ... We remind ourselves of the relative standpoint we occupy in history and faith. We are not trying to describe a common human certainty gained in a common human experience; yet on the other hand we are not seeking to set forth a private and mystic assurance which is not subject to the criticism of the community, that is all those who occupy the same standpoint and look in the same direction toward the same reality to which we look as individuals.[259]

Barbour admits that the limitations here are not that different from the limitations of the *testability of paradigms in science*. Scientific paradigms are not the fruit of logical proofs and have a tremendous impact on the thinking and experience of the scientist. Barbour decides that religious beliefs in a specific community are

256 Ibid.
257 Paul Tillich, *Dynamics of Faith* (New York: HarperOne, 2009), 13.
258 Barbour, *Issues in Science and Religion*, 258.
259 H. Richard Niebuhr, *The Meaning of Revelation* (Louisville: Westminster John Knox Press, 2006), 11, 74.

similar to the axioms of Euclidean geometry: "One does not try to prove axioms, but one asks what happens if one assumes them."[260] He concludes that no unambiguous evaluation of theological propositions can be made. Yet, he also concedes that there is no absolute certainty in science—theories are not unambiguously derived from data.

Barbour thinks that it is much more fruitful to compare particular religious world-views with naturalistic, i.e., atheistic, beliefs about the fundamental nature of reality, rather than with the actual practice of science. While no *Weltanschauung* is capable of formal proof, the consequences of one's choice cannot be underestimated. Highlighting the role of *personal involvement* in theology, Barbour makes the important point that "*revelation* is something given to us to which we respond in gratitude,[261] not an intellectual conclusion we have established on our own."[262] Barbour finds religious commitment and reflective inquiry to be in *tension*, not conflict. Finally, given the depth of the mystery of God, the limits and symbolic character of human language, and the need for apophatic theology, Barbour advises his critical realist perspective in theological formulations—all claims have some tentative character.[263]

Overall, Barbour observes that the "subjective" features of science seem to be more evident in religion. Specifically, he identifies

1) the influence of interpretation on data,
2) the resistance of comprehensive theories to falsification, and
3) the absence of rules for choice among paradigms.[264]

Furthermore, he notes that the "objective" features of science are less evident in their respective religious cases. In particular, Barbour names

1) the presence of common data on which disputants can agree,
2) the cumulative effort of evidence for or against a theory, and
3) the existence of criteria which are not paradigm-dependent.[265]

Thus far, we have explored Barbour's notions of theological and scientific experience and interpretation. We examined his understanding of the roles of religious and scientific communities and their paradigms. We also investigated Barbour's use

260 Barbour, *Issues in Science and Religion*, 260.
261 Barbour makes an excellent point here, but his imprecise notion of revelation limits the significance for many Christians. The answer to the question: What is revelation? has a tremendous impact on how one might "respond in gratitude."
262 Barbour, *Issues in Science and Religion*, 260.
263 Ibid., 260–261.
264 Barbour, *Myths, Models, and Paradigms*, 144–145.
265 Ibid., 145.

of analogy and models in theology and science. This section considered Barbour's criteria for evaluating scientific theories and religious beliefs. The chapter concludes with some methodological conclusions.

4.5 Conclusions on Methodology

Ian Barbour believes that theology and science represent profoundly different types of interest. Despite methodological parallels, the two fields "arise from dissimilar areas of experience which reflect dissimilar aspects of reality."[266] Both science and theology are *selective* in their areas of inquiry. Science is interested in patterns in nature that are at least statistically lawful, whereas theology is concerned with man's "ultimate concern(s)," e.g., From where did I come? Where am I going? Where can I find love and meaning?

Barbour does not fall into the error of *scientism*. He quotes the German physicist, Carl Friedrich Freiherr von Weizsäcker, who describes the scientific worldview as "not wrong in what it asserts but in what it omits."[267] Likewise, Barbour appreciates Norman Campbell's perspective: "It must always be remembered that science does not attempt to order all our experience; some parts of it, and the part perhaps that is of most importance to us as active and moral human beings, is omitted altogether from that order."[268]

According to Barbour, theology and science are similar in three important ways. First, both disciplines have a two-way interaction between experience and interpretation. Second, both fields rely on communities and their respective paradigms to guide inquiry. Their interpretative language is referential and therefore epistemologically realistic. Third, science and theology both have webs of interconnected concepts that must be evaluated together with the criteria of coherence, comprehensiveness, and adequacy to experience.[269]

Barbour identifies four substantial areas in which theology and science differ. First, they differ in the degree of "personal involvement" of the researcher. However, Barbour does not endorse the dichotomy that arises from the existentialist perspective. Second, the role of Divine revelation in theology has no clear parallel in natural science. Yet, he does not affirm the neo-orthodox position that drastically discerps revelation from human experience and interpretation. Third, Barbour asserts that the primary function of religious language is to evoke "self-commitment" and express the adoration due to God. He does also affirm the cognitive function of

---

266 Barbour, *Issues in Science and Religion*, 264.
267 Carl F. von Weizsäcker, *History of Nature* (Chicago: University Of Chicago Press, 1949), 2.
268 Norman R. Campbell, *What Is Science?* (London: Methuen & Co, 1921), 71.
269 Barbour, *Issues in Science and Religion*, 267.

religious language, however. This is something that linguistic analysts tend to disregard. Finally, Barbour believes that intersubjective testability in theology is extremely limited compared to the possibilities in science. He does not claim that critical evaluation is, or should be abandoned. *Alla fin fine,* Barbour states that "the choice is not between theism and science, but between theism and naturalism."[270]

Barbour ultimately concludes that given the aforementioned differences, the contrasts between theology and science must be acknowledged by researchers in both fields. Theology's frequent use of "actor-language" vs science's preferred use of "spectator-language" is a reminder of the differences. Nonetheless, Barbour decides that "the contrasts are not as absolute as most recent theologians and philosophers have maintained ... Reason is fulfilled, not abrogated, by revelation; reflective inquiry can coexist with religious commitment."[271]

Both the scientist and the theologian are rightfully concerned with the natural world. The scientist enquiries into the natural laws that govern the physical universe, whereas the theologian studies creation to better understand the mystery of God and His work in the cosmos. Barbour states that "despite the divergence of their interests, it is (according to critical realism) the same natural world to which they look, so their inquiries cannot be totally independent."[272] Ultimately, what is needed are modes of interaction between theology and science that respect one another's integrity.[273] After all, as the American priest and theologian, Michael Himes, puts it, "science and theology are concerned with the clarification of the awesome."[274]

In Chapter Three, we have explicated Ian Barbour's assessment of the similarities and differences between the natural sciences and theology. The goal was to fairly and clearly present Barbour's views on approaches that emphasize contrasts or parallels between theology and science as well as essential methodological issues. The goal of Chapter Four is to critique Barbour's critical realism, process metaphysics, and his theological methodology according to fundamental Catholic theological principles. It will be shown that Barbour's semi-Kantian epistemology leads to a duality of faith and reason, which denies natural theology's need for a first principle—God. Barbour's implicit philosophical disavowal of *actus purus* determines his theology as a process one with all the accompanying difficulties. On the other hand, a Catholic theology of creation can accommodate some of the insights that emerge from Barbour's approach.

---

270 Ibid.

271 Ibid., 268.

272 Ibid., 269.

273 Ibid., 270.

274 Michael Himes, "Reflections of a Theologian" (Presented at the Science in Seminaries Conference, Tucson, January 31, 2016).

CHAPTER FOUR

A Catholic Critique for the Doctrine of Creation

Having attempted to clearly and fairly present Ian Barbour's fundamental principles (Chapter Two), as well as his judgments about the similarities and differences between theological and scientific inquiry (Chapter Three)—*audiatur et altera pars*, we are now in a position to critique his approach. This chapter will evaluate Barbour's epistemology, metaphysics, and salient aspects of his theological method. Throughout, Barbour's approach will be judged by the fundamental norms and criteria of Catholic theology in order to explicate the ramifications of adopting elements of his thought, particularly for the study of creation.

First, in the critique of Barbour's critical realism, we shall address the importance of realism in science and theology, issues around the relationship of perception and the simple actuality of being, as well as concerns related to certainty, the nature of faith, and truth. Second, the evaluation of Barbour's process metaphysics will address Barbour's concern to acknowledge the dynamicity of the cosmos and offer a Catholic alternative. It will also critically engage Barbour's denial of the Biblical teaching of creation *ex nihilo*, his theological anthropology, his implicit panentheism, the theological consequences of neglecting substances and essences, and Barbour's denial of the perfection of God—*bene diagnoscitur, bene curatur*.

Third, the final section of this chapter is concerned with significant aspects of Barbour's methodology. In particular, we address his understanding of experience and interpretation in theology, his notion of religious communities and their paradigms, his approach to analogy and models, and finally his method for evaluating beliefs. While this chapter engages a number of diverse philosophical and theological ideas that arise in the Barbour *corpus*, they are all appurtenant to our fundamental Catholic evaluation for the doctrine of creation.

1. Critical Realism

1.1 Importance of Realism

Paul Haffner sagely remarks that realism "is the metaphysical bridge which guarantees the true relation between the mind and reality and is thus the right approach to link reason with Christian belief in God."[1] The American fundamental theologian, David L. Schindler, observes that "a theology which begins from within faith in the Christian God must concern itself as a matter of inner principle with the reality of nature and the nature of reality."[2] One of Ian Barbour's enduring contributions to the theology-science field in general, and reflection on God's creation in particular, is his philosophical realism.

Throughout his works, Barbour convincingly argues that there indeed exists an objective, mind-independent reality that the human intellect can come to know. He also acknowledges the necessity to avoid a *naïve* "picturability" in epistemology. In his *critical* realism, he asserts that some of the sense-data that forms the basis of cognition accurately represent this objective reality. Yet, Barbour does not ignore the challenges posed by postmodernism. He also attempts (to quote Thomas G. Guarino in his analysis of some nonfoundationalist thinkers) to give "epistemological weight to the cultural and linguistic determinacy of forms of life, to the priority of flux, and to the encompassing horizons of finitude and temporality."[3]

Scientists and theologians can and do come to certain knowledge about creation. Barbour avoids the postmodern tendency toward anti-foundationalism that he believes leads to relativism.[4] For example, there is no trace of *pensiero debole*[5] in

---

1 Paul Haffner, *The Mystery of Reason* (Leominster, UK: Gracewing Publishing, 2001), 12.

2 David L. Schindler, "Theology, Science, and Cosmology," *Communio* 15, no. 3 (Fall 1988): 270.

3 Guarino, *Foundations of Systematic Theology*, 24.

4 Barbour, *Religion and Science*, 149.

5 "Weak thought" is the Italian postmodern philosopher and politician, Gianni Vattimo's "attempt to reconstruct rationality in a postmodern, post-metaphysical way." Thomas Guarino, *Vattimo and Theology* (New York: T&T Clark, 2009), 9. It is a total rejection of the modern quest for the "certainly true," "really real," or "absolutely objective." See Gianni Vattimo and René Girard, *Christianity, Truth, and Weakening Faith: A Dialogue*, ed. Pierpaolo Antonello, trans. William McCuaig (New York: Columbia University Press, 2010). In a sense, Vattimo's call for a

his scientific and theological research. Barbour would likely concur with the expression attributed to Aristotle, "*Amicus Plato, sed magis amica veritas.*"[6] One must not let sources of personal bias obstruct the quest for truth.

Philosophical realism is the noetic and ontological foundation for all human knowledge, especially scientific and theological investigations of creation. As the Spanish priest-physicist and philosopher, Mariano Artigas, points out, "the philosophical realism required to validate the knowledge of experimental science is already implicit in scientific activity, since the central role played by experimental control is incompatible with idealist, empiricist, or skeptical approaches."[7] Artigas insists on three fundamental philosophical principles in the actual practice of science:

1) There exists in nature an order that can be captured by human understanding.
2) One can be certain about possessing the truth.
3) There is continuity between ordinary knowledge and experimental science.[8]

All three principles are found, albeit not always using the same terms, in Barbour's philosophy of science.

Artigas' first point implies three key features. First, real entities exist outside the structure of the human mind. Second, these entities are intelligible to the human intellect. Third, man can investigate and truly understand the order of creation. Artigas' second point about certainty does not deny the fact that in science, as in everyday life, "partial" and "always perfectible" truth is acquired by the intellect. He wisely highlights that "the experience of error is compatible with a realist attitude, and we can only speak about error if we are able to distinguish error from truth."[9]

Artigas classifies the quest for "absolute certainty" as a "rationalist prejudice."[10] His third point about the continuity between scientific research and "every day"

---

post-truth Christianity has its roots in David Hume's thought. See David Hume, *Dialogues and Natural History of Religion*, ed. J.C.A. Gaskin (Oxford: Oxford University Press, 2009).

6 Literally: "Plato is a friend, but the truth is more friend (to me than he is)." This maxim is a paraphrase of the *Nicomachean Ethics* 1096a. See Roger Bacon, *The 'Opus Majus' of Roger Bacon*, trans. Robert Belle Burke, vol. 1 (London: Williams and Norgate, 1900), 16.

7 Mariano Artigas, *Knowing Things for Sure: Science and Truth*, trans. Alan McCone (New York: University Press of America, 2006), 150.

8 Ibid., 150–152.

9 Ibid., 152.

10 Some rationalists restrict certainty to logical demonstrability and dismiss the realist's use of evidence. They might argue that *evidence* is too subjective and can contribute to one's fall into error. However, the experience of error is compatible with realism as one is able to distinguish error from truth.

learning rests on the fact that they both share the same criteria for truth, the process of observation through sense experience, and evidence, and the fact of trial and error in inquiry.[11] Again, Barbour would not disagree with the aforementioned points.[12]

Philosophical realism is fundamental to Catholic theology.[13] All statements about God and creation in Scripture, the writings of the Fathers, the Popes, and Ecumenical Councils presume that man's senses lead him to true knowledge of an extra-mental world. Catholics accept Divine revelation and its transmission and interpretation in the Church "because of the authority of God himself who reveals them, who can neither deceive nor be deceived."[14] In the 1990 "Instruction on the Ecclesial Vocation of a Catholic Theologian," the Congregation for the Doctrine of the Faith reminded Catholics of the importance of strong philosophical realism in theological research:

> Even though it transcends human reason, revealed truth is in profound harmony with it. It presumes that reason by its nature is ordered to the truth in such a way that, illumined by faith, it can penetrate to the meaning of Revelation. Despite the assertions of many philosophical currents, but in conformity with a correct way of thinking which finds confirmation in Scripture, human reason's ability to attain truth must be recognized as well as its metaphysical capacity to come to a knowledge of God from creation.[15]

The Church here affirms both the legitimacy of natural theology and the foundation of realism: man's ability to know truths about creation and Creator.

1.2 Perception and Actuality

Unfortunately, in the wake of Descartes and Kant, Barbour's critical realism does not give an adequate account of the significant metaphysical fact that the *simple actuality of being* precedes the knowing of any particular human subject.[16] His critical realism also could be interpreted as an attempt to elevate potency over

---

11 Artigas, *Knowing Things for Sure*, 152.

12 See Barbour, *Issues in Science and Religion*, 162–174.

13 Contemporary Catholic theology involves a variety of forms of realism. Some of these include a substantial critique of the so-called *naïve* realism. See Hans Urs von Balthasar, *Theo-Logic: The Truth of the World*, vol. 1, 3 vols. (San Francisco: Ignatius Press, 2001), I; Lonergan, *Insight*, 3:437–441; and Karl Rahner, *Spirit in the World* (New York: Continuum, 1994), II.

14 First Vatican Council, "Dei Filius," 3.

15 Congregation for the Doctrine of the Faith, *Donum Veritatis*, 10.

16 We affirm that the human subject plays a necessary role in constituting the truth of creation as well as the one act of being that precedes the human being.

act. This situation presents two, interrelated aspects that are problematic. First, Barbour envisions that being precedes subjective knowledge as "process" or "fluid event," not as actuality. According to Barbour, knowing, even for God, is thus the momentary actualization of what is first only potentially true.[17] This contrasts with a Catholic theology of creation in which the Father "speaks" creation into being *ex nihilo* through His Word, as a share in God's one, eternally actual truth.[18] Second, "being as process" can never be fully known. The mind grasps only changing parts, not the actual whole.[19]

One notices a Kantian tendency in Barbour's epistemology in the claim that being is only known through diverse models that provide momentary glimpses into what is "real," but is in fact always incomplete and *eo ipso* unintelligible. In this way, the mind actualizes "reality" through a process of integrating otherwise separate and unintelligible data. In some respects, modern science focuses on change, e.g., motion, not natures, essences, and substances.[20] According to Barbour's critical realism, reminiscent of Heraclitus, science itself is a *process* of becoming. If being is not *one* prior to being known, but only becomes one through finite knowing, the implication is that all reality is reducible to the process of coming to know.

Barbour's writings indicate a desire to address the partial, cumulative nature of scientific discovery as well as study the dynamicity of creation. Fundamentally, Barbour focuses on potency and the "immediacy" of entities in the world. However, physics, or a philosophy like Whitehead's, that in some aspects is more "physical" than "metaphysical," cannot be used to explore the most fundamental questions of reality, e.g., eternity, creation, and God.[21] Catholic metaphysical theology certainly concurs that there is a progression of knowledge, as well as change in the cosmos. Yet, it also insists that man has to presume an underlying, stable reality in order to

---

17 Barbour, *Religion and Science*, 294.

18 In Catholic theology, *truth* refers both to correspondence of the intellect and a thing, as well as a communication of the intelligibility of being (as other) to the intellect. According to Thomas Aquinas' theology of Divine ideas, created truth is a participation in the Divine essence. Created truth shares in God by an analogy of attribution (God is the primary analogate), not merely by way of extrinsic proportionality. It is a real communication of the Divine essence. See Thomas Aquinas, *Questiones Disputatae de Veritate*, trans. Robert W. Mulligan, James V. McGlynn, and Robert W. Schmidt (Chicago: Henry Regnery Company, 1954), Q 1.

19 Unity is a transcendental property of being—all being is intelligible as one. See *De Veritate*, Q 1, A 8, sc 5.

20 However, contemporary physical scientists also very much want to know the nature of things. After all, the essence of something is that which makes it what it is and not some other kind of thing.

21 See Chapter 1, Fundamentals of the Catholic Doctrine of Creation.

maintain rationality.[22] Absolute, eternal primacy is *in actu*, the ground of potency. In creation (which implies temporality), one moves from potency to act. Catholic theology presupposes that there is a stable truth to discover about a thing, i.e., essences—the quiddity of things. There is also the truth of *esse* known through affirmative judgment. "*Latet enim veritas, sed nihil pretiosius veritate.*"[23]

Classical philosophy explains how creatures exercise causality in the universe and why they cannot cause themselves—"In him we live and move and have our being."[24] Because there are effects, there must be a cause. Ultimately, causality presupposes a stable, metaphysical first cause, a *logos*, as well as metaphysical necessity. Man finds himself surrounded by other contingent beings. As Thomas Aquinas points out, if there is only contingency, i.e., if every being could have failed to exist, then nothing would exist. There must be a Being, a first cause that is necessary, i.e., whose non-existence is impossible. This Being must be eternal and *per se subsistens*. In other words, one needs a perfectly actual first cause to account for the principled order of diverse beings in motion.[25]

Another argument can be made utilizing the notion of potency. Finite, temporal beings cannot actualize themselves. A Being that can actualize others is required. The created world is in act, but it cannot cause itself. A first cause is necessary.[26] Infinite regression is impossible in efficient causality (simultaneously existing dependency relationships) because there would be no effects.[27] Also, if a

---

22   Walter Kasper writes, "God created all reality according to his eternal ideas, that therefore everything that exists is appointed and ordered by the Spirit of God and is thus ultimately rational. It is only because all reality is appointed by the divine Spirit that it is accessible at all to being known by the human mind. Our rational investigation and knowledge of the world is thus ultimately nothing more than a repetition of the thoughts of God." Kasper, "The Logos Character of Reality," 276.

23   Francisco Sánchez de las Brozas, *Minerva, Sive de Causis Latinae Linguae Commentarius* (Amsterdam: Judocum Pluymer, 1664), I, 1, 40, 16.

24   Acts 17:28a (RSV).

25   Aquinas, *Summa Theologiæ*, I, Q 2, A 3.

26   "ἔστι τοίνυν τι καὶ ὃ κινεῖ. ἐπεὶ δὲ τὸ κινούμενον καὶ κινοῦν [καὶ] μέσον, τοίνυν ἔστι τι ὃ οὐ κινούμενον κινεῖ, ἀΐδιον καὶ οὐσία καὶ ἐνέργεια οὖσα." (1066. Therefore there is also something which causes it to move. And since that which is moved and causes motion is intermediate, there must be something which causes motion and is unmoved, which is eternal and both a substance and an actuality.) Thomas Aquinas, *Commentary on the Metaphysics*, ed. Kenny Joseph, trans. John P. Rowan (Washington, D.C: Dominican Province of Saint Joseph, 1961), bk. XII, lec. VI, chap. 7.

27   A "linear series" of causes can, in principle, extend backward to infinity. However, a "hierarchical series" of causes cannot go on into infinity. Their causal power is completely derived and can only be derived from an entity with inherent causal power. This First Cause has the power to produce its effects without being caused by something else. It has inherent causal power while the secondary causes have only derived causal power. Hence, a "hierarchical" (not merely temporally prior) First Cause is necessary. See Gerard M. Verschuuren, *Aquinas and Modern Science: A New*

temporal being were the efficient cause of itself, it would be prior to itself, which is impossible—no man can be his own father. Therefore, the *primum movens* must be *actus purus* and hence possess no potency.[28] Thus, Catholic reflection on creation necessarily begins with God's perfect actuality and consequently secures causal reason.

Whether in the form of full-fledged subjective (dogmatic) idealism, or in the more modest approach of Barbour's critical realism, there is an inclination for those who adopt a post-Kantian, critical epistemology to offer a "correction" to the spontaneous certainty of methodical/moderate realism which they classify as "acritical." Stanley Jaki, OSB, was very critical of the post-Kantian critique of knowledge. Jaki argues

> that even the fact, let alone the nature, of external reality, however ordinary, cannot be proven by mere logic or mathematical formulas does not make one's immediate registering of external reality a less than fully rational process. To know the existence of things is in fact the very first step in reasoning. Any critical knowledge or philosophy which does not accept this will remain a mere criticism of criticism and not a criticism of the external reality one registers, and not even one's own registering it.[29]

Jaki also emphasizes that "for Aquinas it is natural for man to be in a cognitive unity with nature."[30]

Synthesis of Faith and Reason (Kettering, OH: Angelico Press, 2016), 47. Another way to analyze this question is to distinguish between *per accidens* and *per se* causes. An infinite series of causes is only possible if the universe was created from eternity and the causes are *accidentally* connected, i.e., they are only temporally connected in the past, not essentially. A *per accidens* connection means that if the cause ceases its activity, the effect can exist, e.g., parents are accidental causes of their children, for the children can exist without the existence of the parents. In the case of a *per se* (essential) cause, if the cause ceases to act, the effect ceases to exist, e.g., God and the creation.

28 The American philosopher, John Hittinger, makes an insightful observation on the relationship of God and creation: "We can see especially how it was that evidence, for the ancients, being in the last analysis the manifestation of a mystery (that is, of the root intelligibility of created things imposing itself on our mind by becoming luminous within it), a sort of natural relationship existed for them between intelligence and mystery. On the one hand then, in order to avoid the absurd and to remain faithful to the very first evidence—that of sense perception and that of the principle of identity, science itself and philosophy had to recognize a mystery of relative unintelligibility or ontological obscurity in things; that is, potentiality in Aristotle's meaning of the word, witnessing that the created is not God, who is the pure Act of intelligibility." John Hittinger, "Founding the Modern Project," accessed April 26, 2018, https://icucourses.com/pages/021-03-founding-the-modern-project-cartesian-doubt. Also, Aquinas, *Summa Theologiæ*, I, Q 2, A 3. In addition, it is helpful to note that all beings receive (*qua* potency) a share in the act of being from beyond themselves and, thus, require a pure act that grants existence. Aquinas develops this in *Summa Theologiæ*, I, Q 3 and 4.

29 Stanley L. Jaki, *Is There a Universe?* (New York: Wethersfield Institute, 1993), 108–109.

30 Jaki, *The Road of Science and the Ways to God*, 37.

Jaki explains that in "all major advances in the exact sciences, or physics, a philosophy was used, that of moderate realism, which is also the philosophy implied in the classical proofs of the existence of God."[31] His "moderate realism" is completely consistent with Gilson's "methodical realism."[32] Gilson himself writes that

> the critique of knowledge is essentially incompatible and irreconcilable with metaphysical realism. There is no middle ground. You must either begin as a realist with being, in which case you will have a knowledge of being, or begin as a critical idealist with knowledge, in which case you will never come in contact with being.[33]

Gilson's *punctum saliens* is that "a realist theory of knowledge and a realist critique of knowledge are both possible and necessary, but neither the one nor the other is equivalent to critical realism, and they should not be called by that name."[34] Gilson argues that the fundamental problem is the impossibility of reconciling a critical epistemology that systematically suspends belief in the world outside the mind with classical realism.[35] "Common sense spontaneously affirms that normal perception attains real objects."[36] In response to Thomists who sought to construct a critical realism, Gilson points out that "St. Thomas considers the existence of the external world to be self-evident."[37] All knowledge comes to man through the

---

31 Stanley L. Jaki, "The Demarcation Line between Science and Religion," *Angelicum* 87, no. 1 (2010): 81.

32 Given Barbour's familiarity and positive evaluation of many aspects of Gilson's Thomism, we utilize his philosophy in this Catholic engagement with Barbour's thought. There are of course a multiplicity of twentieth century Thomistic schools and our reliance on Gilson here in no way implies that his interpretation of the Angelic Doctor is the only valid one. For example, Congar, Lonergan, Rahner, Wojtyła, and many others attempted to develop and apply the perennial insights of Thomas Aquinas in light of contemporary theological concerns. See Thomas Joseph White, "Thomism after Vatican II," *Nova et Vetera* 12, no. 4 (2014): 1045–1062; Rowland, *Catholic Theology*, 43–90.

33 Gilson, *Thomist Realism and the Critique of Knowledge*, 149.

34 Ibid., 170.

35 Balthasar and Przywara highlight an additional issue. These Catholic philosophers point out that being is not first "being out there" which is then known in a second moment. Rather, being is the intelligible fullness of act. Consequently, there must be a foundational "polarity" of object and subject in being. Otherwise, a danger may arise of slipping back into the idealistic notion that objects are potency for an actualizing subject. "Objectivism" and "subjectivism" can be viewed as two sides of the same dialectical coin. See Erich Przywara, *Analogia Entis: Metaphysics*, trans. John R. Betz and David Bentley Hart (Grand Rapids, MI: Eerdmans, 2014), I.

36 Gilson, *Thomist Realism and the Critique of Knowledge*, 124.

37 Ibid., 100.

senses.[38] As a consequence, man must be capable of genuine learning, i.e., a process of abstracting the form from *informed* matter.[39]

In developing an epistemology, one need not begin with Descartes' methodical doubt or Kant's transcendental/critical method, exploring the capabilities of *a priori* reason.[40] The immediate evidence of sensation penetrates the intellect and manifests an extra-mental world. As the American philosopher, Frederick Wilhelmsen, points out, the fact of this "existence opens the gate to the Thomistic metaphysics of the primacy of the act of existing in being."[41]

While acknowledging that the Book of Exodus is not a philosophy textbook, Wilhelmsen suggests that there is "an invitation to reasonable men to fashion a

---

38 One way of explaining moderate realism goes back to Aristotle himself. Thomas Aquinas later developed his building blocks for the process of cognition. Aquinas' theory is based on three steps: apprehension, judgment, and reasoning. The apprehension of concepts can be formulated in four steps:

    1. The five senses perceive the sensible single in the outside world.

    2. The *sensus comune* unifies the senses and presents this to the mind as an immaterial *phantasma* (i.e., a mental impression of the sensible single. This is neither the sensible single itself [e.g., John Smith himself] nor the universal of the sensible singular [e.g., man in general].)

    3. The (active) *intellectus agens* illuminates the *phantasma* which universalizes it, abstracting the form and impressing it, the *species impressa*, upon the *intellectus passivis*.

    4. The *intellectus passivis* then produces a concept, or *species expressa*.

    See Aristotle, *De Anima*, trans. C.D.C. Reeve (Cambridge: Hackett Publishing Company, Inc., 2017), bk. 3; Thomas Aquinas, *Commentary on Aristotle's De Anima*, trans. Kenelm Foster and Sylvester Humphries (New Haven: Yale University Press, 1951), bk. 3, accessed March 14, 2018, http://dhspriory.org/thomas/english/DeAnima.htm. The intellect's return to the sensible single in the world is necessary for a judgment of truth because *veritas est adæquatio rei et intellectus*. See Aquinas, *Summa Theologiæ*, I, Q 16, A 2; Aquinas, *Quæstiones Disputatæ de Veritate*, I, 1. This definition of truth from antiquity is traced back not only to Thomas Aquinas but also to the Jewish scholar, Isaac Israeli ben Solomon, and the Islamic scholar, Avicenna. See Avicenna, *The Metaphysica of Avicenna: A Critical Translation-Commentary and Analysis of the Fundamental Arguments in Avicenna's Metaphysica in the Danish Nama-I Ala I*, ed. Parviz Morewedge (New York: Routledge, 2016), I, 9.

39 Metaphysics uses a special form of abstraction called *separatio*. It is a judgment operation used to distinguish things. According to Wippel, "it is the process through which the mind explicitly acknowledges and asserts that that by reason of which something is recognized as being need not be identified with that by which it is recognized as material being, or changing being, or being of a given kind." John F. Wippel, *Metaphysical Themes in Thomas Aquinas* (Washington, DC: CUA Press, 1995), 79. Commenting on *separatio*, Armand Maurer, CSB notes that "judgment is primarily pointed to the act of existing of things, whereas simple apprehension has to do rather with their essences and natures." Thomas Aquinas, *The Division and Methods of the Sciences*, ed. Armand Maurer (Toronto: Pontifical Institute of Mediaeval Studies, 1953), xx.

40 As mentioned in Chapter Two, Barbour is an heir of this tradition.

41 Gilson, *Thomist Realism and the Critique of Knowledge*, 9.

metaphysics of the Name of God."[42] It is quite striking that God would reveal His name to the ancient Hebrew people as "I am Who am." Wilhelmsen further states that "the immediate realism of Aquinas [is] a realism beginning with the truth that things are and that I know them to be because I sense and perceive them."[43]

The human person is a single knowing subject. He can grasp particulars with the senses and universals with the intellect.[44] Far from being in conflict with each other, "through their mutual interpenetration the intellect 'sees' the universal in the singular."[45] Echoing Gilson, Wilhelmsen emphasizes that

> when man apprehends being he is no longer in the order of essence, *quod quid erat esse*, but of the act of existence. Thus, Thomism transcends the critical problem. Once it is understood that the knowing subject is in direct, living communion with beings that are in act, the supposed problem of bridging the gap between an abstract mind and an equally abstract being is seen in all its poverty, resting in the last analysis on an essentialist notion of being.[46]

The axiom that being is a first principle—*ens est quod primo cadit in intellectu*[47]—is certainly not *naïve*.[48] A truly *naïve* realism ignores the immateriality of form, the relationship of the concept to the thing, and the abstraction of essences from substances.[49]

Barbour is attracted to what he describes as the "rich and many-faceted" approach to Divine causality as found in Neo-Thomists such as Gilson.[50] Because Gilson always strove to be congruent with Catholic doctrine, his thought serves as

42 Ibid.
43 Ibid., 10.
44 According to Thomistic *moderate* realism, universals do not exist in a Platonic "realm of ideas" (extreme realism), but "*immanent* to the particular things whose essences they are, or as *abstracted* by the intellect." Edward Feser, *Scholastic Metaphysics: A Contemporary Introduction*, vol. 39, Editiones Scholasticae (Heusenstamm, Germany: CPI Books, 2014), 226. Therefore, essences *exist* in particulars that are of course extra-mental, e.g., the universal "man" *exists* in Pope Francis. This approach also avoids the errors of nominalism and conceptualism that denies the existence of universals.
45 Gilson, *Thomist Realism and the Critique of Knowledge*, 19.
46 Ibid.
47 Ibid., 113.
48 It is also quite correct to affirm that *esse creatum* realizes its fullness as truth in intellect.
49 Knowledge of being is not, contrary to Barbour, the process of actualizing what is otherwise a potency. Rather, human knowing is a share in a comprehensive, always actual truth that includes within it the human knower and one's act of knowing. In addition, as mentioned earlier, we affirm the (relative) completion of the knowledge of being as truth. What is known in truth is actual being, requiring both apprehension and judgment (of its *esse*). See Wippel, *The Metaphysical Thought of Thomas Aquinas*, II.
50 Barbour, *Religion and Science*, 310.

a legitimate Catholic dialogue partner with Ian Barbour. Barbour must accept the dependency of one cause on another. God is the first cause of knowledge as *ipsum esse subsistens*. According to Gilson (and most other Neo-Thomists), being precedes and causes knowledge, e.g., if a knowing subject smells a flower, the flower—an extra-mental *ens*—is the cause of that knowledge of the flower. Therefore,

(1) Being precedes perception;
(2) Perception precedes apprehension;
(3) Apprehension precedes judgment; and
(4) Judgment precedes reasoning.

In addition, in the order of philosophical discovery, there is a tension pointing beyond creation to God's perfectly actual intellect. *Actus essendi* is simple and always precedes the contingent human who receives it. However, the act of being attains its fullness as truth in the intellect. Consequently, the difference of object and subject in being points to the Divine intellect/truth as encompassing act.

A Catholic reception of Barbour's approach to theology and science must be rooted in a robust realism and solid notion of causality in order to maintain both utility and intelligibility. One could engage his critical realism using other Catholic philosophers. Gilson is emphasized here given Barbour's own familiarity with, and affinity for, his thought.

1.3 Certainty, Faith, and Truth

Barbour's critical realism places significant emphasis on the subjective character of knowledge. He writes,

> For when human interpretation is present, there is always the possibility of misinterpretation, especially through wishful thinking, which reads into experience more than is warranted. Moreover, any verbal communication requires the use of symbolic language and conceptual structures that are culturally conditioned.[51]

Barbour's general assertion that one cannot know anything *for sure* may seem to represent a healthy modesty in many fields of inquiry, including the natural sciences, given the tentative character of all scientific theories. However, this attitude can become problematic for Catholic theology—*res ipsa loquitur*. Barbour *underscores* that all religious experience is interpreted by subjective, fallible beings. He therefore rules out "immediate and certain" knowledge in theological questions.

---

51 Barbour, *Issues in Science and Religion*, 210–211.

A Catholic understanding of faith presupposes reason's access to God. Metaphysics can attain knowledge of the Creator's perfect act in judgment. Neither revelation nor faith is random or arbitrary *vis-à-vis* created nature. Barbour's conception of faith is quintessentially Protestant[52] in that he denies that faith corresponds fundamentally to the acceptance of God's revealed truths. Barbour states that "faith means trust and commitment [and] it is compatible with considerable doubt about our theological interpretations."[53]

He claims that this notion of faith "enables us to live and act amid the uncertainties of life without the pretensions of intellectual or moral infallibility."[54] Furthermore, Barbour posits that "doubt frees us from illusions of having captured God in a creed. It calls into question every religious symbol. Self-criticism is called for if we acknowledge that no church, book, or creed is infallible and no formulation irrevocable."[55] Barbour believes that "the dangers of Absolutism can be avoided if revelation is not identified with infallible scriptures, revealed doctrines, or authoritative institutions."[56] From a Catholic perspective, a theological balance between apophatic and kataphatic statements would avoid this extreme position—elevating doubt over knowledge.

Since the early patristic period,[57] the Church has believed that Christ's promises to the Twelve: "He who hears you hears me, and he who rejects you

---

52 The Catholic Church has always taught that the act of faith involves the will and intellect. *Dei Verbum*, 5 expresses the doctrine that man "commits his whole self freely to God, offering the full submission of intellect and will to God who reveals." Thomas Aquinas describes the act of faith as "an act of the intellect assenting to the Divine truth at the command of the will moved by the grace of God." Aquinas, *Summa Theologiæ*, II-II, Q 2, A 9. Therefore, faith is a way of knowing. Conversely, Martin Luther's conception of faith emphasized the act of the will. In one instance, he wrote, "Faith is a living, bold trust in God's grace, so certain of God's favor that it would risk death a thousand times trusting in it." Martin Luther, "An Introduction to St. Paul's Letter to the Romans," in *Luther's German Bible of 1522*, trans. Robert E. Smith (Project Wittenberg, 1994), www.iclnet.org/pub/resources/text/wittenberg/luther/luther-faith.txt.

53 Barbour, *Issues in Science and Religion*, 227.

54 Ibid.

55 Barbour, *Religion and Science*, 135.

56 Ibid., 160.

57 For example, Saint Irenæus wrote in 180 AD, "But [it has, on the other hand, been shown], that the preaching of the Church is everywhere consistent, and continues in an even course, and receives testimony from the prophets, the apostles, and all the disciples ... For in the Church, it is said, 'God hath set apostles, prophets, teachers,' and all the other means through which the Spirit works; of which all those are not partakers who do not join themselves to the Church, but defraud themselves of life through their perverse opinions and infamous behavior. For where the Church is, there is the Spirit of God; and where the Spirit of God is, there is the Church, and every kind of grace; but the Spirit is truth." Irenaeus of Lyons, *Against Heresies*, ed. Alexander Roberts, James Donaldson, and A. Cleveland Coxe (Ex Fontibus, 2015), III, 24, 1.

rejects me, and he who rejects me rejects him who sent me"[58] and "When the Spirit of truth comes, he will guide you into all the truth,"[59] were meant not only as a *donum veritatis* for first century Christians, but for all time. The infallibility of the Magisterium is rooted in the indefectibility of the Church.[60] In addition, the nature of Christian faith is that *it is certain*. The Catechism teaches that faith "is more certain than all human knowledge because it is founded on the very word of God who cannot lie. To be sure, revealed truths can seem obscure to human reason and experience, but 'the certainty that the divine light gives is greater than that which the light of natural reason gives.'[61] "[62] "Now faith is the assurance of things hoped for, the conviction of things not seen."[63] Actual being points to the light of truth. This truth, in turn, leads man to God as the perfectly actual light of truth.

The Italian theologian, Angelo Cardinal Scola, suggests that the Second Vatican Council's Dogmatic Constitution on Divine Revelation, *Dei Verbum*, also proposes the perspective of "truth as event." He writes,

> In the language of Vatican II, truth and Jesus Christ are identified: in this way, Vatican II frees the notion of truth from the ahistorical precomprehension that tends to reify it, thus restoring truth to its identity as a historical event. Truth is in fact inseparable from event; otherwise we drift into formalism. The consideration of revelation as an "event which occurred in the past and continue to occur in faith, the event of a new relationship between God and man," presupposes a renewed approach to revealed truth.[64]

58 Luke 10:16 (RSV).
59 John 16:13a (RSV).
60 George Joyce concisely describes the indefectibility of the Church: "By this term is signified, not merely that the Church will persist to the end of time, but further, that it will be preserved unimpaired in its essential characteristics. The Church can never undergo any constitutional change, which will make it, as a social organism, something different from what it was originally. It can never become corrupt in faith or in morals; nor can it ever lose the Apostolic hierarchy, or the Sacraments through which Christ communicates grace to men." George Joyce, "The Church," *The Catholic Encyclopedia* (New York: Robert Appleton Company, 1908), accessed March 16, 2018, http://www.newadvent.org/cathen/03744a.htm. This doctrine is rooted in Jesus' promise to Peter: "And I tell you, you are Peter, and on this rock I will build my church, and the powers of death (literally: Gates of Hades) shall not prevail against it." Matthew 16:16 (RSV). See Second Vatican Council, *Lumen Gentium*, 25.
61 Aquinas, *Summa Theologiæ*, II–II, Q 171, A 5.
62 CCC 157. No falsehood can come from God; he cannot lie as this would imply a logical contradiction. Thomas Aquinas points out that "everything that does not imply a contradiction in terms, is numbered amongst those possible things, in respect of which God is called omnipotent: whereas whatever implies contradiction does not come within the scope of divine omnipotence, because it cannot have the aspect of possibility." Aquinas, *Summa Theologiæ*, I, Q 25, A 3.
63 Hebrews 11:1 (RSV).
64 Angelo Scola, *The Nuptial Mystery* (Grand Rapids, MI: Eerdmans, 2005), 348–349.

This view could provide a basis for dialogue with Barbour's "event-based" metaphysics. Unfortunately, Barbour's process thought lacks the strong Christological dimension expressed in *Dei Verbum*.

Dei Verbum also teaches that what the inspired authors assert in Holy Scripture must be held as asserted by the Holy Spirit. Catholics therefore believe that the Bible teaches the truths of salvation—firmly, faithfully, and without error.[65] The Second Vatican Council's Dogmatic Constitution on the Church, *Lumen Gentium*, also communicates the Catholic belief that the Pope and the College of Bishops have the ability to teach Christ's doctrines infallibly. It states that "this infallibility with which the Divine Redeemer willed His Church to be endowed in defining doctrine of faith and morals, extends as far as the deposit of Revelation extends, which must be religiously guarded and faithfully expounded."[66]

An elegant and concise description of the Magisterium's role is offered in the Catechism of the Catholic Church:

> The mission of the Magisterium is linked to the definitive nature of the covenant established by God with his people in Christ. It is this Magisterium's task to preserve God's people from deviations and defections and to guarantee them the objective possibility of professing the true faith without error. Thus, the pastoral duty of the Magisterium is aimed at seeing to it that the People of God abides in the truth that liberates. To fulfill this service, Christ endowed the Church's shepherds with the charism of infallibility in matters of faith and morals.[67]

It is likely that one aspect of Barbour's objection to the possibility of an infallible teaching authority is a misunderstanding of the actual Catholic doctrine. For example, a common Protestant belief in the twentieth century was that Catholics asserted that the Roman Pontiff enjoyed the privilege of "impeccability," as well as the authority to formulate novel doctrines. In the late nineteenth century, the

---

65 "*Divinitus revelata, quae in Sacra Scriptura litteris continentur et prostant, Spiritu Sancto afflante consignata sunt. Libros enim integros tam Veteris quam Novi Testamenti, cum omnibus eorum partibus, sancta Mater Ecclesia ex apostolica fide pro sacris et canonicis habet, propterea quod, Spiritu Sancto inspirante conscripti (cf. Io 20,31; 2 Tim 3,16; 2 Pt 1,19-21; 3,15-16), Deum habent auctorem, atque ut tales ipsi Ecclesiae traditi sunt. In sacris vero libris conficiendis Deus homines elegit, quos facultatibus ac viribus suis utentes adhibuit, ut Ipso in illis et per illos agente, ea omnia eaque sola, quae Ipse vellet, ut veri auctores scripto traderent. Cum ergo omne id, quod auctores inspirati seu hagiographi asserunt, retineri debeat assertum a Spiritu Sancto, inde Scripturae libri veritatem, quam Deus nostrae salutis causa Litteris Sacris consignari voluit, firmiter, fideliter et sine errore docere profitendi sunt.*" Second Vatican Council, *Dei Verbum*, 11.
66 Second Vatican Council, *Lumen Gentium*, 25.
67 CCC 890.

Church of England chaplain to Anglicans in Rome, Frank Nutcombe Oxenham, published a series of lectures entitled *The Validity of Papal Claims*.[68]

Given the seriousness of the errors contained therein, the Vatican diplomat, Raphael Cardinal Merry del Val, wrote a response entitled *The Truth of Papal Claims*. Merry del Val's explanation is helpful in clarifying the nature of the Papal Office and would likely have been a benefit to Barbour:

> We do not mean that the Roman Pontiff receives special revelations from heaven, or that by a revelation of the Holy Spirit he may invent or teach new doctrines not contained in the deposit of Faith, though, when occasion offers, and especially in times of conflict, he may define a point which all have not clearly recognized in that Faith, or which some may be striving to put out of view. Nor do we mean that every utterance that proceeds from the Pope's mouth, or from the Pope's pen, is infallible because it is his. Great as our filial duty of reverence must be to the guidance of the Chief Shepherd, we do not hold that every word of his is infallible, or that he must always be right. Much less do we dream of teaching that he is infallible, or in any degree superior to other men, when he speaks on matters that are scientific or historical, or political, or that he may not make mistakes of judgment in dealing with contemporary events, with men and things.[69]

Bishop Vincent Gasser's famous *relatio* at Vatican I, offers a theologically rigorous explanation of the meaning of the dogmatic definition of infallibility.[70] The American priests and theologians, Francis A. Sullivan, SJ and Anthony Figueiredo, have also conducted thorough, contemporary studies of the issue.[71]

Another theological concern with Barbour's critical realism is that it does not seem to permit certainty with regard to theological propositions. This is an important issue in fundamental theology.[72] Joseph Ratzinger's theology of faith suggests a special character of certainty for the *Credo* of Christians. Ratzinger writes,

68 Frank Nutcombe Oxenham, *The Validity of Papal Claims: Five Lectures Delivered in Rome* (London: Longmans Green and Co., 1897).

69 Raphael Merry del Val, *The Truth of Papal Claims: A Reply to The Validity of Papal Claims by F. Nutcombe Oxenham* (London: Sands and Company, 1902), 18–19.

70 See Vincent Ferrer Gasser, *The Gift of Infallibility: The Official Relatio on Infallibility of Bishop Vincent Ferrer Gasser at Vatican Council I*, trans. James T. O'Connor, 2nd ed. (San Francisco: Ignatius Press, 2008).

71 See Francis A. Sullivan, *Creative Fidelity: Weighing and Interpreting Documents of the Magisterium* (Eugene, OR: Wipf & Stock Pub, 2003) and Anthony J. Figueiredo, *The Magisterium-Theology Relationship: Contemporary Theological Conceptions in the Light of Universal Church Teaching Since 1835 and the Pronouncements of the Bishops of the United States*, Tesi Gregoriana 75 (Roma: Gregorian & Biblical Press, 2001).

72 For example, Cardinal Newman was very interested in developing a phenomenology of how one comes to certitude in general, but especially on religious matters. Newman highlights the essential role of probability in life. With the *lumen fidei*, a sum of probabilities can lead to a certainty

In reality, for the believing Christian, the words "I believe" articulate a kind of certainty that is in many respects a higher degree of certainty than that of science, yet one that does indeed carry within it the dynamic of the "not yet"... Just as a person becomes certain of another's love without being able to subject it to the methods of scientific experiment, so in the contact between God and man there is a certainty of a quite different kind from the certainty of objectivizing thought. We live faith, not as a hypothesis, but as the certainty on which our life is based.[73]

Ratzinger identifies a unique aspect of the Christian act of faith—a faith that leads to knowledge. He argues that

belief in God does not claim to offer a fictitious and abstract union of different modes of action; it claims to be more than a subjective conviction inexplicably juxtaposed to a godless objectivity. It claims to reveal the essence, the root, of the objective, to bring into sharper focus the demands of objective reality. It does so by leading to that source which unites object and subject and offers the only true explanation of their relationship.[74]

With regard to the problem of empiricism, Ratzinger and Barbour agree on the need to move away from a *naïve* "picturability" in epistemology. For example, Ratzinger writes that "modern natural science is built on the rejection of pure empiricism, on the superiority of thinking over seeing."[75]

Barbour states that he wants to avoid both religious relativism and religious absolutism. However, his concern with theological "exclusivism" or "particularism" is paramount. He cannot accept the "claim that there is only one true religion."[76] Consequently, Barbour explores other alternatives that one may interpret as an "over-reach" of the λόγος σπερματικός (*lógos spermatikós*) theories.[77] These include the "approximation of truth theory" which holds that other religions possess

---

that exceeds the logic of inference. See John Henry Newman, *Grammar of Assent*, ed. Ian T. Ker (Oxford: Oxford University Press, 1988).

73 Joseph Ratzinger, *Pilgrim Fellowship of Faith: The Church as Communion*, ed. Stephan Otto Horn and Vinzenz Pfnur, trans. Henry Taylor (San Francisco: Ignatius Press, 2005), 18–20.

74 Ratzinger, *Principles of Catholic Theology: Building Stones for a Fundamental Theology*, 71.

75 Ibid., 347.

76 Barbour, *Religion and Science*, 154.

77 According to the Congregation for the Doctrine of the Faith, "it is consistent with Catholic doctrine to hold that the seeds of truth and goodness that exist in other religions are a certain participation in truths contained in the revelation of or in Jesus Christ. However, it is erroneous to hold that such elements of truth and goodness, or some of them, do not derive ultimately from the source-mediation of Jesus Christ." Congregation for the Doctrine of the Faith, *Notification on the Book, Toward a Christian Theology of Religious Pluralism*, January 24, 2001, accessed May 14, 2018, http://www.vatican.va/roman_curia/congregations/cfaith/documents/rc_con_cfaith_doc_20010124_dupuis_en.html.

elements of the truth that are present, for example, in Christianity; the "identity of essence" theory that posits that all religions are fundamentally the same and are simply distinguished by cultural expression; and the theory of "pluralistic dialogue" which holds that God is present in all religions while at the same time asserting that one should hold fast to one's particular faith. According to Barbour, an expression of the "pluralistic dialogue" approach is found in the former Catholic cleric, Paul Knitter's,[78] claim that "one can accept the possibility of *other saviors* without undermining *commitment to Christ.*"[79]

This assertion cannot be reconciled with the salvific unicity of Jesus implied in the first century Christian creedal acrostic: ΙΧΘΥΣ[80]—Jesus Christ, Son of God, Savior—"for there is no other name under heaven given among men by which we must be saved."[81] Barbour's "pluralistic dialogue" approach begins to become indistinguishable from the very relativism that he seeks to avoid. The Catholic Church "desires all men to be saved and to come to the knowledge of the *truth*,"[82] Jesus the Christ.[83]

While Barbour does not fall into metaphysical skepticism, his relativistic tendency is rooted in the same fundamental error—confusing truth for theory. Gerhard Cardinal Müller notes that "a theory will of course always be somewhat removed from everyday life. In Christ, by contrast, knowing God's *truth* and observing his commandments in one's *life* always go together. In him the 'light has come into the world.' (Jn 3:19)."[84]

---

78 Joseph Ratzinger critically engaged Knitter's theology of pluralism. According to Ratzinger, Knitter claimed that "interreligious dialogue must be simplified radically and become practically effective by basing it on only one principle: 'the primacy of orthopraxis with regard to orthodoxy.' Putting praxis above knowledge in this way is also a clearly Marxist inheritance. However, whereas Marxism makes only what comes logically from renouncing metaphysics concrete—when knowledge is impossible, only action is left—Knitter affirms: The absolute cannot be known, but it can be made." Joseph Ratzinger, "Relativism: The Central Problem for Faith Today" (presented at the Meeting of the Doctrinal Commissions of the Bishops Conferences of Latin America, Guadalajara, Mexico, 1996), accessed March 19, 2018, https://www.ewtn.com/library/CURIA/RATZRELA.HTM.

79 Barbour, *Religion and Science*, 157.

80 Ιησοῦς Χριστός, Θεοῦ Υἱός, Σωτήρ. See Augustine, *The City of God, Books XVII-XXII*, trans. Gerald G. Walsh, vol. 3, The Fathers of the Church (Washington, DC: CUA Press, 2008), bk. *XVIII*, chap. 23, 114.

81 Acts 4:12 (RSV).

82 I Timothy 2:4 (RSV).

83 "Jesus said to him, 'I am the way, and the truth, and the life; no one comes to the Father, but by me.'" John 14:6 (RSV).

84 Gerhard Müller, "Is There a Saving Truth? | The Salvific Relevance of the Rule of Faith," *First Things* (March 13, 2018), accessed March 19, 2018, https://www.firstthings.com/web-exclusives/2018/03/is-there-a-saving-truth.

In a 2015 homily, Pope Francis concisely proclaimed the fundamental truth about the mission of Jesus: "What, though, is most important?... He is the Savior and we are saved by him: this is the most important thing, and this is the strength of our faith."[85] Francis' magisterium in *Placuit Deo* offers a helpful correction to Barbour's relativistic approach to Jesus. The dogma of the salvific unicity and universality of Christ and the Church is elegantly summarized here:

> The salvation that God offers us is not achieved with our own individual efforts alone, as neo-Pelagianism would contend. Rather, salvation is found in the relationships that are born from the incarnate Son of God and that form the communion of the Church. Because the grace that Christ gives us is not a merely interior salvation, as the neo-Gnostic vision claims, and introduces us into concrete relationships that He himself has lived, the Church is a visible community. In her we touch the flesh of Jesus, especially in our poorest and most suffering brothers and sisters. Hence, the salvific mediation of the Church, "the universal sacrament of salvation," assures us that salvation does not consist in the self-realization of the isolated individual, nor in an interior fusion of the individual with the divine. Rather, salvation consists in being incorporated into a communion of persons that participates in the communion of the Trinity.[86]

Catholics cannot detach the *actus fidei* from the *depositum fidei*. Müller succinctly summarizes this belief:

> Faith in Christ already contains all truths. In Jesus Christ, the Incarnate Word, the *faith in* him and the *knowledge of* him come together as one. He is the one divine Word that has become flesh. The human words that constitute Jesus' teachings have passed over into the "teaching of the apostles" (Acts 2:42) and the Church's doctrine of faith.

Here the classical Thomistic maxim comes to mind: "You cannot love what you do not know."[87] *Fides quæ creditur* matters. You cannot love God unless you accept His self-communication.

Saint John Henry Newman's "dogmatic principle" for interpreting revelation is helpful to consider at this point:

> That there is a truth then; that there is one truth; that religious error is in itself of an immoral nature; that its maintainers, unless involuntarily such, are guilty in maintaining it; that it is to be dreaded; that the search for truth is not the gratification of curiosity; that its attainment has nothing of the excitement of a discovery; that the mind is below truth, not above it, and is bound, not to descant upon it, but to venerate

---

85 Francis, Homily (Chapel of the Domus Sanctæ Marthæ, January 22, 2015), accessed March 19, 2018, http://www.ewtnnews.com/catholic-news/Vatican.php?id=11532.

86 Congregation for the Doctrine of the Faith, *Placuit Deo*, 2018, 12.

87 While completely in line with Thomas Aquinas' thought, this saying is not a direct quote from the Angelic Doctor.

it; that truth and falsehood are set before us for the trial of our hearts; that our choice is an awful giving forth of lots on which salvation or rejection is inscribed; that "before all things it is necessary to hold the Catholic faith;" that "he that would be saved must thus think," and not otherwise; that, "if thou criest after knowledge, and liftest up thy voice for understanding, if thou seekest her as silver, and searchest for her as for hid treasure, then shalt thou understand the fear of the Lord, and find the knowledge of God,"—this is the dogmatical principle, which has strength.[88]

While the term "dogmatic" can have a negative connotation in modern and post-modern thought, Müller points out that "to speak of Christianity as dogmatic … is to say that it is based on God's historical self-revelation. It is to say that the Word made flesh has imparted to us the fullness of truth and life."[89]

All who bear the name Christian ought to profess faith in "God our Savior, who desires all men to be saved and to come to the knowledge of the truth. For there is one God, and there is one mediator between God and men, the man Christ Jesus."[90] The common truth of created being is known by men and women in communion.[91] The *veritas Christi*, which contains it, is handed down authoritatively in the Church. This view of truth contrasts sharply with Barbour's notion that truth is a never-complete process of scrutinizing often dubious data. In Barbour's theology, faith is reduced to a means to cope with this imperfect knowledge. Having evaluated Barbour's epistemology, we now turn our attention to his metaphysics.

2. Process Metaphysics

The critique of Ian Barbour's process thought must attend to a number of concerns. First, we shall address Barbour's approach to exploring the dynamicity of the cosmos and offer a Catholic alternative. Next, we critically engage a number of problematic aspects of Barbour's thought as they relate to the doctrine of creation. These include Barbour's denial of the Biblical teaching of creation *ex nihilo*, his theological anthropology, his implicit panentheism, the theological consequences of neglecting substances and essences, and his denial of the perfection of God.

---

88 John Henry Newman, *An Essay On Development Of Christian Doctrine* (Notre Dame: University of Notre Dame Press, 1994), 182.

89 Müller, "Is There a Saving Truth?"

90 1 Timothy 2:3b–5 (RSV).

91 Knowledge is constituted in communion first as a child in a family and later in collaboration with the larger society and culture. This natural structure is created to be perfected in the Church, where the fullness of revealed truth is passed on in the community of faith.

2.1 Fundamental Issues

In his book *The Philosophical Approach to God*, the American philosopher, W. Norris Clarke, SJ, comments on the phenomenon of Catholic theologians attempting to integrate process philosophy into their approach.[92] Clarke writes,

> A growing number of Catholic thinkers have also been drawing inspiration from the writings of this school. But I have the impression that some of the latter, especially theologians, are a little incautious in speaking of themselves as "Process theologians," or as "using Process philosophy," taking the latter rather vaguely and generally as thinking about God in dynamic terms, without fully realizing all the implications involved in taking on the whole Process philosophical system as such.[93]

Clarke continues,

> On the one hand, Process thought contains a number of *basic insights* that can and should be fruitfully recognized by Christian theism. On the other hand, Process thought *as a system*, at least in its principal presently established forms—the systems of Alfred North Whitehead and Charles Hartshorne—is still in serious tension, if not incompatibility, with traditional Christian theism on several key points, both philosophical and theological, with respect to the nature of God and His relations with the world.[94]

---

92   The American philosopher and theologian, Joseph A. Bracken, SJ, has attempted a "rethinking" of Whitehead's metaphysics. Bracken acknowledges that Whitehead's metaphysical categories need revision in order to accommodate Catholic belief in God as Trinity. In response to Barbour's own critique of Whitehead, Bracken writes, "*In Religion in an Age of Science*, Ian Barbour concludes that the contemporary evolutionary worldview with its emphasis on the interplay of law and chance, relationality and autonomy, can be properly accounted for only by something like the process-relational metaphysics of Alfred North Whitehead. At the same time, he expresses serious reservations about certain features of Whitehead's scheme, notably, his perceived inability to account for the ongoing identity of the human self and for the fact of multilevel organization within organisms and in the world of inanimate compounds ... I suggest that both of these difficulties can be resolved if one adopts a revisionist understanding of the Whiteheadian category of society according to which democratically organized societies possess an ontological unity and exercise a corporate agency proper to their own level of existence and activity. Furthermore, if one applies this revisionist understanding of societies to the Whiteheadian doctrine of God, a Trinitarian understanding of God becomes possible within the overall parameters of process-relational metaphysics. In this way, traditional belief in the doctrine of the Trinity can be reconciled with a scientifically credible worldview." Joseph A. Bracken, "Revising Process Metaphysics in Response to Ian Barbour's Critique," *Zygon* 33, no. 3 (September 1, 1998): 405.

93   W. Norris Clarke, *The Philosophical Approach to God: A New Thomistic Perspective*, 2nd ed. (New York: Fordham University Press, 2007), 91.

94   Ibid.

Some of these tensions, as they are manifest in Ian Barbour's thought, will be explored in this section.

2.2 Addressing Dynamicity

Ian Barbour views nature as a dynamic process.[95] Therefore, a major philosophical concern for Barbour is for the metaphysics underlying a systematic synthesis of theology and science to adequately describe the dynamicity of the cosmos. Following Whitehead, Barbour affirms that *change* is the very basis of reality. While Barbour demonstrates an impressive awareness of elements of Thomistic philosophy, he never mentions the Thomistic philosophy of nature—a pre-cursor to Whitehead's *philosophy of organism*.[96] The philosophy of nature is concerned with changeable being, i.e., a being that has the capability of movement. Some applications of this philosophy relevant to creation are described in this section.

Thomistic *philosophia naturalis* can also serve as a foundation for a broad-spectrum "philosophy of physics" as it studies nature from a comprehensive, philosophical perspective. The philosophy of nature, i.e., philosophical physics, reveals the necessary conditions for the possibility of empirical physics. It studies the movement of material bodies; the notions of space and time; causality in the physical world; the concept of natural laws; and the unity, order, finality, and value of the cosmos.[97]

The classical Aristotelian classification of theoretical philosophy contains three categories based on the levels of abstraction.[98] Thomas Aquinas adds that every science has its own proper *subjectum*. This subject distinguishes it from others and "designates the formal perspective (*ratio*) under which"[99] things are explored within the discipline of the particular science. Basing himself on Maritain, Armand Maurer, CSB observes that "each of the speculative sciences attains its subject by a mode of abstraction which is *sui generis* and irreducible to any other."[100]

95 Ian G. Barbour, "Science and Religion Today," in *Science and Religion: New Perspectives on the Dialogue*, ed. Ian G. Barbour (New York: Harper & Row, 1968), 21.

96 Classically, the philosophical study of the physical universe, i.e., nature, has also been referred to as "cosmology." This is a distinct, although non-conflicting, discipline from "Biblical cosmology" (e.g., the study of God's creation based on the insights from the Book of Genesis) and "physical cosmology" (e.g., the mathematical and experimental study of the largest-scale structures and dynamics of the universe).

97 See Peter Hoenen, *Cosmologia*, 5th ed. (Rome: Gregorian University Press, 1956). Filippo Selvaggi, *Filosofia del Mondo: Cosmologia Filosofica*, 2nd ed. (Rome: Gregorian University Press, 2008).

98 Aristotle, *Metaphysics*, trans. William David Ross (Oxford: Clarendon Press, 1908), V, 1.

99 Aquinas, *The Division and Methods of the Sciences*, xv.

100 Ibid, *xxi*. Also, see Maritain, *Philosophy of Nature*, 24.

The philosophy of nature is used to investigate the natural world in a general way. It therefore removes individuality but retains sensible matter. It studies change primarily through efficient and final causes as well as the intrinsic principles of bodies, e.g., matter and form. At the next level of abstraction is mathematics. This science removes sensible matter but retains intellectual matter.[101] For the ancients and medievals, mathematics was principally arithmetic and Euclidean geometry.[102] The science with the highest level of abstraction is metaphysics. This *first philosophy*[103] admits no matter and ultimately seeks knowledge of the First Cause (who is immaterial). It explains the contingent universe through God.

Both the philosophy of nature and physics share the same *material* object: material bodies (or material entities).[104] They differ in their *formal* objects. The philosophy of nature is concerned with changeable being, i.e., a being that has the capability of movement. Maritain explains that it seeks ontological, i.e., *dianoetic*, knowledge of nature.[105] On the other hand, the formal object of modern physics is all phenomena that can be measured. It is concerned with nature from an empiriological, i.e., *perinoetic*, perspective.[106] Sense experience is the starting point for both disciplines, but physics also ends with sense experience. Empirical physics begins with a hypothesis that may be verified with observation and experimentation. In philosophy, the process is not hypothetical (in the empirical sense); it is abstractive from essences (hence *dia*-noetic).[107]

One should be careful not to separate the two aspects unduly and excessively. Even physicist can follow their empiriological method only within a certain

---

101 Maritain, *Distinguish to Unite, or, The Degrees of Knowledge*, 35.

102 Aquinas, *The Division and Methods of the Sciences*, xi.

103 Here, the term "first" does not indicate the order of abstraction, but rather the most fundamental. The philosophy of nature is *prior* to metaphysics because in the cognitional process the mind comes to know through sensible, material beings before it can move to a level of abstraction that considers the immaterial.

104 Early modern science often referred to "bodies." The term continues to be used in contemporary physics even though "bodies" is not a technical term, e.g., the "n-body problem" and "rigid body motion."

105 Here Maritain is referring to the Aristotelian phenomenon, which is observable. Many critics of this have a notion of the phenomenon that is close to Kant's phenomenon or phenomenology, which is not realism. Experimental physics is properly about the phenomenon in a *realistic* sense, not in a *phenomenological* sense. And what is observable (the phenomenon) is never the being, or the substance, although the phenomenon is real. Dealing with reality is not dealing *formally* with being as being. See Maritain, *Distinguish to Unite, or, The Degrees of Knowledge*, 55.

106 One can further distinguish empirio-schematic sciences (e.g., anatomy) from the empirio-metric (e.g., thermodynamics).

107 William A. Wallace, *The Modeling of Nature: The Philosophy of Science and the Philosophy of Nature in Synthesis* (Washington, DC: The Catholic University of America Press, 1996), 221–227.

dianoetic context. They need to recognize certain objects as separate entities, attribute to them a certain ontological status and assume certain regularities. All such assumptions are philosophical and are part of the scientific enterprise, even though then the scientific method focuses on measurability and mathematical modeling.

The philosophy of nature uses the word *nature* as the intrinsic principle of motion because the object of this branch of philosophy deals with "mobile" being. Since the intrinsic principle of motion, i.e., substance, is formal and material, nature considers both matter and form, although form is given primary consideration. Because the essence of a material being is its substance, nature is another common term instead of essence. Nature is the principle and cause of motion (and rest) of things in which that principle exists *fundamentally* and *essentially*, and not accidentally. One may say that nature is a cause of motion when it produces movement. Other causes of motion include extrinsic causes. It must be noted that the motion of *artificial* objects, does not originate in a unique form or intrinsic principle, but in something extrinsic.[108]

According to Aristotle, motion is so fundamental that it is above any predicament classification.[109] Movement can be considered both from the perspective of quality (e.g., alteration) and quantity. In Catholic doctrine, God cannot "move" because it would imply that He is an imperfect act.[110] When discussing motion,

---

108 Gardeil, *Introduction to the Philosophy of St. Thomas Aquinas: Cosmology*, vol. 2, chap. 4.

109 Aristotle divides τὰ λεγόμενα (*ta legómena*)—things that are said—into ten distinct categories or predicaments. The first category is *substance*. Substance is further divided, e.g., immobile substances (Unmoved Mover) and mobile substances (bodies). The second category is *quantity* which is divided into discrete and continuous. Within the continuous classification he identifies time, place, etc. See Paul Studtmann, "Aristotle's Categories," ed. Edward N. Zalta, *The Stanford Encyclopedia of Philosophy* (Stanford: Metaphysics Research Lab, Stanford University, November 5, 2013), accessed March 20, 2018, https://plato.stanford.edu/archives/fall2017/entries/aristotle-categories/. Along with the transcendentals, categories constitute the fundamental aspects of the realist metaphysics of Thomas Aquinas. As Charles Thompson puts it, "They express his most fundamental understanding of reality. While much more developed than commonsense realism, they remain essentially compatible with it." Charles Frank Thompson, *The Greatness of God: How God Is the Foundation of All Reality, Truth, Love, Goodness, Beauty, and Purpose* (Bloomington, IN: WestBow Press, 2016), eBook.

110 First Vatican Council, "Dei Filius," 1. This doctrine has numerous Biblical foundations, e.g., "Every good endowment and every perfect gift is from above, coming down from the Father of lights with whom there is no variation or shadow due to change." James 1:17 (RSV) and "So when God desired to show more convincingly to the heirs of the promise the unchangeable character of his purpose, he interposed with an oath, so that through two unchangeable things, in which it is impossible that God should prove false, we who have fled for refuge might have strong encouragement to seize the hope set before us." Hebrews 6:17–18 (RSV).

one must distinguish between act and potency. Both are real beings,[111] as opposed to a privation, which is a being of reason.[112] As Gardeil puts it,

> What is in potency is not yet in motion: a thing that is not yet being warmed, is not in motion toward warmth. On the other hand, what has reached its term, what is in completed act, is not in motion either: a thing that is warm is no longer in motion toward warmth. Consequently, to be in motion is to be in an intermediate state, between the initial potency and the terminal act, hence partly in potency and partly in act. In a word, the warmth of a thing that is being warmed is in imperfect act, and thus imperfect act is motion, but on condition that the thing remained headed toward further warming.[113]

The medieval axiom captures this concept succinctly: "*actus existentis in potentia in quantum est in potentia.*"[114] According to Gardeil, *actus*

> indicates that motion itself is a kind of fulfillment or realization; in the warming of a thing there is already a degree of actualization present ... of what exists in potency affirms that the act in question is not at a standstill, as though fully realized, but that the subject of the act remains in potency to still more actualization ... so far as it is in potency means that the act identified with motion determines or actuates its subject, not in every respect, but in the respect by which it is in potency.[115]

Barbour desires a philosophy that can handle the interconnection of events and view nature as an organic process.[116] It is unfortunate that he does not explore the capabilities of Thomistic philosophy, which supports reciprocal causality and the interconnection of the mutually dependent, changing substances. Reciprocal causality happens all the time in nature because every material being that causes something necessarily changes itself.[117] Barbour instead adopts the metaphysical

---

111 The American philosopher, Edward Feser, offers an elegant explanation for the relationship of "being-in-act" and "being-in-potency." He writes, "1. Act is real, i.e., it has being. 2. Potency is real, i.e., it has being. 3. Potency is really distinct from act. 4. If potency had being in the same, univocal sense in which act does, then it wouldn't be really distinct from act. 5. If potency has being only in an equivocal sense then it wouldn't have being at all. 6. The only sense remaining in an analogous sense. 7. So potency has being in a sense that is analogous to that in which act has." Feser, *Scholastic Metaphysics*, 39:261.

112 Thomas Aquinas makes the helpful distinction between beings *in nature* (e.g., an oak tree) and *beings of reason* (e.g., Sherlock Holmes). See Aquinas, *Commentary on the Metaphysics*, IV, lec. 4, n. 574.

113 Gardeil, *Introduction to the Philosophy of St. Thomas Aquinas: Cosmology*, 2:88.

114 Ibid., 2:89.

115 Ibid.

116 Barbour, *Religion and Science*, 285.

117 See P. De Letter, "Reciprocal Causality: Some Applications in Theology," *The Thomist* 25, no. 3 (1962): 382–418. Gloria Frost, "Aquinas' Ontology of Transeunt Causal Activity," *Vivarium* 56,

category of *event* in light of Whitehead's notions of actual entities/occasion and nexūs.

The Thomistic philosophy of nature describes change (*ens mobile*) in a rigorous way. All moveable beings require privation, subject, and form. In the words of Gardeil, "every change in the physical world requires: a subject that undergoes the change: matter, a determination received by the subject: form, [and] a precedent absence of this determination: privation."[118] The two primary principles of change can be discerned from common experience. For example, consider a color transition from black to white: the term acquired (*terminus ad quem*), e.g., whiteness, and the starting point (*terminus a quo*), e.g., blackness—the "non-possession" of whiteness. One may define the ultimate term of such a change as form, and its initial condition as a privation.[119] In addition, matter provides the basis for the process of change and the terms that constrain its evolution.[120]

Building on ideas first developed in his Φυσική ἀκρόασις (*Phusikè akróasis*), in Latin: *Physica*, Aristotle wrote Περί γενέσεως καὶ φθορᾶς (*Perì genéseos kaì phthoras*), in Latin: *De Generatione et Corruptione*,[121] in which he further explored issues in causality and the nature of reality. Many of his insights have perennial value. In this framework, changes to matter may be either *absolute* (i.e., substantial) or *relative* (i.e., accidental). An absolute change involves a profound transformation of one thing into something else. The subject of such a change is the prime (or *proto*) matter. A relative change takes place when a subject endures in its essence but is modified in a non-essential way. Relative changes pertain to accidents, such as quantity or quality. Motion and growth are examples of changes in quantity while alteration is the hallmark of quality changes.[122]

It is important to point out that change, i.e., transformation, implies a common subject, i.e., *prime matter*, that receives a new *form*. Therefore, when discussing, for example the Holy Eucharist, transubstantiation is not properly called a change. The *accidents* of bread and wine remain after the consecration while the *substance*, i.e., the form-matter composite, is converted into the Body and Blood of Christ.

Reflecting on the mystery of matter, the American fundamental theologian, John M. McDermott, SJ, writes,

no. 1–2 (2018): 47–82. Francis Xavier Meehan, "Efficient Causality in Aristotle and St. Thomas" (PhD, The Catholic University of America, 1940).

118 Gardeil, *Introduction to the Philosophy of St. Thomas Aquinas: Cosmology*, 2:23.

119 Ibid., 2:20–21.

120 Ibid., 2:22.

121 Aristotle, *On the Generation and Corruption*, trans. Harold Henry Joachim (Adelaide, South Australia: eBooks@Adelaide, 2015), accessed May 2, 2018, https://ebooks.adelaide.edu.au/a/aristotle/corruption/.

122 Gardeil, *Introduction to the Philosophy of St. Thomas Aquinas: Cosmology*, 2:25.

> Certainly Christian belief in *creatio ex nihilo* bursts the parameters of ancient philosophy and forced Christian thinkers to reevaluate matter's role. The infinity of matter demands an infinite God capable of comprehending it, and its unintelligibility to the human mind preserves the space for human freedom and God's free interventions in history.[123]

Prime matter is a strange object of study because according to itself it is unknown and is *accidental* non-being. Thomas Aquinas points out that "matter alone is neither a principle of knowledge, nor is it that by which something is assigned to a genus or to a species; rather a thing is so assigned by reason of its being something actual."[124]

The reference by McDermott to the "infinity of matter" should be clarified, as it is completely different from the infinity of God. Based on Aquinas' distinction, McDermott points out that

> God's infinity is infinity in act, consisting of a most perfect *esse*, which is the most formal of all and possesses the characteristic of perfection (*ratio perfecti*)... Matter, on the contrary, is infinite because it is deprived of termination by form and is therefore capable of every further division.[125]

Thus, prime matter is only infinite in potency and paradoxes emerge in man's quest to understand it.[126]

Aquinas' metaphysics and philosophy of nature, can clearly offer a strong philosophical foundation for a systematic synthesis of Catholic theology with the natural sciences. His second level of abstraction in the speculative sciences, which removes sensible matter but retains intellectual matter, mathematics, has less utility in theology but plays an indispensable role in natural science. Whitehead's doctoral advisor, the applied mathematician, Edward J. Routh, was a specialist in dynamical systems theory, making contributions both in mechanics and control theory.[127] Whitehead's early career work as a mathematician was also in applied mathematics and his process metaphysics patently shows the influence of his "dynamical systems perspective" on the world. This approach has proven invaluable in

---

123 John M. McDermott, "The Mystery of Matter," *Angelicum* 87, no. 4 (2010): 993.

124 Thomas Aquinas, *De Ente et Essentia*, trans. Robert T. Miller, Internet Medieval Source Book (New York: Fordham University, 1997), 15, accessed May 2, 2018, https://sourcebooks.fordham.edu/basis/aquinas-esse.asp.

125 McDermott, "The Mystery of Matter," 994.

126 McDermott notes that "despite the obvious perspectival shifts, from Newton to string theory, modern physicists face the same conundrums which perplexed Plato, Aristotle, and Aquinas, and led them to ascribe unintelligibility and 'non being' to the principle of individuality." McDermott, "Matter, Modern Science, and God," 484.

127 See Anthony Thomas Fuller, "Edward John Routh," *International Journal of Control* 26, no. 2 (August 1, 1977): 169–173.

the modeling of nature, whether in physics, chemistry, or biology, and should be emphasized in a Catholic appropriation of Barbour's thought.

A *dynamical* system is a mathematical formalization that describes how one state of a system evolves into another with the passage of time. Whether solved analytically or numerically, one can ideally predict the future state of the system, e.g., the position and velocity of a celestial body in motion. More formally, a dynamical system is often defined as a triple $\{T, X, \varphi^t\}$, where T is a time set, X is a state space (e.g., in mechanics, the state space could be a set of positions and corresponding velocities for the system), and $\varphi^t\colon X \to X$ is a family of evolution operators parameterized by $t \in T$. The time set may treated as continuous ($t \in \mathrm{R}$) or discrete (e.g., $t = 0, 1, 2$, etc.).[128] The state space may be finite or infinite (as well as continuous or discrete). Finally, the evolution operator may be deterministic or stochastic (i.e., probabilistic, as in radioactive decay), as well as autonomous or time-dependent. Differential equations are typically used to define a continuous-time dynamical system.[129]

For example, consider a simple, idealized example of a pendulum with a mass M on the end of a rigid, massless rod of length L. The rod is connected to a point P on a ceiling and under the force of gravity with acceleration g. The pendulum is brought to motion by displacing the mass M some distance ϑ away from the rest position. Regular, periodic motion is observed. This system is described by the second-order differential equation:

$$\ddot{\theta} + \frac{g}{L}\sin\theta = 0.$$

This equation states that the rate of change of the rate of change (hence the *second* derivative) of the angle position plus the product of the ratio of the acceleration due to gravity and the length of the rod with the sine function of the angle must equal zero.

In this dynamical system, there are two state variables: the angle ϑ of the pendulum and the angular velocity ω (i.e., the first derivative of $\vartheta(t)$ with respect to time). We can consider angle, velocity, and time to be continuous. The two-dimensional state space (or phase space) (ϑ, ω) is periodic in ϑ. The evolution of the system indicates the state (i.e., angle and angular velocity) at time t: ($\vartheta(t)$, $\omega(t)$).

---

128 R is the set of *real numbers*. A real number is a continuous quantity that can represent a distance along a line, e.g., -2, ¾, $\sqrt{7}$, π.

129 See Morris W. Hirsch, Stephen Smale, and Robert L. Devaney, *Differential Equations, Dynamical Systems, and an Introduction to Chaos*, 3rd ed. (Waltham, MA: Academic Press, 2012) and Yuri Kuznetsov, *Elements of Applied Bifurcation Theory*, 3rd ed., Applied Mathematical Sciences 112 (New York: Springer, 2004).

Interestingly, even in this very simple case, no closed-form solution of this non-linear system is known. One has to assume that the pendulum is displaced a small amount, thus making the "small angle approximation" noting that $\sin\vartheta \approx \vartheta$ for small ϑ, or one must linearize the system locally around the equilibria. This is done by rewriting the original second-order differential equation as a system of two first-order differential equations, creating the Jacobian matrix,[130] and solving it at the equilibria.

Sir Isaac Newton's study of applied mathematics laid the first foundation for dynamical systems theory with his famous book, *Philosophiæ Naturalis Principia Mathematica*.[131] A significant step forward occurred with Henri Poincaré's research on celestial mechanics which contributed to the general, qualitative theory of dynamical systems. Poincaré's work established the approaches for the local and global analysis of nonlinear differential equations, e.g., the use of Poincaré maps, stability theory for fixed points and periodic orbits, and notions of stable and unstable manifolds.[132]

In the twentieth century, major advances in dynamical systems, both theoretical and practical, occurred in the USSR, UK, and USA.[133] These contributions have born great fruit in the study of biological, chemical, physical, engineering, social, and financial systems. From the chaotic motion of the moons of Pluto, to the Josephson (superconductive) effect in electrical engineering, to the Black–Scholes–Merton model of financial markets containing derivative investment instruments, dynamical systems theory has provided insights into some of the most complex phenomena.

Barbour employs process thought for his systematic synthesis of theology and science because he judges it to be consistent with the contemporary "evolutionary, many-leveled view of nature."[134] He admires Whitehead's attempt to formulate a "complete cosmology" that brings together "aesthetic, moral, and religious interests into relation with those concepts of the world which have their origin in natural science."[135] We believe that this noble objective can accomplished in the Catholic intellectual tradition with some of the enduring insights of Thomas Aquinas.

Aquinas builds on the philosophical insights of Aristotle who himself was natural scientist and concerned with developing a philosophical foundation consistent

130 Named after the brilliant, German mathematician Carl Gustav Jacob Jacobi. Interestingly, Jacobi was the first Jewish mathematician to be appointed professor at a German university. For more on his life and works, see Eric T. Bell, *Men of Mathematics* (New York: Simon & Schuster, 1986), chap. 18.

131 Isaac Newton, *Philosophiæ Naturalis Principia Mathematica* (London: Royal Society, 1687).

132 Jules Henri Poincaré, *Les Méthodes Nouvelles de La Mécanique Céleste*, 3 vols. (Paris: Gauthiers-Villars, 1899).

133 See Philip Holmes, "A Short History of Dynamical Systems Theory: 1885–2007," in *History of Mathematics*, ed. Vagn Lundsgaard Hansen and Jeremy Gray (Oxford: Eolss Publications, 2010), 115–138.

134 Barbour, *Religion and Science*, 284.

135 Whitehead, *Process and Reality*, vi.

with the natural world that he studied as a biologist. In the Thomistic view, echoed by William Carroll, "the self-sufficiency of nature, [and] the dynamism of natural processes which science discovers, does not mean that God is superfluous, since He is the cause of nature itself; He is a cause in such a way that nature has its own integrity, its own self-organizing principles."[136]

While some elements of Barbour's system, e.g., implying potency in God, are inconsistent with Thomistic philosophy and indeed Catholic doctrine, several of Barbour's concerns about the centrality of time, the interconnection of events, and the view of reality as an organic process can be addressed developing and applying concepts from the philosophy of nature.[137] In conclusion, many aspects of dynamicity in creation (physical and ontological) of interest to Barbour, which he attempts to study with his process philosophy, can be investigated in a Catholic context using Thomistic metaphysics and philosophy of nature, as well as dynamical systems theory, e.g., for mathematical modeling in the sciences.

2.3 God the Creator

Having acknowledged the dynamicity of the cosmos and proposed a Catholic alternative for addressing it in the study of creation, we move to an even more fundamental metaphysical question: Why does the cosmos exist?[138] *Ex nihilo nihil*

---

136 William E. Carroll, "Creation and the Foundations of Evolution," *Angelicum* 871, no. 1 (2010): 59.

137 Mariusz Tabaczek, OP's Thomistic response to/interpretation of the theory of evolution will be discussed in section 2.4. His research offers a clear and insightful application of traditional Thomistic concepts to modern questions in biology.

138 In antiquity, a number of diverse answers were given to this question. The Australian philosopher, John Kilcullen, concisely summarizes some of the most influential: "According to Aristotle, Plotinus, Avicenna and Averroes the universe has always existed; according to Aristotle the world is self-subsistent, in no sense created by God. According to Plotinus the world has always existed as an emanation from the First, which is its source or principle, as the sun is the source of light. Avicenna adopted this view, and said that God is therefore the creator of the world, meaning its source: so according to Avicenna the world is created eternally. According to Christians the world of creatures was created a finite time ago. Thomas Aquinas's position is that it is impossible for philosophy either to prove or disprove Christian belief on this point: philosophically it is possible that the world is created eternally, but philosophically it cannot be proved that the world is eternal. We know that the world is not eternal because the creator has revealed that fact to us in the Bible: that the world is not eternal is a truth of faith, not provable or disprovable by philosophy." John Kilcullen, "Thomas Aquinas, Summa Theologica (Cont.)" (Medieval Philosophy Lecture presented at the Macquarie University, Sydney, Australia, 1996),

fit.[139] The Australian priest and theologian, Denis Edwards, identifies the fundamental insight of Karl Rahner, SJ's theology of creation as the fact that God chooses to give Himself in love to what is not divine: creation.[140] In a beautiful articulation of Catholic belief in creation, John M. McDermott, SJ, writes, "God is the universe's intelligent and free creator, its efficient as well as final cause. He is an infinite act of *esse* who intuits material singulars. In Him matter's intelligibility is ultimately grounded even if human minds are stymied in seeking to penetrate its infinity."[141]

Barbour, on the other hand, follows Whitehead in asserting that God and the world are mutual collaborators. Whitehead himself asserts that "metaphysics requires that the relationships of God to the world should lie beyond the accidents of the will, and that they be founded upon the necessities of the nature of the world."[142] Barbour maintains that "creation 'out of nothing' is not a biblical concept [and that] most scholars hold that it is not stated or implied in the biblical narrative."[143]

This is no anodyne assertion and probably represents the nadir of his scholarship. While the majority of Catholic, Orthodox, and Protestant Christians would be flummoxed by this statement, it is not surprising that Barbour takes this position. Barbour concurs with Whitehead in declaring that God is not a creator, but an entity among entities who has a special role: providing a primordial

---

accessed May 21, 2018, http://pandora.nla.gov.au/pan/98441/200905041534/www.humanities.mq.edu.au/Ockham/x52t10.html.

139 Ratzinger engages the question of origins and existence with his logos-centric Christology: "The question is whether reason, or rationality, stands at the beginning of all things and is grounded in the basis of all things or not. The question is whether reality originated on the basis of chance and necessity (or, as Popper says, in agreement with Butler, on the basis of luck and cunning) and, thus, from what is irrational; that is, whether reason, being a chance by-product of irrationality and floating in an ocean of irrationality, is ultimately just as meaningless; or whether the principle that represents the fundamental conviction of Christian faith and of its philosophy remains true: *'In principio erat Verbum'*—at the beginning of all things stands the creative power of reason." Joseph Ratzinger, "Lecture at the Sorbonne: November 27, 1999," in *Truth and Tolerance*, trans. Henry Taylor (San Francisco: Ignatius Press, 2004), 181.

140 Denis Edwards, *How God Acts: Creation, Redemption, and Special Divine Action* (Minneapolis: Fortress Press, 2010), 39.

141 McDermott, "The Mystery of Matter," 999.

142 Alfred North Whitehead, *Adventures of Ideas* (New York: The Free Press, 1967), 168.

143 Barbour, *Issues in Science and Religion*, 384. The Anglican cleric and biochemist, Sjoerd Bonting, is another science-theology scholar that rejects the Biblical doctrine of creation *ex nihilo*. However, Bonting does not follow Barbour in utilizing a process metaphysics and theology. He asserts that God must have created the world from an already existing chaos. God is the great organizer, but chaos always exists. Bonting sees this chaos as the cause of evil, but also as a source of freedom

ground of order and novelty.[144] The process God is influenced by events in the cosmos.[145] He acts in the world by *being experienced* by nature—an experience akin to persuasion.[146]

Walter Kasper writes that "in contradistinction to polytheism, which stands for an inabrogable and ultimate disintegration of reality, biblical monotheism stands for the inner unity of reality and thus for the rationality of the world."[147] In Whitehead and Barbour's universe, the only basis of unity in the cosmos, to quote Clarke, "seems to be pushed back even beyond God to an inscrutable, necessary, and eternal amorphous force of 'creativity' or self-creativity (of which God is the primary and highest instance, but not, it seems, the ultimate source)."[148] Clarke notes how this is reminiscent of the ancient Greek's primordial goddess, Ανάγκη (*Anánke*),[149] who is a personification of necessity, inevitability, and compulsion.

From where does this creativity come? It is not an actuality in itself. From where does the *actus essendi* of entities in Barbour's universe come? Barbour's

---

and creativity. He calls his development "chaos theology." See Sjoerd Lieuwe Bonting, *Creation and Double Chaos: Science and Theology in Discussion* (Minneapolis: Fortress Press, 2009).

144 Whitehead cannot accept a doctrine of God the creator for at least two reasons. First, he resents what he describes as the "unfortunate habit" of paying God metaphysical compliments. Whitehead does not want to accept God as the "foundation of the metaphysical situation." He believes that this would necessarily imply God as the "origin of all evil." See Whitehead, *Science and the Modern World*, 258. Second, Whitehead posits his doctrine that every actual entity is a "self-creative act." W. Norris Clarke describes the Whiteheadian view as "a novel autonomous integration of the prior actual occasions." God is at most "co-creator" in ever "actual occasion." See Clarke, *The Philosophical Approach to God: A New Thomistic Perspective*, 96. The process philosopher, Lewis Ford, summarizes Whitehead's perspective stating that God's role in the world is to supply "the actuality's ideal of itself (the initial subjective aim) which functions as the principle of selective appropriation of past causes." Lewis Ford, "The Immutable God and Fr. Clarke," *New Scholasticism* 49, no. 2 (1975): 191. Process thinkers tend to posit a false dichotomy between God's omnipotence and man's freedom. The Catholic doctrine does not imply in any way a lack of freedom of man or a real role in causality by creatures. According to Clarke, God "communicates to creatures their own being and their own native power and supports them in its use, so that without Him they could neither exist nor act. But since He really has given them a share in His own power, they determine the use to which this power is put, even to use it against the express conditional will of God (=sin). This is a free self-limitation of God's exercise of His own unlimited power: a self-limitation inherent in every notion of participated perfection and hence part of the very logic of participation." Clarke, *The Philosophical Approach to God: A New Thomistic Perspective*, 123–124.

145 For a historical investigation by whom, where, when, how, and why the thesis of the creation of the world was introduced in philosophy, see Paul Clavier, *Ex Nihilo: L'introduction en philosophie du concept de création*, 2 vols. (Paris: Hermann, 2011).

146 Barbour, *Issues in Science and Religion*, 440–442.

147 Kasper, "The Logos Character of Reality," 275.

148 Clarke, *The Philosophical Approach to God: A New Thomistic Perspective*, 99.

149 Her name comes from the ancient Greek word, ἀνάγκη, meaning "force" or "constraint."

process thought does not provide answers to these questions. Whitehead's philosophical move seems to have "turned back the clock" of metaphysics to a pre-Neoplatonic position by reintroducing a dualism of God versus the world that cannot be resolved. How can "creativity" emerge without the *donum acti essendi* and without an "active causal influx"?[150] Whitehead and Barbour's position contrasts sharply with the ancient Christian profession of faith, expressed in the *Symbolum Apostolicum*, in one God who is creator of all that is, heaven and Earth.[151]

Without Divine revelation, an eternal, created universe is possible. Such a cosmos would have no first moment of existence but would still have a cause, a source of its *actus essendi*. In *De Aeternitate Mundi*, Thomas Aquinas argues that philosophically speaking, "it is clear that there is no contradiction in saying that something made by God has always existed."[152] Aquinas, as well as contemporary Catholic theologians, acknowledge that the *creatio mundi ex nihilo et cum tempore* is known by Divine revelation alone.

However, the very *fact* of creation is accessible to man through reason alone, as taught clearly by the Old and New Testaments. In the Book of Wisdom it is written,

> For all men who were ignorant of God were foolish by nature; and they were unable from the good things that are seen to know him who exists, nor did they recognize the craftsman while paying heed to his works; but they supposed that either fire or wind or swift air, or the circle of the stars, or turbulent water, or the luminaries of heaven were the gods that rule the world. If through delight in the beauty of these things men assumed them to be gods, let them know how much better than these is their Lord, for the author of beauty created them. And if men were amazed at their power and working, let them perceive from them how much more powerful is he who formed them. For from the greatness and beauty of created things comes a corresponding perception of their Creator. Yet these men are little to be blamed, for perhaps they go astray while seeking God and desiring to find him. For as they live among his works they keep searching, and they trust in what they see, because the things that are seen are beautiful. Yet again, not even they are to be excused; for if they had the power to know so much that they could investigate the world, how did they fail to find sooner the Lord of these things?[153]

---

150 Clarke, *The Philosophical Approach to God: A New Thomistic Perspective*, 101–103.

151 *Credo in Deum Patrem omnipotentem, Creatorem cæli et terræ*. As early as the second century, there was already unanimity among orthodox Christians about the doctrine of creation *ex nihilo*. For an example from the year 181, see Theophilus of Antioch, *Ad Autolcum*, 2, 4 (*Sources Chretiennes* 20, 102).

152 Thomas Aquinas, "De Aeternitate Mundi," in *Internet Medieval Sourcebook*, trans. Robert T. Miller (New York: Fordham University, 1997), accessed March 15, 2018, https://sourcebooks.fordham.edu/basis/aquinas-eternity.asp.

153 Wisdom 13:1–9(RSV).

In his Epistle to the Romans, Saint Paul writes,

> For what can be known about God is plain to them, because God has shown it to them. Ever since the creation of the world his invisible nature, namely, his eternal power and deity, has been clearly perceived in the things that have been made. So they are without excuse;[154]

The doctrine of creation is also *revealed* in Scripture. Belief in God the Creator is a major theme in the Old Testament.[155] In the Book of Genesis we read, "In the beginning God created[156] the heavens and the earth."[157] Michael Schmaus, posits that the *Sitz im Leben* of the creation stories in Genesis 1 and 2 is of "decisive significance" because "the texts rose out of the faith of the people in their covenant with God."[158] He further points out that the holy writer's point was not to explain "how" the world came to be using scientific language, but "'that' the world comes from God, and he stresses that because of this, God has complete sovereignty over it."[159] The God of the Book of Genesis is not some local Israelite deity, but the Lord of the whole universe.[160]

The prophet Isaiah proclaims, "For thus says the Lord, who created the heavens (he is God!), who formed the earth and made it (he established it; he did not create

---

154 Romans 1:19–20 (RSV).

155 The American Old Testament scholar, Richard J. Clifford, SJ, notes the central importance of the Biblical doctrine of creation. He argues against Gerhard von Rad's significant 1936 article that attempted to claim that faith in creation never attained to the status of an independent doctrine. Von Rad asserted that it was subordinated to soteriology. See Richard J. Clifford, "The Hebrew Scriptures and the Theology of Creation," *Theological Studies* 46 (1985): 507–523. The German Protestant pastor and Biblical scholar, Claus Westermann, concurs that the Old Testament possesses a clear teaching on Creator and creation. See Claus Westermann, *Creation*, trans. John J. Scullion (Philadelphia: Fortress Press, 1974), 175. The Swiss Reformed theologian and pastor, Walter Zimmerli's, position that wisdom theology (e.g., from Proverbs, Job, Sirach, etc.) is creation theology is widely accepted by many scholars. See Walther Zimmerli, "Ort und Grenze der Weisheit im Rahmen der altestamentlichen Theologie," in *Gottes Offenbarung, Gesammelte Aufsätze zum Alten Testament, Theologische Bücherei*, vol. 19 (Munich: Kaiser, 1963), 302. For a useful commentary, see Roland E. Murphy, *The Tree of Life: An Exploration of Biblical Wisdom Literature* (New York: The Anchor Bible Reference Library, 1990), 118.

156 "He created" in English comes from the Hebrew, ברא (*bārā'*). Schmaus argues that while the idea of creation *ex nihilo* is not explicit in this Hebrew word alone, the idea is implicit when one acknowledges that it is a "technical term in the theological language of the priests, and it is used exclusively for divine operations." Schmaus, *God and Creation: The Foundations of Christology*, 2:70.

157 Genesis 1:1 (RSV).

158 Schmaus, *God and Creation: The Foundations of Christology*, 2:68.

159 Ibid., 2:70.

160 Ibid., 2:72.

it a chaos, he formed it to be inhabited!): 'I am the Lord, and there is no other.'"[161] In addition, the Psalmist writes,

> By the word of the Lord the heavens were made, and all their host by the breath of his mouth. He gathered the waters of the sea as in a bottle; he put the deeps in storehouses. Let all the earth fear the Lord, let all the inhabitants of the world stand in awe of Him! For He spoke, and it came to be; He commanded, and it stood forth.[162]

Within Judith 13, we read, "Blessed be the Lord God, who created the heavens and the earth (ἔκτισε τοὺς οὐρανοὺς καὶ τὴν γῆν[163])."[164] Sirach 43 states, "For the Lord has made (*created*) all things (πάντα γὰρ ἐποίησεν ὁ κύριος), and to the godly he has granted wisdom."[165] In 2 Maccabees, the *ex nihilo* aspect of the teaching becomes explicit: "I beseech you, my child, to look at the heaven and the earth and see everything that is in them, and recognize that God *did not make them out of things that existed* (οὐκ ἐξ ὄντων[166]). Thus also mankind comes into being."[167]

Saint Paul, writing to the Church of Rome, states, "As it is written, 'I have made you the father of many nations'—in the presence of the God in whom he believed, who gives life to the dead and *calls into existence the things that do not exist* (καλοῦντος τὰ μὴ ὄντα ὡς ὄντα[168])."[169] With regard to the supremacy of Christ over creation, Paul's Epistle to the Colossians states, "For in him all things were created, in heaven and on earth, visible and invisible, whether thrones or dominions or principalities or authorities—all things were created through him and for him (τὰ πάντα δι' αὐτοῦ καὶ εἰς αὐτὸν ἔκτισται)."[170] The Letter to the Hebrews states, "In many and various ways God spoke of old to our fathers by the prophets; but in these

---

161 Isaiah 45:18 (RSV).

162 Psalm 33:6–9(RSV).

163 LXX, Rahlfs and Hanhart, *Septuaginta*, 996. It should be noted that this Greek word for creation-proper, ἔκτισε (dictionary form κτίζω), is found elsewhere in the Bible. For example, Tobit 8:5 uses the noun form, κτίσεις, to refer to creation or creatures. Sirach 24:8 uses the noun, κτίστης, to refer to the Creator. Forms of κτίζω are also found in the New Testament, e.g., Matthew 19:4, Mark 13:19, Romans 1:25, 1 Corinthians 11:9, Ephesians 2:10, Ephesians 2:15, Ephesians 3:9, Ephesians 4:24, Colossians 1:16, Colossians 3:10, 1 Timothy 4:3, Revelation 4:11, and Revelation 10:6.

164 Judith 13:18b (RSV). This pericope is verse 24 in the *Vulgata Antica*.

165 Sirach 43:33 (RSV).

166 LXX [A], Rahlfs and Hanhart, *Septuaginta*, 1117.

167 2 Maccabees 7:28 (RSV).

168 All Greek New Testament quotes are from the Institute for New Testament Textual Research, *Novum Testamentum Graece: Nestle-Aland*, 28th ed. (Peabody, MA: Hendrickson Publishers, Inc., 2012).

169 Romans 4:17 (RSV).

170 Colossians 1:16 (RSV).

last days he has spoken to us by a Son, whom he appointed the heir of all things, through whom also he *created the world* (ἐποίησεν τοὺς αἰῶνας[171])."[172] Later in the book, the holy author writes, "By faith we understand that the world was created by the word of God, so that *what is seen was made out of things which do not appear* (μὴ ἐκ φαινομένων τὸ βλεπόμενον γεγονέναι)."[173]

Finally, in the Book of Revelation, it is written, "Worthy art thou, our Lord and God, to receive glory and honor and power, *for thou didst create all things, and by thy will they existed and were created* (σὺ ἔκτισας τὰ πάντα, καὶ διὰ τὸ θέλημά σου ἦσαν καὶ ἐκτίσθησαν)."[174] While Barbour may not have accepted the canonicity of the Deuterocanonical books, there are abundant other Biblical sources that speak of God the Creator giving existence to the world. Barbour's insouciant stance toward the Biblical witness on creation is perplexing.

In addition, Christian belief in creation *ex nihilo* goes back to the earliest Tradition of the Church. For example, Tertullian (ca. 155–ca. 240), Hippolytus of Rome (170–240), and Origen (ca. 184–ca. 253) all defend this teaching in the post-Apostolic period.[175] Ernan McMullin shows how in the face of Neo-Platonic assertions of an ungenerated principle independent of God, and Gnostic belief in lesser "perfect" beings who were responsible for the "imperfections" of creation, the Fathers formulated a Biblically-justified doctrine of creation. McMullin identifies Augustine of Hippo as the crucial Father whose Biblically-inspired metaphysics of creation was unambiguously *ex nihilo*.[176]

In fact, creation properly speaking, must be *ex nihilo* according to Thomas Aquinas. Aquinas specifically asks whether to create is to make something from nothing. He writes,

> We must consider not only the emanation of a particular being from a particular agent, but also the emanation of all being from the universal cause, which is God; and this emanation we designate by the name of creation. Now what proceeds by particular emanation, is not presupposed to that emanation; as when a man is generated, he was not before, but man is made from 'not-man,' and white from 'not-white.' Hence if the

---

171 This Greek word properly means "the ages." It is often used to signifiy "in perpetuity," e.g., "for the ages and ages." By implication, it signifies the world, hence the RSV translation of "created the world." This intimate link of time and the world is consistent with the doctrine of *creatio ex nihilo et cum tempore*.

172 Hebrews 1:1–2(RSV).

173 Hebrews 11:3 (RSV).

174 Revelation 4:11 (RSV).

175 See Gerhard May, *Creatio Ex Nihilo: The Doctrine of "Creation Out of Nothing" in Early Christian Thought*, trans. A.S. Worrall (Edinburgh: T&T Clark International, 2004), 178.

176 Ernan McMullin, "Creation Ex Nihilo: Early History," in *Creation and the God of Abraham*, ed. David B. Burrell et al. (Cambridge: Cambridge University Press, 2010), 11–23.

emanation of the whole universal being from the first principle be considered, it is impossible that any being should be presupposed before this emanation. For nothing is the same as no being. Therefore as the generation of a man is from the 'not-being' which is 'not-man,' so creation, which is the emanation of all being, is from the 'not-being' which is 'nothing'.[177]

This implies no contradiction. It is beneficial to read Aquinas' reply to that objection *in extenso*:

When anything is said to be made from nothing, this preposition 'from' [*ex*] does not signify the material cause, but only order; as when we say, 'from morning comes midday,' i.e., after morning is midday. But we must understand that this preposition 'from' [*ex*] can comprise the negation implied when I say the word 'nothing,' or can be included in it. If taken in the first sense, then we affirm the order by stating the relation between what is now and its previous non-existence. But if the negation includes the preposition, then the order is denied, and the sense is, 'It is made from nothing, i.e., it is not made from anything,' as if we were to say, 'He speaks of nothing,' because he does not speak of anything. And this is verified in both ways, when it is said, that anything is made from nothing. But in the first way this preposition 'from' [*ex*] implies order, as has been said in this reply. In the second sense, it imports the material cause, which is denied.[178]

In an address to the Pontifical Academy of Sciences, Benedict XVI offers helpful context to the Church's teaching on creation. He emphasizes the essential aspect of the Catholic doctrine that creation is not merely "movement" or "mutation":

To state that the foundation of the cosmos and its developments is the provident wisdom of the Creator is not to say that creation has only to do with the beginning of the history of the world and of life. It implies, rather, that the Creator founds these developments and supports them, underpins them and sustains them continuously. Thomas Aquinas taught that the notion of creation must transcend the horizontal origin of the unfolding of events, which is history, and consequently all our purely naturalistic ways of thinking and speaking about the evolution of the world. Thomas observed that creation is neither a movement nor a mutation. It is instead the foundational and continuing relationship that links the creature to the Creator, for he is the cause of every being and all becoming (cf. *Summa Theologiæ*, I, q.45, a. 3).[179]

---

177 Aquinas, *Summa Theologiæ*, I, Q 45, A 1.

178 Ibid, I, Q 45, A 1.

179 Benedict XVI, "Address of His Holiness Benedict XVI to Members of the Pontifical Academy of Sciences on the Occasion of Their Plenary Assembly" (Clementine Hall, Vatican City State, October 31, 2008), accessed April 24, 2018, https://w2.vatican.va/content/benedictxvi/en/speeches/2008/october/documents/hf_ben-xvi_spe_20081031_academy-sciences.html.

Contemporary, Catholic fundamental theology emphasizes that Divine revelation is not merely propositional, but dialogical/relational. Creation—natural revelation—certainly has this relational aspect.

While denying the classical belief in God the Creator, Barbour does not adequately address the question of why there is a universe. Why / how is there something rather than nothing? Catholics may ask, Why did God create?[180] This was a question engaged by the First Vatican Council. *Dei Filius* states,

> This one true God, by his goodness and almighty power, not with the intention of increasing his happiness, nor indeed of obtaining happiness, but in order to manifest his perfection by the good things which he bestows on what he creates, by an absolutely free plan, together from the beginning of time brought into being from nothing the twofold created order, that is the spiritual and the bodily, the angelic and the earthly, and thereafter the human which is, in a way, common to both since it is composed of spirit and body.[181]

Ernan McMullin eloquently and concisely summarizes the Council's teaching: "God's purpose in creating the world is to manifest and communicate His perfections."[182]

John Haught contributes to the discussion by writing that "the universe is neither self-originating nor necessary. The universe is the contingent product of God's unlimited graciousness ... The ultimate foundation of the world's existence is the goodness and power of God."[183] The German Reformed theologian, Jürgen Moltmann, notes that it is a sign of God's humility and kenotic love that He allows something/someone else to exist at all.[184] This kenotic act of creation, according to the Anglican clergyman and theologian, Simon Oliver, "is analogically related to God's kenotic self-relation" in the mystery of the Holy Trinity.[185]

In fact, the First Vatican Council promulgated five canons on the doctrine of creation that concisely summarize Catholic belief. While some modern readers

---

180 Luis Ferrer Ladaria, SJ's analysis of the question emphasizes the fact that God created the world freely and for His glory. For more, see Luis F. Ladaria, *Introducción a La Antropología Teológica* (Estella, Spain: Editorial Verbo Divino, 1993), 50–54.

181 First Vatican Council, "Dei Filius," chap. 1, no. 3.

182 Ernan McMullin, "Science and the Catholic Tradition," in *Science and Religion: New Perspectives on the Dialogue*, ed. Ian G. Barbour (New York: Harper & Row, 1968), 189.

183 John Haught, *Christianity and Science: Toward a Theology of Nature* (Maryknoll, NY: Orbis Books, 2007), 108.

184 Jürgen Moltmann, *God in Creation: A New Theology of Creation and the Spirit of God*, trans. Margaret Kohl (San Francisco: Harper & Row, 1985), 88.

185 Simon Oliver, "Trinity, Motion, and Creation Ex Nihilo," in *Creation and the God of Abraham*, ed. David B. Burrell et al. (Cambridge: Cambridge University Press, 2010), 151.

may not be comfortable with the strong language of *anathemata*, they should not dismiss these and other dogmas:

1) If anyone denies the one true God, creator and lord of things visible and invisible: let him be anathema.

2) If anyone is so bold as to assert that there exists nothing besides matter: let him be anathema.

3) If anyone says that the substance or essence of God and that of all things are one and the same: let him be anathema.

4) If anyone says that finite things, both corporal and spiritual, or at any rate, spiritual, emanated from the divine substance; or that the divine essence, by the manifestation and evolution of itself becomes all things or, finally, that God is a universal or indefinite being which by self-determination establishes the totality of things distinct in genera, species, and individuals: let him be anathema.

5) If anyone does not confess that the world and all things which are contained in it, both spiritual and material, were produced, according to their whole substance, out of nothing by God; or holds that God did not create by his will free from all necessity, but as necessarily as he necessarily loves himself; or denies that the world was created for the glory of God: let him be anathema.[186]

These canons summarize Catholic belief in God the Creator, the existence of the spiritual realm, and the essential distinction between God and the world. Unfortunately, Barbour does not measure up in any of the three areas of concern. Barbour denies the Biblical teaching of *creatio ex nihilo*. Barbour also rebuffs the existence of spiritual realities in his rejection of distinctions such as living and non-living, human and non-human, mind and matter.[187] We concur with Polkinghorne that Barbour's process theology is a "very qualified form of panentheism."[188] This particular issue will be discussed later in the chapter in Section 2.5.

Christian belief in creation *ex nihilo* is also fully compatible with contemporary physical cosmology. Big bang theories based on the Friedmann-Lemaître-Robertson-Walker models[189] describe the evolution and structure of the universe but cannot speak about ultimate origins. The Vatican astronomer, William R. Stoeger, SJ, points out that

---

186 First Vatican Council, "Dei Filius," Canons I:1–5.

187 Barbour, *Religion and Science*, 289.

188 Polkinghorne, *Scientists as Theologians*, 33.

189 For a systematic presentation of a 1 + 3 covariant approach to studying the geometry, dynamics, and observational properties of relativistic cosmological models, see George F.R. Ellis and Henk Van Elst, *Cosmological Models: Cargèse Lectures 1998* (Cape Town, South Africa: University of Cape Town, 2008), accessed July 21, 2018, https://arxiv.org/pdf/gr-qc/9812046.pdf.

the basic reason why *creatio ex nihilo* is complementary to any scientific explanation, including whatever quantum cosmology theoretically and observationally reveals about the "earliest" stages of our universe—or multiverse—and not an alternative, is that it does not and cannot substitute for whatever the sciences discover about origins. It simply provides an explanation or ground for the existence and basic order of whatever the sciences reveal. The Creator empowers or enables the physical processes—including whatever primordial originating processes and entities, whatever they are—to be what they are.[190]

While Barbour cannot accept a *creatio ex nihilo*, he does strongly affirm a belief in *creatio continua*,[191] again, following Whitehead's doctrine of "creative advance."[192] On this issue, there is some agreement with Catholic thought. There is a diversity of opinions by theologians on how God accomplishes *creatio continua*. Aquinas' position was that God gave a tendency to exist in bestowing *esse* to the creature. Bonaventure posited that God carries out two distinct acts from the point of view of creatures: the initial bestowal of being and then the conservation of that being in existence.[193] Summarizing the Thomistic position with which we concur, William Carroll writes,

It is true that material bodies tend to corrupt, but matter itself, prime matter is incorruptible. The whole of the universe, considered in itself, has its own being, and tends to continue in being. Of itself, it has no potency, or tendency to non-being. However true it may be to say that a creature would be absolutely nothing without the creative causality of God, still, the creature really has its own being: its own autonomy, and, in a way its own self-sufficiency.[194]

McMullin nicely encapsulates the fundamental Catholic belief in a chapter included in a book edited by Barbour:

Since He is the cause not only of the essence of things, but of their very existence, His creative activity must endure in a positive manner. Without this conservation the world would simply cease to exist. Hence we say that God continually creates the world. His activity never ceases and the products of this creative activity continually manifest the divine perfections.[195]

190 William R. Stoeger, "The Big Bang, Quantum Cosmology, and Creatio Ex Nihilo," in *Creation and the God of Abraham*, ed. David B. Burrell et al. (Cambridge: Cambridge University Press, 2010), 169.

191 Barbour, *Issues in Science and Religion*, 383.

192 Whitehead, *Process and Reality*, 125.

193 Bonaventure, *Commentaria in Quatuor Libros Sententiarum Magistri Petri Lombardi: Tomus II - In Secundum Librum Sententiarum* (Quaracchi, Italia: Ex typographia Colegii S. Bonaventurae, 1885), Dist. 37, A 1, Q 2, accessed April 25, 2018, http://archive.org/details/doctorisseraphic02bona.

194 Carroll, "Creation and the Foundations of Evolution," 58.

195 McMullin, "Science and the Catholic Tradition," 190.

However, there are problems with Barbour's conception of God and *creatio continua*. Because Barbour denies God as creator, properly speaking, and places Him ontologically only slightly above man, Barbour gives them both co-responsibility in *creatio continua*. However, only God can create. Man can only manufacture or produce (*facere*). It is worth quoting at some length Thomas Aquinas' argument:

> It sufficiently appears at the first glance, according to what precedes, that to create can be the action of God alone. For the more universal effects must be reduced to the more universal and prior causes. Now among all effects the most universal is being itself: and hence it must be the proper effect of the first and most universal cause, and that is God. Hence also it is said (*De Causis prop.*, *iii*) that "neither intelligence nor the soul gives us being, except inasmuch as it works by divine operation." Now to produce being absolutely, not as this or that being, belongs to creation. Hence it is manifest that creation is the proper act of God alone. It happens, however, that something participates the proper action of another, not by its own power, but instrumentally, inasmuch as it acts by the power of another; as air can heat and ignite by the power of fire. And so some have supposed that although creation is the proper act of the universal cause, still some inferior cause acting by the power of the first cause, can create. And thus Avicenna asserted that the first separate substance created by God created another after itself, and the substance of the world and its soul; and that the substance of the world creates the matter of inferior bodies. And in the same manner the Master says (*Sent. iv*, D, 5) that God can communicate to a creature the power of creating, so that the latter can create ministerially, not by its own power. But such a thing cannot be, because the secondary instrumental cause does not participate in the action of the superior cause, except inasmuch as by something proper to itself it acts dispositively to the effect of the principal agent. If therefore it affects nothing, according to what is proper to itself, it is used to no purpose; nor would there be any need of certain instruments for certain actions. Thus we see that a saw, in cutting wood, which it does by the property of its own form, produces the form of a bench, which is the proper effect of the principal agent. Now the proper effect of God creating is what is presupposed to all other effects, and that is absolute being. Hence nothing else can act dispositively and instrumentally to this effect, since creation is not from anything presupposed, which can be disposed by the action of the instrumental agent. So therefore it is impossible for any creature to create, either by its own power or instrumentally—that is, ministerially. And above all it is absurd to suppose that a body can create, for no body acts except by touching or moving; and thus it requires in its action some pre-existing thing, which can be touched or moved, which is contrary to the very idea of creation.[196]

In conclusion, the Protestant pastor and theologian, James A. Fowler, beautifully captures the orthodox Christian belief: "God, the non-contingent Being, created all things to be contingent upon Himself. The created order is not self-existent, self-generative, self-sustaining, autonomous, independent, eternal or infinite. Only God is such; and what God is only God is."[197] God created "from pure freedom and pure love."[198] It is regrettable that Barbour does not subject his process thought to the Biblical doctrine of *creatio ex nihilo*. As a Christian theologian, he goes *ultra vires* when he allows his metaphysics to "overwhelm" revelation. Scripture must be the soul of theology.[199] Having critically engaged Barbour's understanding of God the Creator, we now turn our attention to the specific *creatio hominis*.

2.4 Creation of Man

It is appropriate at this point to begin to examine Barbour's understanding of the creation of man. The conclusion of the first chapter of the Book of Genesis highlights the special status of mankind in creation.[200] In a clear articulation of the Catholic theological tradition, Schmaus writes,

> God did not create the world simply to have it on hand, but because he wanted to enter into communication and conversation with it. This has meaning only if we see man as the essential element in creation. It implies that creation without man would be senseless. Here we find the beginnings of that personal ontology, that I-Thou metaphysics of personality ... which distinguishes Old Testament thought from that of the Greeks.[201]

According to Schmaus, "in his self-giving love God desires to grant to the non-divine a share in the fulfilling dialogue of his own inner divine life."[202] *Bonum est diffusivum sui.* God the Creator prepares all of creation for the benefit of Adam and Eve and to give Him glory. Our first parents were to be in communion with God and responsible stewards of His work.

The second chapter of Genesis, emphasizes the unique, spiritual dimension of the human person: "The Lord God formed man of dust from the ground, and breathed into his nostrils the breath of life; and man became a living being."[203] Barbour would certainly concur with Schmaus that "the concept of a purely material creation devoid of the spiritual principle would not do justice to the meaning of creation."[204] While the existence of the soul is accessible *sola*

---

197 James A. Fowler, *In the Beginning God Created* (Fallbrook: C.I.Y. Publishing, 2007), 39–40.
198 Kasper, "The Logos Character of Reality," 282.
199 Second Vatican Council, *Dei Verbum*, 24.
200 See Genesis 1:26–31 (RSV).
201 Schmaus, *God and Creation: The Foundations of Christology*, 2:71.
202 Ibid., 2:90.
203 Genesis 2:7 (RSV).
204 Schmaus, *God and Creation: The Foundations of Christology*, 2:91.

ratio,[205] the fuller, Christian understanding of the human soul relies on Divine revelation. Therefore, Catholics profess the soul to be "substantial, spiritual, immortal, individual, and unique."[206]

In a 2008 address to a plenary gathering of the Pontifical Academy of Sciences, Benedict XVI highlighted the important fact of the *spiritual* nature of the human person:

> The distinction between a simple living being and a spiritual being that is *capax Dei*, points to the existence of the intellective soul of a free transcendent subject. Thus the Magisterium of the Church has constantly affirmed that "every spiritual soul is created immediately by God—it is not 'produced' by the parents—and also that it is immortal"

205 Aristotle points out that man has knowledge of two types of things, particulars and universals. Universals have no materiality, e.g., "orangeness," "kindness," and "priesthood." Universal concepts cannot be instantiated as a particular in any material substrate, e.g., brain tissue or a "brain state." The American neurosurgeon, Michael Egnor, identifies that brain states are intrinsically particulars, and concepts are universals. Therefore, a concept cannot be a particular brain state. While concepts can have a material representation, representation presupposes that which it represents. A representation is inherently a representation of some particular. Consequently, the representation cannot be the total instantiation of that object. If the representation were the complete instantiation of a particular, the representation is the particular itself, not a representation. If a concept is represented in a brain state, then that concept is presupposed by the representation; therefore one hasn't explained the concept. One has merely explained the representation. Even if a materialist could demonstrate that a concept is represented in a brain state, e.g., as an accidental form (rather than a substantial form), he cannot explain the concept "materialistically." The material representation of a concept by accidental form presupposes the concept! For more details on this line of argumentation, see Michael Egnor, "Aristotle on the Immateriality of Intellect and Will," *Evolution News & Science Today*, January 26, 2015, accessed November 8, 2018, https://evolutionnews.org/2015/01/aristotle_on_th/. Edward Feser also offers a compelling syllogistic argument in favor of the immateriality of the rational faculty. 1. Formal thought processes can have exact or unambiguous conceptual content (if not we couldn't do natural science). 2. Nothing material can have exact or unambiguous conceptual content. 3. Therefore, formal thought processes are not material. Edward Feser, "The Immateriality of the Intellect" (Lecture presented at the The Spiritual Soul and Contemporary Neuroscience: A Thomistic Perspective Conference, The Pontifical University of Saint Thomas Aquinas, December 1, 2018). Ultimately, the mind thinks through the material cause of the brain. The mathematician and cyberneticist, Norbert Wiener writes, "The mechanical brain does not secrete thought 'as the liver does bile,' as the earlier materialists claimed, nor does it put it out in the form of energy, as the muscles puts out its activity. Information is information, not matter or energy. No materialism which does not admit this can survive at the present day." Wiener, *Cybernetics, Second Edition*, 132.
206 Haffner, *Mystery of Creation*, 107.

(CCC 366). This points to the distinctiveness of anthropology, and invites exploration of it by modern thought.[207]

Ratzinger also points out how "in the language of the Bible the word 'body'— 'This is my Body'—does not mean just a body, in contradistinction to the spirit, for instance. Body, in the language of the Bible, denotes rather the whole person, in whom body and spirit are indivisible one."[208] Unfortunately, Ian Barbour misses this fact because he rejects Thomistic metaphysics for his systematic synthesis of theology and science. He wants to avoid what he perceives as a dualist view of reality: man as matter *and* spirit.[209] However, Catholic anthropology is hylomorphic, not dualistic. The soul is coextensive with the body.

To understand the hylomorphic theory it is useful to look at the etymology. The Greek word, ὕλη (*húle*), denotes matter, and μορφή (*morphé*) denotes form. In Aristotle's ontology, all material substances are composed of two co-principles: substantial form and prime matter. Prime matter is the ultimate subject of any change. As McDermott puts it, "classical hylopmorphism binds matter, the principle of individuality, to a universal form in producing a composite nature, a principle of rest and activity, which develops according to its own internal laws."[210]

These philosophical concepts enjoy a special status in the Catholic Tradition as they have been used to formally define dogmas. For example, the Church proclaimed the dogma that the human soul is the substantial form of the body at the Council of Vienne:

> Moreover, with the approval of the said Council, we reject as erroneous and contrary to the truth of the Catholic faith every doctrine or proposition rashly asserting that the substance of the rational or intellectual soul is not of itself and essentially the form of the human body, or casting doubt on this matter. In order that all may know the truth of the faith in its purity and all error may be excluded, we define that anyone who presumes henceforth to assert defend or hold stubbornly that the rational or

---

207 Benedict XVI, "Address of His Holiness Benedict XVI to Members of the Pontifical Academy of Sciences on the Occasion of Their Plenary Assembly."

208 Joseph Ratzinger, *God Is Near Us: The Eucharist, the Heart of Life*, ed. Stephan Otto Horn and Vinzenz Pfnur, trans. Henry Taylor (San Francisco: Ignatius Press, 2003), 79.

209 In Karl Rahner, *Hominisation: The Evolutionary Origin of Man as a Theological Problem*, trans. W.T. O'Hara, Quaestiones Disputatae 13 (Freiburg-im-Breisgau: Herder and Herder, 1965), Rahner develops a fundamental theology of the origin of man as well as his existence, and future, in light of evolutionary theory. He engages issues in causality, the distinction between spirit and matter, the unity of spirit and matter, and the creation of the spiritual soul. Rahner emphasizes that the fulfillment of man's existence is only possible through God's self-gift, not only in heaven, but also in the present in seminal form through His grace.

210 McDermott, "Matter, Modern Science, and God," 481.

intellectual soul is not the form of the human body of itself and essentially, is to be considered a heretic.[211]

In addition, the first section of the Constitutions of the Fourth Lateran Council, affirms the doctrine that God, "at the beginning of time created from nothing both spiritual and corporeal creatures, that is to say angelic and earthly, and then created human beings composed as it were of both spirit and body in common."[212] This teaching was also echoed at the First Vatican Council in light of nineteenth century pantheism and materialism.[213]

The theory of hylomorphism is certainly comprehensible in itself, but due to the limitations of the finite and imperfect human intellect, it is not understood absolutely. In this way, it is like knowledge of God. God is knowable in Himself but the human intellect cannot completely comprehend Him in His majesty— *Deus quoad se vs Deus quoad nos*. One notes that the human mind moves from things more "noble" to us but more "confused" in themselves (e.g., physical creation) to things more "noble" in themselves and less "confused" in themselves (e.g., the spiritual realm).[214] The intellectual move from creation to Creator is elegantly expressed by the Apostle Paul in his Letter to the Romans: "For what can be known about God is plain to them, because God has shown it to them. Ever since the creation of the world his invisible nature, namely, his eternal power and deity, has been clearly perceived in the things that have been made."[215]

Thomas Aquinas acknowledges the soul-body tension. He writes that "the intellect, which is the principle of intellectual operation, is the form of the human body."[216] Nonetheless, he admits that the human person also engages in activities that exceed the physical body, e.g., intellection itself.[217] Aquinas attempts to reconcile these positions by positing that the soul has its own *actus essendi*. Furthermore,

---

211 Council of Vienne, "Decrees," in *Decrees of the Ecumenical Councils*, ed. Norman P. Tanner, vol. 1, 2 vols. (Washington, DC: Georgetown University Press, 1990), Decree 1.

212 Lateran Council IV, "Constitutions," in *Decrees of the Ecumenical Councils*, ed. Norman P. Tanner, vol. 1, 2 vols. (Washington, DC: Georgetown University Press, 1990), 1.

213 "Dei Filius," chap. 1, no. 3.

214 "*Sed altera scientia est magis bona et honorabilis altera dupliciter. Aut quia est magis certa, ut dictum est: unde dicit secundum certitudinem, aut ex eo quod meliorum, illorum scilicet quae sunt in sua natura bona, et mirabiliorum, idest illorum quorum causa ignoratur, propter utraque, idest propter haec duo animae historiam.*" Thomas Aquinas, *Commentary on Aristotle's De Anima*, trans. Kenelm Foster and Sylvester Humphries (New Haven: Yale University Press, 1951), Book 1, Lectio 1, § 6 accessed March 14, 2018, http://dhspriory.org/thomas/english/DeAnima.htm.

215 Romans 1:19–20 (RSV).

216 Aquinas, *Summa Theologiæ*, I, Q 76, A 1.

217 Thomas Aquinas, *Summa Contra Gentiles*, ed. Joseph Kenny, trans. James F. Anderson (New York: Hanover House, 1957), II, 56.

he suggests that the soul communicates this act of existence to the body. However, the soul without the body is not a complete substance; the act of understanding of the intellect requires physical organs. Consequently, prior to the resurrection of the body, the souls in heaven cannot "know" without the supernatural infusion of knowledge by God.[218]

Barbour simply wants to avoid this tension by denying the spirituality of the soul.[219] But if everything is material, creation is pure potency, i.e., it is all flux. By assuming that *complementary* principles—body and soul—are dualistic, Barbour himself falls into dualism; he is caught *in flagrante delicto* introducing dualism.

Unfortunately, Barbour also does not acknowledge the reality and salvation of body and soul, a very important issue for Christian theology.[220] Stanley Jaki persuasively shows how these mysteries are intimately connected with the mystery of Christ and our salvation:

> [Christian philosophy] was a philosophy propelled by the gigantic historic fact of Christ, taken for that unsurpassable unity of mind and matter which became known under such words as *incarnation* and *hypostatic union*. A chief and favorable consideration of that philosophy devolved from the fact that it implied consciousness of its being anchored in Christ, the God-become-man, who remained alive as a man even when his body lay dead for three days in the grave. No intellectually sensitive Christian could recall Christ's words to the good thief—"Today you will be with me in paradise"—and not think of them as a promise with absolute certainty that the

---

218 Ibid, II, 69.

219 Barbour, *Issues in Science and Religion*, 360–364.

220 *Character sacramentalis* is a foundational notion in Sacramental theology to explain Baptism, Confirmation, and Holy Orders. It is a supernatural seal impressed upon the soul and is ineffaceable. With regard to the long history of the doctrine, Michael James Ryan writes, "Though first solemnly defined by the Council of Trent, it had already been officially declared in the Council of Florence; and it was the unanimous opinion of all theologians, long before the time of Wyclif, who questioned it. It was set forth with the utmost explicitness by St. Augustine in the controversies of the fifth century ... At the end of the second century we find in the work known as "Excerpta Theodoti" (n. *lxxvi*), generally attributed to Clement of Alexandria, historical evidence of the existence of the doctrine. As the coin circulating in Judea in Christ's time bore the image and superscription of Cæsar, so, the writer says, does the believer obtain through Christ the name of God as an inscription, and the Holy Spirit as an image, upon his soul; as even brute animals by a mark show their owner and by a mark are distinguished, so the believing soul, which has received the seal of truth, bears the marks (*stigmata*) of Christ." Michael James Ryan, "Character (in Catholic Theology)," *The Catholic Encyclopedia* (New York: Robert Appleton Company, 1908), accessed November 8, 2018, http://newadvent.org/cathen/03586a.htm. It is very unclear how one could maintain this Catholic doctrine if one accepts Barbour's metaphysics. With all the cosmos in constant flux, the notion of a permanent sacramental seal (permanent both in time and eternity) seems impossible.

most precious part of this repentant wretch would survive the imminent destruction of his body.[221]

The crucial link between anthropology and Christology is highlighted in one of the most oft cited sections of the Second Vatican Council's Pastoral Constitution on the Church, *Gaudium et Spes*: "Christ, the final Adam, by the revelation of the mystery of the Father and His love, fully reveals man to man himself and makes his supreme calling clear. It is not surprising, then, that in Him all the aforementioned truths find their root and attain their crown."[222] Benedict XVI beautifully echoes this belief, pointing back to Genesis 1 and the creation of Adam: "In Jesus Christ the creation of man first attains its true goal; in Him the Creator's conception of man finds its full expression; in Him the beast that lurks in all of us is overcome for the first time, and what is truly human is made present for us."[223]

One area where Barbour concurs with Jaki, and with the broader Catholic intellectual tradition, is the fact of man's complete dependence on God. Utilizing Thomistic language, William Carroll writes, "The complete dependence of the creature on the Creator means that there is a kind of priority of non-being to being in any creature, but this priority is not fundamentally temporal. It is, as Aquinas said, a priority according to nature, not according to time."[224] Barbour appreciates the fact that the ground and order of science, and the cosmos itself, is from God:

> Man is seen as totally dependent upon God at every moment of his existence. Everything that he is or makes himself to be, the very fact that he is at all, all these find their ultimate ground in the Creator. Man accepts things as they are, tries to understand them and modify them. But the whole order of space and time, of man and materials, takes its being from One who stands alone, who conserves the world in being and does not merely modify it. The scientific quest itself takes on its full significance only within this context of *creation*, of the universe as God's handiwork. This insight is probably the principal legacy that the Judeo-Christian tradition has bequeathed to philosophy.[225]

The metaphysics underlying a systematic synthesis between theology and science should be able to intelligently describe the order and structure of creation. For Barbour, it must also be able to incorporate the contemporary theory

221 Jaki, *The Savior of Science*, 173.

222 Second Vatican Council, *Gaudium et Spes*, 22.

223 Benedict XVI, *Dogma and Preaching: Applying Christian Doctrine to Daily Life* (San Francisco: Ignatius Press, 2011), 278.

224 William E. Carroll, "Creation, Evolution, and Thomas Aquinas," *Revue des Questions Scientifiques* 171, no. 4 (2000): n14.

225 Barbour, "Science and Religion Today," 40–41.

of evolution.[226] Recently, the Polish theologian, Mariusz Tabaczek, OP, has done very impressive work showing how Thomistic concepts can be developed and applied in light of modern evolutionary biology. Tabaczek acknowledges that neither Aristotle nor Thomas were aware of the evolution of species. Nonetheless, he argues articulately that their systems of thought remain open to this new data.[227]

Starting with Aristotle's theory of hylomorphism, Tabaczek emphasizes how

> Aristotle notices that substantial form persists through accidental change, but this in no way excludes the possibility of a process in which a thing can change as a whole. It is possible that a thing may change in a way that brings about not only an alteration of an existent being, but also the coming-to-be of a new substance. In other words, when the primary matter of an already existing being is properly disposed, it may receive a new substantial form in a process of the coming-to-be of a new substance, that is "generation" or "corruption." What is more, this idea of the proper disposition of matter is related to a natural tendency of matter to be in-formed by more perfect forms. Aristotle recognizes an ascending gradation in the perfection of beings in nature.[228]

Tabaczek's analysis offers a basis with which to specify some metaphysical aspects of the process of evolution. Evolution can be understood as a series of accidental changes in the structure of DNA. Such changes to the genetic material would certainly have implications for the disposition of prime matter. These changes could foreseeably create the conditions for a specific moment at which the prime matter of the male and female gametes, when fused, is not disposed to the old substantial form of the parents (e.g., species Γ), but to a new substantial form (e.g., species Δ).[229]

Tabaczek acknowledges that it would likely take many mutations (the results guided by natural selection) to produce such an effect. In addition, the actual event of speciation would be extremely difficult to observe. However, these issues do not exclude the possibility of such events. Tabaczek suggests the concrete situation "where members of a species migrate to a new environment and can be modified gradually in subsequent generations, to the point where they can no longer mate with the descendants of their ancestors."[230]

His exploration of this topic is impressive, especially in how he goes beyond offering a metaphysical explanation in terms of material and formal causes. Tabaczek

---

226 Barbour, *Religion and Science*, 104.
227 Mariusz Tabaczek, "Thomistic Response to the Theory of Evolution: Aquinas on Natural Selection and the Perfection of the Universe," *Theology and Science* 13, no. 3 (July 3, 2015): 325.
228 Ibid., 327.
229 Ibid.
230 Ibid.

identifies that for Aristotle, "chance" is a strange accidental cause because it lacks a τέλος (*télos*) and is therefore non-deterministic:

> Chance events are due to nothing in the substance or *per se* cause that happens to concur with these unexpected occurrences. And yet, as an accidental cause, chance occurs always and only in reference to a *per se* cause. Therefore, chance for Aristotle is posterior and inherently related to nature (φύσις) and intellect (νοῦς), and thus it is associated with formal and final causality rather than with material necessity.[231]

Tabaczek's application of Aristotelian principles to Neo-Darwinist theory is helpful in understanding the character of random mutations. Mutations of genetic material provides the *necessary but not sufficient conditions* for evolution. A mutation may simply create a cancerous tumor that will destroy the organism. Tabaczek notes that mutations have

> a *per accidens* character in reference to the *per se* cause of living beings that strive to survive and produce offspring. The acceptance of this plural notion of causality helps us understand that the absence of a direct efficient cause of mutations does not exclude other kinds of causality from being active. Aristotle's philosophy of nature reminds us that we need to take formal and final causality into account in our attempt to explain the nature of evolutionary changes.[232]

While acknowledging that it would be anachronistic to claim that Thomas Aquinas had a formal theory of biological evolution, there is a very interesting section of Aquinas' *Commentary on Aristotle's Physics* in which he seems to suggest a notion of natural selection:

> For example, one might say that because of the necessity of matter some teeth, i.e., the front teeth, happen to be sharp and suitable for cutting food, and the molars happen to be broad and useful for grinding food. Nevertheless, nature did not make the teeth such and so for the sake of these utilities. Rather after teeth have been made by nature in such a way as they develop from the necessity of matter, it is accidental that they acquired such a form. And once this form exists, this utility follows. And the same thing can be said of all other parts which seem to have some determinate form for the sake of some end. But one might say that such utilities follow always or in many cases, and what is always or in most cases suitable exists by nature. In order to forestall this objection they say that from the beginning of the formation of the world the four elements were joined in the constitution of natural things, and thus the many and varied dispositions of natural things were produced. And in all these things only that which happened to be suitable for some utility, as if it were made for that utility, was preserved. For such things had a disposition which made them suitable for being

---

231 Ibid., 329.
232 Ibid.

preserved, not because of some agent intending an end, but because of that which is per se vain, i.e., by chance. On the other hand, whatever did not have such a disposition was destroyed, and is destroyed daily. Thus Empedocles said that in the beginning things which were part ox and part man were generated.[233]

Following Aristotle's conception, Aquinas recognizes that an efficient cause can work through another in order to achieve an end that is proportionate to the natural capacity of the second. This leads to the notion, very pleasing to Barbour, of primary and secondary causality as well as principal and instrumental causality. Tabaczek posits that

these philosophical assertions prove to be very useful when applied to the causation of God. Nature consists of beings which, due to their forms, generate other beings. However, they can only cause the production of beings like themselves by causing forms like their own to be educed from properly disposed matter. They are not the cause of the form as such (by which they also are particular kinds of being), nor of the act of being, by which they also exist. As secondary causes, they can make a thing "become" what it is, by educing its form from the potentiality of primary matter, but they cannot make it exist (*causa fiendi* is distinct from *causa essendi*).[234] Only God is the source of the absolute *esse*. If we can speak of one creature as a source of being of the other in the process of generation, it is only because it acts as an instrumental cause "in the hands of God" who creates the being of a new organism.[235]

Barbour's theological anthropology, while seeking to engage the latest developments in modern science, especially the Neo-Darwinian synthesis, never reduces man to an automaton. He seeks to respect man's freedom in the face of attacks from determinism in physics.[236] Obviously, he also wants to maintain man's religious nature, seeking answers to questions about origins, love, destiny, and the Infinite.

In this area, one notices much compatibility with Catholic thought. Barbour would likely agree with the following excerpt from Benedict XVI's second volume in the *Jesus of Nazareth* series:

At this point, modern man is tempted to say: Creation has become intelligible to us through science. Indeed, Francis S. Collins, for example, who led the Human Genome Project, says with joyful astonishment: "The language of God was revealed" (*The Language of God*, p. 122). Indeed, in the magnificent mathematics of creation, which

---

233 Thomas Aquinas, *Commentaria in Octo Libros Physicorum*, trans. Richard J. Blackwell, Richard J. Spath, and W. Edmund Thirlkel (New Haven: Yale University Press, 1963), II, lec. 12, chap. 8, para. 252–253.

234 A cause of *becoming* is not identical to a cause of *being*.

235 Tabaczek, "Thomistic Response to the Theory of Evolution," 334–335.

236 See Chapter Two, Section 2.4 of this work.

today we can read in the human genetic code, we recognized the language of God. But unfortunately not the whole language. The functional truth about man has been discovered. But the truth about man himself—who he is, where he comes from, what he should do, what is right, what is wrong—this unfortunately cannot be read in the same way. Hand in hand with growing knowledge of functional truth there seems to be an increasing blindness toward "truth" itself—toward the question of our real identity and purpose.[237]

Certainly a reason that Barbour dedicated most of his professional career to the interaction of theology and science was because he was aware that the existential questions mentioned by Benedict (e.g., Who am I? Where do I come from? What is right?) cannot be answered by the methods of natural science. "Our real identity and purpose" can only be discovered in our relationship to God. Answers to these existential questions take time; hence Italians wisely say, "*Tutti noi siamo in cammino, tutti noi siamo pellegrini.*"

2.5 Panentheism

Having examined aspects of the special relationship between the Creator and the pinnacle of His creation, mankind, in the previous section, we now explore Barbour's understanding of the *fundamental* distinction between God and the creation. Ian Barbour's implicit panentheism was mentioned earlier in this chapter. The origins of contemporary panentheism can be traced back to nineteenth century Germany.

The philosopher and Freemason, Karl Friedrich Krause, in an attempt to synthesize what he perceived to be the positive aspects of pantheism[238] and monotheism, formulated a doctrine that "all is in God"—*Allingottlehre*. He speculated that "the One in itself and through itself also is the All."[239] According to the

---

237 Benedict XVI, *Jesus of Nazareth: Holy Week* (San Francisco: Ignatius Press, 2011), 193.

238 Pantheism can be considered a "pre-Christian heresy" because it is so ancient. The Church has always condemned any pantheistic system as inconsistent with Biblical revelation. For example, Amaury of Bène (AKA Amalric of Bena) attempted to use Aristotelian science to justify a belief that "*omnia unum, quia quidquid est, est Deus.*" See Hugh Chisholm, ed., "Amalric of Bena," *The Encyclopædia Britannica* (Cambridge: Cambridge University Press, 1910), 779. Amaury was excommunicated for his pantheistic views posthumously by the Provincial Synod of Sens, also known as the "Council of Paris," in 1210. See Edward Grant, ed., "The Condemnation of Aristotle's Books on Natural Philosophy in 1210 at Paris," in *A Source Book in Medieval Science*, trans. Lynn Thorndike, Source Books in the History of the Sciences (Cambridge: Harvard University Press, 1974), 42.

239 Karl Krause, *Vorlesungen über das System der Philosophie* (Göttingen: Dieterich, 1828), 255–256. Translated and cited in John W. Cooper, *Panentheism—The Other God of the Philosophers: From Plato to the Present* (Grand Rapids, MI: Baker Academic, 2013), 122.

Christian Reformed Church minister and theologian, John Cooper, Krause believed that "the distinction between God and the world is that of whole and part."[240]

It was not long before German Lutherans, British Anglicans, and American transcendentalists[241] began to explore this blurring of the distinction of Creator and creation. The influential German idealist philosopher, Georg Wilhelm Friedrich Hegel, also advanced the banner of panentheism. Ian Barbour's panentheism flows from his reliance on the thought of Alfred Whitehead, Charles Hartshorne, and David Griffin.

However, in his particular process metaphysics, Barbour diverges from the aforementioned authors in various ways. For example, the American Protestant theologian, Philip Clayton,[242] notes how Barbour acknowledges Divine *transcendence* more than the father of process thought, Whitehead.[243] According to Whitehead's notion of the symmetrical co-relation between God and the world, "it is as true to say that God transcends the World, as that the World transcends God. It is as true to say that God creates the world, as that the World creates God."[244]

With regard to the relationship of God and the world, Barbour sides with Hartshorne who posits that "the world is in God (*panentheism*), a view that neither identifies God with the world (*pantheism*) nor separates God from the world (*theism*). 'God includes the world but is more than the world.'"[245] Barbour writes,

> Hartshorne points out that we have only dim awareness of some portions of our bodies and our pasts, whereas God knows the world completely at every point and forgets nothing. Hartshorne proposes the mind-body analogy, if appropriately extended, provides an image of God's finitely sympathetic and all-embracing participation in the world process, a mode of influence that is internal rather than external.[246]

---

240 Cooper, *Panentheism—The Other God of the Philosophers*, 122.

241 Transcendentalism is an intellectual heir of German and British Romanticism, modernist Biblical criticism (e.g., Johann Gottfried Herder and Friedrich Schleiermacher), the philosophical skepticism of David Hume, and German idealism (e.g., Immanuel Kant). See Russell Goodman, "Transcendentalism," ed. Edward N. Zalta, *The Stanford Encyclopedia of Philosophy* (Stanford: Metaphysics Research Lab, Stanford University, May 6, 2017), accessed May 3, 2018, https://plato.stanford.edu/archives/sum2017/entriesranscendentalism/.

242 Philip Clayton, "Barbour's Panentheistic Metaphysic," *Theology and Science* 15, no. 1 (January 2, 2017): 55.

243 Barbour, *Religion in an Age of Science*, 263–265.

244 Whitehead, *Process and Reality*, 410.

245 Hartshorne, *The Divine Relativity*, 90.

246 Barbour, *Religion in an Age of Science*, 260.

Barbour believes that his panentheist process ontology resolves a number of complex issues examined in Chapter Two of this work, e.g., the status of human freedom, the problem of evil, the challenge of interreligious dialogue, the evolutionary nature of the cosmos, and the tension between change and law.[247]

In addition to Whitehead's notion of *actual occasions*, Barbour also adopts a theory of emergent properties. Whitehead's process metaphysics describes reality at different levels in exactly the same sense. As Clayton describes it, "all reality consists of moments of experience or 'actual occasions.'"[248] Barbour's incorporation of a theory of emergence modifies this description by positing that there are real differences at various levels that establish what it is for each class of entities to exist. The tension is most manifest in the discussion of "consciousness."

Is Whitehead's unitary metaphysic of actual occasions which posits that reality is composed of moments of conscious experience, even at the lowest level, valid? Or does consciousness *emerge* at higher levels? Whitehead's process thought emphasizes the "mental" as a fundamental description of reality. Hence, this ontology is sometimes referred to as *panpsychism* or *panexperientialism*.

Barbour prefers "two-aspect theories" in his engagement with the mind-body problem. He develops a theory of *dipolar monism* from Whitehead's foundation. Barbour states,

> The process view has much in common with the two-language theories or a parallelism that takes mental and neural phenomena to be two-aspects of the same events ... All integrated entities at any level have an inner reality and an outer reality, but these take very different forms at different levels.[249]

With regard to the status of subjectivity, Barbour notes that his own view is "very similar to the *emergent monism* defended by Philip Clayton and Arthur Peacocke."[250] All three concur that consciousness is an emergent property only present at higher levels of complexity.

Barbour's "non-reductionist emergentism" implies that the whole emerges from the parts, that is, as its result. Even if he claims that the whole is more than the sum of its parts, he is not accounting for this claim using adequate ontological language. An actual whole must "first" cause the parts as their formal cause. This is true even if the parts in turn interact with the whole, so to speak, causing

---

247 Ibid., 261–262.

248 Clayton, "Barbour's Panentheistic Metaphysic," 56.

249 Ian G. Barbour, "Neuroscience, Artificial Intelligence, and Human Nature," in *Neuroscience and the Person: Scientific Perspectives on Divine Action*, ed. Robert John Russell (Vatican City State: Vatican Observatory, 1999), 276.

250 Barbour, *Nature, Human Nature, and God*, 98.

emergent novelty for the whole. To say otherwise is to nonsensically elevate what is derivative—potency—over what is actual.

One of the most obvious theological problems with any form of panentheism is the implication that God is dependent on the world. The Christian doctrine of *creatio ex nihilo* is an effective safeguard against this error. As stated earlier in this chapter, all of creation is utterly dependent on the Creator; there is no mutual dependence. For God to be God, it must be affirmed that His acts of creating and redeeming the world are completely free. If the world were "in God" in a panentheistic way, He would necessarily be redeeming Himself—a *contradiction*.

All relationships between beings of the same "order" involve mutual dependence—the larger in relation to the smaller, the parent in relation to the child. Barbour's panentheism puts God on the same ontological order as creatures and so makes God interdependent with the world, growing in value (or not) as the world progresses. In the Catholic theological tradition, utilizing the insights of Thomas Aquinas, God is acknowledged as a being of a wholly different order from creatures. This gives rise to Aquinas' doctrine of the "mixed" relation between God and creatures (*real* in the creature, *ideal* only regarding God). Though sometimes misinterpreted as making God indifferent, it actually preserves God's intimacy with creation and the gratuity of Divine love. For the creature, there is always "something in it for us" whenever we act. For God, there is not; His love is pure ἀγάπη (*agápe*).[251]

A rejection of Barbour's panentheism does not imply a distant deism. Thomas Aquinas argued that God is indeed in all of creation, but not as part of its essence or accidence. To exist in things may refer to being part of a being as in pantheism or as a cause exists in an effect (*per se*). God is present "as an agent is present to that upon which it works."[252] Aquinas further states,

> For an agent must be joined to that wherein it acts immediately and touch it by its power; hence it is proved in *Phys. vii* that the thing moved and the mover must be joined together. Now since God is very being by His own essence, created being must be His proper effect; as to ignite is the proper effect of fire. Now God causes this effect in things not only when they first begin to be, but as long as they are preserved in being; as light is caused in the air by the sun as long as the air remains illuminated.

251 "Some things, however, are both agent and patient at the same time: these are imperfect agents, and to these it belongs to intend, even while acting, the acquisition of something. But it does not belong to the First Agent, Who is agent only, to act for the acquisition of some end; He intends only to communicate His perfection, which is His goodness; while every creature intends to acquire its own perfection, which is the likeness of the divine perfection and goodness." Aquinas, *Summa Theologiæ*, I, Q 44, A 4.

252 Aquinas, *Summa Theologiæ*, I, Q 8, A 1.

Therefore as long as a thing has being, God must be present to it, according to its mode of being. But being is innermost in each thing and most fundamentally inherent in all things since it is formal in respect of everything found in a thing, as was shown above (I:7:1). Hence it must be that God is in all things, and innermostly.[253]

The nature of God is *actus essendi* whereas we humans have *actus essendi*. The proper effect of God is also *actus essendi*.

One can affirm that God's existence in things occurs *per essentiam* (cause in the effect), *per potentiam* (by the power of God), and *per presentiam* (God sees everything). In the human person, He is present in the aforementioned cause-effect relationship, in apprehensions (i.e., the intentional presence of God acquired through intellect), and by grace (e.g., by Baptism we are adopted sons or daughters of God). Therefore, Thomas Aquinas affirms that God is everywhere in substance, power, and presence. He is present

> in one way after the manner of an efficient cause; and thus He is in all things created by Him; in another way he is in things as the object of operation is in the operator; and this is proper to the operations of the soul, according as the thing known is in the one who knows; and the thing desired in the one desiring. In this second way God is especially in the rational creature which knows and loves Him actually or habitually. And because the rational creature possesses this prerogative by grace ... He is said to be thus in the saints by grace.[254]

For the aforementioned reasons, a Catholic reception of Barbour's thought cannot accept his panentheistic metaphysics. Panentheistic confusion about God's essence, and the essences or substances of creation, requires a rectification. In the next section, we explore the important, fundamental theological concepts of substance and essence.

2.6 Substances and Essences

The concept of *substance* is important in Catholic theology for many different reasons.[255] Creation theology (e.g., Created substances are not Divine; God is

253 Ibid.
254 Ibid, I, Q 8, A 3.
255 It is worth noting two far-reaching twentieth century attempts to "transpose" the terminology of substance along modern philosophical lines. For example, Karl Rahner, SJ defines substances as active ontological events. Stephen Fields clearly and concisely summarizes Rahner's theory. He writes, "[Substances] are constituted by the emanation and return of form in and through matter. Substances are real-symbols, because their fundamental reality, their meaning and intelligibility, is grasped in and through matter. Matter is the means by which a substance's accidents are perceived by the senses. The accidents thus incarnate and express form, which is the principle

self-subsistent being.), theological anthropology (e.g., Man is a distinct substance
of a rational nature.), sacramental theology (e.g., Transubstantiation), Christology
(e.g., Jesus is begotten, not made, consubstantial with the Father.), soteriology
(e.g., the status of the soul and body after death acknowledging that the soul is the
substantial form of the body during life), and other areas of theology, utilize this
fundamental notion.[256] In the Thomist tradition, a substance is "that whose nature
is to exist in its own right and not in another (*id cui competit existere in se and non
in alio*)."[257] It is a principle of action and *operatio sequitur esse*.

In examining Barbour's theology of God and creation, it is quite apparent
that his process metaphysics lacks a satisfactory theory of the perdurance of the
individual through time and into eternity. Regrettably, the fundamental, ontological principle of substance has been misunderstood by William of Ockham,

of the substance's identity." Stephen Fields, "God's Labor, Novelty's Emergence: Cosmic Motion
as Self-Transcending Love," in *Love Alone Is Credible: Hans Urs Von Balthasar as Interpreter of
the Catholic Tradition*, ed. David L. Schindler, vol. 1 (Grand Rapids, MI: Wm. B. Eerdmans
Publishing, 2008), 121. Fundamentally, for Rahner, the "substance" of an entity is its meaning
and purpose. Consequently, in his Eucharistic theology, the transubstantiation of the bread
and wine at the Eucharist implies that after the consecration, the bread and wine have a new
"meaning" of spiritual food because they are now a "symbol" of Jesus Christ. See Engelbert
Gutwenger, "Transubstantiation," in *Encyclopedia of Theology: A Concise Sacramentum Mundi*, ed.
Karl Rahner (London: Burns & Oates, 1975), 1754–1755. The influential Belgian theologian,
Edward Schillebeeckx, OP, concurred with Rahner that the physical bread and wine become
"fully signs" of Christ. See Edward Schillebeeckx, *The Eucharist* (New York: Burns & Oates,
2005), 120.

256   The British priest and theologian, Edward Holloway, was interested in an alternative notion to
Aristotelian substance. His basic notion is presented in a series of essays originally written 1945–
1946, but not published until 1994, entitled *Perspectives in Philosophy*. Holloway believes that the
medieval Scholastic synthesis, which he characterizes as abstract and essentialist, is largely irrel-
evant to the philosophy of science. His "existential" reformulation emphasizes a cosmic Unity-
Law of control and purposive direction which culminates in the Incarnation of God in Christ.
Unfortunately, his nascent ideas in this area are very un-developed and remain inchoate. See
Edward Holloway, *Perspectives in Philosophy: A Critique of an Abstract Scholasticism and Principles
Towards Replacement*, E-Book., vol. 1 (Glasgow: Faith-Keyway Publications, 1994), chaps. 7–9.
The aforementioned "Unity-Law of control and purposive direction" requires some explanation.
According to Holloway, "the Law of Control and Direction … is not a law of matter in a specific
sense. It is not the law of this event and effect, or of that event and effect, it is a law in matter
that is cosmic and all-inclusive, so that the entire universe is one equation of meaningful devel-
opment, in mutual relativity of part on part, at all times throughout space." Edward Holloway,
Catholicism: A New Synthesis (Surrey: Keyway Publications, 1970), 64.

257   Foley, *A Critique of the Philosophy of Being of Alfred North Whitehead in the Light of Thomistic
Philosophy*, 109.

Descartes, Locke, Hume, Kant, and Whitehead[258] as something inert underlying the accidents.[259] Therefore, it is not surprising that Barbour wants to sideline the notion of substance when describing reality with his process metaphysics.[260]

Barbour places reality only in events. However, all being is event *and* substance. While one could argue that event, defined as the dynamic interrelation of beings, is in a sense prior to substance, Barbour does not define event in this way. Tracey Rowland's research illustrates the importance and relevance of this issue. She describes how the development of a metaphysical framework wherein relationality and substantiality are treated as equally primordial aspects of being has been pursued by significant twentieth century Catholic theologians, e.g., W. Norris Clarke, Joseph Ratzinger, David L. Schindler, and Walter Kasper.[261]

For example, W. Norris Clarke, SJ's excellent Aquinas Lecture entitled *Person and Being* argues that Aquinas defends a twofold idea: substance and relationality. Clarke's accent is on relationality, since many have argued that this idea is missing from Aquinas. However, he also shows why substantiality is an essential idea for Saint Thomas as well:

> It turns out, then, that relationality and substantiality go together as two distinct but inseparable modes of reality. Substance is the primary mode, in that all else, including relations, depend on it as their ground. But since "every substance exists for the sake of its operations," as St. Thomas has told us, being as substance, as existing *in it-self*, naturally flows over into being as relational, as turned *towards others* by it self-communicating action. To be fully is to be *substance-in-relation*.[262]

Barbour follows Whitehead in describing "event" as intersecting activities.[263] However, Barbour never clearly defines *what* is acting in these intersecting

---

258 Whitehead inveighs against an erroneous concept of substance. Foley points out how Whitehead is confronting the Cartesian definition, i.e., substance is that which exists *by* itself. In the Thomistic tradition, substance is "that which, having depended upon other entities, exists in itself with a certain measure of subsistence." Ibid., 127. Whitehead also falsely assumes that the notion of substance implies isolation of entities. In reality, Thomistic metaphysics has a robust notion of interdependence and causality (explained in terms of potency and act).

259 Ibid., 109. One notices that the emphasis today is on social-cultural specificity, historicity, and finitude, rather than perduring substance.

260 Barbour, *Issues in Science and Religion*, 129–130.

261 Tracey Rowland, *Culture and the Thomist Tradition: After Vatican II* (New York: Routledge, 2003), 96.

262 W. Norris Clarke, *Person and Being* (Milwaukee: Marquette University Press, 1993), 14.

263 An inadequate notion of substances is found throughout modern philosophy. Hume developed an extreme form of empiricism called "sensationalism"—mental concepts are just the result of intuitive impressions. His deficient notion of substance is the result of an associative process. Julián Marías concisely describes Hume's theory: "Perception and reflection provide us with a number of elements which we attribute to substance, which acts as a basis or support for them;

activities. Recall that Barbour adopts Whitehead's actual entities, also referred to as actual occasions, which are spatio-temporally extended *processes*. Barbour misses the elemental fact that every act in nature is rooted in a substance. As a consequence of the modern "turn to the subject," and a lack of "contact" with creation, process philosophers lose sight of this fundamental reality.

While the first argument for the existence of substances, prime matter, and substantial forms was made in the fourth century BC, it remains a foundational metaphysical concept. Aristotle defined the concept of substance, or second matter, as a composition of a *substantial* form and *prime* matter. This matter-form composition is the essential principle of natural being and is involved in substantial change. He posited that a similar composition exists in the union of *second* matter and *accidental* form, i.e., between a substance and its accidents. In this case, second matter is the underlying substance that is already composed of substantial form and prime matter. This is the union altered by an accidental change. If an accident is gained or lost, or if one accident succeeds another, the substance remains the same.[264] According to Gardeil,

> Substantial form, like prime matter, is an intrinsic, non-accidental principle of mobile being. It is the first act of corporeal or physical substance; which means it is the principle by reason of which this substance exists as well as the principle that causes this substance to be one kind of thing instead of another.[265]

Aristotle maintains that prime matter is "the primary substratum of each thing, from which a thing comes to be but not as an accident, and which remains throughout."[266] The Scholastics developed the axiom that matter is "*neque quid,*

---

but nowhere do we find the impression of substance ... sensible impressions have more vitality than imagined impressions, and this causes us to believe in the reality of what is represented." Marías, *History of Philosophy*, 258. Hume's critique of substance goes beyond Berkeley's critique of material and corporeal substance to the ego itself. Hume reduces the ego to an amalgamation of successive perceptions. As Marías puts it, "Thus the ego does not have substantial reality; it is a result of imagination." Ibid., 258–259. Not surprising, Hume ends up in philosophical skepticism, denying that human knowledge attains metaphysical truth. For more details, see David Hume, *A Treatise of Human Nature*, 2 vols. (London: Thomas and Joseph Allman, 1817).

264 Gardeil, *Introduction to the Philosophy of St. Thomas Aquinas: Cosmology*, 2:29.

265 Ibid., 2:32.

266 Aristotle, *Physics*, I, 9, 192 a 31–32, translated and cited in Gardeil, *Introduction to the Philosophy of St. Thomas Aquinas: Cosmology*, 2:30. Saint Thomas translates this into Latin as "*Primum subiectum ex quo aliquid fit per se et non secundum accidens, et inest rei iam factae.*" Aquinas, *Commentaria in Octo Libros Physicorum*, I, lect. 15, no. 281. Also, see H. M. Robinson, "Prime Matter in Aristotle," *Phronesis* 19, no. 2 (1974): 168–188.

neque quale, neque quantum, neque aliquid eorum quibus ens determinatur.[267] One can state that prime matter's chief property is its absolute indetermination. Matter is pure potency, i.e., *"non est ens actu sed potentia tantum."*[268] Therefore, properly speaking, matter is not what exists nor what is generated. The real subject of existence is the *union* of form and matter.[269] In light of the paradoxical nature of matter, McDermott notes that Catholic

> thinkers as diverse as Maritain, Rahner, and Lonergan recognize the basic choice which matter involves. Faced with its unintelligibility they choose to trust the basic goodness of nature and refer their efforts beyond matter … to God … In Jesus Christ the infinite and the finite have been reconciled.[270]

In his work, *De Ente et Essentia* (*On Being and Essences*), Thomas Aquinas develops a rigorous notion of *essence*—what is sometimes referred to as *nature*. It is beneficial to quote at length an excerpt from the first chapter to clearly present Aquinas' notion:

> Since that through which a thing is constituted in its proper genus or species is what is signified by the definition indicating what the thing is, philosophers introduced the term quiddity to mean the same as the term essence; and this is the same thing that the Philosopher frequently terms what it is to be a thing, that is, that through which something has being as a particular kind of thing. Essence is also called form, for the certitude of every thing is signified through its form, as Avicenna says in his *Metaphysicæ* I, cap. 6. The same thing is also called nature, taking nature in the first of the four senses that Boethius distinguishes in his book *De Persona et Duabus Naturis* cap. 1, in the sense, in other words, that nature is what we call everything that can in any way be captured by the intellect, for a thing is not intelligible except through its definition and essence. And so the Philosopher says in V *Metaphysicæ* cap. 4 that every substance is a nature.[271]

Unfortunately, given his reliance on Whitehead and Hartshorne, Barbour does not have an adequate sense of essences. Being is always and everywhere in flux. Potency always has priority since potency allows for an infinite number of possibilities in terms of development and change. A consequence of Barbour not

267 Gardeil, *Introduction to the Philosophy of St. Thomas Aquinas: Cosmology*, 2:31. In English: Matter is "neither actual substance, nor quality, nor quantity, nor anything else by which being is determined."
268 Ibid.
269 Ibid., 2:31–32.
270 McDermott, "Matter, Modern Science, and God," 507.
271 Aquinas, *De Ente et Essentia*, chap. 1.

accepting the doctrine of *creatio ex nihilo* is the implication that prime matter is constantly and continually open to change.

A Catholic, metaphysically justified view must maintain that creation has a stable nature and actuality. This still of course permits dynamicity and development with time. However, this change is in accord with the fundamental essence or nature of a created entity.

This kind of stability is absent from Barbour's process thought, which regards it as limiting and constraining. His stance on metaphysics and creation has serious consequences. Barbour asserts that God cannot possibly be omniscient because the universe is in radical flux, open to unlimited development, which comes about through creative, mutual interaction between God and other entities.

In the context of attempting to adumbrate a new Christology, Barbour identifies "history" and "relationship" as the central theological categories, rather than substance. He posits that "what was unique about Christ ... was his relationship to God, not his metaphysical 'substance.'"[272] Barbour acknowledges that this implies that what makes Christ unique compared to us is simply a matter degree— Jesus is better at being authentically human.[273]

This position grossly contradicts the orthodox Christian dogma that Jesus Christ is a Divine person (ὁμοούσιος [*homooúsios*], or in Latin, *consubstantialis*, with the Father) who assumed a human nature identical to ours in all things save sin— *Deum verum et hominem verum*. Furthermore, Barbour's position is incongruous with Saint Paul's Christocentric teaching on creation: "There is one God, the Father, from whom are all things and for whom we exist, and one Lord, Jesus Christ, through whom are all things and through whom we exist."[274] The consequences of denying that Jesus is one in being with the Father, with the Godhead, is also devastating for soteriology. In Saint Gregory Nazianzen's letter to the priest, Cledonius, against the heretic Apollinarius, he eloquently wrote, "For that which He [Christ] has not assumed He has not healed; but that which is united to His Godhead is also saved."[275]

An aspect of man's mission entrusted to him by the Creator is to develop and cultivate some entity—whether it be the world or *la condition humaine*— according to its stable, created nature or essence. Kant created a problem in philosophy when he declared that natures are unknowable because of the limitations of

---

272 Barbour, *Religion in an Age of Science*, 210.
273 Ibid., 213.
274 1 Corinthians 8:6 (RSV).
275 Gregory of Nazianzen, "Epistle to Cledonius the Priest Against Apollinarius," in *Nicene and Post-Nicene Fathers*, ed. Philip Schaff and Henry Wace, trans. Charles Gordon Browne and James Edward Swallow, vol. 7, 2 (Buffalo: Christian Literature Publishing Co., 1894), 440.

human reasoning.[276] However, he did not completely deny the existence of natures. Barbour takes a step beyond Kant. He implicitly asserts that *there are no stable, created natures*. His description of the cosmos implies only fluidity *ad infinitum* in the interactions that take place between entities, e.g., God and man. In fact, the disappearance of this notion of stable essences or natures is behind much of postmodern thought today, e.g., Gianni Vattimo.[277]

A consequence of Barbour's panentheism and misunderstanding around substances and essences enables him to err in the area of the perfection(s) of God. An immutable, eternal, omnipotent, and omniscient God is not possible according to Barbour's theological, and most fundamentally philosophically commitments. In this next section we critique his denial of the perfection of God.

2.7 Perfection of God

Michael Schmaus wisely notes that "the [Catholic] doctrine of creation presupposes a God separate from the world, transcendent, free, unique, omnipotent, other."[278] Unfortunately, in adopting elements of Whitehead's philosophy of God, Barbour places "process" or "creativity" as the ultimate principle of reality rather than God Himself. However, God is eternal, not "in" and limited to time.[279] In the words of W. Norris Clarke, God's "eternal Now is outside the flow of our motion-dependent time, but present in its own unique time-transcending way to all points of time without internal succession in God."[280] God enjoys a life, without beginning or end, or succession, and of the most perfect kind.[281] Thomas Aquinas points out that

> the idea of eternity follows immutability, as the idea of time follows movement, as appears from the preceding article. Hence, as God is supremely immutable, it supremely belongs to Him to be eternal. Nor is He eternal only; but He is His own eternity; whereas, no other being is its own duration, as no other is its own being. Now

---

276 Kant posited that man cannot have *a priori* knowledge about anything whose existence and nature are completely independent of the mind, i.e., "things in themselves." See Kant, *Critique of Pure Reason*, Bxviii.

277 See Guarino, *Vattimo and Theology*.

278 Schmaus, *God and Creation: The Foundations of Christology*, 2:85.

279 According to Saint Augustine, "The eternity of God is His Essence itself, which has nothing mutable in it. In It there is nothing past, as if it were no longer, nothing future, as if it had not been. In It there is only 'is,' that is, the present." Augustine, *Enarrationes in Psalmos*, Ps. 101, 2, 10 translated and cited in Ludwig Ott, *Fundamentals of Catholic Dogma*, 4th ed. (Rockford, IL: TAN Books and Publishers, Inc., 1974), 37.

280 Clarke, *The Philosophical Approach to God: A New Thomistic Perspective*, 134.

281 See Walter McDonald, "Eternity," *The Catholic Encyclopedia* (New York: Robert Appleton Company, 1909), accessed May 2, 2018, http://www.newadvent.org/cathen/05551b.htm.

God is His own uniform being; and hence as He is His own essence, so He is His own eternity.[282]

The fact that God is *ipsum esse per se subsistens* is significant in and of itself, but also in relation to man. For humans, using the metaphorical language of gift and reception, our actuality, *actus essendi*, is received by our essence which is a potential. In other words, there is ontological receptivity built into one's being, that is, as a potency for the *actus essendi*. God on the other hand is a purely self-existent being that exists in complete actuality. According to Aquinas, this relationship between Creator and creatures is rooted in the fundamental fact that

> all created perfections are in God. Hence He is spoken of as universally perfect, because He lacks not any excellence which may be found in any genus … Whatever perfection exists in an effect must be found in the effective cause: either in the same formality, if it is a univocal agent—as when man reproduces man; or in a more eminent degree, if it is an equivocal agent—thus in the sun is the likeness of whatever is generated by the sun's power. Now it is plain that the effect pre-exists virtually in the efficient cause: and although to pre-exist in the potentiality of a material cause is to pre-exist in a more imperfect way, since matter as such is imperfect, and an agent as such is perfect; still to pre-exist virtually in the efficient cause is to pre-exist not in a more imperfect, but in a more perfect way. Since therefore God is the first effective cause of things, the perfections of all things must pre-exist in God in a more eminent way. Dionysius implies the same line of argument by saying of God: "It is not that He is this and not that, but that He is all, as the cause of all."[283]

In the context of this ontological discussion, it is also imperative to affirm that the God of the Bible is a personal God. Without abandoning the valuable metaphysical analysis of God, Benedict XVI offers an articulate relational approach to the Triune God. He writes,

> God has all the essential characteristics of what we mean by a "person," in particular conscious awareness, the ability to recognize and the ability to love. In that sense he is someone who can speak and who can listen. That, I think, is what is essential about God. Nature can be marvelous. The starry heaven is stupendous. But my reaction to that remains no more than an impersonal wonder, because that, in the end, means that I am myself no more than a tiny part of an enormous machine. The real God, however, is more than that. He is not just nature, but the One who came before it and who sustains it. And the whole of God, so faith tells us, is the act of relating. That is what we mean when we say that he is a Trinity, that he is threefold. Because he is in

---

282 Aquinas, *Summa Theologiæ*, I, Q 10, A 2.
283 Aquinas, *Summa Theologiæ*, I, Q 4, A 2.

himself a complex of relationships, he can also make other beings who are grounded in relationships and who may relate to him, because he has related them to himself.[284]

Barbour and other process thinkers tend to over-emphasize God's "personalistic" attributes at the expense of other aspects of the Divine, e.g., immutability.[285] In Catholic theology, one does not speak of God *suffering* in a way that would imply some deficiency (e.g., physical, emotional, or spiritual) and/or the result of external actions imposed upon Him which would force some change in His being. This is certainly affirmed in Jesus in His human nature, but not for the Triune God *qua Deus*. In the early Church, the Fathers articulated repeatedly a doctrine of God as unchangeable and perfect. He is impassible—ἀπαθής (*apathés*)[286]—since He has no needs and cannot be involuntarily acted upon.

At the same time, the Church Fathers equally rejected any idea that God is an indifferent Creator who simply set the world in motion and "left it alone." More recently, the American theologian, Thomas Weinandy, OFM Cap, arguing from the Bible as well as from the philosophical and theological tradition of the Fathers and Aquinas, asserts that a God who is impassible is more loving and compassionate than a suffering God. He also avers that Jesus' experience of suffering *qua homo* is the truly redemptive and life-giving aspect of His passion.[287]

How does this doctrine of the immutability of God relate to the aspects of Biblical revelation, particularly in the Old Testament, where God is described with many anthropomorphisms? God is sometimes depicted as "emotional" in a way similar to us, e.g., experiencing anger.[288] Our emotions can be the result of

284 Benedict XVI, *God and the World* (San Francisco: Ignatius Press, 2002), 96–97.
285 The Fourth Lateran Council and the First Vatican Council teach that God is immutable (*incommutabilis*) and eternal (*æternus*). See DS 428 and 1782. Ludwig Ott summarizes the teaching stating, "Holy Scripture excludes all change from God and positively ascribes to Him absolute immutability ... The Fathers exclude all change from God ... St. Thomas bases the absolute immutability of God on His pure actuality, on His absolute simplicity and on His infinite perfection." Ott, *Fundamentals of Catholic Dogma*, 35–36.
286 See Clement of Alexandria in Philip Schaff et al., eds., *Ante-Nicene Fathers - Fathers of the Second Century: Tatian, Theophilus of Antioch, Athenagoras of Athens, Clement of Alexandria*, vol. 2 (CreateSpace Independent Publishing Platform, 2017), chap. IX, 425.
287 See Thomas Weinandy, *Does God Suffer?* (Notre Dame, IN: University of Notre Dame Press, 2000).
288 Saint Augustine addresses this issue with great clarity: "God's anger implies no perturbation of the divine mind; It is simply the divine judgment passing sentence on sin. And when God 'thinks and then has second thoughts' this merely means that changeable realities come into relation with his immutable reason. For God cannot 'repent' as human beings repent, of what he has done, since in regard to everything his judgment is fixed as his foreknowledge is clear ... But it is only by the use of such human expressions that Scripture can make its many kinds of readers whom it wants to help to feel, as it were, at home. Only thus can Scripture frighten the proud and

imperfections, e.g., unrighteous anger resulting from an uncontrolled temper. The Incarnation of the Word certainly intensified this tension. In Catholic theology, one can speak of God "suffering" as an active or positive openness, accessibility, or approachability because of love. This does not imply a passive, negative state of weakness.

The Triune God is a Being Who is absolutely good, Who is love, Whose very will is act and Whose every act is love. The only Being capable of reciprocally giving and receiving that will/act/love is that Being Himself. This is reflected in many of the formulations in Trinitarian theology about the Persons *in se*. It is only within that relationship that such a love can experience no deficiency in Giver and Receiver.

When such a Being creates creatures in His image and likeness, a connection is made that, on the one hand establishes conditions for a relationship analogous to how that interior life operates, while on the other hand involves unavoidably a wide variance from the same, since the creature is immeasurably less than the Creator. The Incarnation heightens this dynamic since it tightens the connection between the creatures and the Creator, e.g., the "shock" of Christ's statement that He could call His disciples friends[289]—something previously unthinkable in the *historia salutis*. Similarly, in Catholic doctrine, the fatherhood of God is not something completely static or purely metaphysical, but also dynamic and relational. Thus, theologians have focused much on the lessons to be learned from the Lord's Prayer, the Parable of the Prodigal Son, and the two names of God given at the burning bush.

In order to articulate a metaphysically justified doctrine of God, faithful to Sacred Scripture, as well as to respond to the challenges posed by process thinkers, such as Whitehead and Barbour, contemporary Catholic theologians have engaged the issue of God's perfection.[290] There is evident theological diversity on the issue among Catholics. W. Norris Clarke, SJ makes a distinction between two orders in God: *esse reale* and *esse*

---

arouse the slothful, provoke inquiries and provide food for the convinced. This is possible only when Scripture gets right down to the level of the lowliest readers." Augustine, *The City of God, Books VIII–XVI*, trans. Gerald G. Walsh and Grace Monahan, vol. 14, The Fathers of the Church (Washington, DC: CUA Press, 2008), bk. *XV*, chap. 25, 476–477.

289 John 15:15.

290 Hans Urs von Balthasar describes his own thought in this area as a "meta-anthropology," for which being culminates in the perfection of persons-in-communion. "The perfect actuality of love" encapsulates his ontology. In his view, person and being are not opposed, but one is the key to understanding the other. Balthasar was careful to avoid the false option of either metaphysics *or* personalism. See Hans Urs von Balthasar, "A Résumé of My Thought," *Communio* 15, no. 4 (1988): 468–473.

intentionale.[291] On the order of *esse reale,* God's intrinsic perfection always remains an Infinite Plenitude.[292] Yet, when considering *esse intentionale,* one can also speak of the "divine field of consciousness as related to creatures."[293] In this way, creation "affects" the personal life of God. Clarke writes,

> Our metaphysics of God must certainly allow us to say that in some real and genuine way God is affected positively by what we do, that He receives love from us and experiences joy *precisely because* of our responses: in a word, that His consciousness is contingently and qualitatively *different* because of what we do. All this difference remains, however, on the level of God's *relational consciousness* and therefore does not involve change, increase or decrease, in the Infinite Plenitude of God's *intrinsic inner being* and perfection—what St. Thomas would call the "absolute" (non-relative) aspect of His perfection.[294]

Clarke further notes that "if we examine the matter more fully, we realize that God's 'receiving' from us, being delighted at our response to His love, is really His original delight in sharing with us in His eternal Now His own original power of loving and infinite goodness which has come back to Him in return."[295] A key point for Clarke is to acknowledge that the "consciousness" of the Triune God can be present to our dynamic, contingent cosmos without implying our flow of time.[296] Man's notion of the movement of time is based on our experience of

---

291 Some people misunderstand the Thomistic claim that there is *logical relation* between God and world rather than a *real one.* Clarke maintains the proper intention of that language, without suggesting that the God-world relation is "less than real." He writes, "For when God creates, bestows existence itself on creatures 'out of nothing' (no preexisting subject), He is not relating himself to anything real, since there is nothing there yet. He posits in existence the whole other pole of the relation by his creative act alone. This obviously cannot be a real relation, which requires two real poles to be already there." Clarke, *The Philosophical Approach to God: A New Thomistic Perspective,* 135.

292 Clarke perhaps emphasizes more than Thomas Aquinas himself the paradox that *esse,* though perfectly complete and simple, is intrinsically differentiated. This may be most clearly demonstrated with inter-personal terms, e.g., love, intention, and "affectivity." However, it must also apply *analogously* with regard to the Creator-creation relation.

293 Clarke, *The Philosophical Approach to God: A New Thomistic Perspective,* 132.

294 Ibid., 136.

295 Ibid., 137.

296 We wish to emphasize that God is not "in motion" as Barbour would suppose. The entire "flow of time" is present to Him simultaneously, as one complete plan (*esse intentionale*): the act of a potency insofar as it is in act. However, the natural motion (the act of the potency *qua* potency) is still real in God; the self-movement of the nature contributes to being, that is, in distinction from God. Yet, paradoxically, it adds nothing, since the plenitude of God's *actus essendi* always already contains it.

motion, i.e., change, within ourselves and the world around us. However, as Clarke points out,

> In God there is only the relational order of the contents of God's intentional consciousness as related to us, without any "moving around" or physical motion inside His own intrinsic being ... God knows and responds ... *in* His eternal Now, simply present to each event as it actually takes place.[297]

Thomas Weinandy, OFM Cap, finds Clarke's distinction to be ill-founded. Weinandy believes that Clarke distinguishes *esse reale* and *esse intentionale* because he classifies impassibility as incompatible with relating to human beings in a loving and compassionate way. Weinandy argues that this assumption is false and that it is illegitimate to "divide up" God into *esse reale* and *esse intentionale*. He emphasizes that who God is determines how He relates.[298] One cannot separate part of Him, i.e., the impassible part, that does not relate, and another part of Him, i.e., the intentional part, that does. Weinandy believes that if God were divided in this way, man could never relate to God as He really is. Weinandy writes, "God's immutability is not a detriment which must be held in dialectic with his relatedness nor an 'evil' that must be overcome for God to be 'actually' related to the created order."[299]

Because God is *ipsum esse—ego sum qui sum*,[300] He "has no self-constituting potency which needs to be actualized."[301] God is not "something" *in actum*, but *actus purus*. In fact, as Trinity, Weinandy emphasizes that the Father, Son, and Holy Spirit are fully in act "in that they are constituted and defined only in the act of being inter-related to one another."[302] As *esse* must be the actuality of all acts and the perfection of perfections, God is most perfect and therefore immutable. Weinandy goes on to affirm that "the immutability of God is the primary

---

297 Clarke, *The Philosophical Approach to God: A New Thomistic Perspective*, 138–139.

298 "I have argued, from revelation, that the persons of the Trinity are subsistent relations fully in act, and therefore are immutable and impassible, not in the sense of being static and inert, but as being unconditionally active and supremely passionate. I have equally argued, from reason, that God is pure act, and therefore consummately dynamic in his immutability and wholly passionate in his impassibility. Moreover, I proceeded to demonstrate that because the persons of the Trinity are subsistent relations fully in act, in that they share the one pure act of divine existence, they possess no self-constituting relational potential, and therefore, they are fully relational ... The act of creation, as a mixed relation, specifies that the persons of the Trinity relate the creature to themselves as they are, and so, reciprocally, are actually related to the creature as the creature is. Thus, this relationship is immediate, dynamic, intimate, and enduring." Weinandy, *Does God Suffer?*, 144.

299 Weinandy, *Does God Suffer?*, 137, n. 69.

300 Exodus 3:14 (Vulgate).

301 Weinandy, *Does God Suffer?*, 122.

302 Ibid., 127.

presupposition for his dynamic and intimate actual relation to the created order."[303]
He also offers a helpful clarification on what Divine immutability implies:

> One should not be misled into thinking that God's immutability is like the immuta-
> bility of a rock only more so. What God and rocks appear to have in common is only
> the fact that they do not change. The reason for their unchangeableness is for polar-
> opposite reasons ... God is unchangeable not because he is inert or static like a rock,
> but for just the opposite reason. He is so dynamic, so active that no change can make
> him more active. His is act pure and simple.[304]

Of course, as with any theological discourse on the Triune God,[305] the veil of mystery is never completely lifted.

Process thinkers, like Barbour, posit change in God in order to make Him
more dynamic. They miss the crucial fact that Divine immutability as pure act
"guarantees and authenticates his pure vitality and absolute dynamism."[306] Process
theologians also focus on the perfection of finite causes and they make God a finite
cause.[307] In adopting elements of the philosophy of Whitehead and Hartshorne,
Barbour argues for a Divine causality in which God's causality is limited to
"influence."

However, God's causality is completely effective. Aquinas concisely articulates
a Catholic view that we quote *in extenso*:

> Divine providence imposes necessity upon some things; not upon all, as some for-
> merly believed. For to providence it belongs to order things towards an end. Now
> after the divine goodness, which is an extrinsic end to all things, the principal good in
> things themselves is the perfection of the universe; which would not be, were not all
> grades of being found in things. Whence it pertains to divine providence to produce
> every grade of being. And thus it has prepared for some things necessary causes, so
> that they happen of necessity; for others contingent causes, that they may happen by
> contingency, according to the nature of their proximate causes. The effect of divine

---

303 Ibid., 137.

304 Thomas Weinandy, *Does God Change?*, Studies in Historical Theology 4 (Still River, MA: St.
     Bede's Press, 2002), 78–79.

305 When discussing the mystery of the Trinity, it is always beneficial to state clearly the Catholic
     doctrine on the distinction between the three Persons. W. Norris Clarke, SJ faithfully presents
     this teaching when he writes, "The only distinction of any kind between the Three Persons in
     the Trinity is that stemming from the relation of *origin*, originator-originated, giver-receiver, not
     from anything in *what* is given and received, the identical, intrinsic, infinite fullness of perfec-
     tion of the absolute divine nature." Clarke, *The Philosophical Approach to God: A New Thomistic
     Perspective*, 145. Hence, there is a real relational multiplicity in a God who is also perfect
     simplicity.

306 Weinandy, *Does God Suffer?*, 124.

307 Barbour, *Religion and Science*, 294.

providence is not only that things should happen somehow; but that they should happen either by necessity or by contingency. Therefore whatsoever divine providence ordains to happen infallibly and of necessity happens infallibly and of necessity; and that happens from contingency, which the plan of divine providence conceives to happen from contingency.[308]

An inadequate sense of eternal act leads Barbour to posit a conflict between God's omniscience (classically understood) and human freedom. However, God always includes the novelty and creative freedom of events as "other" to Him. Catholic theologies of God describe Him as the perfection of being that includes all beings in advance. Unfortunately, Barbour simply has not grasped the thought of the classical expositors of the doctrine of God, e.g., Augustine, Anselm, and Aquinas. In his critique of the orthodox position, Barbour is implicitly imputing a mistaken view of God as being from them.[309]

Barbour does not want to grant God omnipotence because then he cannot explain the source of evil. If God is all good and all powerful, why does He permit sin, suffering, and evil?[310] Theodicy is a complex area of natural theology.[311] Nevertheless, we can securely state that Barbour unfortunately misses the fundamental fact that evil is an absence, a *privatio boni*. Evil is insubstantial and not part of God's creation. The Fathers of the Church were very careful never to identify *matter*, or creation more generally, with evil, in their articulations of the doctrine of *creatio ex nihilo*.

The heretics of the patristic period, e.g., the Marcionites, the Manichees, and the Gnostics, posited that if matter were evil, it could not be dependent on God. Therefore, matter cannot not be a creation of God; it must be eternal like him.[312] Unfortunately, Barbour places man and all of creation on the same ontological level as God. His notion of God as an entity among entities in the (possibly eternal?) cosmos is dangerously similar to this ancient heresy.

---

308 Aquinas, *Summa Theologiæ*, I, Q 22, A 4.

309 See Barbour, *Religion and Science*, 306–307.

310 Summarizing Irenæus of Lyons in *Against Heresies*, II, 9, 2, Gerhard May writes, "Only the heretics would, contrary to reason and Scripture, have the creator God ... responsible for all imaginable evil." May, *Creatio Ex Nihilo*, 177.

311 Gottfried Wilhelm Leibniz coined the term "théodicée" in his 1710 book, *Essais de Théodicée sur la bonté de Dieu, la liberté de l'homme et l'origine du mal* (*Essays of Theodicy on the Goodness of God, the Freedom of Man and the Origin of Evil*). His intention was to show that our experience of evil in the world does not conflict with the Christian doctrine of the goodness of God. See Gottfried Wilhelm Leibniz, *Essais de Théodicée sur la Bonté de Dieu, La Liberté de L'homme et L'origine du Mal* (Charleston, SC: Nabu Press, 2010).

312 Aquinas, *Aquinas on Creation*, 9–10.

Barbour does not accept the Christian doctrine that evil entered the world when our first parents, abusing their God-given freedom, chose against the good that God had offered to them. He specifically rejects the writings of the Apostle Paul, Augustine, and Thomas Aquinas, on the topic, stating that "neither a primeval state of perfection nor a historical fall are credible today."[313] Pope Francis' magisterium, expressed in *Placuit Deo*, clearly expresses the Catholic doctrine:

> It is also necessary to affirm that, according to biblical faith, the origin of evil is not found in the material, corporeal world experienced as a boundary or a prison from which we need to be saved. On the contrary, this faith proclaims that all the universe is good because it was created by God (cf. Gen 1:31; Wis 1:13-14; 1 Tim 4:4), and that the evil that is most damaging to man is that which comes from his heart (cf. Mt 15:18-19; Gen 3:1-19). By sinning, man abandoned the source of love, and loses himself in false forms of love that close him ever more into himself.[314]

Articulating the thought of Thomas Aquinas, the British theologian, Simon Tugwell, OP, writes, "The fact that things exist and act in their own right is the most telling indication that God is existing and acting in them."[315] "God saw everything that he had made, and behold, it was very good."[316]

Unfortunately, Barbour's commitment to process thought does not allow him to develop an adequate notion of *participation* in God's power and other perfections. Barbour posits a false dichotomy where either God has all the power and other entities have none, or God is not omnipotent and entities have power completely independent of him—*tertium non datur*. He is very close to the solution with his knowledge and appreciation of the Thomistic notion of primary and secondary causality. Yet, he never takes the steps to develop these principles further in his work.

This section concludes our critique of Barbour's process metaphysics. The next section begins our analysis of his theological method as it relates to the doctrine of creation. We shall critique Barbour's notion of experience and interpretation in theology, his understanding of the role of religious communities and their paradigms, his view of analogy and models in theology, and his approach for evaluating religious beliefs.

---

313 Barbour, *Religion and Science*, 301.
314 Congregation for the Doctrine of the Faith, *Placuit Deo*, 7.
315 Simon Tugwell, ed., *Albert & Aquinas: Selected Writings* (New York: Paulist Press, 1988), 213.
316 Genesis 1:31a (RSV).

3. Issues in Theological Method

Having analyzed the theological consequences of Barbour's epistemology and metaphysics for creation, we now study the impact of Ian Barbour's views on the similarities and differences between science and religion for his theological method. In this section, we critically engage a variety of important issues from the perspective of Catholic fundamental theology. Creation remains our "lens" for this investigation.

3.1 Experience and Interpretation

In Chapter Three we developed Barbour's position on religious experience. He posits that just as there are no un-interpreted facts in the natural sciences, there are no un-interpreted experiences in religious life. Barbour suggests that all religious experience requires some theological interpretation. On this point, he follows Whitehead who writes,

> The dogmas of religion are the attempts to formulate in precise terms the truths disclosed in the religious experience of mankind. In exactly the same way the dogmas of physical science are the attempts to formulate in precise terms the truths disclosed in the sense-perception of mankind.[317]

Here, a Catholic must be careful not to follow a modernist approach and reduce the Bible, and Divine revelation in general, to a record of historically conditioned, personal religious experiences. Catholic theology is not simply derived from private experience. For example, the doctrine of the Trinity is directly revealed throughout Sacred Scripture[318] but few Christians, even the most learned and devout, would claim to have a personal "experience" of the Trinity *qua Trinitas*. The relationship of faith and experience is complex. Ratzinger observes that "it is clear that faith without experience can only be verbiage of empty formulas [and] to reduce faith to experience is to rob it of its kernel."[319]

Of course, the "devil is in the details" when it comes to how one identifies and interprets the data of religion, particularly Sacred Scripture. Barbour does not clearly explicate his notion of the "data of religion" and at one point asks, "Whether anything so subjective [i.e., religious beliefs] can be called 'data'?"[320] In

---

317 Whitehead, *Religion in the Making*, 47.
318 For example: "Go therefore and make disciples of all nations, baptizing them in the name of the Father and of the Son and of the Holy Spirit." Matthew 28:19 (RSV).
319 Joseph Ratzinger, "Sources and Transmission of the Faith," *Communio* 10, no. 1 (1983): 23.
320 Barbour, *Issues in Science and Religion*, 253.

234 | THEOLOGY AND SCIENCE IN THE THOUGHT OF IAN BARBOUR

Catholic theology, the interpretation of Sacred Scripture, received from Sacred Tradition, would certainly constitute a datum. The Sacred Liturgy would also be a datum. In addition, within the Catholic Church, there is the reality of "theological theories" being raised to the level of a dogma, e.g., the Conciliar definitions of the equality of the Father, Son, and Holy Spirit in the face of Arianism and Pneumatomachianism. Therefore, since the fourth century, the *dogma* of the Trinity itself is a datum of the Christian religion.

In Barbour's denial of the Biblical foundations of the doctrine *creatio ex nihilo*, one sees a striking example of flawed interpretation of the data of religion. Barbour's writings do not manifest a systematic approach for the interpretation of Scripture. It is unfortunate that he does not seem aware of the richness of the various Catholic approaches to Biblical theology.[321] For example, in Barbour's interpretation of the creation account in the beginning of the Book of Genesis, he does not acknowledge the important Thomistic distinction between *primary* and *secondary* material in Sacred Scripture. The supernatural revelation of creation may be obscured if one cannot distinguish the pre-scientific, Near East cosmology of the ancient Hebrew people from the profound religious doctrines that are taught in Genesis 1.

In this regard, Thomas Aquinas' interpretative approach is helpful. Aquinas acknowledges that not everything contained in Holy Scripture is a matter of faith. He writes,

> Of things to be believed some of them belong to faith, whereas others are purely subsidiary, for, as happens in any branch of knowledge, some matters are its essential interest, while it touches on others only to make the first matters clear. Now because faith is chiefly about the things we hope to see in heaven, "for faith is the substance of things hoped for," [Hebrews *xi*.1] it follows that those things which order us directly to eternal life essentially belong to faith; such as the three Persons of almighty God, the mystery of Christ's incarnation, and other like truths ... Some things, however, are proposed in Holy Scripture, not as being the main matters of faith, but to bring them out; for instance, that Abraham had two sons, that a dead man came to life at the

---

321 For example, see Augustin Bea, *The Word of God and Mankind*, trans. Dorothy White (London: Geoffrey Chapman Ltd., 1967); Paul Beauchamp, *L'un et l'autre Testament: Accomplir les Écritures*, vol. 2, 2 vols. (Paris: Seuil, 1990); Ratzinger, *In the Beginning*; Joseph A. Fitzmyer, *The Biblical Commission's Document—The Interpretation of the Bible in the Church: Text And Commentary* (Rome: Gregorian & Biblical Press, 1995); Peter S. Williamson, *Catholic Principles for Interpreting Scripture: A Study of the Pontifical Biblical Commission's The Interpretation of the Bible in the Church* (Rome: Gregorian & Biblical Press, 2001); Jean-Dominique Barthélemy, *God and His Image: An Outline of Biblical Theology*, Revised. (San Francisco, CA: Ignatius Press, 2007); James R. Pambrun, *God's Signature: Understanding Paul Beauchamp on Creation in the First Testament*, Terra Nova 3 (Leuven: Peeters, 2018).

touch of Elisha's bones, and other like matters narrated in Scripture to disclose God's majesty or Christs incarnation.[322]

It was mentioned in the last chapter that Barbour identifies four fundamental aspects of religious experience in the Judæo-Christian tradition:

(1) awe and reverence,
(2) humility and guilt,
(3) acceptance of forgiveness, and
(4) responsibility for action in society.

As these aspects can be found throughout the Old and New Testaments, they are certainly congruent with Catholic theology. They are also instantiated in the Sacramental life of the Church. For example, in the Sacrament of Reconciliation, a penitent approaches the Sacrament acknowledging the power of God (Category 1), confesses his guilt to the priest in humility (Category 2), receives counsel and absolution from the priest (Category 3), and goes forth to do penance and live a renewed life of grace in the world (Category 4). However, one must be careful to avoid the modern tendency toward *reductionism*. In Catholic theology, the sacred mysteries of God's self-communication cannot be reduced to four categories.

Barbour is certainly correct in his assertion that religious experience is interpreted systematically within the discipline of theology. We concur with the feedback mechanism mentioned earlier through which theological concepts affect religious communities from which the "data of religion" arises. Barbour is also quite right when he states that theological "beliefs have implications for worship, ethics, and all aspects of corporate and individual life, and thereby influence the data."[323] Interpretation of religious experiences and beliefs takes place within religious communities and according to particular paradigms. In the next section, we critically engage Barbour's notion of religious communities and paradigms.

3.2 Religious Communities and Paradigms

Thomas G. Guarino points out that both in academic theology as well as the broader life of the Church, a "dynamic tension" can arise between the preservation and development of doctrine.[324] While one does not speak of paradigm shifts in Catholic theology in terms of revelation *in se*, one can speak of new paradigms of

---

322 Aquinas, *Summa Theologiæ*, II-II, Q 1, A 6.
323 Barbour, *Issues in Science and Religion*, 210.
324 Thomas Guarino, *Vincent of Lérins and the Development of Christian Doctrine* (Grand Rapids, MI: Baker Academic, 2013), 3.

interpretation, expression, or *methodology.*[325] For example, a change in paradigms can be seen as similar to a change in hermeneutic. This is consistent with Barbour's definition of a paradigm as "key examples from the past that influence all its activities."[326] Throughout history, theologians have applied diverse "lenses" in their study of revelation. For example, with regard to *interpretation,* one can say that the adoption and adaptation of concepts from Aristotelian metaphysics by Saints Anselm, Albert the Great, and Thomas Aquinas represented a paradigmatic shift in how the Christian faith was expressed in the medieval period.

With regard to *expression,* one can note the change in language (e.g., literary tone) in the Dogmatic Constitutions of the Second Vatican Council compared to the First, e.g., the absence of anathema canons. Over the last 2000 years, there have been a wide variety of *methodologies* in theology. The mystery of God certainly exceeds any particular method or system, and orthodoxy is definitely not reductive to a system.[327]

Among the various theological pedagogical *methodologies,* the Decree on Priestly Training, *Optatam Totius,* recommends the genetic method for seminarian education in order to facilitate a renewal of theology.[328] This method is the norm at the Pontifical Gregorian University and many American seminaries. The Irish theologian, Gerard Whelan, SJ, notes how Pope Francis often adopts an "inductive" method in his pastoral theology.[329] In all three situations, i.e., new paradigms of *interpretation, expression,* or *methodology,* the "key examples from the past" do not change. A real and substantial continuity is present between early (e.g., patristic) doctrinal formulations and those that are articulated with a new philosophical

---

325 The 1989 document of the International Theological Commission, *The Interpretation of Dogma,* is a helpful tool when considering new paradigms of interpretation. It offers a strong defense of the permanent values of dogmatic formulæ as well as guiding principles for contemporary interpretation. For Catholic theologians, the indissoluble bond between Scripture, Tradition and the communion of the Church is foundational. The ITC document echoes the magisterial teaching of Pope Paul VI who wrote that while greater clarity of expression is always possible with dogmas, any new formulations "must always be done in such a way that they retain the meaning in which they have been used, so that with the advance of an understanding of the faith, the truth of faith will remain unchanged. For it is the teaching of the First Vatican Council that 'the meaning that Holy Mother the Church has once declared, is to be retained forever, and no pretext of deeper understanding ever justifies any deviation from that meaning.'" Paul VI, *Mysterium Fidei,* 1965, 25.
326 Barbour, *Issues in Science and Religion,* 214.
327 See Rowland, *Catholic Theology,* 1–15.
328 Second Vatican Council, *Optatam Totius,* 1965, 16.
329 Gerard Whelan, "Evangelii Gaudium come 'Teologia Contestuale': Aiutare la Chiesa ad 'Alzarsi al Livello dei sui Tempi,'" in *Evangelii Gaudium: il testo ci interroga: Chiavi di lettura, testimonianze e prospettive,* ed. Miguel Yáñez Humberto (Rome: Gregorian & Biblical Press, 2014), 37.

approach, modern language, or innovative method. The British New Testament scholar, Richard Bauckham, points out that

> John's original variation of the salutation in [Revelation] 1:4b-5a[330] strongly suggests that his understanding of the divine is deliberately "trinitarian." I put the word in inverted commas only to warn us that, of course, we must not attribute to John the particular conceptuality of the patristic doctrine of the Trinity which became the norm for the later Christian tradition. As we shall see ... the theological concern that gives John's understanding of the divine a Trinitarian character is fundamentally the same as that which led to the patristic development of trinitarian doctrine: a concern to include Jesus, as well as the Spirit, in the Jewish monotheistic faith in God.[331]

There is indeed authentic continuity between the Trinitarian faith of the Apostle John and that of the Church in the twenty-first century.

As the Church reflects on the mystery of the Trinity, and doctrines develop under the inspiration of the Holy Spirit, a theologian would not reject a dogmatic proposition based on some "experience" (in the Barbourian sense) and attempt to instigate a paradigm shift as can happen in the natural sciences. For example, the belief in the hypostatic union of the human and divine natures of Jesus Christ will not be declared "false" by new "data"—"Jesus Christ is the same yesterday and today and forever."[332] Similarly, the Church will not retract its belief in the creation of the spiritual and material orders of the cosmos *ex nihilo et cum tempore* given its foundation in Sacred Scripture and Tradition. It is impossible to add or subtract anything from the substance of the articles of faith.[333]

Around the year 180, Saint Irenæus of Lyon, published the well-known work entitled *Adversus Hæreses*. In confronting the Gnostic heresy, Irenæus identifies three fundamental principles for Catholic doctrine. First, Divine revelation must be accepted as a historical fact. Second, the teaching of the Apostles faithfully preserves and transmits this revelation. Finally, the authoritative interpretation of revelation requires the integration of Sacred Scripture and Apostolic Tradition under the guidance of the Magisterium, i.e., the men entrusted with Sacred Office who are the successors to the Apostles.[334] These basic principles continue to guide

---

330 "Grace to you and peace from him who is and who was and who is to come, and from the seven spirits who are before his throne, and from Jesus Christ the faithful witness, the first-born of the dead, and the ruler of kings on earth." Revelation 1:4b–5a (RSV).

331 Richard Bauckham, *The Theology of the Book of Revelation* (Cambridge: Cambridge University Press, 1993), 24.

332 Hebrews 13:8 (RSV).

333 In fact, Thomas Aquinas wrote that all the articles of faith "are contained implicitly in certain primary matters of faith, such as God's existence and His providence." *Summa Theologiae*, II–II, Q 1, A 7.

334 See Irenaeus of Lyons, *Against Heresies*.

the Church's reflection on the deposit of the faith and should be considered in a Catholic reception of Barbour's exploration of paradigm shifts and doctrinal revision. As with the challenge of second century Gnostics, so too today Irenæus' principles serve to prevent God's authoritative, self-communication from being obscured or corrupted.

In the fifth century, Saint Vincent of Lérins insisted that "in the Catholic Church itself, all possible care must be taken, that we hold that faith which has been believed everywhere, always, by all."[335] Vincent writes that "we shall follow universality [Catholicity] if we confess that one faith to be true, which the whole Church throughout the world confesses; [and] antiquity, if we in no wise depart from those interpretations which it is manifest were notoriously held by our holy ancestors and fathers."[336] This theological insight has become an official criteria for the discernment of authentic doctrinal development. At the First Vatican Council, the Fathers adopted one of Vincent's fundamental principles for development found in his *Commonitorium*.[337] *Dei Filius* teaches that doctrinal development must always be growth "*in eodem scilicet dogmate, eodem sensu, eademque sententia*"[338] (in the same doctrine, in the same sense, and the same understanding).

In a 2013 interview, Pope Francis commented on a passage from the Office of the Readings of the *Feria Sexta* of the Twenty-Seventh Week of Ordinary Time taken from the *Commonitorium Primum* of Vincent of Lérins,[339] Francis notes how doctrine progresses, solidifying with years, growing over time, deepening with age. He states,

> St. Vincent of Lerins makes a comparison between the biological development of man and the transmission from one era to another of the deposit of faith, which grows and is strengthened with time ... So we grow in the understanding of the truth. Exegetes and theologians help the church to mature in her own judgment. Even the other sciences and their development help the church in its growth in understanding ... Even the forms for expressing truth can be multiform, and this is indeed necessary for the transmission of the Gospel in its timeless meaning ... The Church has experienced times of brilliance, like that of Thomas Aquinas.[340]

---

335 Vincent of Lerins, *The Commonitory of St. Vincent of Lerins*, ed. Paul A. Boer, trans. Charles A. Heurtley (New York: Veritatis Splendor Publications, 2012), chap. 2, para. 6.

336 Ibid.

337 Ibid., chap. 23, para. 54.

338 First Vatican Council, "Dei Filius," 4.

339 "*Ita étiam christiánae religiónis dogma sequátur has decet proféctuum leges, ut annis scílect consolidétur, dilatétur témpore, sublimétur aetát.*" *Liturgia Horarium*, vol. 4, 4 vols. (Vatican City State: Libreria Editrice Vaticana, 2000), 300.

340 Francis, "A Big Heart Open to God."

The theology of the development of doctrine was a great concern of Saint John Henry Newman. His interest was to identify and explain true developments in doctrine, i.e., the way Catholic teaching has become more detailed and explicit over the last 2000 years, as well as distinguish cases of doctrinal corruption.[341]

Gerhard Müller points out that the need for doctrinal development flows from the very nature of revelation. He describes it is a "consequence of the presence of the divine Word in our human words and understanding."[342] The *intellectus fidei* of the present develops from the *auditus fidei* of the first century. Müller is careful to point out that doctrinal development in the Catholic theological tradition does not justify interpreting the historical Christian faith in terms of German idealism, historicism, and modernism:

> Proponents of these currents think of God, or the Absolute, as a so-called "transcendental a priori," that is, as the subjective necessary condition of our reason and experience, which is itself prior to our experience and can never be the object of experience. Inasmuch as the Absolute is the condition for our thought and language, it cannot itself be expressed in words and concepts. According to this approach, then, all the dogmas of the Catholic faith are only provisional conceptual formulas that give expression to the ever-changing religious sentiment found in the Church's collective consciousness.[343]

Modern philosophy has made manifest the "problem" of the relationship between *truth* and *history*. This is an issue that fundamental theology must engage. As Müller concisely explains,

> In its temporality, history seems to be the realm of the transient, the changeable, the contingent, whereas truth is beyond time, always valid, and found in the realm of divine ideas. As such, truth is never completely within the reach of finite human beings, who can approach it ever more closely but ultimately can never get ahold of it. Christian theology, in contrast, does not start with the question of how—under the conditions of historical existence—it is *possible* to know the truth. Rather, it begins with the *fact* of God's self-revelation in time.[344]

Whether one is considering Barbour's notion of doctrinal "revision" in a *theology of nature* or if one believes that there are grounds for a *paradigmatic-shift* in an aspect of theology, doctrinal development in the Catholic Church should always refer to

---

341 See Newman, *An Essay On Development Of Christian Doctrine.*

342 Gerhard Müller, "Development, or Corruption?," *First Things* (February 20, 2018), accessed March 8, 2018, https://www.firstthings.com/web-exclusives/2018/02/development-or-corruption.

343 Ibid.

344 Ibid.

the process by which the People of God come to a more profound understanding of God's self-communication—Divine revelation.

Müller makes the important point that "the doctrinal formulas are not themselves the object of the act of faith. Rather, the believer's faith refers to the very reality of God and God's truth in Christ."[345] Here, he follows Thomas Aquinas who wrote that "the act of the believer does not terminate in a proposition, but in a thing."[346] Hence, the *formulæ fidei* are truly *referential* (to use Barbour's term). Again, to echo Müller, "they are not just fortuitous expressions of our subjective consciousness of God."[347]

When considering Barbour's notion of religious paradigms and the possibility of "shifts," it is helpful to consider *Dei Verbum*. In paragraph eight, it beautifully and succinctly summarizes the Catholic understanding of doctrinal development. *Dei Verbum* states that Catholic Tradition

> which comes from the Apostles develops in the Church with the help of the Holy Spirit. For there is a growth in the understanding of the realities and the words which have been handed down. This happens through the contemplation and study made by believers, who treasure these things in their hearts (see Luke, 2:19, 51) through a penetrating understanding of the spiritual realities which they experience, and through the preaching of those who have received through Episcopal succession the sure gift of truth. For as the centuries succeed one another, the Church constantly moves forward toward the fullness of divine truth until the words of God reach their complete fulfillment in her.[348]

In Catholic theology, Sacred Tradition is not understood simply to be a transmission of concepts, but of the very presence of the Risen Jesus. Benedict XVI expressed this belief powerfully at a Wednesday Audience in 2006:

> [The] ongoing actualization of the presence of Jesus—through the work of the Spirit and through the Church's apostolic ministry and fraternal communion—is what we mean by the term Tradition; it is not just a transmission of "things" but the efficacious presence of the Lord who accompanies and guides the gathered community. The Holy Spirit nurtures this communion, assuring the connection between the apostolic faith experienced by the first communities of disciples and our experience today of Christ in his Church.[349]

---

345 Ibid.
346 Aquinas, *Summa Theologiæ*, II–II, Q 1, A 2.
347 Müller, "Development, or Corruption?"
348 Second Vatican Council, *Dei Verbum*, 8.
349 Benedict XVI, "Tradition: Communion in Time" (General Audience, Vatican City State, April 26, 2006), accessed April 30, 2018, https://zenit.org/articles/role-of-church-tradition/.

Having analyzed Ian Barbour's understanding of religious communities and their paradigms, we now critique his notion of analogy and models in theology and science.

3.3 Analogy and Models

Barbour's approach to models cannot be separated from his critical realist theory of knowledge. A critical realist view of models emphasizes their selective character. Barbour wants to avoid what he classifies as two unhelpful extremes: the *literalist* view of models that comes from *naïve* realism and the *fictionalist* view from instrumentalism. Although one would be hard-pressed to find a "non-critical" realist, e.g., a Gilsonian realist, who subscribes to a literalist interpretation of models.

Barbour also rejects the positivist claim that theories can be inferred directly from observations through induction. As with Sacred Scripture, Barbour advocates that models be taken *seriously but not literally*.[350] Barbour correctly points out that religious language is often metaphorical. He acknowledges that while "a metaphor is *not literally true* … [it] is not a useful fiction, a mere pretense, a game of make-believe with no relation to reality; it asserts that there are significant analogies between the things compared."[351]

Unfortunately, Barbour does not distinguish between the "literal" and "literalist" interpretations of Sacred Scripture. The *literal* meaning of a passage from the Bible is not the fundamentalist interpretation. The Pontifical Biblical Commission (PBC) has defined the literal sense in a very helpful way that is worth quoting *in extenso*:

> The literal sense is not to be confused with the "literalist" sense to which fundamentalists are attached. It is not sufficient to translate a text word for word in order to obtain its literal sense. One must understand the text according to the literary conventions of the time. When a text is metaphorical, its literal sense is not that which flows immediately from a word-to-word translation (e.g., "Let your loins be girt": Lk. 12:35), but that which corresponds to the metaphorical use of these terms ("Be ready for action"). When it is a question of a story, the literal sense does not necessarily imply belief that the facts recounted actually took place, for a story need not belong to the genre of history but be instead a work of imaginative fiction. The literal sense of Scripture is that which has been expressed directly by the inspired human authors. Since it is the fruit of inspiration, this sense is also intended by God, as principal author. One arrives at this sense by means of a careful analysis of the text, within its literary and historical context. The principal task of exegesis is to carry out this analysis, making use of all the

---

350 Barbour, *Myths, Models, and Paradigms*, 36–38.
351 Ibid., 13.

resources of literary and historical research, with a view to defining the literal sense of the biblical texts with the greatest possible accuracy (cf "*Divino Afflante Spiritu*: Ench. Bibl.," 550). To this end, the study of ancient literary genres is particularly necessary (ibid. 560).[352]

Barbour's writings demonstrate a well-researched and consequently rich understanding of analogy in science and theology. Regrettably, in light of the Barthian influence at Yale Divinity School, Barbour does not fully appreciate the legitimacy and power of the analogy of being in theology (discussed in Chapter Two). His *a priori* rejection of most natural theologies does not allow him to make the important "theological movement" from creation to Creator. This hapless *intellektuelles Gepäck* restricts Barbour from acknowledging the simple fact, recognized by most Christians, that the beauty and order in creation points to the perfections of the Triune God.

In *Issues in Science and Religion*, Barbour writes,

> There is little interest today in looking to nature for support for religious beliefs; the once-popular arguments of "natural theology"—such as the claim that evidences of design prove the existence of a Designer—appear dubious logically and, more significantly, reflect a speculative approach very different from the attitudes characteristic of religion itself.[353]

Even with forty years of further reflection, Barbour still maintains that "even if the argument [of the existence of God from natural theology] is accepted, it leads only to the distant God of deism … not the God of theism actively involved with the world and human life."[354] Barbour's rejection of natural theology may indicate a "subconscious" divorce between faith and reason.

Barbour is generally very careful with his treatment of models. His discussion of the similarities and differences between scientific and religious models would find little disagreement from most Christian theologians or practicing scientists. Barbour's observation that (informal) religious models can have greater influence in faith communities than official doctrines formulated with theological propositions is particularly interesting. Perhaps one sees an example of this in Catholic popular piety and devotions. Of course, this situation is not problematic as long as the popular religious models do not contradict Church doctrine.

---

352 Pontifical Biblical Commission, *The Interpretation of the Bible in the Church* (Boston: Pauline Books & Media, 1996), II, B, 1.
353 Barbour, *Issues in Science and Religion*, 2.
354 Barbour, *Nature, Human Nature, and God*, 3.

3.4 Evaluating Beliefs

Because of the conceptul and methodological parallels that he sees between the-ology and science, Barbour suggests that religious beliefs may be evaluated ac-cording to the same criteria as scientific theories: relation to data, coherence, and comprehensiveness. Nonetheless, there are substantial differences. Barbour acknowledges that theology and science diverge in their criteria of evaluation with regard to the influence of interpretation on experience, the fact that the criteria of evaluation are themselves influenced by religious beliefs, and the fact that in-tersubjective testability occurs only within particular religious communities. He recognizes that the influence of interpretation on experience is much greater in theology compared to science. All scientific facts are theory-laden, but in theology Barbour asserts that the "feedback" from interpretative to experiential aspects is much more significant. For example, when a person professes Christian faith and receives Baptism, he interprets reality in a new way and experiences the world differently.[355]

Regrettably, Barbour's theology of faith does not include the fundamental Catholic concept of the *obœdientia fidei*. The Catechism states that "to obey (from the Latin *ob-audire*, to 'hear or listen to') in faith is to submit freely to the word that has been heard, because its truth is guaranteed by God, who is Truth itself. Abraham is the model of such obedience offered us by Sacred Scripture. The Virgin Mary is its most perfect embodiment."[356] *Obœdientia fidei* can never place the be-liever in a compromised position with regard to natural reason in the Catholic theological tradition. *Dei Filius* teaches that

> although faith is above reason, nevertheless, between faith and reason no true dis-sension can ever exist, since the same God, who reveals mysteries and infuses faith, has bestowed on the human soul the light of reason; moreover, God cannot deny Himself, nor ever contradict truth with truth. But, a vain appearance of such a contra-diction arises chiefly from this, that either the dogmas of faith have not been under-stood and interpreted according to the mind of the Church, or deceitful opinions are considered as the determinations of reason. Therefore, "every assertion contrary to the truth illuminated by faith, we define to be altogether false" [Lateran Council V].[357]

The Second Vatican Council, rooting itself in the doctrine of creation, echoes this teaching on the compatibility of natural reason and supernatural faith. As God is the author of the natural and supernatural orders, it is unreasonable to suppose

---

355 Barbour, *Issues in Science and Religion*, 258.
356 CCC 144.
357 First Vatican Council, "Dei Filius," 4.

a contradiction between a truth of the natural sciences and the Catholic faith. Failing to respect the legitimate autonomy of the natural sciences and theology can instigate the conflict mode of interaction. *Gaudium et Spes* states,

> For by the very circumstance of their having been created, all things are endowed with their own stability, truth, goodness, proper laws and order. Man must respect these as he isolates them by the appropriate methods of the individual sciences or arts. Therefore if methodical investigation within every branch of learning is carried out in a genuinely scientific manner and in accord with moral norms, it never truly conflicts with faith, for earthly matters and the concerns of faith derive from the same God. Indeed whoever labors to penetrate the secrets of reality with a humble and steady mind, even though he is unaware of the fact, is nevertheless being led by the hand of God, who holds all things in existence, and gives them their identity. Consequently, we cannot but deplore certain habits of mind, which are sometimes found too among Christians, which do not sufficiently attend to the rightful independence of science and which, from the arguments and controversies they spark, lead many minds to conclude that faith and science are mutually opposed.[358]

This teaching has implications that will be explored later in Chapter Five for Barbour's notion of theologies of nature—the revision of doctrine based on contemporary science.

Given his "liberal" Protestant orientation, critical realist epistemology, process metaphysics, and his classification of the similarities and differences in the methods of theology and science, Barbour generally emphasizes the parallel perspectives on the two disciplines. Hence, Barbour concludes that "the contrasts are not as absolute as most recent theologians and philosophers have maintained ... Reason is fulfilled, not abrogated, by revelation; reflective inquiry can coexist with religious commitment."[359]

Another similarity that Barbour rightly highlights is the fact that both the scientist and the theologian are rightly interested with the natural world. The scientist investigates the natural laws that govern the cosmos, whereas the (Catholic) theologian studies creation in search of the Creator. Barbour states that "despite the divergence of their interests, it is (according to critical realism) the same natural world to which they look, so their inquiries cannot be totally independent."[360] Barbour is quite correct that what is needed are modes of interaction between theology and science that respect one another's integrity.[361]

---

358 Second Vatican Council, *Gaudium et Spes*, 36.
359 Barbour, *Issues in Science and Religion*, 268.
360 Ibid., 269.
361 Ibid., 270.

In Chapter Four, using the doctrine of creation as a "lens," our goal was to offer a Catholic critique of Ian Barbour's approach to relating theology and science. This chapter examined Barbour's epistemology, metaphysics, and aspects of his theological method. In light of the findings, we now consider in Chapter Five how Barbour's approach can, or cannot, facilitate the *dialogue* and *integration* of the Catholic doctrine of creation with the natural sciences. Within the interaction typology of dialogue, the notions of presuppositions and limit questions as well as methodological and conceptual parallels will be explored from a Catholic perspective. Within the typology of integration, we shall consider natural theology, theologies of nature, and the move toward a systematic synthesis between theology and science in the Catholic tradition. This final chapter will also offer some conclusions on Ian Barbour's overall contribution to the field as well as suggestions for future research.

CHAPTER FIVE

Toward Dialogue and Integration

At the beginning of this book, we stated our goal to evaluate Ian Barbour's approach to relating theology and science for the purpose of exploring the possibility of it enriching the *dialogue* and *integration* of the Catholic doctrine of creation with the natural sciences. Toward this end, the second chapter was dedicated to an explication of the sources of Barbour's fundamental theological principles, his critical realist epistemology, and his process metaphysics. Having established those foundations, we elucidated Barbour's assessment of the similarities and differences between theology and science in the third chapter. This allowed us to explain his methodologies for carrying out theology and science as independent, truth seeking activities, as well as for relating the two fields. Chapter Four offered a critique of Barbour's epistemology, metaphysics, and theological method according to fundamental Catholic theological criteria.

In this final chapter, we explore how Barbour's approach can facilitate *dialogue* and *integration* between the Catholic doctrine of creation and the natural sciences. In our application of Barbour's dialogue and integration insights that could possibly contribute to Catholic theology, we are attentive to the following criteria:

(1) Fidelity to Divine revelation and its definitive interpretation in the Church,

(2) The selection and application of a suitable metaphysics and epistemology for both natural science and Catholic theology. We reject any philosophy that "overwhelms" revelation, and

(3) Consistency with the best of contemporary natural science.

Ultimately, we offer some conclusions on Barbour's contributions to the field of theology and science.

The perennial insights of Thomas Aquinas on creation guide many aspects of this analysis. We have chosen him as the standard for a Catholic theology of creation because he develops the grammar and logic for speaking about creation. His metaphysics also ensures the intelligibility of science. As in Chapter Four, we shall show how Aquinas fulfills and corrects certain "drifts" in Barbour's thought. As William Carroll puts it, "Thomas Aquinas did not have the advantage of the Hubble Space Telescope, but in many ways he was able to see farther and more clearly than those who do."[1]

The Austrian theologian, Christoph Cardinal Schönborn, OP, argues that mistakes made in the past when relating Christian faith and natural science should not lead theologians simply to declare a truce and avoid engagement.[2] Ian Barbour has shown that when one precludes certain contrasting perspectives on theology and science, e.g., fundamentalism or scientific materialism, the *conflict* between the two fields can be avoided. Other contrasting perspectives support the *independence* of theology and science, e.g., neo-orthodoxy.[3]

Still other perspectives sustain *dialogue* through conceptual and methodological parallels and permit limit questions, e.g., Why is there a universe? Finally, according to Barbour, a true *integration* between theology and science can emerge through natural theology, theologies of nature, and a metaphysically supported systematic synthesis.

---

1 William E. Carroll, "Aquinas and the Big Bang," *First Things*, no. 97 (November 1999): 20.

2 See Christoph Schönborn, "Schöpfungskatechese un Evolutionstheorie. Vom Burgfrieden zum konstruktiven Konflikt," in *Evolutionismus und Christentum*, ed. Robert Spaemann, Reinhard Löw, and Peter Koslowski (Weinheim: Wiley-VCH, 1986), 91–116.

3 In 1997, the American paleontologist and historian of science, Stephen Jay Gould, introduced the idea of non-overlapping magisteria (NOMA) in the theology-science field. NOMA fits into Barbour's typology of independence. Gould, an agnostic, maintains that science and theology represent different areas of inquiry, e.g., facts vs. values. Each field exercises a legitimate magisterium and the two domains must never overlap. Gould believes that scientists should not deal with limit questions, e.g., Why is there a universe? He also thinks that theologians should stay away from science, e.g., believing that God created the universe. For more information, see Stephen Jay Gould, *Rocks of Ages: Science and Religion in the Fullness of Life* (New York: Ballantine Books, 2002), chap. 2.

In this final chapter, we endeavor to continue to develop answers to questions posed in Chapter One such as: How can Barbour help Catholics relate the doctrine of creation to the natural sciences? Where are his ideas problematic? How can these problems nevertheless unveil something of the truth? Can he aid in deepening our understanding of doctrine?

While Barbour does not personally assent to the full, Catholic doctrine of creation, his *dialogue* interaction modality can bring the doctrine into a fruitful and informative exchange with the natural sciences. It will be shown that his focus on presuppositions and limit questions as well as methodological and conceptual parallels does not necessarily bring with it the problematic aspects of his thought identified in the last chapter. The *dialogue* typology is not explicitly coupled to critical realism or process metaphysics. Similarly, aspects of Barbour's theological method critiqued in Chapter Four are not implied in the typology. On the other hand, Catholic scholars must exercise greater care in naïvely adopting Barbour's preferred mode of *integration*. The next two sections of this chapter will explicate and apply these two typologies of interaction in the context of the Catholic doctrine of creation.

Barbour's overall quest is very significant. Therefore, Catholic engagement with his thought is of great importance. The German Protestant theologian, Wolfhart Pannenberg, makes the keen observation that "if the God of the Bible is creator of the universe, then it is not possible to understand fully or even appropriately the processes of nature without any reference to God."[4] Summarizing the Christocentric thought of John Paul II, David L. Schindler writes, "the Incarnation of the Word carries an ontological force: it affects internally the being of everything."[5] In the decision to move beyond *conflict* and *independence* typologies of interaction, Catholics and many Protestants are generally in strong agreement. Christian faith in creation and the scientific study of nature should be in some relationship of *dialogue* and perhaps *integration*.

---

4 Wolfhart Pannenberg, "Theological Questions to Scientists," *Communio* 15, no. 3 (1988): 319.

5 Schindler, "Theology, Science, and Cosmology," 270. John Paul II writes, "The Incarnation of God the Son signifies the taking up into unity with God not only of human nature, but in this human nature, in a sense, of everything that is 'flesh': the whole of humanity, the entire visible and material world. The Incarnation, then, also has a cosmic significance, a cosmic dimension. The 'first-born of all creation,' becoming incarnate in the individual humanity of Christ, unites himself in some way with the entire reality of man, which is also 'flesh' and in this reality with all 'flesh,' with the whole of creation." John Paul II, *Dominum et Vivificantem*, 1986, 50.

1. Dialogue

1.1 Presuppositions and Limit Questions

According to the Italian theologian, Michelina Tenace, Catholic fundamental theology has a particular role in proposing [limit] questions (*proporre le domande*).[6] As mentioned in the first chapter, Barbour writes that "limit questions are ontological questions raised by the scientific enterprise as a whole but not answered by the methods of science,"[7] e.g., Why is there a universe?[8] or Why is it comprehensible?

Between the fields of physical cosmology and the theology of creation, Ian Barbour identifies various classes of limit questions related to the *intelligibility* and the *contingency*[9] of the universe. Why is the cosmos rationally intelligible? This is obviously not a question that can be answered by mathematics, physics, chemistry, or biology. Barbour also identifies four forms of contingency that characterize the universe:

(1) *Contingent existence*, e.g., Why is there anything at all?
(2) *Contingent boundary conditions*, e.g., A singularity at the beginning of spacetime would be inaccessible to the methods of science.
(3) *Contingent laws*, e.g., A universe could exist with different laws.
(4) *Contingent events*, "The cosmos is a unique and irreversible sequence of events."[10]

All four contingencies offer substantial areas for the dialogue of the Catholic doctrine of creation with the natural sciences.

Barbour points out that dialogue between theology and science may arise from considering the *presuppositions* of the scientific enterprise as a whole. Here he makes a clear contribution to bringing the Catholic doctrine of creation into deeper dialogue with modern science. For example, surprising to many, the

---

6 Michelina Tenace, "Incontro del Dipartimento di Teologia Fondamentale" (Presentation, Pontificia Università Gregoriana, October 12, 2017).

7 Barbour, *Religion and Science*, 90.

8 It is worth nothing that von Balthasar believes that "the adage that God created the world for his own glorification is acceptable only if one says that God's glory consists in his love." Hans Urs von Balthasar, "Creation and Trinity," trans. Stephen Wentworth Arndt, *Communio* 15, no. 3 (1988): 285.

9 Pannenberg wisely points out how natural laws, such as the laws of physics, appear to theologians as "contingent products of the creative freedom of God." Wolfhart Pannenberg, "The Doctrine of Creation and Modern Science," *Zygon* 23, no. 1 (1988): 9.

10 Barbour, *When Science Meets Religion*, 54–56.

question, Is there a universe? has baffled distinguished cosmologists from Einstein to Hawking, leading them to fail to face up to the question.[11]

Stanley Jaki diagnoses the origin of this problem. He observes that in post-Kantian philosophy, the "universe" is often reduced to a mere word, if it is employed at all. Jaki writes,

> The word "universe" had no place in the positivism of Auguste Comte and of J.S. Mill. The pluralistic universe of W. James's pragmatism is just as illogical as is the universe within Dewey empiricism. There is no room for the universe in existentialism and in phenomenology. Whatever else the universe may be, it is not a phenomenon. And insofar as the universe means coherence, it is irreconcilable with the radical separation among all events as postulated by Sartre. It should be no surprise that deconstructionists can at most repeat Kant's false arguments about the universe. As if to prove how far they are behind times, they are the least willing to construct a philosophy about the universe in this age of scientific cosmology.[12]

Jaki also notices that the "universe" in Berkeleyan and Hegelian idealism is reduced to a *mental* entity. The Dutch mathematician, Willem de Sitter, in the context of discussing the formal construction of scientific laws as the sole true reality, states that the universe is a mere mathematical formula.[13]

Jaki comments,

> The recognition by the human mind of the existence of the Creator by means of created things implies a philosophical framework which makes no sense unless there is a totality of things, real, orderly and contingent, which is the notion of a universe proclaimed by the dogma of creation and claimed by science as well.[14]

The Filipino philosopher of science, Noel Villajin, wisely remarks that "totality, universe, contingency, creation, God and full intelligibility in science point out to some presuppositions that lie beyond science. These presuppositions are essential for science."[15] Barbour would certainly agree.

In an article on the importance of the reality of the universe as a "strict totality of things,"[16] the American academic, John-Peter Pham, highlights the fact that

11 See Jaki, *Is There a Universe?*
12 Stanley L. Jaki, "The Reality of the Universe" (Lecture presented at the International Congress on the Philosophy of Nature, Pontificia Università Lateranense, January 10, 1992) cited in John-Peter Pham, "The Importance of the Reality of the Universe in the Work of Stanley L. Jaki," *Faith & Reason* (December 26, 1995): 337–354.
13 Willem de Sitter, *Kosmos* (Cambridge, MA: Harvard University Press, 1932), 133–134.
14 Stanley L. Jaki, *Cosmos and Creator* (Edinburgh: Scottish Academic Press, 1980), 86.
15 Noel Ma. N. Villajin, "The Universe as a Creation: The Ontological Presupposition of Science" (PhD, Universidad de Navarra, 1995), 482.
16 Jaki, *Is There a Universe?*, 10.

by achieving a contradiction-free account of the totality of gravitationally interacting entities,[17] modern cosmology implicitly discredits the very foundations of Kantian idealist agnosticism which, for two centuries, called into doubt the very validity of the notion of the universe and, by implication, the very notion of its Creator and his objective laws which can be known by reason as well as revelation. For the real genius, and consequently danger, of Kant's strategy "lay precisely in his claim that in order to make impossible the step from the universe to God, one had to destroy access to the universe itself by declaring it a notion unworthy of the intellect.[18]"[19]

Pham continues,

> Furthermore, by showing over the mind-boggling span of seventy orders of magnitude a most specific universe, modern cosmology has also provided a powerful demonstration of the contingency of creation. Like any specific thing, the specific universe has to be the result of a choice among many other possibilities. But since the universe is the totality of things, the choice for its specificity can only be looked for "outside" that totality.[20]

The contingent yet intelligibly ordered status[21] of this "totality of things" is a clear pointer to the Christian *Deus Creator*. He is the reason why the universe exists and why it is precisely the way it is. Barbour's exhortation to fellow scientists to consider the *presuppositions* of their work[22] certainly advances the theology-science interaction in general and the dialogue of creation theology and physical cosmology in particular.

Barbour's colleague, Arthur Peacocke, makes the important point that "any affirmations about God's relation to the world, any doctrine of creation, if it is not to become vacuous and sterile, must be about the relation of God to, the creation by God of, the world that the natural sciences describe."[23] This connection is another essential *presupposition* that in itself constitutes a point of dialogue between

---

17   Here, Pham refers to Jaki's point about the significant of the "power or ability of General Relativity to treat in a scientifically consistent manner the totality of material particles endowed with gravitation." See Stanley L. Jaki, "The Absolute Beneath the Relative: Reflections on Einstein's Theories," in *The Absolute Beneath the Relative and Other Essays* (Lanham, MD: University Press of America, 1988), 9.

18   Stanley L. Jaki, *God and the Cosmologists* (Washington, DC: Regnery Gateway Inc., 1991), 22–23.

19   John-Peter Pham, "The Importance of The Reality of The Universe in the Work of Stanley L. Jaki," *Faith & Reason* (December 26, 1995): 337–354, accessed 10/31/2018 https://www.catholicculture.org/culture/library/view.cfm?recnum=3731.

20   Ibid.

21   The hierarchical order of contingent motion is what necessitates a first cause, that is, as the guarantee of the universe's apparent intelligibility.

22   Barbour, *Religion and Science*, 90.

23   Arthur Peacocke, "God's Action in the Real World," *Zygon* 26, no. 4 (1991): 456.

the natural sciences and the doctrine of creation. While the natural scientist studies creation from the point of view of *measure* and *change*, and the fundamental theologian from the point of view of *being* and *revelation*, it is the *eadem creatio* under investigation. In the view of Thomas Aquinas, this connection, and therefore *dialogue*, is extremely important:

> The opinion is false of those who asserted that it made no difference to the truth of the faith what anyone holds about creatures, so long as one thinks rightly about God ... For error concerning creatures ... spills into false opinions about God, and takes men's minds away from Him, to whom faith seeks to lead them.[24]

In the next section we explore the particularly important presupposition of the intelligibility of the universe. We then investigate four areas of contingency (existence, boundaries, laws, and events) that suggest presuppositions as well as limit questions. Finally, we examine methodological and conceptual parallels between theology and science.

1.1.1 Intelligibility

In Chapter One we discussed the influence of Ian Barbour on the Anglican theologian and physicist, John Polkinghorne. In his book, *One World: The Interaction of Science and Theology*, Polkinghorne advances Barbour's program of dialogue focused on the *intelligibility* of creation. According to Polkinghorne's perspective, the key to understanding the universe is mathematics—a creation of the God-given intellect.[25] The ability of the human mind to understand creation, particularly with the tools of quantitative reasoning, is no accident because God is the common ground of rationality and creation. As Ratzinger puts it, "everything that is, is reasonable in terms of its origin, for it comes from creative reason."[26] Scientists can have faith in the regularity and order of the cosmos because of the fidelity of the *logos*.[27]

Barbour's identification of the *intelligibility* of the universe as a presupposition for the practice of science is significant. While certainly not the first Christian thinker to make the observation,[28] and not the only one in the contemporary

---

24 Aquinas, *Summa Contra Gentiles*, bk. II, chap. 3, 6.

25 John Polkinghorne, *One World: The Interaction of Science and Theology* (Philadelphia: Templeton Press, 2007), 56.

26 Joseph Ratzinger, *A Turning Point for Europe*, trans. Brian McNeil, 2nd ed. (San Francisco: Ignatius Press, 2010), 111.

27 Polkinghorne, *One World*, 116.

28 The Fathers of the Church, e.g., Saint Maximus the Confessor, reflected deeply on the intelligibility of the universe and its theological implications. See Alexei V. Nesteruk, *Light from the East: Theology, Science, and the Eastern Orthodox Tradition* (Minneapolis: Fortress Press, 2003), 52.

era,[29] Barbour's influence in the Anglophonic theological world brought this issue to the forefront for many theologians in the United States and the United Kingdom. From the Catholic perspective, the *logos*-centric theology of Benedict XVI offers a convincing explanation for this intelligibility:

> All things come from the Creator Spirit, from the Creator God. And if he is called "the Word," that means that in the beginning there was a God who is mind. In the beginning was the creative mind who called the world into being; and this mind is, so to speak, the firm foundation that supports the universe, the source from whom we come, in whom we exist, in whom we can put our trust. But when the Bible says: "In the beginning was the Word," it says much more as well. It is not just a mind that, as it were, governs the universe like an idea in higher mathematics, while remaining itself untouchable and uninvocable; this God, who is truth, spirit, mind, is likewise Word, that is, he is also gift. He is for us the constant new beginning, and thus also a new hope and a new way.[30]

At the University of Regensburg, Benedict noted, "'In the beginning was the λόγος.' This is the very word used by the emperor: God acts, σὺν λόγω, with *logos*. *Logos* means both reason and word—a reason which is creative and capable of self-communication, precisely as reason."[31] Creation is intelligible to man because he is given a share in the *logos* of God who is Creator and whose signature is present in His work. As Ratzinger puts it, "God himself shines through the reasonableness of his creation."[32]

Barbour makes the significant observation that the very fact that physicists are seeking a grand unified theory,[33] the "Holy Grail" of modern science, implies the deep conviction that the universe is "orderly, simple, and *rationally intelligible*."[34] Ratzinger emphasizes the significance of this order, simplicity, and intelligibility: "The universe is not the product of darkness and unreason. It comes from intelligence, freedom, and from the beauty that is identical with love."[35] Albert

29 See George V. Coyne and Michael Heller, *A Comprehensible Universe: The Interplay of Science and Theology* (New York: Springer, 2008).
30 Excerpt from a homily given at the 88th Deutschen Katholikentag, July 5, 1984 and published in Joseph Ratzinger, *Co-Workers of the Truth: Meditations for Every Day of the Year*, ed. Irene Grassl, trans. Mary Frances McCarthy (San Francisco: Ignatius Press, 1992), 48–49.
31 Benedict XVI, *The Regensburg Lecture*, ed. James V. Schall (South Bend: St. Augustines Press, 2007), 135.
32 Ratzinger, *In the Beginning*, 24.
33 The acronym GUT (Grand Unified Theory) was first coined in 1978 by CERN researchers John Ellis, Andrzej Buras, Mary K. Gaillard, and Dimitri Nanopoulos. See Andrzej J. Buras et al., "Aspects of the Grand Unification of Strong, Weak and Electromagnetic Interactions," *Nuclear Physics B* 135, no. 1 (1978): 66–92.
34 Barbour, *When Science Meets Religion*, 52.
35 Ratzinger, *In the Beginning*, 25.

Einstein once wrote that "the most incomprehensible thing about the universe is that it is comprehensible."[36]

Barbour is correct that a quest for an aesthetically beautiful and conceptually simple theory certainly creates a dialogue opportunity with the doctrine of creation. One cannot help but ask about the origins of unified laws. Human reason seeks complete, unified knowledge in correspondence to the intelligible order of creation.

The popular science educator and one of the founders of modern quark theory,[37] James S. Trefil, echoes Barbour's position on the intelligibility of the universe:

> But who created those laws?... Who made the laws of logic?... No matter how far the boundaries are pushed back, there will always be room both for religious faith and a religious interpretation of the physical world. For myself, I feel much more comfortable with the concept of God who is clever enough to devise the laws of physics that make the existence of our marvelous universe inevitable than I do with the old-fashioned God who had to make it all, laboriously, piece by piece.[38]

Having shown how Barbour's notion of the intelligibility of the cosmos can introduce dialogue between the doctrine of creation and natural science, we now explore dialogue opportunities around the contingency of the cosmos.

1.1.2 Contingent Existence

Barbour also advances the dialogue between the doctrine of creation and natural science in his reflection on the contingency of creation. On the topic of the *contingent existence* of the universe, Barbour writes,

> Why is there anything at all? This is the question of greatest interest to theologians, and it corresponds to the religious meaning of creation *ex nihilo* ... The existence of the cosmos as a whole is not self-explanatory, regardless of whether it is finite or infinite in time. It now appears that the Big Bang was an absolute beginning, a singular event, but if scientists were to discover new evidence for a cyclic universe or infinite time, the contingency of existence would remain. The details of particular scientific cosmologies are irrelevant to the contingency of the world.[39]

---

36 Albert Einstein, "Physics and Reality," in *Ideas and Opinions*, trans. Sonja Bargmann (New York: Bonanza, 1954), 292.

37 For a description of the evolution of atomic theory through the discoveries of subatomic particles such as the quark, the meson, the lepton, and others, see James Trefil, *From Atoms to Quarks*, Revised. (New York: Anchor, 1994).

38 James Trefil, *The Moment of Creation: Big Bang Physics from before the First Millisecond to the Present Universe* (New York: Collier Books, 1983), 223.

39 Barbour, *When Science Meets Religion*, 54–55.

This statement accords very well with Aquinas' metaphysics of creation. As mentioned earlier, Aquinas believed in a moment of creation according to Divine revelation. However, he also posits that a Creator would be necessary, even assuming an eternal universe, in order to account for the existence of contingent causes whose forms are not identical to their *esse*. Again, as previously stated, Aquinas also offers an argument for God's existence from contingency.[40]

Barbour is very aware of Stephen Hawking's contributions to physical cosmology and cites him often in his books and articles. It is interesting to note that although Hawking stated that he did not believe in eternity or a Creator God,[41] he wrote,

> Even if there is only one possible unified theory, it is just a set of rules and equations. What is it that breathes fire into the equations and makes a universe for them to describe? The usual approach of science of constructing a mathematical model cannot answer the questions of why there should be a universe for the models to describe. Why does the universe go to all the bother of existing? Is the unified theory so compelling that it brings about its own existence? Or does it need a creator, and if so, does he have any other effect on the universe? Who created him?[42]

Barbour's favorite twentieth century Catholic philosopher, Étienne Gilson, would likely respond to Hawking by stating that God, who is self-subsistent being, gives the act of existence to creation.

Thomas Torrance concurs with Barbour on the importance of the contingent existence of the cosmos as a point of dialogue. Torrance has focused much of his research on the notion of "contingent order." He examines the implications of the Judæo-Christian belief that the cosmos was freely created by God *ex nihilo*, and has an existence, freedom, and rational order of its own while still being dependent on Him.[43] In his analysis of Torrance's work, Barbour writes, "He stresses God's freedom in creating as an act of voluntary choice. God alone is infinitely free, he says, and both the existence and the structure of the world are contingent in the sense that they might not have been."[44]

The universe studied by the natural sciences need not exist. Barbour's reflection on the contingent existence of the cosmos is a beneficial contribution toward facilitating dialogue between creation and natural science. The dependence of the

---

40 Aquinas, *Summa Theologiæ*, I, Q 2, A 3.
41 Mlodinow and Hawking, *The Grand Design*, 180.
42 Hawking, *A Brief History of Time*, 190. In his last book, Hawking writes, "There is no God. No one created the universe and no one directs our fate." Stephen Hawking, *Brief Answers to the Big Questions* (New York: Bantam Books, 2018), 38.
43 Thomas F. Torrance, *Divine and Contingent Order* (Edinburgh: T&T Clark, 2005).
44 Barbour, *When Science Meets Religion*, 53.

universe (on the order of being) on a Creator who provides the *actus essendi* is an important aspect of Catholic belief in creation. As Barbour puts it, "The existence of the cosmos as a whole is not self-explanatory."[45] In the next section, we explicate Barbour's analysis of *contingent boundary conditions* and apply it to the Catholic doctrine of creation.

1.1.3 Contingent Boundary Conditions

Barbour's exploration of contingency identifies a very significant point: there is always a *boundary condition* whether one assumes a creation *cum tempore* or an eternally (created) universe. In the orthodox doctrine of *creatio ex nihilo et cum tempore* defended in the last chapter, God creates the material and spiritual orders of creation from nothing and with time. In contemporary scientific language, one could say that God created the natural order (e.g., spacetime and mass-energy) and the supernatural order. While not falling into the error of concordism, Barbour does acknowledge the likely possibility that the Big Bang[46] (13.8 billion years ago) could represent an *absolute* beginning of the cosmos.[47]

On the other hand, in the *Gedankenexperiment* of an infinite universe, Barbour highlights the fact that "we would still have contingent boundary conditions; however far back we went, we would have to deal with a situation or state that we would have to treat as an unexplained given."[48] Barbour concurs with Aquinas' logic

---

45 Ibid., 54.

46 The father of the Big Bang, Monsignor Georges Lemaître, challenged the prevailing view of his colleagues in the 1920s and 1930s, such as Albert Einstein, who promoted a static, eternal model of the universe. Lemaître's model was novel in that it described a dynamic universe with a beginning. In a Big Bang cosmology, as time moves forward, the universe expands, temperature drops, density decreases, asymmetry increases, and stability increases. Lemaître solved the equation assuming a positive curvature ($k = 1$) and the cosmological constant (Λ) above the critical value to enable unending expansion. Also, $k = + 1$ implies a spherical geometry and a closed, finite universe ($k = 0$ is a flat, unbounded, and infinite universe while $k = - 1$ is a saddle shaped, open, unbounded, and infinite universe). Modern observation indicates that the curvature is very near zero. However, the intrinsically inaccurate nature of measurement means that we may never know if the universe is actually flat, spherical, or saddle shaped. See Ray D'Inverno, *Introducing Einstein's Relativity* (Oxford: Clarendon Press, 1992), 331–341. The Friedmann–Lemaître–Robertson–Walker (FLRW) model of the universe is considered to be without boundaries, in which case the term "compact universe" would describe a universe that is a closed manifold, mathematically speaking. In topology, a closed manifold is compact without boundary and an open manifold is one that is not compact and without boundary. A "closed universe" is necessarily a closed manifold, but an "open universe" could either be a closed or open manifold. See Daniel Martin, *Manifold Theory: An Introduction for Mathematical Physicists* (Cambridge: Woodhead Publishing, 2002).

47 Barbour, *When Science Meets Religion*, 54.

48 Ibid., 55.

which is unsurpassable here: no "horizontal" cause can be the all-encompassing, purposive first cause.[49] One can also hypothesize about a third scenario: neither creation *ex nihilo* nor Aristotle's eternal world,[50] but Hawking's theory of quantum gravity. Barbour points out that if one agrees with Hawking's theory of quantum gravity (mentioned at the end of the Introduction in Chapter One) in which there is neither infinite time nor a beginning of time—time is finite but unbounded (i.e., there is no edge)—a contingent boundary condition still exists! Space and imaginary time[51] are finite but unbounded, and real time emerges[52] gradually according to Hawking.[53] However, one must still assume a particular structure of physical relationships from which spacetime develop—a contingent boundary condition.

A Creator God is a logical and metaphysically reasonable explanation for the "unexplained given" of universe. Scientists utilize, revise, and refute scientific laws that explain our universe. From where do these laws come? The next section explores the contingent nature of the laws of physics.

1.1.4 Contingent Laws

The *contingent nature of physical laws* is a distinct but related area of contingency that Barbour identifies as an opportunity for dialogue. He writes, "While many of the laws of cosmology appear to be arbitrary, some of them may turn out to be necessary implications of more fundamental theories. If a unified theory is found, however, it will itself be contingent, and the argument only moves back a stage."[54]

---

49   Aquinas, *Commentary on the Metaphysics*, bk. *XII*, lec. *VI*, chap. 7.

50   Aristotle argues that everything that exists came from a material substratum: ὑποκείμενον (*hupokeímenon*)—the "underlying thing." However, he points out that the nature of matter is to be the substratum from which other entities come. As a result, the underlying matter of the world could have come into existence only from an already existing matter exactly like itself. To assume that the *underlying* matter of the world came into existence this way would require assuming that underlying matter already existed. This assumption is self-contradictory so the world must be eternal. See Aristotle, *Physics*, I, 7.

51   Mathematically speaking, imaginary time τ is calculated by a Wick rotation of $\pi/2$ in the complex plane: $\tau = it$ where $i^2 = -1$. See Gian Carlo Wick, "Properties of Bethe-Salpeter Wave Functions," *Physical Review* 96, no. 4 (November 15, 1954): 1124–1134.

52   The meaning of the "emergence" of real time from imaginary time seems to imply *time*. Hawking's theory is very nebulous.

53   The Hartle-Hawking model of the cosmos has no boundary in the way that classical general relativity predicts, e.g., the Big Bang model, because the incorporation of quantum effects has removed the boundary. See Chris J. Isham, "Quantum Theories of the Creation of the Universe," in *Quantum Cosmology and the Laws of Nature*, ed. Robert J. Murphy, Nancey Murphy, and Chris J. Isham (Rome: Vatican Observatory, 1993), 51–92.

54   Barbour, *When Science Meets Religion*, 56.

Relying on principles from systems theory, Barbour also acknowledges that laws governing the behavior of higher level, complex systems are not necessarily derivable from more fundamental laws due to the existence of emergent properties.[55] He gives the examples of "life" and "consciousness" as phenomena that cannot be explained only with the laws of physics. Barbour is quick to point out however that these phenomena at the same time do not violate any physical laws.

Barbour is critical of attaching the label, a "theory of everything,"[56] to the quest for a unified theory of particle physics. If a model emerges in which, at high energy, the four fundamental interactions/forces of the Standard Model are merged into a single force,[57] such a model would "leave out all of the diversity and particularity of events in the world and the emergence of more complex levels of organization from simpler ones."[58] The so-called "theory of everything" would tell humanity little about the life and work of William Shakespeare and Ludwig van Beethoven.

Barbour's non-reductionism accords well with a traditional Catholic theory of form and the hierarchy of being. Lower causes do not account for the higher; matter is potency *vis-à-vis* form. Acknowledging this fact can lead one to Aquinas's argument for the Creator God from exemplarity.[59]

What (or who) is the origin of scientific laws? For example, while Maxwell's name is attached to the a set of partial differential equations that, together with the

55   See Bertalanffy, *General System Theory*, chap. 3.

56   John D. Barrow, *Theories of Everything: The Quest for Ultimate Explanation* (Oxford: Oxford University Press, 1991).

57   The Standard Model accurately describes experimental predictions regarding three of the four fundamental forces of nature, and is a gauge theory with the gauge group $SU(3) \times SU(2) \times U(1)$. Although the physics of special relativity is incorporated in the Standard Model, general relativity is not. The Standard Model will fail at energies or distances where the graviton is expected to emerge. Modern theories, e.g., string theory and general relativity, are, in one way or another, gauge theories. For more information, see Robert Mann, *An Introduction to Particle Physics and the Standard Model* (New York: CRC Press, 2009).

58   Barbour, *When Science Meets Religion*, 56.

59   "Among beings there are some more and some less good, true, noble and the like. But 'more' and 'less' are predicated of different things, according as they resemble in their different ways something which is the maximum, as a thing is said to be hotter according as it more nearly resembles that which is hottest; so that there is something which is truest, something best, something noblest and, consequently, something which is uttermost being; for those things that are greatest in truth are greatest in being, as it is written in *Metaph. ii.* Now the maximum in any genus is the cause of all in that genus; as fire, which is the maximum heat, is the cause of all hot things. Therefore there must also be something which is to all beings the cause of their being, goodness, and every other perfection; and this we call God." Aquinas, *Summa Theologiæ*, I, Q 2, A 3.

Lorentz force law,[60] form the foundation of classical electromagnetism, optics, and electronics, Maxwell and Lorentz did not *create* the fundamental laws governing electricity and magnetism.[61] The doctrine of creation provides a reasonable answer to the question of origins of laws: the Creator. Having investigated the utility of theological reflection on the contingent laws of nature for promoting dialogue between the natural sciences and the doctrine of creation, we now turn our attention to the contingency of events.

1.1.5 Contingent Events

The final area of contingency that Barbour suggests for dialogue is the *contingency of events*. He writes, "The cosmos is a unique and irreversible sequence of events in which genuine novelty appears. Our account of it must take a historical form rather than consisting in general laws alone."[62] In light of the Second Law of Thermodynamics[63] and his adoption of Heisenberg's interpretation of quantum mechanics that posits a strong form of indeterminacy,[64] Barbour rejects necessity in events. He rebuffs the assertion of determinism that all events, including human acts, are ultimately determined by causes external to the will.

Barbour's perspective on the contingency of events aligns well with the Catholic doctrine of creation. There is true freedom in creation and the origin of this freedom points to the Creator God. As early as Genesis 3, one finds an abuse of free will in the fall of Adam and Eve.[65] If man were not free, he could not sin. While it would be irresponsible to assert *prima facie* that free will is possible

---

60 See Olivier Darrigol, *Electrodynamics from Ampère to Einstein* (Oxford: Oxford University Press, 2003), 322–331.

61 See James Clerk Maxwell, *Treatise on Electricity and Magnetism*, 3rd ed., 2 vols. (New York: Dover Publications, 1954).

62 Barbour, *When Science Meets Religion*, 56.

63 In all spontaneous, natural processes, the total entropy (a measure of disorder) increases. Such processes are said to be "irreversible." The increase in entropy accounts for the irreversibility of natural processes, and the asymmetry between future and past. A mathematical definition of entropy that was developed by Ludwig Boltzmann is: "The entropy of a state is the logarithm of the number of molecular configurations in the state." Phil Attard, *Non-Equilibrium Thermodynamics and Statistical Mechanics: Foundations and Applications* (Oxford: Oxford University Press, 2012), 2.

64 It was mentioned in Chapter Two that Werner Heisenberg maintained that indeterminacy is an objective feature of nature. He believed that "the transition from the 'possible' to the 'actual' takes place during the act of observation." Heisenberg, *Physics and Philosophy: The Revolution in Modern Science*, 54.

65 We emphasize the important dogmatic point that Adam and Eve's fall into sin does not imply that God is the author of sin, nor that he tempted Adam and Eve to sin. "Let no one say when he is tempted, 'I am tempted by God'; for God cannot be tempted with evil and he himself tempts no one." James 1:13 (RSV) Even though the fall was foreknown by God in His omniscience,

because of entropy and quantum theory,[66] it is worthwhile for Catholics to reflect theologically on the relationship of natural laws and freedom in God's contingent creation as Barbour does inchoately.

Thus far, we have explored how the intelligibility, contingent existence, contingent boundary conditions, contingent laws, and contingent events, according to Barbour, can promote dialogue between the natural sciences and the doctrine of creation. These areas suggest salient presuppositions to the scientific enterprise, as well as suggest questions that arise in science but cannot be answered by the scientific method. We now turn our attention to Barbour's use of methodological and conceptual parallels to support his dialogue typology.

1.2 Methodological and Conceptual Parallels

On the topic of methodological and conceptual parallels, D.L. Schindler writes,

> The theologian who takes up cosmological reflection today is of necessity drawn, at least by implication, into the question of the relation between theology and science. What is the character and legitimacy of a distinctly theological inquiry into nature and the cosmos, that is, relative to the methods and methodical inquiry of science?[67]

Barbour seeks to answer this fundamental theological question. He states that "one form of dialogue is a comparison of the methods of the two fields [science and theology], which may show similarities even when the differences are acknowledged."[68] Barbour contributes positively to the interaction of theology and science with his approach to dialogue based on *methodological congruencies*.

As mentioned earlier, Barbour regards the Neo-Thomism of Gilson and Garrigou-Lagrange in a generally positive light. He considers their approach to causality as "rich and many-faceted."[69] For example, he notes that the Thomistic notion of God influencing final causality (e.g., by creating man to be attracted to the *bonum*) has "much in common with process thought."[70] Strangely, in *When*

human freedom is not violated because our free choices are one means by which God's will is carried out in His creation.

66 Some scholars who assert an ontological indeterminism in quantum theory, i.e., that indeterminacy is an objective feature of nature, posit that free will is possible because the mind is responsible for the wave function collapse in matter, which leads to a choice among the different possibilities for the human person. The idea was first proposed in the 1930s. See John von Neumann, *Mathematische Grundlagen Der Quantenmechanik* (Berlin: Springer-Verlag, 1932); Arthur H. Compton, *The Freedom of Man* (New Haven, CT: Yale University Press, 1935).

67 Schindler, "Theology, Science, and Cosmology," 270.

68 Barbour, *When Science Meets Religion*, 2–3.

69 Barbour, *Religion and Science*, 310.

70 Ibid.

Science Meets Religion (2000), Barbour classifies the Thomistic approach of primary and secondary causality as an example of the *independence* interaction mode, rather than the one of *dialogue*.[71] We strongly disagree with this categorization based on his own criteria. In fact, in *Religion and Science: Historical and Contemporary Issues* (1997), he correctly categorizes the Thomistic approach to causality within the dialogue typology.[72]

A clear methodological parallel is present in the Thomistic perspective of affirming God as the first and primary cause of the cosmos as well as maintaining the reality of secondary causes in nature that can be studied with the methods of the natural sciences. For example, according to the Catholic doctrine of creation, God is the *primary* cause of the Earth—its existence and properties.[73] Physics also properly speaks of *instrumental* causes 4.5 billion years ago through which the Earth formed from debris around the solar protoplanetary disk[74] and through which it continues to move in an orbit around the sun, also interacting gravitationally with the moon and other planets.[75]

In summary, Ian Barbour's approach to *dialogue* emphasizes parallels in method and concepts as well as the important, metaphysical presuppositions and limit questions that arise in the course of carrying out modern science. These various components of his dialogue typology are very conducive to bringing the natural sciences into a beneficial interaction with the doctrine of creation. In the next section, we explore how Ian Barbour's preferred typology of interaction between theology and science, *integration*, can be applied for the Catholic doctrine of creation.

2. Integration

Natural theology, *theologies of nature*, and *systematic syntheses* of theology and science (through a comprehensive metaphysics) are all opportunities for *integration* according to Barbour. While he does not place great value in natural theology,[76] Barbour does acknowledge the potential for the Anthropic Principle[77] to undergird

---

71 Barbour, *When Science Meets Religion*, 159–160.

72 Barbour, *Religion and Science*, 245.

73 "In the beginning God created the heavens and the earth." Genesis 1:1 (RSV).

74 See G. Brent Dalrymple, *The Age of the Earth* (Stanford: Stanford University Press, 1991).

75 See Konstantin Batygin and Gregory Laughlin, "On the Dynamical Stability of the Solar System," *The Astrophysical Journal* 683, no. 2 (August 20, 2008): 1207–1216.

76 Barbour, *Issues in Science and Religion*, 2.

77 As mentioned in Chapter One, the anthropic principle acknowledges that the laws of physics and key parameters of the cosmos take on values that are consistent with conditions for life as we know it, including human life. The universe could be conceivably have been defined by a different

a new natural theology. Fine-tuned phenomena such as an expansion rate of the universe that allows galaxies to form, the relative strength of the strong nuclear force that enables the formation of elements more massive than hydrogen, and the asymmetry of the particle/antiparticle ratio that allows for ordinary matter, can all contribute to a modern natural theology enriched by physical cosmology.[78]

In the context of developing his notion of a theology of nature, Barbour proposes the doctrines of creation, Divine providence, and human nature as possible areas of theological development in light of modern science. For example, theological models of God the (Continuing) Creator "updated" in light of modern science would fit in this category. Barbour writes,

> Our understanding of the general characteristics of nature will affect our models of God's relation to nature. Nature is today understood to be a dynamic evolutionary process with a long history of emergent novelty, characterized throughout by chance law. The natural order is ecological, interdependent, and multi-leveled ... God creates "in and through" the process of the natural world that science unveils.[79]

In summary, we may ask, What does our current knowledge about the natural world say about God whose fingerprints may be discerned in His ongoing work?

In his reflection on opportunities for a theology of nature focused on human nature, Barbour asks, "What are the implications of current cosmology for our self-understanding? Can they be reconciled with the Biblical view of man?"[80] Despite the immensity of time and space, a higher level of complexity is present in the human person than in physical phenomena of distant galaxies. In addition, when cosmology is considered in relation to evolutionary biology, molecular biology, and ecology, the interdependence of all creation is made manifest.[81] Nonetheless, mankind is the most advanced form of life that we have encountered.

Barbour's highest level of integration between theology and science is found in a systematic synthesis rooted in a common metaphysics. As developed in Chapters Three and Four, Barbour adopts and simplifies the process metaphysics of Alfred North Whitehead. A systematic synthesis for the Catholic doctrine of creation can be proposed using the metaphysics of Thomas Aquinas. In Sections 2.1–2.3, we now explore Barbour's three integration methods: natural theology, a theology of nature, and a systematic synthesis.

---

set of values and fundamental laws that would have been inconsistent with life on Earth. See Barrow and Tipler, *The Anthropic Cosmological Principle*.

78 Barbour, *When Science Meets Religion*, 57–58.
79 Barbour, *Religion and Science*, 101.
80 Barbour, *When Science Meets Religion*, 61.
81 Ibid., 62.

2.1 Natural Theology

On the topic of natural theology, Paul Haffner astutely remarks, "Creation itself ... is already a first modulation of the Word of God. In a certain analogous and limited sense, creation is a 'sacrament,' a sign and efficacious means, of God's Self-revelation and His gift of Himself."[82] Walter Kasper notes that Copernicus, Kepler, Galileo, Newton, Heisenberg, and many other scientists "were filled with the conviction that they encountered traces of the divine Spirit ordering all in the regularities and order of the world."[83]

Unfortunately, *au contraire*, Barbour writes, "Even if the argument [of the existence of God from natural theology] is accepted, it leads only to the distant God of deism ... not the God of theism actively involved with the world and human life."[84] Regrettably, the Barthian obloquy of the analogy of being[85] that Barbour

---

82 Paul Haffner, *Towards a Theology of the Environment* (Leominster, UK: Gracewing Publishing, 2008), 195.

83 Kasper, "The Logos Character of Reality," 274.

84 Barbour, *Nature, Human Nature, and God*, 3.

85 In the General Introduction section, treating the Prima Pars, Questions 1–4, A.M. Fairweather offers the following very helpful synthesis of Aquinas' approach to the *analogia entis* and natural theology: "As the first active principle and first efficient cause of all things, God is not only perfect in himself, but contains within himself the perfections of all things, in a more eminent way. It is this that makes possible the celebrated analogia entis, whereby the divine nature is known by analogy from existing things, and not only by analogy based on the memory, intellect, and will of man, as Augustine had maintained. It is a fundamental principle of Aquinas that every agent acts to the producing of its own likeness. Every creature must accordingly resemble God at least in the inadequate way in which an effect can resemble its cause. The analogy is especially an analogy of 'being,' which the mediaeval mind apparently conceived as in some way active, not merely passive. All created things resemble God in so far as they are, and are good. Goodness and beauty are really the same as 'being,' from which they differ only logically. Names which are derived from creatures may therefore be applied to God analogously, that is, proportionately, or we may say relatively, in the manner which the passages appended to Q. 3 should be sufficient to explain (cf. *S. Contra Gentiles* I, ch. 30). The application of them must, however, respect the principle of 'negative knowledge,' which is observed by most thinkers of the millennium following Plotinus when speaking of the transcendent. Plotinus had maintained that anything whatever could be truly denied of the divine being, and also that whatever we affirm, we must forthwith affirm the opposite (*Enneads* V). Aquinas maintains that we can know of God's essence only what it is not, not what it is, but that this is properly knowledge of God. Names may be applied in so far as they are intended to affirm what applies to him in a more eminent way than we can conceive, while they must at the same time be denied of him on account of their mode of signification. The principle is in keeping with the practice of the Old Testament, which repeatedly has recourse to negatives in reference to the divine." Thomas Aquinas, *Nature and Grace: Selections from the Summa Theologica of Thomas Aquinas*, ed. A. M. Fairweather (London: Catholic Way Publishing, 2013), 28.

acquired in the atmosphere of Yale Divinity School remained a clear aspect of his thought for the rest of this life. Interestingly, some of Barbour's best intellectual tendencies are toward the analogy of being. Barbour spontaneously grants himself a dispensation from his neo-orthodox position when he discusses the Anthropic Principle. He classifies it as "a new version of natural theology that starts from cosmology."[86] As mentioned earlier, there are a variety of "fine-tuning" arguments. These lines of reasoning acknowledge the fact that various universal, fundamental physical constants must lie within an incredibly small range for matter to emerge, galaxies to form, and the initial conditions for life to transpire, thus making their precise values very special, perhaps pointing to some greater *logos*.

Scientists acknowledge that there are numerous possible universes consistent with Einstein's field equations.[87] However, the universe that we inhabit is one in which the arbitrary parameters are "fine-tuned" for the existence of life as we know it.[88] According to Barbour, fine-tuned phenomena such as an expansion rate of the universe that allows galaxies to form, the relative strength of the strong nuclear force that enables the formation of elements larger than hydrogen, and the asymmetry of the particle/antiparticle ratio that allows for ordinary matter, can all contribute to a modern natural theology rooted in cosmology.[89]

Reflecting on the sensitivity of the universe to its initial conditions, Stephen Hawking observes that "if the rate of expansion after the Big Bang had been smaller by even one part in a hundred thousand million, it would have recollapsed before it reached its present size."[90] Conversely, if the rate of expansion had been greater by one part in a million, the overly rapid expansion would have prevented the formation of stars and planets. The rate of expansion is governed by many factors, e.g., the strength of gravity, the mass of the universe, and the initial explosive energy of the Big Bang. Barbour succinctly captures the situation when he writes that "the cosmos seems to be balanced on a knife edge."[91]

86 Barbour, *When Science Meets Religion*, 57.
87 These are the set of ten equations that describe the fundamental interaction of gravitation as a result of spacetime being curved by energy and mass. See Albert Einstein, "Grundlage Der Allgemeinen Relativitätstheorie," *Annalen der Physik* 49, no. 7 (1916): 769–822.
88 See Luke A. Barnes, "The Fine-Tuning of the Universe for Intelligent Life," *Publications of the Astronomical Society of Australia* 29, no. 04 (2012): 529–564; Geraint F. Lewis and Luke A. Barnes, *A Fortunate Universe: Life in a Finely Tuned Cosmos* (Cambridge, UK: Cambridge University Press, 2016).
89 Barbour, *When Science Meets Religion*, 57–58.
90 Hawking, *A Brief History of Time*, 121.
91 Barbour, *When Science Meets Religion*, 57.

Another interesting aspect of the Anthropic Principle has to do with the formation of elements—a process that involves *many* technical subtleties.[92] Stellar nucleosynthesis occurs via the deuteron, ^2H, also known as heavy hydrogen, due to the presence of one neutron (in addition to the proton). However, only a small change in the strong nuclear force[93] is required to unbind the deuteron and prevent nuclear fusion in stars as we know it.[94] In a universe where the strong nuclear force is even slightly weaker, hydrogen might be the only element because almost all of the elements in the periodic table would be unstable. On the other hand, a more attractive strong nuclear force could have converted all the hydrogen ($Z = 1$) into

92   The initial mass of a star determines its gravity and the ability of a star to compress elements in its core into heavier elements until iron is produced. A star, like our sun, spends most of its life making helium. When it fuses all its hydrogen and the core is just helium, it becomes a red giant. While it is a red giant, the pressure on the helium nucleus will keep increasing due to gravity. It is analogous to a trash compactor. Gravity squeezes the helium core to such a degree that there is fusion of helium atoms. Then the star becomes a horizontal branch star and triple alpha reactions take place that produce carbon and oxygen. This might go on for 10 million years. Then the star will have burnt all its helium and the core will be carbon and oxygen. It will be surrounded by a thin layer of helium and a thin layer of hydrogen. Gravity compresses the star's carbon and oxygen core. Our sun's mass is not sufficient generate enough pressure and heat to fuse the carbon and oxygen. It will eventually become a white dwarf star and no longer produce energy through nuclear fusion. A star 10 times as big as our sun could generate enough gravity to squeeze the carbon and oxygen core to a higher temperature and produce higher elements and continue to build up the periodic table. A star about 50 times as big as the sun could keep "crunching" until it generates a big iron core surrounded by a layer of the previous element it had been fusing, surrounded by (previous element–1),…,to hydrogen. Now a "problem" arises. The fusion of iron is endothermic, i.e., it consumes energy rather than produces it. As a result, the star eventually collapses in on itself. Supernovæ may expel much of the stellar material away from a star. Depending on the progenitor star mass and metallicity, one can eventually end up with a neutron star or a black hole. During a supernova, a star releases extremely large amounts of energy as well as neutrons. This produces elements heavier than iron, such as uranium and gold. For more details on stellar structure and evolution, see Rudolf Kippenhahn, Alfred Weigert, and Achim Weiss, *Stellar Structure and Evolution*, 2nd ed., Astronomy and Astrophysics Library (New York: Springer, 2012).

93   The strong nuclear force is one of the four known fundamental interactions, with the others being electromagnetism, the weak nuclear force, and gravitation. It is an attractive force that ties the nucleons (e.g., protons and neutrons) in the nucleus. See Joseph H. Hamilton and Fujia Yang, *Modern Atomic and Nuclear Physics*, Revised. (Hackensack, NJ: World Scientific Publishing Company Inc., 2010), chap. 11.

94   Luke A. Barnes and Geraint F. Lewis, "Producing the Deuteron in Stars: Anthropic Limits on Fundamental Constants," *Journal of Cosmology and Astroparticle Physics* 2017, no. 7 (July 20, 2017), https://iopscience.iop.org/article/10.1088/1475-7516/2017/07/036/pdf.

helium ($Z = 2$), initially producing a pure helium universe.[95] Barbour points out that such a universe would not likely support stable stars to produce elements like oxygen ($Z = 8$) in their cores, as normally occurs. As a consequence, there might not be water (H_2O) or breathable air (O_2).[96] Also, such helium fusion stars would burn out too fast to support a planet while life forms.

It is very important to note that because of the coupling strength of strong nuclear interactions, there is no stable element or isotope with mass number, $A = 5$. Therefore, there is no way to "go beyond helium" by adding just a neutron or a proton. For example, the only way to normally form carbon ($Z = 6$) is by the "triple-α" process that fuses three helium nuclei, i.e., alpha particles, into carbon. This can only happen at sufficiently high density and pressure, e.g., as found in most large stars.

However, one must also carefully consider the lifetime of ^{8}Beryllium ($Z = 4$) because the triple-α process from helium to carbon relies on the presence of some ^{8}Be to capture another He nucleus. This happens because the ^{8}Be ground state binding equals almost exactly the binding energy of two He nuclei. This would not be the case for a different coupling. Moreover, there is a resonance in ^{12}C that equals the ^{8}Be + ^{4}He energy. If this resonance[97] were not where it is (because of a different strong force), carbon might not have formed in stars. In our universe, this resonance significantly increases the probability that an incoming α-particle combines with ^{8}Be to form carbon.[98] Although, strengthening the strong force might bind ^{8}Be and thus allow carbon production without the resonance.[99] In any

95 *Atomic number*, the number of protons in the nucleus of an atom, in German is *Atomzahl*. The "*Z*" comes from the first letter for the word "number" in German. The *mass number* in German is *Atomgewicht* (atomic weight), hence the symbol is "*A*."

96 Barbour, *When Science Meets Religion*, 57–58. In our universe, the formation of carbon is enhanced by a "resonance" that lowers the energy needed for the interaction. Oxygen is also made in the triple-α fusion process so the cores of stars have both carbon and oxygen in their center after helium fusion. For more information, see Lillian Huang, Fred C. Adams, and Evan Grohs, "Sensitivity of Carbon and Oxygen Yields to the Triple-Alpha Resonance in Massive Stars," *Astroparticle Physics* 105 (February 1, 2019): 13–24.

97 Certain nuclear reactions take place only when the energy of the incident particles is at or very close to a characteristic value.

98 The existence of this resonance was predicted by the British astrophysicist, Sir Fred Hoyle, before its actual observation, based on his theoretical work on the formation of carbon. See Fred Hoyle, "The Universe: Past and Present Reflections," *Engineering and Science* (November 1981): 8–12. The "Hoyle resonance" is very interesting because oxygen does not have it, thus preventing all of the carbon from being converted into oxygen, and leaving roughly equal amounts in normal stellar nucleosynthesis.

99 See Fred C. Adams and Evan Grohs, "Stellar Helium Burning in Other Universes: A Solution to the Triple Alpha Fine-Tuning Problem," *Astroparticle Physics* 87 (January 2017): 40–54.

case, carbon is an essential component of all life on Earth, representing approximately 45–50% of all dry biomass.[100] For example, carbon is a crucial component of proteins, DNA, carbohydrates, and lipids. Finally, in a cosmic scenario with a more powerful strong force, oxygen might not be very abundant because it could be destroyed by captures of protons and α-particles.[101]

The particle/antiparticle ratio also supports the Anthropic Principle. Barbour notes that for every billion antiprotons created after the Big Bang, there were one billion and *one* protons. After the pairs annihilated each other, only protons remained to provide the building blocks of the material universe. Barbour asks, "If the laws of physics are symmetrical between particles and antiparticles, why was there a tiny asymmetry here?"[102] Later he writes, "The simultaneous occurrence of many independent improbable features appears *wildly* improbable."[103]

Even Stephen Hawking, widely known for his atheistic statements, notices, "The odds against a universe like ours emerging out of something like the Big Bang are enormous … I think there are clearly religious implications whenever you start to discuss the origins of the universe."[104] The famous English-American theoretical physicist and mathematician, Freeman Dyson, also concurs. Dyson, a Christian, even if an idiosyncratic one, writes, "The more I examine the universe and the details of its architecture, the more evidence I find that the universe in some sense must have known we were coming."[105]

Barbour's use of the Anthropic Principle certainly points to a Creator God and makes a contribution to natural theology. The fine-tuning arguments, pointing to a creative Reason, are completely consistent with Catholic doctrine, which, as mentioned earlier, teaches that:

(1) God is the *creator mundi*,
(2) God created *ex nihilo*,
(3) God created directly, *sine causis secundariis*, and
(4) God created the universe *cum tempore*.[106]

100 Food and Agriculture Organization of the United Nations, "Knowledge Reference for National Forest Assessments - Modeling for Estimation and Monitoring," last modified May 12, 2005, accessed October 16, 2018, http://www.fao.org/forestry/17111/en/.

101 The author is grateful to Wolfgang Hillebrandt of the Max Planck Institute for Astrophysics, Luke Barnes of Western Sydney University, and David Brown, SJ of the Vatican Observatory for sharing some of their in-depth knowledge of nucleosynthesis.

102 Barbour, *When Science Meets Religion*, 58.

103 Ibid.

104 John Boslough, *Stephen Hawking's Universe* (New York: Morrow, 1985), 109.

105 Freeman Dyson, *Disturbing the Universe* (New York: Harper & Row, 1981), 250.

106 Aquinas, *Aquinas on Creation*, 22.

It is unfortunate that Barbour's *general* stance toward natural theology is dismissive, particularly given its long intellectual heritage in the Church.[107] For example, Lucius Cæcilius Firmianus Lactantius (c. 250–c. 325), the Catholic religious policy advisor to the first Christian Roman emperor, Constantine I, writes,

> For there is no one so unformed, so untouched by civilized custom, who, when he raises his eyes toward the sky, even though he does not know by the providence of what god all this which he beholds is governed, does not understand that there is something, however, from the very magnitude, motion, arrangement, constancy, utility, beauty, and proportion of nature, and that this could not be possible if it were not for the fact that it is established in a marvelous manner and has been fashioned by some greater plan.[108]

In the twenty-first century, Benedict XVI echoes Lactantius' point, framing it in such a way as to establish an *analogia rationis*:

> And the more we can delve into the world with our intelligence, the more clearly the plan of Creation appears. In the end, to reach the definitive question I would say: God exists or he does not exist. There are only two options. Either one recognizes the priority of reason, of creative Reason that is at the beginning of all things and is the principle of all things—the priority of reason is also the priority of freedom—or one holds the priority of the irrational, inasmuch as everything that functions on our earth and in our lives would be only accidental, marginal, an irrational result—reason would be a product of irrationality.[109]

Catholics must never forget that "creation itself is the self-revelation of God."[110] In an elegant application of Thomistic ideas, McDermott observes that "since there is a similarity between cause and effect which allows the human mind to mount from created effect to Creator and because creation is utterly dependent upon God, a participation schema is established whereby all created being participate in God's infinite *esse*."[111]

---

107 For a modern, rigorous, Thomistic argument for the existence of God, see Edward Feser, *Five Proofs of the Existence of God* (San Francisco: Ignatius Press, 2017), 128–131.

108 Lactantius, *The Divine Institutes, Books I–VII*, trans. Mary Francis McDonald, Fathers of the Church 49 (Washington, DC: CUA Press, 2008), 21.

109 Benedict XVI, "Meeting with the Young People of the Diocese of Rome in Preparation for the Celebration of the 21st World Youth Day," April 6, 2006, accessed January 22, 2018, http://w2.vatican.va/content/benedict-xvi/en/speeches/2006/april/documents/hf_ben-xvi_spe_20060406_xxi-wyd.html.

110 Clifford, "Creation," 196. Although this analogy implies similarity with greater dissimilarity.

111 McDermott, "The Mystery of Matter," 1012.

In the history of humanity, one notices that it is quite "natural" to carry out natural theology.[112] Barbour's use of the Anthropic Principle to develop a natural theology is clearly beneficial for integrating scientific insights with the Catholic doctrine of creation. In the next section, we explore the applicability of his second integration typology: theologies of nature.

2.2 Theology of Nature

At the end of his ground-breaking work, *Issues in Science and Religion*, Barbour concludes that "theology should not be based primarily on nature."[113] He also reiterates his critique of natural theology and claims that "in the biblical tradition, faith in *God as Redeemer* is more important that faith in God as Creator."[114] This is a strange position given that there would be no cosmos (and man) to redeem if there had not been a creation.[115] This placing of a wedge between the ontological and soteriological orders is likely the fruit of Barbour's neo-orthodox theological education—creation is fallen and corrupted and the focus should be on the work of the Redeemer. *Crux probat omnia.*[116]

---

112 *Documented* evidence of man engaging in natural theology goes back to at least the fifth century BC. For example, in the *Timæus*, Plato writes, "And that which has come into existence must necessarily, as we say, have come into existence by reason of some Cause. Now to discover the Maker and Father of this Universe were a task indeed; and having discovered Him, to declare Him unto all men ..." Plato, *Timaeus. Critias. Cleitophon. Menexenus. Epistles*, trans. Robert G. Bury, Plato vol. 9, Loeb Classical Library 234 (Cambridge, MA: Harvard University Press, 1929), 28.

113 Barbour, *Issues in Science and Religion*, 452.

114 Ibid., 453.

115 On the relationship of God the Creator and God the Redeemer, Ratzinger points out that "the primacy of the Logos and the primacy of love proved to be identical. The Logos was seen to be, not merely a mathematical reason at the basis of all things, but a creative love taken to the point of becoming sympathy, suffering with the creature. The cosmic aspect of religion, which reverences the Creator in the power of being, and its existential aspect, the question of redemption, merged together and became one." Ratzinger, "Lecture at the Sorbonne: November 27, 1999," 182.

116 This phrase is a key principle for Martin Luther and the Reformation in general. Alister McGrath writes, "*Crux probat omnia.* For Luther, Christian thinking about God comes to an abrupt halt at the foot of the cross. The Christian is forced, by the very existence of the crucified Christ, to make a momentous decision. Either he will seek God elsewhere, or he will make the cross itself the foundation and criterion of his thought about God. The 'crucified God'—to use Luther's daring phrase—is not merely the foundation of the Christian faith, but is also the key to understanding the nature of God." Alister E. McGrath, *Luther's Theology of the Cross* (Oxford, UK: Blackwell Publishers Ltd., 1985), 1.

On the contrary, faith in God should be rooted in His *full* revelation. The Christian must acknowledge God for who He is, e.g., Alpha, Omega, creator, redeemer, sanctifier, I am who am, Lord, Emmanuel, Father, Son, and Holy Spirit. It would erroneous to suggest that "God as Redeemer" is more important than "God as Creator" or that "God the Son" is more important that "God the Holy Spirit."

Nevertheless, Barbour does urge that theology, rooted in "historical revelation" and "personal experience," include a *theology of nature* "which does not disparage or neglect the natural order."[117] His critical realism rejects the two-language approach of linguistic analysis, for example, when addressing creation. Barbour suggests that certain theological doctrines must be reformulated in light of mature science. As mentioned earlier, Barbour proposes the doctrines of creation, providence, and human nature.[118] In particular, he advocates for a novel synthesis of the doctrines of creation and providence for a new notion of *creatio continua* without *creatio ex nihilo*. His stated goal in developing a theology of nature is to bring theological positions into greater harmony with the best scientific knowledge.[119]

The integration of cosmological data is certainly consistent with the aims and principles of Catholic theology. For example, the American astronomer and theologian, William R. Stoeger, SJ, writes,

> Obviously, philosophy and theology must take these new cosmic and human perspectives and possibilities seriously ... To the extent that they do not critically assimilate and confront these truths and perspectives, they will fail to articulate authentically and truthfully who we are, what the world and the universe really is, and who God really is or is not. For God has expressed the divine nature in the reality we experience around us and experience in ourselves.[120]

Barbour recognizes that the reformulation of Christian doctrines cannot be inconsistent with the *core* of the Christian Tradition. Surprisingly, he only posits one "core" belief: God as "creative love revealed in Christ."[121] God's immutability, for example, and indeed any other statement about God based on reason and revelation, is classified as an "auxiliary hypothesis." Barbour asserts that auxiliary hypotheses can be modified by "new" data, e.g., contemporary reflection on human

---

117 Barbour, *Issues in Science and Religion*, 453.

118 The connection between creation and providence is implicit in the Book of Wisdom: "But thou hast arranged all things by measure and number and weight." Wisdom 11:20 (RSV). Although, in Barbour's United Church of Christ, this book is classified as ἀπόκρυφος.

119 Barbour, *Religion and Science*, 100–101.

120 William R. Stoeger, "Key Developments in Physics Challenging Philosophy and Theology," in *Religion and Science: History, Method, and Dialogue*, ed. W. Mark Richardson and Wesley J. Wildman (New York: Routledge, 1996), 194.

121 Barbour, *Religion and Science*, 328.

freedom and suffering, the interpretation and experience of evil, and our relatively new, evolutionary understanding of the universe.

To select one element, albeit significant, at the exclusion of all others, from the datum of Divine revelation, as the "core" of Christian faith, is grievously slipshod. It is an uncharacteristically inexpert move on Barbour's part. Barbour's fundamental mistake is to focus on partial propositions (akin to models) to describe the *depositum fidei*. Rather, revelation is the complete self-communication of the Triune God in Jesus Christ (*Verbum Dei*) that Tradition mediates to us in time. Barbour's error likely flows from his "semi-Kantian" epistemology, which does not allow for access to God's immutable essence. Further objections to his selection of a "core" of the Christian Tradition include: Who identifies this core? How is it known? Does Divine revelation itself identify its own core?

Barbour is correct that integrating contemporary data from the natural sciences can enrich theological reflection. For example, a more precise science of human reproduction has the potential to enhance sexual bioethics. In addition, a more detailed account of the specificity of the cosmos could further develop a theology of creation. Therefore, Barbour can make a contribution here in a *theology of nature integration* of cosmology and the doctrine of creation.

New "data" is always welcome. John Henry Newman writes, "Nor are we afraid to allow, that, even after His coming, the Church has been a treasure-house, giving forth things olds and new, casting the gold of fresh tributaries into her refiner's fire, or stamping upon her own, as time required it, a deeper impress of her Master's image."[122] However, one must proceed extremely carefully in theological reflection, and especially in doctrinal development, based on new science. Science as a field is always in flux. McDermott writes,

> Indeed, insofar as mathematics is the language of the physical sciences and Gödel has shown that no mathematical system can be simultaneously consistent and complete— the original postulated axioms cannot be logically justified by the subsequent arguments depending on them—no theoretical physics can claim to be the last word, much less produce the unified field theory or the "theory of everything."[123]

In his 1958 book, *Physics and Philosophy*, Heisenberg advances a very Kantian philosophy of science. His interpretation of quantum mechanics is dependent on many "idealizations."[124] McDermott notes that "because these concepts are ideal, quantum mechanics affirms the priority of the possible over the actual, of potentialities over actualities or facts. As a result, classical logic's principles

---

122 Newman, *An Essay On Development Of Christian Doctrine*, 382.
123 McDermott, "Matter, Modern Science, and God," 498.
124 See Heisenberg, *Physics and Philosophy: The Revolution in Modern Science*.

of excluded middle and contradiction are no longer absolute in quantum mechanics."[125] One example would be in an application of the principle of superposition, e.g., Schrödinger's cat[126] being simultaneously dead and alive.[127] To attempt to revise/develop a theological doctrine based on a scientific theory and its associated philosophy of science that denies the axioms of logic would be disastrous.

In addition, a theologian must avoid the temptation to improperly elevate natural science to an idolatrous position. No matter how advanced the science of any place and time may be, it cannot offer an exhaustive view of reality. Barbour approaches an internal "contradiction" in his approach. He generally rejects natural theology, and strongly emphasizes knowledge of God as revealed in the Bible as a loving redeemer, but then gives science a preeminent place in theological inquiry. He should acknowledge that the same *logos* underlies both the natural knowledge of God and the natural knowledge of His creation.

Natural science studies change in the material universe (*ens mobile*), particularly under the aspect of measure. McDermott astutely notes,

> Although the growth of scientific knowledge may approximate ever more closely the fullness of being, its conceptual formulations can never replace the existential predicate. Reality is always more than human abstractions and there is some knowledge of it that transcends concepts, however it is characterized: existential, personal, intuitive, connatural, illative, etc. Because the mind can reflect upon itself and gain distance

125 McDermott, "Matter, Modern Science, and God," 500.
126 See Erwin Schrödinger, "Die Gegenwärtige Situation in Der Quantenmechanik," *Naturwissenschaften* 23, no. 48 (November 1, 1935): 807–812.
127 Schrödinger explicates what he saw as the problem of the Copenhagen interpretation of quantum mechanics applied to everyday objects. He writes, "One can even set up quite ridiculous cases. A cat is penned up in a steel chamber, along with the following device (which must be secured against direct interference by the cat): in a Geiger counter, there is a tiny bit of radioactive substance, so small, that perhaps in the course of the hour one of the atoms decays, but also, with equal probability, perhaps none; if it happens, the counter tube discharges and through a relay releases a hammer that shatters a small flask of hydrocyanic acid. If one has left this entire system to itself for an hour, one would say that the cat still lives if meanwhile no atom has decayed. The first atomic decay would have poisoned it. The psi-function of the entire system would express this by having in it the living and dead cat (pardon the expression) mixed or smeared out in equal parts. It is typical of these cases that an indeterminacy originally restricted to the atomic domain becomes transformed into macroscopic indeterminacy, which can then be resolved by direct observation. That prevents us from so naively accepting as valid a 'blurred model' for representing reality. In itself, it would not embody anything unclear or contradictory. There is a difference between a shaky or out-of-focus photograph and a snapshot of clouds and fog banks." John D. Trimmer, "The Present Situation in Quantum Mechanics: A Translation of Schrödinger's 'Cat Paradox' Paper," *Proceedings of the American Philosophical Society* 124, no. 5 (1980): 328.

from its objectifications of reality, the mind can never successfully be reduced to a mechanical computer.[128]

Catholic theology must concern itself not only with *ens mobile* but *esse* in general and He who provides the *actus essendi* to both the material and spiritual orders of reality. Ultimately, theology must cast its gaze on *ipsum esse subsistens*: God Himself.

We now consider Ian Barbour's last mode of integration: the systematic synthesis. Barbour considers this to be the supreme form of integration. He also acknowledges that it is the most challenging. While it would be highly problematic for Catholic theology to adopt Barbour's process metaphysics, it will be shown that the Thomistic alternative offers a very appealing alternative.

2.3 Systematic Synthesis

One of Barbour's significant scholarly contributions is to confront the unhealthy dichotomy, adopted by some Christians, to compartmentalize "science and reason" in one part of their life, and "religion and faith" in another. John Henry Newman elegantly expressed his concern with this illegitimate disjunction:

> It will not satisfy me, what satisfies so many, to have two independent systems, intellectual and religious, going at once side by side, by a sort of division of labour, and only accidentally brought together. It will not satisfy me, if religion is here, and science there, and young men converse with science all day, and lodge religion in the evening. It is not touching the evil, to which these remarks have been directed, if you men eat and drink and sleep in one place, and think in another: I want the same roof to contain both the intellectual and the moral discipline. Devotion is not a sort of finish given to the sciences; nor is science a sort of feather in the cap, if I may express myself, an ornament and setoff to devotion. I want the intellectual layman to be religious, and the devout ecclesiastic to be intellectual.[129]

Barbour writes, "A more systematic integration can occur if both science and religion contribute to a coherent world view elaborated in a comprehensive metaphysics ... The Thomistic framework provided such a metaphysics."[130] Thomistic metaphysics (which establishes causal order) encompasses physics, so to speak. This metaphysical way of articulating causality allows for an integration of physical

---

128 McDermott, "Matter, Modern Science, and God," 502.
129 John Henry Newman, "Intellect, the Instrument of Religious Training" (Sermon, University Church, Dublin, Sunday after Ascension 1856) cited in John Henry Newman, *Sermons Preached on Various Occasions* (London: Longmans Green and Co., 1908), 13.
130 Barbour, *Religion and Science*, 103.

causality into the order of eternal being. Theology's dialogue with science occurs within this primary "integration."

Regrettably, as already mentioned, Barbour's eisegetical reading of Aquinas is infused with seventeenth century Cartesian dualism. Instead of adopting the metaphysics of twentieth century Thomists that he respects, e.g., Gilson, Barbour looks elsewhere for a comprehensive metaphysics, i.e., Whitehead. It is unfortunate that Barbour doubts the value of Thomism. The sapient epistemological and metaphysical insights of Thomas Aquinas have shown themselves to have perennial relevance for theology and science.

This situation is particularly lamentable for the integration of the doctrine of creation and the natural sciences. With regard to the theory of evolution, William Carroll writes,

> If we follow Thomas' lead, we can see that there is no need to choose between a robust view of creation as the constant exercise of divine omnipotence and the causes disclosed by the natural sciences ... The account he offers of divine agency and the autonomy and integrity of nature is not merely an artifact from the past, but an enduring legacy. Not only is there no contradiction between creation and evolution, without creation, there would be no evolution.[131]

Regarding the origins of the cosmos and the human person, creation is concerned with the Primary Cause, while evolutionary theories address secondary causes.[132]

As explained in Chapter Four, Section 2.4, Mariusz Tabaczek, OP's application of Aristotelian-Thomistic principles to Neo-Darwinist theory can be helpful in understanding the character of random mutations in genetic material. The universal applicability of Thomas Aquinas' metaphysics is rooted in the fundamental principles of *essentia* and *actus essendi*,[133] which encapsulates the notions of substance, accidents, act, potency, form, matter, qualities, quantities, and therefore, causality. A Thomistic integrative framework relating external causality, internal causality, and God's act of creation is highly beneficial in a Catholic systematic synthesis of theology and science.

Aristotle, Aquinas, and a myriad of other philosophers, distinguish between *intrinsic* (material and formal) causality and *extrinsic* (efficient and final[134])

---

131 Carroll, "Creation and the Foundations of Evolution," 60.

132 For a fascinating Thomistic exploration of evolutionary biology, see Verschuuren, *Aquinas and Modern Science*, chap. 9.

133 For God, there is no distinction of any kind between His essence and His existence.

134 We should clarify that final causality has both an internal and external dimension. The external dimension is the good to which a thing is inclined. The internal is the inclination toward that good determined by the form. Specifically, insofar as form is the end of generation (generation is movement toward form in matter), form—an intrinsic principle—is a final cause (of generation). In addition, in the realm of accidental change, the desire for or inclination toward a good (arising

causality.[135] Any corporeal being is caused by the intrinsic principles of form and matter. Therefore, these are internal causes. But the internal causes are affected by causes that are not internal. If they are not internal, they are external. Efficient causality is the power behind it. However, efficient causality does not act if it is not for a goal, i.e., final causality. In addition, in the Thomistic tradition, there are two "levels" of causality: horizontal and vertical, or categorical and transcendental. The first is the causality in the created world studied by natural science; the second is the causality of God in all creation. God's immutable causality ensures the universal intelligibility of ongoing scientific discovery.

This is exactly the type of integrative view that Barbour was seeking. In addition, for Catholics, Aquinas' perspective on causality and creation does not carry the problematic baggage of Alfred North Whitehead's process metaphysics. Barbour's commitment to Whitehead's process thought does not allow him to develop an adequate notion of participation in God's power and other perfections. He therefore posits a false dichotomy where either God has all the power and other entities have none, or God is not omnipotent, and entities have power completely independent of him. Barbour is very close to the solution with his knowledge and appreciation of the Thomistic notion of primary and secondary causality. Yet, he never takes the steps to develop these principles further in his work.

3. Conclusion

In the last century, the Catholic Church has been blessed with several influential figures who have promoted a mutually beneficial interaction between the natural sciences and Christian faith. The Belgian priest and physical cosmologist, Georges Lemaître; the British theoretical nuclear physicist, Peter Hodgson; the Hungarian-American priest, theologian, and philosopher of science, Stanley Jaki; the American theoretical particle physicist and cosmologist, Stephen Barr; the British priest and fundamental theologian, Paul Haffner; and others have made lasting contributions to the field. While much work remains in the ministries of catechetics and apologetics, solid intellectual foundations have been established.

---

from the substantial form of a sensitive or rational being) which causes the agent to act is an end which can be understood as intrinsic. For more on this topic, see Thomas Aquinas, *De Principiis Naturæ*, ed. Joseph Kenny, trans. Roman A. Kocourek (St. Paul, MN: North Central, 1948), III, 19–20, accessed November 21, 2018, https://dhspriory.org/thomas/DePrincNaturae.htm.

135 Matter and form are internal co-principles.

The unique collaboration of Benedict XVI and Francis in *Lumen Fidei*[136] offers a powerful reminder of the importance ongoing work in this area. They write,

> The gaze of science thus benefits from faith: faith encourages the scientist to remain constantly open to reality in all its inexhaustible richness. Faith awakens the critical sense by preventing research from being satisfied with its own formulæ and helps it to realize that nature is always greater. By stimulating wonder before the profound mystery of creation, faith broadens the horizons of reason to shed greater light on the world which discloses itself to scientific investigation.[137]

David L. Schindler notes that "theology and science cannot properly be understood merely as indifferent or neutral to one another."[138] He emphasizes that "the necessary *distinction* between theology and science cannot be rightly understood as one of *separation*."[139]

Tout bien considéré, Ian Barbour makes a significant contribution to the interaction of theology and science. Indeed, Barbour's perspicuous goal throughout his life as a scholar was to promote a mutually beneficial relationship between the natural sciences and Christian theology. His typologies of dialogue and integration offer a generally helpful guide for relating the Catholic doctrine of creation with cosmology and other natural sciences.

Barbour's knowledge of the natural sciences, particularly physics, is very up-to-date and his analysis of scientific issues is unquestionably methodical and logical. This expertise allows him to introduce the science of theology to many academics in the physical and biological sciences. Barbour is a highly original thinker with a mind untrammelled by convention; he is no epigone. Barbour also distinguishes himself in his dedication to "wide-ranging dialogue" and the "culture of encounter," (to use Pope Francis' terms) as well as a commitment to interdisciplinary and cross-disciplinary approaches to research.[140]

The work of Ian Barbour is indeed prescient, especially in his insistence on realism in theology and science as well as his promotion of a systematic synthesis of the fields through a common metaphysics. On this issue, Ratzinger writes, "To separate religion, belief in God, from objective truth is to fail to recognize

---

136 According to Pope Francis, Benedict XVI "himself had almost completed a first draft of an encyclical on faith. For this I am deeply grateful to him, and as his brother in Christ I have taken up his fine work and added a few contributions of my own. The Successor of Peter, yesterday, today and tomorrow, is always called to strengthen his brothers and sisters in the priceless treasure of that faith which God has given as a light for humanity's path." Francis, *Lumen Fidei*, 7.

137 Ibid., 34.

138 David L. Schindler, "Theology, Science, and Cosmology," *Communio* 15, no. 3 (Fall 1988): 271.

139 Ibid., 272.

140 Francis, *Veritatis Gaudium*, 2017, 4b–c.

its innermost nature."[141] In a period when it was *de rigueur* to abandon realism in science in favor of idealism, instrumentalism, and positivism, as well as completely dismiss first philosophy, Barbour merits a paean. With his critical realism, he affirms man's ability to come to know objective truth, albeit partially and imperfectly. We concur with McMullin that the aspect of Barbour's critical realism emphasizing the "approximation of reality in a cumulative sense," is more applicable to sciences like physics and chemistry, not Catholic theology. In a Catholic theological context, a more robust realism, such as that of Gilson, Barbour's favorite Thomist, is preferred.

With his process thought, despite the Catholic fundamental theological difficulties identified in Chapter Four, Barbour demonstrates the relevance of ontology, identity and change, causality, as well as necessity and contingency in theology and science. Barbour should be commended for his perseverance in the face of the critique from non-foundationalist, postmodern thinkers, e.g., Sallie McFague.[142] As Thomas G. Guarino points out, "Christian doctrine needs some kind of (commodious) metaphysical approach in order to support logically its claims to be universal, perduring, self-same, and normative."[143] Barbour's appreciation of metaphysics for the rationality of theology and science, e.g., the ability to make truth claims, places him in good company with Catholic theologians. In this vein, Guarino writes,

> Catholic "foundationalist" thinkers like Rahner and Lonergan ... thought that some foundationalist ontology is necessary if one is adequately to defend fundamental Catholic positions on doctrine. If one accepts postmodernity more fully, thereby abandoning some form of foundationalist ontology, one's entire understanding of revelation, especially the role of Christian doctrine, is deeply affected. Either the truth of the gospel must simply be asserted, breaking its link with a rationally elaborated infrastructure. Or, by opening a fissure between ontology and theology, one develops a quite different understanding of what the deposit of faith is, how it develops, and the type of continuity and identity proper to it. Particularly affected is the type of truth mediated by it.[144]

141 Ratzinger, *Principles of Catholic Theology: Building Stones for a Fundamental Theology*, 70.
142 McFague laments areas where Barbour's thought is *modern*, rather than *postmodern*. She disagrees with his critique of the feminist and "two-thirds-world" (e.g., distinctively African, Asian, South American) position on the social construction of science. McFague also asserts that Barbour's preference for a unified worldview comes at the cost of slighting issues of diversity and particularity. She strongly disputes "his defense of objectivity in both science and theology, especially in conversation with feminist critiques of Western science." McFague, "Ian Barbour: Theologian's Friend, Scientist's Interpreter," 25.
143 Guarino, *Foundations of Systematic Theology*, 25.
144 Thomas Guarino, "Postmodernity and Five Fundamental Theological Issues," *Theological Studies* 57, no. 4 (December 1996): 660–661.

We selected *creation* as the lens through which to study Ian Barbour's approach to relating theology and science. The doctrine of creation is a foundational teaching of the Catholic faith.[145] The French philosopher, Paul Clavier, writes,

> There is a strong claim that the world's createdness, if true, cannot be known but through revelation. We ... dismiss this claim by arguing that creation cannot be merely a revealed truth (*revelabile tantum*), since it is on the contrary the very preamble to any genuine revelation. Ontologically, no revelation can happen in a self-existent world. No creation, no revelation. Epistemically, no revelation is to be admitted but on the assumption that the world depends, for its existence and operation, on a supernatural agent. No admittance of creative power, no justified identification of any revelatory activity.[146]

The doctrine of creation is so important for Catholics and many other Christians that it has Creedal status: "*Credo in Deum Patrem omnipotentem, Creatorem cæli et terræ.*"

Stanley Jaki points out that "it was the Biblical doctrine of creation, especially in its Christological form that God created everything through his Son, that prompted the notion of an autonomous, though contingent set of laws of nature that can and should be investigated by science."[147] According to William Carroll,

---

145 Benedict emphasized this important doctrine in the context of his Apostolic Journey to München, Altötting, and Regensburg: "We believe in God. This is a fundamental decision on our part. But again the question has to be asked: is this still possible today? Is it reasonable? From the Enlightenment on, science, at least in part, has applied itself to seeking an explanation of the world in which God would be unnecessary. And if this were so, he would also become unnecessary in our lives. But whenever the attempt seemed to be nearing success—inevitably it would become clear: something is missing from the equation! When God is subtracted, something doesn't add up for man, the world, the whole universe. So we end up with two alternatives. What came first? *Creative* Reason, the *Creator* Spirit who makes all things and gives them growth, or Unreason, which, lacking any meaning, yet somehow brings forth a mathematically ordered cosmos, as well as man and his reason. The latter, however, would then be nothing more than a chance result of evolution and thus, in the end, equally meaningless. As Christians, we say: 'I believe in God the Father, the *Creator* of heaven and earth'—I believe in the *Creator* Spirit. We believe that at the beginning of everything is the eternal Word, with Reason and not Unreason. With this faith we have no reason to hide, no fear of ending up in a dead end. We rejoice that we can know God! And we try to help others see the reasonableness of faith, as Saint Peter in his First Letter explicitly urged the Christians of his time to do, and with them, ourselves as well (cf. 3:15)." (emphasis added) Benedict XVI, Homily (Islinger Feld, Regensburg, September 12, 2006), accessed March 23, 2018, https://w2.vatican.va/content/benedict-xvi/en/homilies/2006/documents/hf_ben-xvi_hom_20060912_regensburg.html.

146 Paul Clavier, "No Creation, No Revelation," *International Journal for Philosophy of Religion* 73, no. 3 (2013): 255.

147 Jaki, "The Demarcation Line between Science and Religion," 81.

"Creation, as a metaphysical and theological notion, affirms that all that is, in whatever way or ways it is, depends upon God as cause. The natural sciences ... have as their subject the world of changing things: from subatomic particles to acorns to galaxies."[148] In a similar vein, the Dutch-American geneticist and philosopher of science, Gerard M. Verschuuren, concisely states that "the empirical sciences study the nature and activity of secondary causes, but metaphysics and theology study God's providence and divine action in creation. These two perspectives are different and complementary, but are certainly not opposed to each other."[149]

The doctrine of creation is intimately connected with other aspects of the Catholic faith. For example, Joseph Ratzinger illustrates the fundamental connection between the doctrine of creation and the doctrine of salvation for θέωσις (*théosis*):

> We can only be saved—that is, be free and true—when we stop wanting to be God and when we renounce the madness of autonomy and self-sufficiency. We can only be saved—that is, become ourselves—when we engage in the proper relationship. But our interpersonal relationships occur in the context of our utter *creatureliness*, and it is there that the damage lies. Since the relationship with *creation* has been damaged, only the *Creator* himself can be our savior. We can be saved only when he from whom we have cut ourselves off takes the initiative with us and stretches out his hand to us. Only being loved is being saved, and only God's love can purify damaged human love and radically reestablish the network of relationships that have suffered from alienation.[150] (emphasis added)

Unlike the great polytheistic civilizations of antiquity who developed cosmogonic myths centered on capricious minor deities, a distinctive feature of historic Judaism and Catholic Christianity is belief in one Creator God. Unfortunately, Barbour's adoption of process theology, which reduces God to an entity among entities, capable of some level of influence or persuasion, does not do justice to the rich Biblical belief in an all knowing, all powerful God who creates out of love *ex nihilo et cum tempore*.

Barbour's belief in the "self-creation" of entities is a result of elevating evolution to the status of a *philosophia universalis*. Carroll astutely writes, "The very intelligibility of evolution itself depends upon a source which transcends the process of nature ... Creation is the foundation of the reality and the intelligibility

148 William E. Carroll, "Creation and a Self-Sufficient Universe," in *Evolutionstheorie und Schöpfungsglaube: Neue Perspektiven der Debatte*, ed. Hubert Philipp Weber and Rudolf Langthaler (Göttingen, Germany: Vandenhoeck & Ruprecht, 2013), 239.

149 Verschuuren, *Aquinas and Modern Science*, 50.

150 Ratzinger, *In the Beginning*, 73–74. The fact that the Creator's *eros* for man is also totally *agape* is further developed by Ratzinger later as pope. See Benedict XVI, *Deus Caritas Est*, 2005, 10.

of evolutionary change."[151] Thomas Aquinas sapiently taught that "*creatio non est mutatio*."[152]

Both Barbour and Aquinas affirm *creatio continua*. However, they understand the concept in a different way. To quote Carroll, "for Thomas, creation is not primarily some distant event; rather, it is the on-going complete causing of the existence of all that is."[153] Aquinas is aware that "over and above the mode of becoming by which something comes to be through change or motion, there must be a mode of becoming or origin of things, without any mutation or motion through the influx of being."[154]

According to Barbour's panentheistic view of God and the world, God is a source of order and novelty. In the context of evolution, a major concern for Barbour, God is "continuously active, influencing events through persuasive love but not controlling them unilaterally."[155] However, God does not need to exercise "top-down influence" in the face of quantum indeterminacy[156] to act in creation, as Barbour sometimes speculates.[157] God's all-pervasive creativity operates in eternal

---

151 Carroll, "Creation and the Foundations of Evolution," 52.

152 For example, see Thomas Aquinas, *Quæstiones Disputatæ de Potentia Dei*, ed. Kenny Joseph, trans. English Dominican Father (Westminster, MD: The Newman Press, 1952), Q 3, A 2, https:// dhspriory.org/thomas/QDdePotentia.htm.

153 Carroll, "Creation and the Foundations of Evolution," 53.

154 Thomas Aquinas, *De Substantiis Separatis*, ed. Joseph Kenny, trans. Francis J. Lescoe (West Hartford, CT: Saint Joseph College, 1959), chap. 9, 49.

155 Robert J. Russell, *Theology and Science: Current Issues and Future Directions* (Berkeley, CA: Center for Theology and the Natural Sciences, 2000), II, C, 2.

156 Barbour suggests that God actualizes one among a range of possibilities already present in nature through top-down causality. See Barbour, *Religion and Science*, 315.

157 Thomas Aquinas offers a very comprehensive response to how God acts in every agent: "Some have understood God to work in every agent in such a way that no created power has any effect in things, but that God alone is the ultimate cause of everything wrought; for instance, that it is not fire that gives heat, but God in the fire, and so forth. But this is impossible. First, because the order of cause and effect would be taken away from created things: and this would imply lack of power in the Creator: for it is due to the power of the cause, that it bestows active power on its effect. Secondly, because the active powers which are seen to exist in things, would be bestowed on things to no purpose, if these wrought nothing through them. Indeed, all things created would seem, in a way, to be purposeless, if they lacked an operation proper to them; since the purpose of everything is its operation. For the less perfect is always for the sake of the more perfect: and consequently as the matter is for the sake of the form, so the form which is the first act, is for the sake of its operation, which is the second act; and thus operation is the end of the creature. We must therefore understand that God works in things in such a manner that things have their proper operation. In order to make this clear, we must observe that as there are few kinds of causes; matter is not a principle of action, but is the subject that receives the effect of action. On the other hand, the end, the agent, and the form are principles of action, but in a certain order. For the first principle of action is the end which moves the agent; the second is the agent; the

simultaneity. There is no need for Him to respond to discrete possibilities "in the moment." The ordered convergence of all causes is from His eternal wisdom.

It is unfortunate that in his quest to overcome Cartesian dualism, Barbour consistently attempts to deny the important distinction between the supernatural and the natural. Natural science and revealed theology are not of the same order. Merriam-Webster defines *supernatural* in the following way: "of or relating to an order of existence beyond the visible observable universe; *especially*: of or relating to God." The *Dictionary of Fundamental Theology* describes the supernatural as "that which was not created and, as something uncreaturely, has effects on nature as the creaturely."[158] The study of created natures often leads the honest seeker to contemplate "an order of existence beyond the visible, observable universe," i.e., to the *Increatum*.[159] Theology is the noblest of the sciences, the *regina*

---

third is the form of that which the agent applies to action (although the agent also acts through its own form); as may be clearly seen in things made by art. For the craftsman is moved to action by the end, which is the thing wrought, for instance a chest or a bed; and applies to action the axe which cuts through its being sharp. Thus then does God work in every worker, according to these three things. First as an end. For since every operation is for the sake of some good, real or apparent; and nothing is good either really or apparently, except in as far as it participates in a likeness to the Supreme Good, which is God; it follows that God Himself is the cause of every operation as its end. Again it is to be observed that where there are several agents in order, the second always acts in virtue of the first; for the first agent moves the second to act. And thus all agents act in virtue of God Himself: and therefore He is the cause of action in every agent. Thirdly, we must observe that God not only moves things to operated, as it were applying their forms and powers to operation, just as the workman applies the axe to cut, who nevertheless at times does not give the axe its form; but He also gives created agents their forms and preserves them in being. Therefore He is the cause of action not only by giving the form which is the principle of action, as the generator is said to be the cause of movement in things heavy and light; but also as preserving the forms and powers of things; just as the sun is said to be the cause of the manifestation of colors, inasmuch as it gives and preserves the light by which colors are made manifest. And since the form of a thing is within the thing, and all the more, as it approaches nearer to the First and Universal Cause; and because in all things God Himself is properly the cause of universal being which is innermost in all things; it follows that in all things God works intimately. For this reason in Holy Scripture the operations of nature are attributed to God as operating in nature, according to Job 10:11: 'Thou hast clothed me with skin and flesh: Thou hast put me together with bones and sinews.'" Aquinas, *Summa Theologiæ*, I, Q 105, A 5.

158 Karl H. Neufeld, "Supernatural," ed. René Latourelle and Rino Fisichella, *Dictionary of Fundamental Theology* (New York: The Crossroad Publishing Company, February 1, 2000), 1016.

159 The connection between what is "seen" and "unseen" is particularly important in Sacramental theology. McDermott writes, "Catholic thought has always sought to preserve the sane balance between intelligibility and mystery, between the finite and the infinite. For the sacrament is fundamental to the Catholic vision of reality: in a through a finite sign, which is humanly intelligible, the infinite God, the mystery of infinite love, makes Himself present, calling me to the free

scientiarum,[160] because of its formal object: God in His very being.[161]

We now come to the end of our study. In Chapter One we showed how, as an experimental physicist and theologian, Ian Barbour was a key figure in the twentieth century effort to promote a positive relationship between theology and science. In Chapter Two we attempted to present clearly and fairly Barbour's fundamental principles. Chapter Three offered an explication of Barbour's methodology for relating theology and science based on his assessment of the two disciplines' similarities and differences. Chapter Four provided a Catholic critique of Barbour's thought for the doctrine of creation. We focused on the consequences of his epistemology, metaphysics, and theological method. Finally, in this last chapter, we attempted to apply Barbour's insights to promote great dialogue and integration between the natural sciences and the Catholic doctrine of creation.

Ian Barbour's metaphysician, Alfred North Whitehead, acknowledges that "the two strongest general forces ... which influence men ... [are] the force of religious intuitions, and the force of our impulse to accurate observation and logical deduction."[162] He later writes, "When we consider what religion is for mankind and what science is, it is no exaggeration to say that the future course of history depends upon the decision of this generation as to the relations between them."[163] It is our hope that this endeavor at a Catholic evaluation of Ian G. Barbour's thought, according to fundamental theological criteria, for the doctrine of creation, contributes to "the work of evangelization at the service of peace."[164] As the Church continues her pilgrim journey toward the fullness of the Kingdom, we pray that this research contributes to passage of the *populus Dei "ex umbris et imaginibus in veritatem."*[165]

Laudetur Iesus Christus!

4. Future Work

As in most scholarly endeavors, there are often opportunities for future research to extend the results of particular study. An important ethical and scientific issue

response of love. That structure is found preeminently in Jesus Christ, the God-man, and in the Eucharist, the source and goal of the Church's other sacraments." McDermott, "The Mystery of Matter," 1013–1014.

160 The Divine *Logos* is the magnificent font of all knowledge.

161 Aquinas, *Summa Theologiæ*, I, Q 1, A 7.

162 Whitehead, *Science and the Modern World*, 260.

163 Ibid.

164 Francis, *Evangelii Gaudium*, 242.

165 Inscription on the original tomb of John Henry Cardinal Newman.

today is the care for our common home, the Earth. In recent years, pioneering Catholic theologians, such as Paul Haffner, have begun to identify and study the salient issues.[166] Pope Francis has also recently reminded the Church and the global community of man's responsibility to be a good steward of God's creation.[167] Some of Ian Barbour's later writings deal with ecological issues. For example, in *Ethics in An Age of Technology*, he engages topics in environmental values, energy, conservation, and sustainability.[168] A Catholic evaluation of Barbour's theology of environment might be a fruitful follow-up study.

Barbour was also interested in process metaphysics as a proper dialogue partner for theology. While process philosophy is in eclipse at the moment, it may return as a significant philosophical and theological option. The relationship of *being* and *becoming* is one of the eternal philosophical problems. In our treatment of Barbour's metaphysics, we analyzed his creative approach to the act of being. Process metaphysics provides one thoughtful, although from the standpoint of Catholic theology, ultimately inadequate response. A second follow-up research project could seek to deepen ontological reflection on the act of being as inherently novel. Metaphysically speaking, the act of being is not a static monad, but a gift given over, eternally to the Son and Spirit, and then to countless others in creation. The simple act of being is also differentiated communion. The Triune structure of eternal act is reflected in creation in the way that the created *actus essendi* depends on form for its concreteness. Act is indivisible wholeness, but it is the act *of* beings.

Likewise, form is act *vis-à-vis* the potency of matter; but natural form is dependent on matter for its ongoing propagation in a species. Perfect act in some sense receives from what it generates in and through itself. In *De Potentia*, Thomas Aquinas says, accordingly, that act receives from potency, but *qua* potency, not *qua* act. In other words, a potency is moved into being by a prior act, which does not depend on it; but just to this extent, that act is enriched by potency.[169] It is enriched by gratuitously actuating another in and through itself. This issue is splendidly

---

166 Haffner, *Towards a Theology of the Environment*.

167 Francis, *Laudato Si'*, 116.

168 Barbour, *Ethics in an Age of Technology*.

169 See Aquinas, *Quæstiones Disputatæ de Potentia Dei*, Q 7, A 2. Aquinas refers to the relation of *esse* and form, as well as that of form and matter. His analysis implies more generally that act is open to determination "from below" or "from within" by its potency. This stance has to be squared with Aquinas' frequent claim that perfect act is not passive to any prior or external act. So the key seems to be that determination of act by potency must primarily be from act itself. The perfection of act includes the power for intrinsic but gratuitous "self"-determination. The key metaphysical issue connected to this is the non-subsistence of created *esse*—in being given over wholly to *ens*—as the ontological image of Divine goodness.

introduced in *Divine Love as Event: A Study in the Trinitarian Theology of Hans Urs von Balthasar*,[170] but more work remains.

A third area for further study could be the metaphysical issue of "physical events" as an ontological category (in light of modern science) and the related issue of the mutuality of form and matter. For example, it is correct to state that biological forms are in some sense "receptive" *vis-à-vis* matter. Of course, forms transcend and "inform" matter, but they also depend on it, and are intimately bound to it. More generally, the receptivity or openness of metaphysical principles may allow one to both affirm the priority of act over potency and affirm the novelty of act itself, manifested in and through its potencies. Act is intrinsically receptive and novel. Barbour's process theology is wrong to deny the priority of act over potency, but it is right that being is ever new. Likewise, physics today is correct as it affirms the priority of intelligible laws of nature, yet also insists that various levels of contingency are built into them.

A fourth area of future research might be to assess the impact and reception of Barbour' approach to relating religious inquiry and scientific research for non-Christian religions. Does Barbour have something to offer for a distinctly Jewish engagement with science?[171] Can he contribute to relating natural science with Eastern religions and philosophies, e.g., Hinduism, Buddhism, Jainism, Sikhism, Taoism, Shinto, or Confucianism? Inter-cultural dialogue is an important aspect of the Christian apostolate and at the service of peace.[172]

170 John T. Laracy, "Divine Love as Event: A Study in the Trinitarian Theology of Hans Urs von Balthasar" (PhD, The Pontifical John Paul II Institute for Studies on Marriage and the Family at the Catholic University of America, 2017).

171 For a thorough introduction to Jewish reflection and engagement with the sciences, see Hava Tirosh-Samuelson, "Judaism and the Dialogue of Religion and Science: A Personal Journey," *Theology and Science* 16, no. 4 (November 2018): 388–414.

172 See Sylwia Górzna, "Intercultural Dialogue in the Teaching of Pope Benedict XVI," *Philosophy Study* 7, no. 7 (July 28, 2017): 373–384; Francis, "Address of Pope Francis to Participants in the Plenary Session of the Congregation for Catholic Education" (Clementine Hall, Vatican City State, February 13, 2014), accessed October 23, 2018, https://w2.vatican.va/content/francesco/en/speeches/2014/february/documents/papa-francesco_20140213_congregazione-educazione-cattolica.html.

Major Scholarly Works of Ian G. Barbour

(by publication date)

Barbour, Ian G. "An Automatic Low Frequency Analyzer." *Review of Scientific Instruments* 18, no. 7 (July 1, 1947): 516–522.

———. "Magnetic Deflection of Cosmic-Ray Mesons Using Nuclear Plates." PhD, University of Chicago, 1950.

———. "Integration as an Objective in the Physical Sciences." *American Journal of Physics* 20 (1952): 565.

———. "Karl Heim on Christian Faith and Natural Science." *The Christian Scholar* 39, no. 3 (1956): 229–237.

———. *Christianity and the Scientist*. New York: Association Press, 1960.

———. *Issues in Science and Religion*. Upper Saddle River, NJ: Prentice-Hall, 1966.

———. "Commentary on Theological Resources from the Physical Sciences." *Zygon* 1, no. 1 (March 1966): 27–30.

———. "Science and Religion Today." In *Science and Religion: New Perspectives on the Dialogue*, edited by Ian G. Barbour, 3–29. New York: Harper & Row, 1968.

———. "Teilhard's Process Metaphysics." *Journal of Religion* 59 (1969): 136–159.

———. *Science & Secularity: The Ethics of Technology*. New York: Harper & Row, 1970.

———. *Myths, Models, and Paradigms*. New York: HarperCollins College Division, 1974.

———. "Paradigms in Science and Religion." In *Paradigms & Revolutions: Applications and Appraisals of Thomas Kuhn's Philosophy of Science*, edited by Gary Gutting, 223–245. Notre Dame, IN: University of Notre Dame Press, 1980.

———. *Technology, Environment, and Human Values.* New York: Praeger, 1980.

———. *Religion in an Age of Science.* San Francisco: Harper Collins, 1990.

———. *Ethics in an Age of Technology.* San Francisco: Harper Collins, 1992.

———. *Religion and Science: Historical and Contemporary Issues.* San Francisco: Harper, 1997.

———. "Neuroscience, Artificial Intelligence, and Human Nature." In *Neuroscience and the Person: Scientific Perspectives on Divine Action*, edited by Robert John Russell, 249–280. Vatican City State: Vatican Observatory, 1999.

———. *When Science Meets Religion: Enemies, Strangers, or Partners?* San Francisco: HarperOne, 2000.

———. *Nature, Human Nature, and God.* Minneapolis: Fortress Press, 2002.

———. "Remembering Arthur Peacocke: A Personal Reflection." *Zygon* 43, no. 1 (March 1, 2008): 89–102.

———. "John Polkinghorne on Three Scientist-Theologians." *Theology and Science* 8, no. 3 (August 1, 2010): 247–264.

———. "A Personal Odyssey." *Theology and Science* 15, no. 1 (January 2, 2017): 5–16.

Co-authored

Barbour, Ian G., Sanford Lakoff, and John Opie. *Energy and American Values.* New York: Praeger, 1982.

Bibliography

Adams, Fred C., and Evan Grohs. "Stellar Helium Burning in Other Universes: A Solution to the Triple Alpha Fine-Tuning Problem." *Astroparticle Physics* 87 (January 2017): 40–54.

Ade, P. a. R., N. Aghanim, M. Arnaud, M. Ashdown, J. Aumont, C. Baccigalupi, A. J. Banday, et al. "Planck 2015 Results—XIII. Cosmological Parameters." *Astronomy & Astrophysics* 594 (October 2016). Accessed February 27, 2018. https://www.aanda.org/articles/aa/abs/2016/10/aa25830-15/aa25830-15.html.

Agamben, Giorgio. "What Is a Paradigm?" Lecture presented at the European Graduate School, Saas-Fee, Switzerland, October 1, 2002. Accessed March 6, 2018. https://www.youtube.com/watch?v=G9Wxn1L9Er0.

Albeverio, Sergio, Rafael Høegh-Krohn, and Sonia Mazzucchi. *Mathematical Theory of Feynman Path Integrals: An Introduction.* 2nd ed. Berlin: Springer-Verlag, 2008.

Allen, Paul L. *Ernan McMullin and Critical Realism in the Science-Theology Dialogue.* Burlington: Routledge, 2006.

———. "Is There Verification in Theology?" *Open Theology* 3, no. 1 (September 2, 2017): 417–433.

Angelo, Bernard Jerold. "Conceptual Frameworks: Their Uses and Potential Abuses." PhD, Syracuse University, 2000. Accessed October 10, 2017. https://search.proquest.com/dissertations/docview/304649084/abstract/CDD323051D654D77PQ/2.

Aquinas, Thomas. *Aquinas on Creation.* Translated by Steven Baldner and William E. Carroll. Toronto: Pontifical Institute of Mediaeval Studies, 1997.

———. *Commentaria in Octo Libros Physicorum.* Translated by Richard J. Blackwell, Richard J. Spath, and W. Edmund Thirlkel. New Haven, CT: Yale University Press, 1963. Accessed April 27, 2018. https://dhspriory.org/thomas/Physics.htm.

———. *Commentary on Aristotle's De Anima.* Translated by Kenelm Foster and Sylvester Humphries. New Haven, CT: Yale University Press, 1951. Accessed March 14, 2018. http://dhspriory.org/thomas/english/DeAnima.htm.

———. *Commentary on the Metaphysics.* Edited by Kenny Joseph. Translated by John P. Rowan. Washington, D.C: Dominican Province of Saint Joseph, 1961. Accessed March 14, 2018. http://dhspriory.org/thomas/Metaphysics.htm.

———. "De Aeternitate Mundi." In *Internet Medieval Sourcebook.* Translated by Robert T. Miller. New York: Fordham University, 1997. Accessed March 15, 2018. https://sourcebooks. fordham.edu/basis/aquinas-eternity.asp.

———. *De Ente et Essentia.* Translated by Robert T. Miller. Internet Medieval Source Book. New York: Fordham University, 1997. Accessed May 2, 2018. https://sourcebooks.fordham. edu/basis/aquinas-esse.asp.

———. *De Principiis Naturæ.* Edited by Joseph Kenny. Translated by Roman A. Kocourek. St. Paul, MN: North Central, 1948. Accessed November 21, 2018. https://dhspriory.org/ thomas/DePrincNaturae.htm.

———. *De Substantiis Separatis.* Edited by Joseph Kenny. Translated by Francis J. Lescoe. West Hartford, CT: Saint Joseph College, 1959.

———. *Nature and Grace: Selections from the Summa Theologica of Thomas Aquinas.* Edited by A. M. Fairweather. London: Catholic Way Publishing, 2013.

———. *Quæstiones Disputatæ de Potentia Dei.* Edited by Kenny Joseph. Translated by English Dominican Father. Westminster, MD: The Newman Press, 1952. https://dhspriory.org/ thomas/QDdePotentia.htm.

———. *Quæstiones Disputatæ de Veritate.* Translated by Robert W. Mulligan, James V. McGlynn, and Robert W. Schmidt. Chicago: Henry Regnery Company, 1954.

———. *Summa Contra Gentiles.* Edited by Joseph Kenny. Translated by James F. Anderson. New York: Hanover House, 1957. Accessed March 14, 2018. http://dhspriory.org/thomas/ ContraGentiles.htm.

———. *Summa Theologiæ.* Translated by Fathers of the English Dominican Province. 2nd ed. London, 1920. Accessed February 1, 2018. http://www.newadvent.org/summa/.

———. *The Division and Methods of the Sciences.* Edited by Armand Maurer. Toronto: Pontifical Institute of Mediaeval Studies, 1953.

Aristotle. *De Anima.* Translated by C.D.C. Reeve. Cambridge: Hackett Publishing Company, Inc., 2017.

———. *Metaphysics.* Translated by William David Ross. Oxford: Clarendon Press, 1908.

———. *On the Generation and Corruption.* Translated by Harold Henry Joachim. Adelaide, South Australia: eBooks@Adelaide, 2015. Accessed May 2, 2018. https://ebooks.adelaide. edu.au/a/aristotle/corruption/.

———. *Physics.* Translated by C.D.C. Reeve. Indianapolis: Hackett Publishing Company, Inc., 2018.

Artigas, Mariano. *Knowing Things for Sure: Science and Truth*. Translated by Alan McCone. New York: University Press of America, 2006.

Ashley, Benedict M. *The Way Toward Wisdom: An Interdisciplinary and Intercultural Introduction to Metaphysics*. Notre Dame: University of Notre Dame Press, 2006.

Attard, Phil. *Non-Equilibrium Thermodynamics and Statistical Mechanics: Foundations and Applications*. Oxford: Oxford University Press, 2012.

Augustine. *On Genesis*. Edited by John E. Rotelle. Translated by Edmund Hill. Vol. 13. The Works of St. Augustine 1. Hyde Park, NY: New City Press, 2002.

———. *The City of God, Books VIII–XVI*. Translated by Gerald G. Walsh and Grace Monahan. Vol. 2. The Fathers of the Church. Washington, DC: CUA Press, 2008.

———. *The City of God, Books XVII-XXII*. Translated by Gerald G. Walsh. Vol. 3. The Fathers of the Church. Washington, DC: CUA Press, 2008.

———. *The Confessions*. Edited by David Vincent Meconi. Translated by Maria Boulding. Ignatius Critical Editions. San Francisco: Ignatius Press, 2012.

Auld, Sandra B. "Barbour, Whitehead, and Bohm: Can Process Philosophy Reveal a Metaphysical Basis for Both Religion and Science?" MA, University of Guelph (Canada), 2002. Accessed October 10, 2017. https://search.proquest.com/dissertations/docview/305582962/abstract/CDD323051D654D77PQ/5.

Aveling, Francis. "Rationalism." In *Catholic Encyclopedia*. New York: Robert Appleton Company, 1911. Accessed March 2, 2018. http://www.newadvent.org/cathen/12652a.htm.

Avicenna. *The Metaphysica of Avicenna: A Critical Translation-Commentary and Analysis of the Fundamental Arguments in Avicenna's Metaphysica in the Danish Nama-I Ala I*. Edited by Parviz Morewedge. New York: Routledge, 2016.

Ayer, Alfred J. *Language, Truth and Logic*. 2nd ed. New York: Dover Publications, 1952.

Bacon, Francis. *The Advancement of Learning*. London: Cassell & Company, 1893. Accessed January 25, 2018. http://www.gutenberg.org/files/5500/5500-h/5500-h.htm.

Bacon, Roger. *The 'Opus Majus' of Roger Bacon*. Translated by Robert Belle Burke. Vol. 1. London: Williams and Norgate, 1900.

Baillie, John. *Our Knowledge of God*. New York: Charles Scribner's Sons, 1939.

Bainton, Roland Herbert. *Yale and the Ministry: A History of Education for the Christian Ministry at Yale from the Founding in 1701*. New York: Harper & Brothers, 1957.

von Balthasar, Hans Urs. "A Résumé of My Thought." *Communio* 15, no. 4 (1988): 468–473.

———. "Creation and Trinity." Translated by Stephen Wentworth Arndt. *Communio* 15, no. 3 (1988): 285–293.

———. *Karl Barth: Darstellung Und Deutung Seiner Theologie*. Köln: Verlag Jakob Hegner, 1951.

———. *Theo-Drama: The Last Act*. Translated by Graham Harrison. Vol. 5. 5 vols. San Francisco: Ignatius Press, 2003.

———. *Theo-Logic: The Truth of the World*. Vol. 1. 3 vols. San Francisco: Ignatius Press, 2001.

Barbour, George B. *In the Field with Teilhard de Chardin*. New York: Herder, 1965.

———. "Letter to His Sons," April 11, 1955.

———. "The Geological Background of Peking Man (Sinanthropus)." *Science* 72, no. 1877 (December 19, 1930): 635–636.

Barbour, Hugh S. "Memorial to George Brown Barbour." *Geological Society of America* 9 (1979): 1–5.

Barbour, Ian G. "A Personal Odyssey." *Theology and Science* 15, no. 1 (January 2, 2017): 5–16.

———. "An Automatic Low Frequency Analyzer." *Review of Scientific Instruments* 18, no. 7 (July 1, 1947): 516–522.

———. "Commentary on Theological Resources from the Physical Sciences." *Zygon* 1, no. 1 (March 1966): 27–30.

———. *Ethics in an Age of Technology.* San Francisco: Harper Collins, 1992.

———. "Integration as an Objective in the Physical Sciences." *American Journal of Physics* 20 (1952): 565.

———. *Issues in Science and Religion.* Upper Saddle River, NJ: Prentice-Hall, 1966.

———. "Karl Heim on Christian Faith and Natural Science." *The Christian Scholar* 39, no. 3 (1956): 229–237.

———. "Magnetic Deflection of Cosmic-Ray Mesons Using Nuclear Plates." PhD, University of Chicago, 1950.

———. *Myths, Models, and Paradigms.* New York: HarperCollins College Division, 1974.

———. *Nature, Human Nature, and God.* Minneapolis: Fortress Press, 2002.

———. "Neuroscience, Artificial Intelligence, and Human Nature." In *Neuroscience and the Person: Scientific Perspectives on Divine Action*, edited by Robert John Russell, 249–280. Vatican City State: Vatican Observatory, 1999.

———. "Paradigms in Science and Religion." In *Paradigms & Revolutions: Applications and Appraisals of Thomas Kuhn's Philosophy of Science*, edited by Gary Gutting, 223–245. Notre Dame, IN: University of Notre Dame Press, 1980.

———. *Religion and Science: Historical and Contemporary Issues.* San Francisco: Harper, 1997.

———. *Religion in an Age of Science.* San Francisco: Harper Collins, 1990.

———. "Remembering Arthur Peacocke: A Personal Reflection." *Zygon* 43, no. 1 (March 1, 2008): 89–102.

———. "Science and Religion Today." In *Science and Religion: New Perspectives on the Dialogue*, edited by Ian G. Barbour, 3–29. New York: Harper & Row, 1968.

———. *Technology, Environment, and Human Values.* New York: Praeger, 1980.

———. "Teilhard's Process Metaphysics." *Journal of Religion* 59 (1969): 136–159.

———. *When Science Meets Religion: Enemies, Strangers, or Partners?* San Francisco: HarperOne, 2000.

Barbour, Ian G., Sanford Lakoff, and John Opie. *Energy and American Values.* New York: Praeger, 1982.

Barbour, John. "The Life of Ian Barbour: An Interview with His Son, John." Interview by Joseph R. Laracy. Email, November 14, 2017.

Barnes, Luke A. "The Fine-Tuning of the Universe for Intelligent Life." *Publications of the Astronomical Society of Australia* 29, no. 04 (2012): 529–564.

Barnes, Luke A., and Geraint F. Lewis. "Producing the Deuteron in Stars: Anthropic Limits on Fundamental Constants." *Journal of Cosmology and Astroparticle Physics* 2017, no. 7 (July 20, 2017): 1–18. https://iopscience.iop.org/article/10.1088/1475-7516/2017/07/036/pdf.

Barrett, Mary Ellen. *Encyclopedia of Catholic Social Thought, Social Science, and Social Policy: Supplement*, edited by Michael L. Coulter, Richard S. Myers, and Joseph A. Varacalli. Vol. 3. Lanham, UK: Scarecrow Press, 2012.

Barrow, John D. *Theories of Everything: The Quest for Ultimate Explanation*. Oxford: Oxford University Press, 1991.

Barrow, John D., and Frank J. Tipler. *The Anthropic Cosmological Principle*. Revised. Oxford: Oxford University Press, 1988.

Barrs, Jerram. "Echoes of Eden." *CS Lewis*. Last modified November 10, 2009. Accessed March 7, 2018. http://www.cslewis.com/echoes-of-eden/.

Barth, Karl. *Church Dogmatics*. Translated by Geoffrey W. Bromiley. 2nd ed. Edinburgh: T&T Clark, 1975.

———. *Die Kirchliche Dogmatik*. 14 vols. Zürich: TVZ Theologischer Verlag, 1993.

Barthélemy, Jean-Dominique. *God and His Image: An Outline of Biblical Theology*. Revised. San Francisco, CA: Ignatius Press, 2007.

Barut, Asim Orhan. *The Theory of the Scattering Matrix for the Interactions of Fundamental Particles*. New York: Macmillan, 1967.

Batygin, Konstantin, and Gregory Laughlin. "On the Dynamical Stability of the Solar System." *The Astrophysical Journal* 683, no. 2 (August 20, 2008): 1207–1216.

Bauckham, Richard. *The Theology of the Book of Revelation*. Cambridge: Cambridge University Press, 1993.

Bea, Augustin. *The Word of God and Mankind*. Translated by Dorothy White. London: Geoffrey Chapman Ltd., 1967.

Beards, Andrew. "Generalized Empirical Method." *The Lonergan Review* 3, no. 1 (2011): 33–87.

———. *Method in Metaphysics: Lonergan and the Future of Analytical Philosophy*. Toronto: University of Toronto Press, 2008.

Beauchamp, Paul. *L'un et l'autre Testament: Accomplir les Écritures*. Vol. 2. 2 vols. Paris: Seuil, 1990.

Bechtel, William, and Robert C. Williamson. "Vitalism." Edited by Edward Craig. *Routledge Encyclopedia of Philosophy*. New York: Routledge, 1998. Accessed January 19, 2018. https://www.rep.routledge.com/articles/thematic/vitalism/v-1.

Bell, Eric T. *Men of Mathematics*. New York: Simon & Schuster, 1986.

Benedetto, Arnold J. "Divine Concurrence." Edited by Thomas Carson. *New Catholic Encyclopedia*. Farmington Hills: Thompson Gale, 2003. Accessed February 7, 2018. http://www.encyclopedia.com/religion/encyclopedias-almanacs-transcripts-and-maps/concurrence-divine.

Benedict XVI. "Address of His Holiness Benedict XVI to Members of the Pontifical Academy of Sciences on the Occasion of Their Plenary Assembly," Clementine Hall, Vatican City State, October 31, 2008. Accessed April 24, 2018. https://w2.vatican.va/content/benedict-xvi/en/speeches/2008/october/documents/hf_ben-xvi_spe_20081031_academy-sciences.html.

———. *Deus Caritas Est*, 2005.

———. *Dogma and Preaching: Applying Christian Doctrine to Daily Life*. San Francisco: Ignatius Press, 2011.

———. *God and the World*. San Francisco: Ignatius Press, 2002.

———. "Homily at the Vespers in the Cathedral of Aosta." *L'Osservatore Romano*, July 24, 2009. Accessed February 17, 2018. https://w2.vatican.va/content/benedict-xvi/en/homilies/2009/documents/hf_ben-xvi_hom_20090724_vespri-aosta.html.

———. *Jesus of Nazareth: Holy Week*. San Francisco: Ignatius Press, 2011.

———. "Meeting with the Young People of the Diocese of Rome in Preparation for the Celebration of the 21st World Youth Day," April 6, 2006. Accessed January 22, 2018. http://w2.vatican.va/content/benedict-xvi/en/speeches/2006/april/documents/hf_ben-xvi_spe_20060406_xxi-wyd.html.

———. *The Regensburg Lecture*, edited by James V. Schall. South Bend: St. Augustines Press, 2007.

———. "Tradition: Communion In Time." General Audience, Vatican City State, April 26, 2006. Accessed April 30, 2018. https://zenit.org/articles/role-of-church-tradition/.

———. Homily, Islinger Feld, Regensburg, September 12, 2006. Accessed March 23, 2018. https://w2.vatican.va/content/benedict-xvi/en/homilies/2006/documents/hf_ben-xvi_hom_20060912_regensburg.html.

Benjamin, Abram Cornelius. *Introduction to the Philosophy of Science*. New York: The Macmillan Co., 1937.

Berg, Christian. *Theologie Im Technologischen Zeitalter: Das Werk Ian Barbours Als Beitrag Zu Verhältnisbestimmung von Theologie Zu Naturwissenschaft Und Technik*. Stuttgart: Kohlhammer, 2002.

Bertalanffy, Ludwig von. *General System Theory: Foundations, Development, Applications*. Revised. New York: George Braziller Inc., 2015.

Betten, Francis S., ed. *The Roman Index of Forbidden Books*. 5th ed. London: B. Herder Book Co., 1920.

Bhaskar, Roy. "A Realist Theory of Science." DPhil, University of Oxford, 1975.

Bohr, Niels. "Discussions with Einstein on Epistemological Problems in Atomic Physics." In *Albert Einstein: Philosopher–Scientist*, by Albert Einstein. Cambridge: Cambridge University Press, 1949.

———. "The Quantum Postulate and the Recent Development of Atomic Theory." *Nature* 121 (April 14, 1928): 580–590.

Bolger, Robert Kevin. "Kneeling at the Altar of Science: Miscues and Mishaps in the Contemporary Dialogue between Science and Religion." PhD, The Claremont Graduate University, 2009. Accessed October 10, 2017. https://search.proquest.com/dissertations/docview/304863534/abstract/CDD323051D654D77PQ/6.

Bonaventura. *The Mind's Road to God*. Translated by George Boas. New York: Macmillan, 1953.

Bonaventure. *Commentaria in Quatuor Libros Sententiarum Magistri Petri Lombardi: Tomus II—In Secundum Librum Sententiarum*. Quaracchi, Italia: Ex typographia Colegii S. Bonaventurae, 1885. Accessed April 25, 2018. http://archive.org/details/doctorisseraphic02bona.

Bonino, Serge-Thomas. "To Be a Thomist." *Nova et Vetera* 8, no. 4 (2010): 763–775.

Bonting, Sjoerd Lieuwe. *Creation and Double Chaos: Science and Theology in Discussion*. Minneapolis: Fortress Press, 2009.

Boslough, John. *Stephen Hawking's Universe*. New York: Morrow, 1985.

Bostrom, Nick. "Where Are They?" *MIT Technology Review*, April 22, 2008. Accessed November 21, 2017. https://www.technologyreview.com/s/409936/where-are-they/.

Bourke, Vernon J. "Rationalism." Edited by Dagobert D. Runes. *Dictionary of Philosophy*. Totowa, NJ: Littlefield, Adams, and Company, 1962.

Bracken, Joseph A. "Revising Process Metaphysics in Response to Ian Barbour's Critique." *Zygon* 33, no. 3 (September 1, 1998): 405–414.

Breuvart, Jean-Marie. *Le Questionnement métaphysique d'A.N. Whitehead*. Louvain-la-Neuve, Belgium: Chromatika, 2013.

Brewer, Elmer Woodson. "The Approaches of John Polkinghorne, Arthur Peacocke, and Ian Barbour for the Integration of Natural Science and Christian Theology." PhD, The Southern Baptist Theological Seminary, 1995. Accessed October 10, 2017. https://search.proquest.com/dissertations/docview/304218674/abstract/D0BD7AB8396D4439PQ/1.

Brozas, Francisco Sánchez de las. *Minerva, Sive de Causis Latinae Linguae Commentarius*. Amsterdam: Judocum Pluymer, 1664.

Bruno, Giordano. *The Expulsion of the Triumphant Beast*. Translated by Arthur D. Imerti. 2nd ed. Lincoln, NE: Bison Books, 2004.

Brüntrup, Godehard, and Ludwig Jaskolla, eds. *Panpsychism: Contemporary Perspectives*. Philosophy of Mind. New York: Oxford University Press, 2016.

Buber, Martin. *I and Thou*. Translated by Ronald G. Smith. Edinburgh: T&T Clark, 1937.

Budge, Ernest Alfred Thompson Wallis. *The Gods of the Egyptians*. Vol. 1. 2 vols. London: Methuen & Co, 1904.

Bultmann, Rudolf. *Jesus Christ and Mythology*. London: Hymns Ancient & Modern Ltd, 2012.

———. "New Testament and Mythology." In *Philosophy, Religious Studies, and Myth*, edited by Robert A. Segal, 29–72. New York: Garland Publishing Inc., 1996.

———. *The Gospel of John: A Commentary*. Edited by Paul N. Anderson. Translated by G. R. Beasley-Murray. Eugene: Wipf & Stock, 2014.

Bultmann, Rudolf K. "Faith in God the Creator." In *Existence and Faith: Shorter Writings of Rudolf Bultmann*, translated by Schubert M. Ogden. New York: Meridian Books, 1960.

Buras, Andrzej J., John R. Ellis, Mary K. Gaillard, and Dimitri V. Nanopoulos. "Aspects of the Grand Unification of Strong, Weak and Electromagnetic Interactions." *Nuclear Physics B* 135, no. 1 (1978): 66–92.

Buxton, Graham. *The Trinity, Creation and Pastoral Ministry: Imaging the Perichoretic God*. Eugene, OR: Wipf & Stock Publishers, 2007.

Campbell, Norman R. *Physics: The Elements*. Cambridge: Cambridge University Press, 1920.

———. *What Is Science?* London: Methuen & Co, 1921.

Carnap, Rudolf. "The Elimination of Metaphysics through Logical Analysis of Language." In *Logical Empiricism at Its Peak: Schlick, Carnap, and Neurath*, edited by Sahotra Sarkar, 10–31. New York: Garland Publishing Inc., 1996.

Carroll, William E. "Aquinas and the Big Bang." *First Things*, no. 97 (November 1999): 18–20.

——. "Creation and a Self-Sufficient Universe." In *Evolutionstheorie und Schöpfungsglaube: Neue Perspektiven der Debatte*, edited by Hubert Philipp Weber and Rudolf Langthaler, 231–248. Göttingen, Germany: Vandenhoeck & Ruprecht, 2013.

——. "Creation and the Foundations of Evolution." *Angelicum* 871, no. 1 (2010).

——. "Creation, Evolution, and Thomas Aquinas." *Revue des Questions Scientifiques* 171, no. 4 (2000): 319–347.

Chamberlain, Stephen. "The Dispute between Gilson and Maritain over Thomist Realism." *Studia Gilsoniana* 2, no. 2 (2017): 177–195.

Chardin, Pierre Teilhard de. *The Phenomenon of Man*. New York: Harper & Row, 1961.

Chesterton, G.K. "Saint Thomas Aquinas." In *Collected Works*. Vol. 2. San Francisco: Ignatius Press, 1986.

Chisholm, Hugh, ed. "Amalric of Bena." In *The Encyclopædia Britannica*. Cambridge: Cambridge University Press, 1910.

Clarke, W. Norris. *Person and Being*. Milwaukee: Marquette University Press, 1993.

——. *The Philosophical Approach to God: A New Thomistic Perspective*. 2nd ed. New York: Fordham University Press, 2007.

Clavier, Paul. *Ex Nihilo: L'introduction en philosophie du concept de création*. 2 vols. Paris: Hermann, 2011.

——. "No Creation, No Revelation." *International Journal for Philosophy of Religion* 73, no. 3 (2013): 255–268.

Clayton, Philip. "Barbour's Panentheistic Metaphysic." *Theology and Science* 15, no. 1 (January 2, 2017): 53–62.

Clifford, Anne M. "Catholicism and Ian Barbour on Theology and Science." In *Fifty Years in Science and Religion: Ian G. Barbour and His Legacy*, edited by Robert John Russell, 287–300. Ashgate Science and Religion Series. Burlington, VT: Ashgate Publishing, 2004.

——. "Catholicism and Ian Barbour on Theology and Science." *Theology and Science* 15, no. 1 (January 2, 2017): 88–100.

——. "Creation." In *Systematic Theology: Roman Catholic Perspectives*, edited by Francis Schüssler Fiorenza and John P. Galvin. Vol. 1. Minneapolis: Fortress Press, 1991.

Clifford, Richard J. "The Hebrew Scriptures and the Theology of Creation." *Theological Studies* 46 (1985): 507–523.

Cobb, John B. "Spiritual Discernment in a Whiteheadian Perspective." In *Religious Experience and Process Theology*, edited by Harry J. Cargas and Bernard J. Lee. New York: Paulist Press, 1976.

Cobb, John B., and David Ray Griffin. *Process Theology: An Introduction*. Philadelphia: Westminster Press, 1976.

Compton, Arthur H. *The Freedom of Man*. New Haven, CT: Yale University Press, 1935.

Congregation for the Doctrine of the Faith. "Declaration in Defense of the Catholic Doctrine on the Church Against Certain Errors of the Present Day," June 24, 1973. Accessed April 17, 2018. http://www.vatican.va/roman_curia/congregations/cfaith/documents/rc_con_cfaith_doc_19730705_mysterium-ecclesiae_en.html.

———. *Donum Veritatis*, 1990. Accessed December 1, 2017. http://www.vatican.va/roman_curia/congregations/cfaith/documents/rc_con_cfaith_doc_19900524_theologian-vocation_en.html.

———. *Notification on the Book, Toward a Christian Theology of Religious Pluralism*, January 24, 2001. Accessed May 14, 2018. http://www.vatican.va/roman_curia/congregations/cfaith/documents/rc_con_cfaith_doc_20010124_dupuis_en.html.

———. *Placuit Deo*, 2018.

Cooper, James Fenimore. *Tenacious of Their Liberties: The Congregationalists in Colonial Massachusetts*. Oxford: Oxford University Press, 2002.

Cooper, John W. *Panentheism—The Other God of the Philosophers: From Plato to the Present*. Grand Rapids, MI: Baker Academic, 2013.

Coulson, Charles Alfred. *Science and Christian Belief*. Chapel Hill: University of North Carolina Press, 1955.

Council of Vienne. "Decrees." In *Decrees of the Ecumenical Councils*, edited by Norman P. Tanner. Vol. 1. Washington, DC: Georgetown University Press, 1990.

Coyne, George V., and Michael Heller. *A Comprehensible Universe: The Interplay of Science and Theology*. New York: Springer, 2008.

Cronin, K.J. *The Name of God as Revealed in Exodus 3:14*. Exodus-314.com, December 16, 2017. Accessed January 24, 2018. http://exodus-314.com/images/banners/the_name.pdf.

Dalrymple, G. Brent. *The Age of the Earth*. Stanford: Stanford University Press, 1991.

Danielou, Jean. "The Meaning and Significance of Teilhard de Chardin." Translated by John Lyon. *Communio* 15, no. 3 (1988): 350–360.

Darrigol, Olivier. *Electrodynamics from Ampère to Einstein*. Oxford: Oxford University Press, 2003.

Davidson, Mark. *Uncommon Sense: The Life and Thought of Ludwig von Bertalanffy, Father of General Systems Theory*. Los Angeles: J.P. Tarcher, 1983.

Dawkins, Richard. *The God Delusion*. Boston: Mariner Books, 2008.

De Brasi, Richard, and Joseph R. Laracy. "An Empirical Critique of Empiricism." *Logos: A Journal of Catholic Thought and Culture* 16, no. 4 (October 3, 2013): 124–163.

De Letter, P. "Reciprocal Causality: Some Applications in Theology." *The Thomist* 25, no. 3 (1962): 382–418.

Dennett, Daniel C. *Consciousness Explained*. New York: Little Brown, 1991.

———. *Darwin's Dangerous Idea: Evolution and the Meanings of Life*. New York: Simon & Schuster, 1996.

Descartes, René. *Discourse on Method*. Edited by Pamela Kraus and Frank Hunt. Translated by Richard Kennington. Indianapolis: Hackett Publishing Company, Inc., 2012.

———. *Meditations on First Philosophy in Which the Existence of God and the Distinction of the Soul from the Body Are Demonstrated.* Translated by Donald A. Cress. Indianapolis: Hackett Publishing Company, Inc., 1979.

———. *Principia Philosophiæ.* Amsterdam: Ludovicum Elzevirium, 1644.

———. *The Passions of the Soul: Les Passions De l'Âme.* Translated by Stephen Voss. Indianapolis: Hackett Publishing Company, Inc., 1989.

DeWolf, Harold. *A Theology of the Living Church.* New York: Harper & Brothers, 1953.

D'Inverno, Ray. *Introducing Einstein's Relativity.* Oxford: Clarendon Press, 1992.

Dodd, Charles Harold. *The Parables of the Kingdom.* London: James Nisbet and Co., 1935.

Doig, James C. *Aquinas on Metaphysics: A Historico-Doctrinal Study of the Commentary on the Metaphysics.* The Hague: Martinus Nijhoff, 1972.

Dombrowski, Dan. "Charles Hartshorne." In *The Stanford Encyclopedia of Philosophy*, edited by Edward N. Zalta. Stanford: Metaphysics Research Lab, Stanford University, 2017. Accessed January 15, 2018. https://plato.stanford.edu/archives/spr2017/entries/hartshorne/.

Draper, John William. *History of the Conflict between Religion and Science.* CreateSpace Independent Publishing Platform, 2014.

Drees, Willem B. *Religion, Science and Naturalism.* Cambridge: Cambridge University Press, 1998.

Duhem, Pierre. *The Aim and Structure of Physical Theory.* Translated by Philip P. Wigner. Princeton: Princeton University Press, 1954.

Dunne, Tad. "Bernard Lonergan." Edited by James Fieser and Bradley Dowden. *Internet Encyclopedia of Philosophy*, 2018. Accessed January 19, 2018. http://www.iep.utm.edu/lonergan/.

Dyck, John M. *Faith under Test: Alternative Service during World War II in the U.S. and Canada.* Gospel Publishers, 1997.

Dyson, Freeman. *Disturbing the Universe.* New York: Harper & Row, 1981.

Eddington, Arthur. *The Nature of the Physical World.* Cambridge: Cambridge University Press, 1928.

———. *The Philosophy of Physical Science.* Cambridge: Cambridge University Press, 1949.

Editors of Encyclopædia Britannica. "Pierre Teilhard de Chardin." *Encyclopedia Britannica*, April 26, 2013. Accessed January 10, 2018. https://www.britannica.com/biography/Pierre-Teilhard-de-Chardin.

Edwards, Denis. *How God Acts: Creation, Redemption, and Special Divine Action.* Minneapolis: Fortress Press, 2010.

Egnor, Michael. "Aristotle on the Immateriality of Intellect and Will." *Evolution News & Science Today*, January 26, 2015. Accessed November 8, 2018. https://evolutionnews.org/2015/01/aristotle_on_th/.

Ehrbar, Hans G. "Marxism and Critical Realism." Salt Lake City, 1998.

Einstein, Albert. *Albert Einstein: Autobiographical Notes.* Translated by Paul Arthur Schlipp. La Salle, IL: Open Court, 1979.

———. "Die Feldgleichungen Der Gravitation." *Sitzungsberichte der Preussischen Akademie der Wissenschaften zu Berlin* (1915): 844–847.

———. "Grundlage Der Allgemeinen Relativitätstheorie." *Annalen der Physik* 49, no. 7 (1916): 769–822.

———. "Letter to Max Bohm." In *Natural Philosophy of Cause and Chance*, by Max Bohm, 122. London: Oxford University Press, 1949.

———. "On the Method of Theoretical Physics." *Philosophy of Science* 1, no. 2 (April 1934): 163–169.

———. "Physics and Reality." In *Ideas and Opinions*, translated by Sonja Bargmann. New York: Bonanza, 1954.

———. "Remarks Concerning the Essays Brought Together in This Co-Operative Volume." In *Albert Einstein: Philosopher-Scientist*, edited by Paul Arthur Schilpp, 665–688. Library of Living Philosophers 7. Evanston, IL: Northwestern University Press, 1949.

Eisler, Rudolf. "Realismus." *Wörterbuch Der Philosophischen Begriffe*. Berlin: Mittler, 1929.

Elliger, Karl, and Willhelm Rudulph, eds. *Biblia Hebraica Stuttgartensia*. Stuttgart: German Bible Society, 1997.

Ellis, George F.R. "Does the Multiverse Really Exist?" *Scientific American* 305, no. 2 (August 2011): 38–43.

Ellis, George F.R., and Henk Van Elst. *Cosmological Models: Cargèse Lectures 1998*. Cape Town, South Africa: University of Cape Town, 2008. Accessed July 21, 2018. https://arxiv.org/pdf/gr-qc/9812046.pdf.

Emmet, Dorothy M. *The Nature of Metaphysical Thinking*. London: Macmillan And Company Limited, 1946.

Feingold, Lawrence. *Faith Comes from What Is Heard: An Introduction to Fundamental Theology*. Steubenville, OH: Emmaus Academic, 2016.

Ferré, Frederick. "Metaphors, Models, and Religion." *Soundings* 51, no. 3 (1968): 327–345.

Feser, Edward. *Five Proofs of the Existence of God*. San Francisco: Ignatius Press, 2017.

———. *Scholastic Metaphysics: A Contemporary Introduction*. Vol. 39. Editiones Scholasticae. Heusenstamm, Germany: CPI Books, 2014.

———. "The Immateriality of the Intellect." Lecture presented at the The Spiritual Soul and Contemporary Neuroscience: A Thomistic Perspective Conference, The Pontifical University of Saint Thomas Aquinas, December 1, 2018.

Feynman, Richard P. "The Reason for Antiparticles." In *Elementary Particles and the Laws of Physics: The 1986 Dirac Memorial Lectures*, by Steven Weinberg and Richard P. Feynman, 1–60. Cambridge, UK: Cambridge University Press, 1999.

Fields, Stephen. "God's Labor, Novelty's Emergence: Cosmic Motion as Self-Transcending Love." In *Love Alone Is Credible: Hans Urs Von Balthasar as Interpreter of the Catholic Tradition*, edited by David L. Schindler, 1:115–140. Grand Rapids, MI: Wm. B. Eerdmans Publishing, 2008.

Figueiredo, Anthony J. *The Magisterium-Theology Relationship: Contemporary Theological Conceptions in the Light of Universal Church Teaching Since 1835 and the Pronouncements of the Bishops of the United States*. Tesi Gregoriana 75. Roma: Gregorian & Biblical Press, 2001.

First Vatican Council. "Dei Filius." In *Decrees of the Ecumenical Councils*, edited by Norman P. Tanner. Vol. 2. Washington, DC: Georgetown University Press, 1990. Accessed March 22, 2018. https://www.ewtn.com/library/councils/v1.htm.

Fitzmyer, Joseph A. *The Biblical Commission's Document—The Interpretation of the Bible in the Church: Text And Commentary*. Rome: Gregorian & Biblical Press, 1995.

Fleischmann, Martin, and Stanley Pons. "Electrochemically Induced Nuclear Fusion of Deuterium." *Journal of Electroanalytical Chemistry and Interfacial Electrochemistry* 261, no. 2, Part 1 (April 10, 1989): 301–308.

Florescu, Ionut. *Probability and Stochastic Processes*. Hoboken, NJ: John Wiley & Sons, 2014.

Floyd, Gregory P. "Review of Transforming Light: Intellectual Conversion for Early Lonergan by Richard M. Liddy." *The Lonergan Review* 9 (2018): 143–148.

Foley, Leo A. *A Critique of the Philosophy of Being of Alfred North Whitehead in the Light of Thomistic Philosophy*. Washington, DC: The Catholic University of America Press, 1946.

Food and Agriculture Organization of the United Nations. "Knowledge Reference for National Forest Assessments—Modeling for Estimation and Monitoring." Last modified May 12, 2005. Accessed October 16, 2018. http://www.fao.org/forestry/17111/en/.

Ford, Lewis. "The Immutable God and Fr. Clarke." *New Scholasticism* 49, no. 2 (1975).

Fourier, Jean-Baptiste-Joseph. *Théorie analytique de la chaleur*. Paris: Chez Firmin Didot, 1822.

Fowler, James A. *In the Beginning God Created*. Fallbrook: C.I.Y. Publishing, 2007.

Fox, Everett. *The Five Books of Moses: The Schocken Bible*. Vol. 1. New York: Schocken, 2000.

Francis. "A Big Heart Open to God." Interview by Antonio Spadaro. America Magazine, September 30, 2013. Accessed May 14, 2018. https://www.americamagazine.org/faith/2013/09/30/big-heart-open-god-interview-pope-francis.

———. "Address of Pope Francis to Participants in the Plenary Session of the Congregation for Catholic Education," Clementine Hall, Vatican City State, February 13, 2014. Accessed October 23, 2018. https://w2.vatican.va/content/francesco/en/speeches/2014/february/documents/papa-francesco_20140213_congregazione-educazione-cattolica.html.

———. *Evangelii Gaudium*, 2013.

———. *Laudato Si'*, 2015.

———. *Lumen Fidei*, 2013.

———. *Veritatis Gaudium*, 2017.

———. Homily, Chapel of the Domus Sanctæ Marthæ, January 22, 2015. Accessed March 19, 2018. http://www.ewtnnews.com/catholic-news/Vatican.php?id=11532.

Frank Frost Productions. "Accessing Teilhard's Past." *The Teilhard de Chardin Project*, November 19, 2017. Accessed January 10, 2018. http://www.teilhardproject.com/accessing-teilhards/.

Frankl, Viktor E. *Man's Search for Meaning*. Translated by Ilse Lasch. Boston: Beacon Press, 2006.

Frost, Gloria. "Aquinas' Ontology of Transeunt Causal Activity." *Vivarium* 56, no. 1–2 (2018): 47–82.

Fuller, Anthony Thomas. "Edward John Routh." *International Journal of Control* 26, no. 2 (August 1, 1977): 169–173.

Gardeil, Henri Dominique. *Introduction to the Philosophy of St. Thomas Aquinas: Cosmology.* Translated by John A. Otto. Vol. 2. Eugene, OR: Wipf & Stock Publishers, 2009.

———. *Introduction to the Philosophy of St. Thomas Aquinas: Metaphysics.* Translated by John A. Otto. Vol. 4. Eugene, OR: Wipf & Stock Publishers, 2012.

Garrigou-Lagrange, Réginald. *God: His Existence and His Nature.* 2 vols. New York: Charter Press, 2016.

———. *Grace: Commentary on the Summa Theologica of St. Thomas, Ia IIae, q. 109–14.* Translated by The Dominican Nuns of Corpus Christi Monastery. New York: B. Herder Book Co., 1952. Accessed February 7, 2018. http://www.ewtn.com/library/theology/gracepref.htm.

———. "Le Réalisme Thomiste et Le Mystere de La Connaissance." *Revue de Philosophie* 38, no. 1–2 (1931): 58–80; 132–156.

Gasser, Vincent Ferrer. *The Gift of Infallibility: The Official Relatio on Infallibility of Bishop Vincent Ferrer Gasser at Vatican Council I.* Translated by James T. O'Connor. 2nd ed. San Francisco: Ignatius Press, 2008.

Gilkey, Langdon. *Reaping the Whirlwind.* New York: Seabury Press, 1981.

Gilson, Etienne. *The Christian Philosophy of Thomas Aquinas.* New York: Random House, 1956.

———. *The Spirit of Mediaeval Philosophy.* Notre Dame: University of Notre Dame Press, 1991.

———. *Thomist Realism and the Critique of Knowledge.* Translated by Mark A. Wauck. San Francisco: Ignatius Press, 2012.

Gindikin, Simon. *Tales of Physicists and Mathematicians.* Boston: Birkhäuser, 1988.

Gironi, Fabio. "The Theological Hijacking of Realism: Critical Realism in 'Science and Religion.'" *Journal of Critical Realism* 11, no. 1 (2012): 40–75.

Goodman, Russell. "Transcendentalism." Edited by Edward N. Zalta. *The Stanford Encyclopedia of Philosophy.* Stanford: Metaphysics Research Lab, Stanford University, May 6, 2017. Accessed May 3, 2018. https://plato.stanford.edu/archives/sum2017/entriesranscendentalism/.

Górzna, Sylwia. "Intercultural Dialogue in the Teaching of Pope Benedict XVI." *Philosophy Study* 7, no. 7 (July 28, 2017): 373–384.

Gould, Stephen Jay. *Rocks of Ages: Science and Religion in the Fullness of Life.* New York: Ballantine Books, 2002.

Grant, Edward, ed. "The Condemnation of Aristotle's Books on Natural Philosophy in 1210 at Paris." In *A Source Book in Medieval Science,* translated by Lynn Thorndike, 42. Source Books in the History of the Sciences. Cambridge: Harvard University Press, 1974.

Greenfield, Ronald A., Brent R. Brown, James B. Hutchins, John J. Iandolo, Rhett Jackson, Leonard N. Slater, and Michael S. Bronze. "Microbiological, Biological, and Chemical Weapons of Warfare and Terrorism." *The American Journal of the Medical Sciences* 323, no. 6 (June 2002): 326–340.

Gregory of Nazianzen. "Epistle to Cledonius the Priest Against Apollinarius." In *Nicene and Post-Nicene Fathers,* edited by Philip Schaff and Henry Wace, translated by Charles Gordon Browne and James Edward Swallow. Vol. 7. Revised and Edited for New Advent by Kevin Knight. 2. Buffalo: Christian Literature Publishing Co., 1894. Accessed May 9, 2018. http://www.newadvent.org/fathers/3103a.htm.

Griffin, David Ray. "Some Whiteheadian Comments." In *Mind in Nature: Essays on the Interface of Science and Philosophy*, edited by John B. Cobb and David Ray Griffin, 97–100. Washington, D.C.: University Press of America, 1977.

Guarino, Thomas. *Foundations of Systematic Theology.* New York: T&T Clark, 2005.

———. "Postmodernity and Five Fundamental Theological Issues." *Theological Studies* 57, no. 4 (December 1996): 654–689.

———. *Vattimo and Theology.* New York: T&T Clark, 2009.

———. *Vincent of Lérins and the Development of Christian Doctrine.* Grand Rapids, MI: Baker Academic, 2013.

Guerrière, Daniel. "Continental Theistic Philosophers." Edited by Richard Popkin. *The Columbia History of Western Philosophy.* New York: Columbia University Press, January 15, 1999.

Gunton, Colin. *Becoming and Being: The Doctrine of God in Charles Hartshorne and Karl Barth.* Oxford: Oxford University Press, 1978.

Gutwenger, Engelbert. "Transubstantiation." In *Encyclopedia of Theology: A Concise Sacramentum Mundi*, edited by Karl Rahner, 1754–1755. London: Burns & Oates, 1975.

Haffner, Paul. *Creation and Scientific Creativity: A Study in the Thought of S. L. Jaki.* 2nd ed. Leominster, UK: Gracewing Publishing, 2009.

———. *Mystery of Creation.* Leominster, UK: Gracewing Publishing, 1995.

———. *The Mystery of Reason.* Leominster, UK: Gracewing Publishing, 2001.

———. *The Tiara and the Test Tube: The Popes and Science from the Medieval Period to the Present.* Leominster, UK: Gracewing Publishing, 2014.

———. *Towards a Theology of the Environment.* Leominster, UK: Gracewing Publishing, 2008.

Hallanger, Nathan, and Ted Peters, eds. *God's Action in Nature's World: Essays in Honour of Robert John Russell.* Burlington: Routledge, 2006.

Hamilton, Joseph H., and Fujia Yang. *Modern Atomic and Nuclear Physics.* Revised. Hackensack, NJ: World Scientific Publishing Company Inc., 2010.

Hanby, Michael. *No God, No Science: Theology, Cosmology, Biology.* Oxford, UK: Wiley-Blackwell, 2016.

Hanson, Norwood R. *Patterns of Discovery.* Cambridge: Cambridge University Press, 1958.

Hartle, James, and Stephen Hawking. "Wave Function of the Universe." *Physical Review D* 28, no. 12 (December 15, 1983): 2960–2975.

Hartshorne, Charles. *Man's Vision of God.* Chicago: Willet Clark, 1941.

———. *Reality as Social Process: Studies in Metaphysics and Religion.* New York: Free Press, 1953.

———. *The Divine Relativity: A Social Conception of God.* New Haven, CT: Yale University Press, 1948.

———. *The Logic of Perfection.* LaSalle: Open Court, 1962.

Haught, John. *Christianity and Science: Toward a Theology of Nature.* Maryknoll, NY: Orbis Books, 2007.

———. *Science & Religion: From Conflict to Conversation.* New York: Paulist Press, 1995.

Hawking, Stephen. *A Brief History of Time.* 10th ed. New York: Bantam, 1998.

———. *Brief Answers to the Big Questions.* New York: Bantam Books, 2018.

———. "Origins of the Universe." J. Robert Oppenheimer Lecture in Physics, University of California, Berkeley, March 13, 2007. Accessed December 7, 2017. http://www.berkeley.edu/news/media/releases/2007/03/16_hawking_text.shtml.

Healy, Nicholas J. "Henri de Lubac on Nature and Grace: A Note on Some Recent Contributions to the Debate." *Communio* 35, no. 4 (2008): 535–564.

Heisenberg, Werner. *Physics and Philosophy: The Revolution in Modern Science.* New York: Harper & Brothers, 1958.

———. "Über Den Anschaulichen Inhalt Der Quantentheoretischen Kinematik Und Mechanik." *Zeitschrift für Physik* 43, no. 3–4 (1927): 172–198.

Hempel, Carl Gustav. "Problems and Changes in the Empiricist Criterion of Meaning." *Revue Internationale de Philosophie* 11 (1950): 41–63.

Hercsik, Donath. *Elementi di teologia fondamentale: Concetti, contenuti, metodi.* Bologna: EDB, 2006.

Herken, Gregg. *Brotherhood of the Bomb: The Tangled Lives and Loyalties of Robert Oppenheimer, Ernest Lawrence and Edward Teller.* New York: Henry Holt and Co., 2002.

Herstein, Gary L. "Alfred North Whitehead." *Internet Encyclopedia of Philosophy*, n.d. Accessed January 23, 2018. https://www.iep.utm.edu/whitehed/.

Hesse, Mary B. "Models in Physics." *British Journal for the Philosophy of Science* 4, no. 15 (1953): 198–214.

Himes, Michael. "Reflections of a Theologian" Presented at the Science in Seminaries Conference, Tucson, January 31, 2016.

Hippolytus. "Refutation of All Heresies." In *Ante-Nicene Fathers*, edited by Alexander Roberts, James Donaldson, and Arthur Cleveland Coxe, translated by John Henry MacMahon. Vol. 5. Buffalo, NY: Christian Literature Publishing Co., 1886. Accessed May 21, 2018. http://www.newadvent.org/fathers/050110.htm.

———. *The Apostolic Tradition of Hippolytus.* Translated by Burton Scott Easton. Cambridge, UK: Cambridge University Press, 2014.

Hirsch, Morris W., Stephen Smale, and Robert L. Devaney. *Differential Equations, Dynamical Systems, and an Introduction to Chaos.* 3rd ed. Waltham, MA: Academic Press, 2012.

Hittinger, John. "Founding the Modern Project." Web Lecture presented at the International Catholic University, n.d. Accessed April 26, 2018. https://icucourses.com/pages/021-03-founding-the-modern-project-cartesian-doubt.

Hochschild, Joshua P. *The Semantics of Analogy: Rereading Cajetan's De Nominum Analogia.* Notre Dame: University of Notre Dame Press, 2010.

Hodge, Charles. *Systematic Theology.* Vol. 1. 3 vols. Peabody, MA: Hendrickson Publishers, Inc., 1999.

Hoenen, Peter. *Cosmologia.* 5th ed. Rome: Gregorian University Press, 1956.

Hogeweg, Paulien. "The Roots of Bioinformatics in Theoretical Biology." Edited by David B. Searls. *PLoS Computational Biology* 7, no. 3 (March 31, 2011). Accessed December 5, 2017. https://www.ncbi.nlm.nih.gov/pmc/articles/PMC3068925/.

Holloway, Edward. *Catholicism: A New Synthesis.* Surrey: Keyway Publications, 1970.

————. *Perspectives in Philosophy: A Critique of an Abstract Scholasticism and Principles Towards Replacement*. E-Book. Vol. 1. 3 vols. Glasgow: Faith-Keyway Publications, 1994.

Holmes, Philip. "A Short History of Dynamical Systems Theory: 1885–2007." In *History of Mathematics*, edited by Vagn Lundsgaard Hansen and Jeremy Gray, 115–138. Oxford: Eolss Publications, 2010.

Hoyle, Fred. "The Universe: Past and Present Reflections." *Engineering and Science* (November 1981): 8–12.

Huang, Lillian, Fred C. Adams, and Evan Grohs. "Sensitivity of Carbon and Oxygen Yields to the Triple-Alpha Resonance in Massive Stars." *Astroparticle Physics* 105 (February 1, 2019): 13–24.

Hume, David. *A Treatise of Human Nature*. 2 vols. London: Thomas and Joseph Allman, 1817.

————. *An Enquiry Concerning Human Understanding*. Hollywood, FL: Simon & Brown, 2011.

————. *Dialogues and Natural History of Religion*. Edited by J.C.A. Gaskin. Oxford: Oxford University Press, 2009.

Hünermann, Peter, ed. *Heinrich Denzinger—Enchiridion Symbolorum: A Compendium of Creeds, Definitions, and Declarations of the Catholic Church*. 43rd ed. San Francisco: Ignatius Press, 2012.

Huyssteen, J. Wentzel Van. *The Shaping of Rationality: Toward Interdisciplinarity in Theology and Science*. Grand Rapids, MI: Wm. B. Eerdmans Publishing Co., 1999.

Institute for New Testament Textual Research. *Novum Testamentum Graece: Nestle-Aland*. 28th ed. Peabody, MA: Hendrickson Publishers, Inc., 2012.

International Theological Commission. *Unity of the Faith and Theological Pluralism*, 1972. Accessed July 30, 2018. http://www.vatican.va/roman_curia/congregations/cfaith/cti_documents/rc_cti_1972_fede-pluralismo_en.html.

Irenaeus of Lyons. *Against Heresies*. Edited by Alexander Roberts, James Donaldson, and A. Cleveland Coxe. South Bend: Ex Fontibus, 2015.

Isham, Chris J. "Quantum Theories of the Creation of the Universe." In *Quantum Cosmology and the Laws of Nature*, edited by Robert J. Murphy, Nancey Murphy, and Chris J. Isham, 51–92. Rome: Vatican Observatory, 1993.

Jaki, Stanley L. *Cosmos and Creator*. Edinburgh: Scottish Academic Press, 1980.

————. *God and the Cosmologists*. Washington, DC: Regnery Gateway Inc., 1991.

————. *Is There a Universe?* New York: Wethersfield Institute, 1993.

————. *Science and Creation*. Lanham: University Press of America, 1990.

————. "The Absolute Beneath the Relative: Reflections on Einstein's Theories." In *The Absolute Beneath the Relative and Other Essays*, 233. Lanham, MD: University Press of America, 1988.

————. "The Demarcation Line between Science and Religion." *Angelicum* 87, no. 1 (2010): 81–89.

————. "The Reality of the Universe." Lecture presented at the International Congress on the Philosophy of Nature, Pontificia Università Lateranense, January 10, 1992.

————. *The Road of Science and the Ways to God*. 3rd ed. Real View Books, 2005.

————. *The Savior of Science*. Grand Rapids: Wm. B. Eerdmans Publishing Company, 2000.

Joest, Wilfried. *Ontologie der Person bei Luther*. Göttingen: Vandenhoeck & Ruprecht, 1967.

John Paul II. *Dominum et Vivificantem*, 1986. Accessed August 2, 2018. http://w2.vatican.va/content/john-paul-ii/en/encyclicals/documents/hf_jp-ii_enc_18051986_dominum-et-vivificantem.html.

———. *Fides et Ratio*, 1998.

Johnson, Daniel L., and Charles Hambrick-Stowe, eds. *Theology and Identity: Traditions, Movements, and Polity in the United Church of Christ*. Revised. Cleveland: United Church Press, 2007.

Journet, Charles. *The Primacy of Peter*. Translated by John Chapin. Westminster, MD: Newman Press, 1954.

Joyce, George. "The Church." *The Catholic Encyclopedia*. New York: Robert Appleton Company, 1908. Accessed March 16, 2018. http://www.newadvent.org/cathen/03744a.htm.

Kant, Immanuel. *Critique of Pure Reason*. Edited by Gary Banham. Translated by Norman K. Smith. 2nd ed. New York: Macmillan And Company Limited, 2007.

Karl Heim. *Christian Faith And Natural Science*. New York: Harper & Brothers, 1953.

Kasper, Walter. "The Logos Character of Reality." Translated by Stephen Wentworth Arndt. *Communio* 15, no. 3 (Fall 1988): 274–284.

Kermack, William Ogilvy, and Anderson Gray McKendrick. "A Contribution to the Mathematical Theory of Epidemics." *Proceedings of the Royal Society A: Mathematical, Physical and Engineering Sciences* 115, no. 772 (August 1, 1927): 700–721.

Kerr, Fergus. "A Different World: Neoscholasticism and Its Discontents." *International Journal of Systematic Theology* 8, no. 2 (April 2006): 128–148.

Kierkegaard, Søren. *Journals of Søren Kierkegaard*. Translated by Alexander Dru. Oxford: Oxford University Press, 1948.

Kilcullen, John. "Thomas Aquinas, Summa Theologica (Cont.)." Medieval Philosophy Lecture presented at the Macquarie University, Sydney, Australia, 1996. Accessed May 21, 2018. http://pandora.nla.gov.au/pan/98441/20090504-1534/www.humanities.mq.edu.au/Ockham/x52t10.html.

Kippenhahn, Rudolf, Alfred Weigert, and Achim Weiss. *Stellar Structure and Evolution*. 2nd ed. Astronomy and Astrophysics Library. New York: Springer, 2012.

Knasas, John F.X. "Transcendental Thomist Methodology and Maritain's 'Critical Realism.'" In *Jacques Maritain and the Many Ways of Knowing*, edited by Douglas A. Ollivant, 66–77. Washington, DC: CUA Press, 2002.

Komonchak, Joseph A. "Augustine, Aquinas, or the Gospel Sine Glossa? Divisions over Gaudium et Spes." In *Unfinished Journey: The Church 40 Years after Vatican II*, edited by Austen Ivereigh, 102–118. New York: Continuum, 2004.

van Kooten Niekerk, Kees. "A Critical Realist Perspective." In *Rethinking Theology and Science: Six Models for the Current Dialogue*, edited by Niels Henrik Gregersen and J. Wentzel van Huyssteen. Grand Rapids: Eerdmans, 1998.

Korf, Werner, Christof Schomerus, and Jörg H. Stehle. *The Pineal Organ, Its Hormone Melatonin, and the Photoneuroendocrine System*. Vol. 146. Advances in Anatomy, Embryology and Cell Biology. New York: Springer, 1998.

Koziol, Michael. "Scientists in the U.S. and Japan Get Serious About Low-Energy Nuclear Reactions." *IEEE Spectrum* 55, no. 12 (November 28, 2018): 10–11.

Krause, Karl. *Vorlesungen über das System der Philosophie*. Göttingen: Dieterich, 1828.

Kuhn, Thomas S. *The Structure of Scientific Revolutions*. 4th ed. Chicago: University of Chicago Press, 2012.

Kuznetsov, Yuri. *Elements of Applied Bifurcation Theory*. 3rd ed. Applied Mathematical Sciences 112. New York: Springer, 2004.

Kysar, Robert. *Voyages with John: Charting the Fourth Gospel*. Waco: Baylor University Press, 2005.

Lactantius. *The Divine Institutes, Books I–VII*. Translated by Mary Francis McDonald. Fathers of the Church 49. Washington, DC: CUA Press, 2008.

Ladaria, Luis F. *Introducción a La Antropología Teológica*. Estella, Spain: Editorial Verbo Divino, 1993.

Lakatos, Imre. "Falsification and the Methodology of Scientific Research Programmes." In *Criticism and the Growth of Knowledge*, edited by Imre Lakatos and Alan Musgrave, 91–195. Cambridge: Cambridge University Press, 1970.

Laplace, Pierre Simon. *A Philosophical Essay on Probabilities*. Translated by Frederick Wilson Truscott and Frederick Lincoln Emory. New York: Dover, 1961.

Laracy, John T. "Divine Love as Event: A Study in the Trinitarian Theology of Hans Urs von Balthasar." PhD, The Pontifical John Paul II Institute for Studies on Marriage and the Family at the Catholic University of America, 2017.

Laracy, Joseph R. "Addressing System Boundary Issues in Complex Socio-Technical Systems." *Systems Research Forum* 2, no. 1 (2007): 19–26.

Laszlo, Ervin. *An Introduction to Systems Philosophy*. New York: Gordon & Breach, 1972.

Lateran Council IV. "Constitutions." In *Decrees of the Ecumenical Councils*, edited by Norman P. Tanner. Vol. 1. Washington, DC: Georgetown University Press, 1990.

Leeuw, Gerardus van der. *Religion in Essence and Manifestation*. Translated by Ninian Smart and John Evan Turner. Princeton: Princeton University Press, 2014.

Lehr, Donald. "Templeton Prize Laureate Arthur Peacocke Dies." *Templeton Foundation*. Last modified October 25, 2006. Accessed November 24, 2017. http://www.templetonprize.org/tplapd.html.

———. "Templeton Prize Laureate Ian Barbour, Pioneer in Science and Religion, Dies at 90." *Templeton Foundation*. Last modified 2014. Accessed November 15, 2017. http://www.templetonprize.org/news_barbour.html.

Leibniz, Gottfried Wilhelm. *Essais de Théodicée sur la Bonté de Dieu, La Liberté de L'homme et L'origine du Mal*. Charleston, SC: Nabu Press, 2010.

Lemaître, Georges. "Un Univers Homogène de Masse Constante et de Rayon Croissant Rendant Compte de La Vitesse Radiale Des Nébuleuses Extragalactiques." *Annales de la Société Scientifique de Bruxelles* 47 (1927): 49–59.

Leo XIII. *Aeterni Patris*, 1879.

Lewis, Geraint F., and Luke A. Barnes. *A Fortunate Universe: Life in a Finely Tuned Cosmos.* Cambridge, UK: Cambridge University Press, 2016.

Lewis, John, ed. *Beyond Chance and Necessity.* London: Garnstone Press, 1974.

Liddy, Richard. "Jaki and Lonergan: Confrontation or Encounter?" In *Stanley Jaki International Congress*, edited by Paul Haffner and Joseph R. Laracy. Leominster, UK: Gracewing Publishing, 2020.

Lippert, Todd. "Interview of Ian Barbour's Pastor, Rev. Todd Lippert." Interview by Joseph R. Laracy. Email, October 31, 2017.

Lokhorst, Gert-Jan. "Descartes and the Pineal Gland." In *The Stanford Encyclopedia of Philosophy*, edited by Edward N. Zalta. Winter 2017. Stanford: Metaphysics Research Lab, Stanford University, 2013. Accessed May 9, 2018. https://plato.stanford.edu/archives/win2017/entries/pineal-gland/.

Lonergan, Bernard. *Insight: A Study of Human Understanding.* Edited by Frederick Crowe and Robert Doran. 5th ed. Vol. 3. Collected Works of Bernard Lonergan. Toronto: University of Toronto Press, Scholarly Publishing Division, 1992.

———. "Metaphysics as Horizon." *CrossCurrents* 16, no. 4 (1966): 481–494.

———. *Method in Theology.* 2nd ed. Toronto: University of Toronto Press, Scholarly Publishing Division, 1990.

Losch, Andreas. "On the Origins of Critical Realism." *Theology and Science* 7, no. 1 (February 1, 2009): 85–106.

———. "On the Relationship of Ian Barbour's and Roy Bhaskar's Critical Realism." *Journal of Critical Realism* 16, no. 1 (February 2017): 70–83.

———. "Wright's Version of Critical Realism." In *God and the Faithfulness of Paul: A Critical Examination of the Pauline Theology of N.T. Wright*, edited by Christoph Heilig, J. Thomas Hewitt, and Michael F. Bird, 101–114. Minneapolis: Fortress Press, 2017.

Louth, Andrew. *Denys the Areopagite.* New York: Continuum, 1989.

Löwenbach, Hans, and Ian G. Barbour. "An Automatic Device for Continuous Frequency Analysis of Electroencephalograms." *Federation Proceedings* 5, no. 1 (1946): II:65.

Luther, Martin. "An Introduction to St. Paul's Letter to the Romans." In *Luther's German Bible of 1522*, translated by Robert E. Smith. Project Wittenberg, 1994. www.iclnet.org/pub/resources/text/wittenberg/luther/luther-faith.txt.

Lyons, Jack. "Epistemological Problems of Perception." In *The Stanford Encyclopedia of Philosophy*, edited by Edward N. Zalta. Stanford: Metaphysics Research Lab, Stanford University, 2016. Accessed January 17, 2018. https://plato.stanford.edu/archives/spr2017/entries/perception-episprob/.

Macquarrie, John. *Existentialism.* Philadelphia: Westminster Press, 1972.

Mann, Robert. *An Introduction to Particle Physics and the Standard Model.* New York: CRC Press, 2009.

Margenau, Henry. *The Nature of Physical Reality.* 2nd ed. New York: McGraw-Hill Book Company, 1950.

Marías, Julián. *History of Philosophy*. Translated by Stanley Appelbaum and Clarence C. Strowbridge. 22nd ed. New York: Dover Publications, 1967.

Maritain, Jacques. *Distinguish to Unite, or, The Degrees of Knowledge*. Translated by Gerald Phelan. 4th ed. New York: Charles Scribner's Sons, 1959.

———. *Philosophy of Nature*. Translated by Imelda C. Byrne. New York: Philosophical Library, 1951.

Martin, Brian R. *Nuclear and Particle Physics: An Introduction*. 2nd ed. Chichester, UK: John Wiley & Sons, 2009.

Martin, Craig. *A Critical Introduction to the Study of Religion*. 2nd ed. New York: Routledge, 2017.

Martin, Daniel. *Manifold Theory: An Introduction for Mathematical Physicists*. Cambridge: Woodhead Publishing, 2002.

Marx, Karl. "French Materialism." In *Selected Writings*, translated by Henry James Stenning. New York: Classic Books International, 2010.

Mascall, Eric L. *Christian Theology and Natural Science: Some Questions in Their Relations*. London: Longmans Green and Co., 1957.

———. *Existence and Analogy*. London: Darton, Longman & Todd Ltd., 1966.

———. *Openness of Being: Natural Theology Today*. London: Darton, Longman & Todd Ltd., 1971.

Maxwell, James Clerk. *Treatise on Electricity and Magnetism*. 3rd ed. 2 vols. New York: Dover Publications, 1954.

May, Gerhard. *Creatio Ex Nihilo: The Doctrine of "Creation Out of Nothing" in Early Christian Thought*. Translated by A.S. Worrall. Edinburgh: T&T Clark International, 2004.

McDermott, John M. "Matter, Modern Science, and God." *Angelicum* 88, no. 2 (2011): 481–508.

———. "The Mystery of Matter." *Angelicum* 87, no. 4 (2010): 993–1014.

McDonald, Walter. "Eternity." *The Catholic Encyclopedia*. New York: Robert Appleton Company, 1909. Accessed May 2, 2018. http://www.newadvent.org/cathen/05551b.htm.

McFague, Sallie. "Ian Barbour: Theologian's Friend, Scientist's Interpreter." *Zygon* 31, no. 1 (March 1, 1996): 21–28.

McGrath, Alister E. *Luther's Theology of the Cross*. Oxford, UK: Blackwell Publishers Ltd., 1985.

———. *Nature*. A Scientific Theology 1. Grand Rapids, MI: William B. Eerdmans Publishing Company, 2001.

———. *Reality*. A Scientific Theology 2. Grand Rapids, MI: William B. Eerdmans Publishing Company, 2002.

———. *Theory*. A Scientific Theology 3. Grand Rapids, MI: William B. Eerdmans Publishing Company, 2003.

McInerny, Ralph M. *Aquinas and Analogy*. Washington, DC: The Catholic University of America Press, 1996.

———. *The Logic of Analogy: An Interpretation of St Thomas*. The Hague: Martinus Nijhoff, 1971.

McMullin, Ernan. "A Case for Scientific Realism." In *Scientific Realism*, edited by Jarrett Leplin. Berkeley: University of California Press, 1984.

———. "Creation Ex Nihilo: Early History." In *Creation and the God of Abraham*, edited by David B. Burrell, Carlo Cogliati, Janet M. Soskice, and William R. Stoeger, 11–23. Cambridge: Cambridge University Press, 2010.

———. "Enlarging the World." In *Physics and Our View of the World*, edited by Jan Hildevoord. Cambridge: Cambridge University Press, 1994.

———. "Realism in Theology and Science: A Response to Peacocke." *Religion and Intellectual Life* 2, no. 4 (1985): 39–47.

———. "Science and the Catholic Tradition." In *Science and Religion: New Perspectives on the Dialogue*, edited by Ian G. Barbour, 30–42. New York: Harper & Row, 1968.

Meehan, Francis Xavier. "Efficient Causality in Aristotle and St. Thomas." PhD, The Catholic University of America, 1940.

Melamed, Yitzhak Y. *Spinoza's Metaphysics: Substance and Thought*. Oxford, UK: Oxford University Press, 2015.

Merry del Val, Raphael. *The Truth of Papal Claims: A Reply to The Validity of Papal Claims by F. Nutcombe Oxenham*. London: Sands and Company, 1902.

Meyer, Ben F. *Critical Realism and the New Testament*. Princeton Theological Monograph Series 17. Allison Park: Pickwick, 1989.

Meyer, Raymond K. "An Evangelical Analysis of the Critical Realism and Corollary Hermeneutics of Bernard Lonergan with Application for Evangelical Hermeneutics." PhD, Southeastern Baptist Theological Seminary, 2007. Accessed October 10, 2017. https://search.proquest.com/dissertations/docview/304719979/abstract/CDD323051D654D77PQ/7.

Michaud, Derek. "Karl Barth (1886–1968)." Edited by Wesley Wildman. *Boston Collaborative Encyclopedia of Western Theology*. Boston, 1994. Accessed February 5, 2018. http://people.bu.edu/wwildman/bce/barth.htm.

Mill, John Stuart. *A System of Logic, Ratiocinative and Inductive*. 2 vols. London: John W. Parker, 1843.

Miller, Robert Moats. *Harry Emerson Fosdick: Preacher, Pastor, Prophet*. New York: Oxford University Press, 1985.

Mlodinow, Leonard, and Stephen Hawking. *The Grand Design*. New York: Bantam, 2012.

Moleski, Martin X. *Personal Catholicism: The Theological Epistemologies of John Henry Newman and Michael Polanyi*. Washington, D.C.: CUA Press, 2000.

Moltmann, Jürgen. *God in Creation: A New Theology of Creation and the Spirit of God*. Translated by Margaret Kohl. San Francisco: Harper & Row, 1985.

Monod, Jacques. *Chance and Necessity: An Essay on the Natural Philosophy of Modern Biology*. Translated by Austryn Wainhouse. New York: Vintage Books, 1972.

Moorhead, Robert K. *Deerfield 1797–1997: A Pictorial History of the Academy*. Deerfield, MA: Deerfield Academy Press, 1997.

Morris, Joe E. *Revival of the Gnostic Heresy: Fundamentalism*. New York: Palgrave Macmillan, 2008.

Müller, Gerhard. "Development, or Corruption?" *First Things* (February 20, 2018). Accessed March 8, 2018. https://www.firstthings.com/web-exclusives/2018/02/development-or-corruption.

————. "Is There a Saving Truth? | The Salvific Relevance of the Rule of Faith." *First Things* (March 13, 2018). Accessed March 19, 2018. https://www.firstthings.com/web-exclusives/2018/03/is-there-a-saving-truth.

Murphy, Francesca Aran. *God Is Not a Story: Realism Revisited.* Oxford: Oxford University Press, 2007.

Murphy, John I. "Analogy of Faith." Edited by Thomas Carson. *New Catholic Encyclopedia.* Farmington Hills: Thompson Gale, 2003. Accessed January 29, 2018. http://www.encyclopedia.com/religion/encyclopedias-almanacs-transcripts-and-maps/analogy-faith.

Murphy, Roland E. *The Tree of Life: An Exploration of Biblical Wisdom Literature.* New York: The Anchor Bible Reference Library, 1990.

Nesteruk, Alexei V. *Light from the East: Theology, Science, and the Eastern Orthodox Tradition.* Minneapolis: Fortress Press, 2003.

Neufeld, Karl H. "Supernatural." Edited by René Latourelle and Rino Fisichella. *Dictionary of Fundamental Theology.* New York: The Crossroad Publishing Company, February 1, 2000.

von Neumann, John. *Mathematische Grundlagen Der Quantenmechanik.* Berlin: Springer-Verlag, 1932.

Neurath, Otto. "Physicalism." *The Monist* 41, no. 4 (1931): 618–623.

Newman, John Henry. *An Essay On Development Of Christian Doctrine.* Notre Dame: University of Notre Dame Press, 1994.

————. *Grammar of Assent.* Edited by Ian T. Ker. Oxford: Oxford University Press, 1988.

————. "Intellect, the Instrument of Religious Training." Sermon, University Church, Dublin, Sunday after Ascension 1856.

————. *Sermons Preached on Various Occasions.* London: Longmans Green and Co., 1908.

Newton, Isaac. *Philosophiæ Naturalis Principia Mathematica.* London: Royal Society, 1687.

Niebuhr, H. Richard. *Christ and Culture.* 2nd ed. San Francisco: Harper & Row, 1975.

————. *The Meaning of Revelation.* Louisville: Westminster John Knox Press, 2006.

Northrop, Filmer Stuart Cuckow. *The Logic of the Sciences and Humanities.* New York: The Macmillan Co., 1947.

Numbers, Ronald L. *The Creationists: From Scientific Creationism to Intelligent Design.* Cambridge: Harvard University Press, 2006.

O'Collins, Gerald. *Rethinking Fundamental Theology.* Oxford: Oxford University Press, 2013.

O'Connor, John J., and Edmund F. Robertson. "Alfred North Whitehead." *MacTutor History of Mathematics.* Scotland: School of Mathematics and Statistics | University of St Andrews, October 2003. Accessed January 10, 2018. http://www-groups.dcs.st-and.ac.uk/history/Biographies/Whitehead.html.

Oliver, Simon. "Trinity, Motion, and Creation Ex Nihilo." In *Creation and the God of Abraham,* edited by David B. Burrell, Carlo Cogliati, Janet M. Soskice, and William R. Stoeger, 133–151. Cambridge: Cambridge University Press, 2010.

Orchin, Milton, Roger S. Macomber, Allan R. Pinhas, and R. Marshall Wilson. *The Vocabulary and Concepts of Organic Chemistry.* 2nd ed. Hoboken: Wiley-Interscience, 2005.

Ott, Ludwig. *Fundamentals of Catholic Dogma.* 4th ed. Rockford, IL: TAN Books and Publishers, Inc., 1974.

Oxenham, Frank Nutcombe. *The Validity of Papal Claims: Five Lectures Delivered in Rome.* London: Longmans Green and Co., 1897.

Pambrun, James R. "Creation Ex Nihilo and Dual Causality." In *Creation and the God of Abraham,* edited by David B. Burrell, Carlo Cogliati, Janet M. Soskice, and William R. Stoeger. Cambridge: Cambridge University Press, 2010.

———. *God's Signature: Understanding Paul Beauchamp on Creation in the First Testament.* Terra Nova 3. Leuven: Peeters, 2018.

Pannenberg, Wolfhart. "The Doctrine of Creation and Modern Science." *Zygon* 23, no. 1 (1988): 3–21.

———. "Theological Questions to Scientists." *Communio* 15, no. 3 (1988): 319–333.

Parker, Dawn. "Lansing-Area Men Played Key Role in Civil Rights Movement." *Lansing State Journal,* March 2, 2015. Accessed November 14, 2017. http://www.lansingstatejournal.com/story/news/local/2015/03/02/okemos-man-recalls-civil-rights-work/24253241/.

Pauck, Wilhelp. *The Heritage of the Reformation.* New York: The Free Press of Glencoe, Inc., 1961.

Paul VI. *Ecclesiam Suam,* 1964.

———. *Mysterium Fidei,* 1965.

———. *Solemni Hac Liturgia,* 1968. http://w2.vatican.va/content/paul-vi/la/motu_proprio/documents/hf_p-vi_motu-proprio_19680630_credo.html.

Peacocke, Arthur. "Articulating God's Presence in and to the World Unveiled by the Science." In *In Whom We Live and Move and Have Our Being: Panentheistic Reflections on God's Presence in a Scientific World,* edited by Philip Clayton and Arthur Peacocke, 137–157. Grand Rapids: William B. Eerdmans, 2004.

———. *Creation and the World of Science: The Re-Shaping of Belief.* 2nd ed. Oxford: Oxford University Press, 2004.

———. "God's Action in the Real World." *Zygon* 26, no. 4 (1991): 455–476.

———. *Intimations of Reality: Critical Realism in Science and Religion.* Notre Dame: University of Notre Dame Press, 1984.

———. *Science and the Christian Experiment.* London: Oxford University Press, 1971.

———. *Theology for a Scientific Age: Being and Becoming–Natural, Divine and Human.* 2nd ed. Minneapolis: Augsburg Fortress Publishers, 1993.

Peacocke, Arthur, and Philip Clayton, eds. *All That Is: A Naturalistic Faith for the Twenty-First Century.* Minneapolis: Fortress Press, 2007.

Pearson, Karl. *The Grammar of Science.* 3rd ed. New York: The Macmillan Co., 1911.

Peirce, Charles. *Chance, Love, and Logic.* New York: Harcourt, 1923.

Peters, Ted. "Theology and Natural Science." In *The Modern Theologians,* edited by David Ford. 2nd ed. Oxford: Blackwell, 1997.

Peterson, Brandon. "Critical Voices: The Reactions of Rahner and Ratzinger to 'Schema XIII' (Gaudium et Spes)." *Modern Theology* 31, no. 1 (January 1, 2015): 1–26.

Pham, John-Peter. "The Importance of The Reality of the Universe in the Work of Stanley L. Jaki." *Faith & Reason* 21, no. 4 (December 26, 1995): 337–354.

Pié-Ninot, Salvador. *La Teologia Fondamentale*. Translated by Pietro Crespi. 3rd ed. Biblioteca di Teologia Contemporanea 121. Brescia: Queriniana, 2007.

Pius XII. *Mediator Dei*, 1947.

Placher, William C. "Postliberal Theology." In *An Introduction to Christian Theology in the Twentieth Century*, edited by David F. Ford, 343–356. Malden: Blackwell Publishers Ltd., 1997.

Planck, Max. "On Irreversible Radiation Processes." In *Physikalische Abhandlungen Und Vorträge*, 1:597. Braunschweig: Friedr. Wieweg & Sohn, 1958.

———. "Science and Faith." In *The Philosophy of Physics*, translated by W.H. Johnston. London: George Allen & Unden Ltd., 1936.

Plato. *Timaeus. Critias. Cleitophon. Menexenus. Epistles*. Translated by Robert G. Bury. Vol. 9. 12 vols. Loeb Classical Library 234. Cambridge, MA: Harvard University Press, 1929.

Poincaré, Jules Henri. *Les Méthodes Nouvelles de La Mécanique Céleste*. 3 vols. Paris: Gauthiers-Villars, 1899.

Polanyi, Michael. *Personal Knowledge*. Chicago: University of Chicago Press, 1958.

———. *Science, Faith, and Society*. Chicago: University of Chicago Press, 1964.

Polkinghorne, John. *Belief in God in an Age of Science*. New Haven, CT: Yale University Press, 1998.

———. "Canon Arthur Peacocke." *The Independent*. London, November 6, 2006, sec. Obituaries. Accessed November 22, 2017. http://www.independent.co.uk/news/obituaries/canon-arthur-peacocke-423175.html.

———. "Contributions to Quantum Field Theory." PhD, University of Cambridge, 1955.

———. *From Physicist to Priest: An Autobiography*. Eugene: Wipf & Stock Publishers, 2008.

———. *One World: The Interaction of Science and Theology*. Philadelphia: Templeton Press, 2007.

———. *Reason and Reality: The Relationship between Science and Theology*. Philadelphia: Trinity Press International, 1991.

———. *Science and Christian Belief: Theological Reflections of a Bottom-up Thinker*. London: SPCK Publishing, 1994.

———. *Science and the Trinity: The Christian Encounter with Reality*. New Haven, CT: Yale University Press, 2004.

———. *Scientists as Theologians*. London: SPCK, 1996.

———. *The Faith of a Physicist: Reflections of a Bottom-Up Thinker*. Princeton: Princeton University Press, 2014.

Polkinghorne, John, and Nicholas Beale. *Questions of Truth: Fifty-One Responses to Questions About God, Science, and Belief*. Louisville: Westminster John Knox, 2009.

Pontifical Biblical Commission. *The Interpretation of the Bible in the Church*. Boston: Pauline Books & Media, 1996.

Popper, Karl R. *The Logic of Scientific Discovery*. Eastford: Martino Fine Books, 2014.

Potworowski, Christophe F. *Contemplation and Incarnation: The Theology of Marie-Dominique Chenu*. London: McGill-Queen's Press, 2001.

Przywara, Erich. *Analogia Entis: Metaphysics*. Translated by John R. Betz and David Bentley Hart. Grand Rapids, MI: Eerdmans, 2014.

———. *Schriften*. Vol. 2. Einsiedeln: Johannes Verlag, 1962.

Pseudo-Dionysius. *Pseudo-Dionysius: The Complete Works*. Translated by Paul Rorem. The Classics of Western Spirituality. Mahwah, NJ: Paulist Press, 1988.

Rahlfs, Alfred, and Robert Hanhart, eds. *Septuaginta*. Stuttgart: Deutsche Bibelgesellschaft, 2006.

Rahner, Karl. *Hominisation: The Evolutionary Origin of Man as a Theological Problem*. Translated by W.T. O'Hara. Quaestiones Disputatae 13. Freiburg-im-Breisgau: Herder and Herder, 1965.

———. "Natural Science and Reasonable Faith: Theological Perspectives for Dialogue with the Natural Sciences." In *Theological Investigations*, translated by Hugh M. Riley, 21:16–55. New York: Crossroad, 1988.

———. "Naturwissenschaft Und Vernünftiger Glaube." In *Christlicher Glaube in Moderner Gesellschaft*, edited by A. Battke, 3:34–78. Weltall—Erde—Mensch 2. Freiburg im Breisgau: Herder, 1981.

———. *Spirit in the World*. New York: Continuum, 1994.

Rapoport, Anatol. "General Systems Theory." In *Systems Science and Cybernetics*, edited by Francisco Parra-Luna. Vol. 1. Oxford: Eolss Publications, 2009.

Ratzinger, Joseph. *A Turning Point for Europe*. Translated by Brian McNeil. 2nd ed. San Francisco: Ignatius Press, 2010.

———. *Co-Workers of the Truth: Meditations for Every Day of the Year*. Edited by Irene Grassl. Translated by Mary Frances McCarthy. San Francisco: Ignatius Press, 1992.

———. *Eschatology: Death and Eternal Life*. Translated by Michael Waldstein. 2nd ed. Washington, DC: The Catholic University of America Press, 2007.

———. *God Is Near Us: The Eucharist, the Heart of Life*. Edited by Stephan Otto Horn and Vinzenz Pfnur. Translated by Henry Taylor. San Francisco: Ignatius Press, 2003.

———. *In the Beginning: A Catholic Understanding of the Story of Creation and the Fall*. Translated by Boniface Ramsey. Grand Rapids, MI: Eerdmans, 1995.

———. "Lecture at the Sorbonne: November 27, 1999." In *Truth and Tolerance*, translated by Henry Taylor, 178–183. San Francisco: Ignatius Press, 2004.

———. *Mary: The Church at the Source*. San Francisco: Ignatius Press, 2005.

———. *Milestones: Memoirs 1927–1977*. San Francisco: Ignatius Press, 2005.

———. *Pilgrim Fellowship of Faith: The Church as Communion*. Edited by Stephan Otto Horn and Vinzenz Pfnur. Translated by Henry Taylor. San Francisco: Ignatius Press, 2005.

———. *Principles of Catholic Theology: Building Stones for a Fundamental Theology*. Translated by Mary Frances McCarthy. San Francisco: Ignatius Press, 1989.

———. "Relativism: The Central Problem for Faith Today." Guadalajara, Mexico, 1996. Accessed March 19, 2018. https://www.ewtn.com/library/CURIA/RATZRELA.HTM.

———. "Sources and Transmission of the Faith." *Communio* 10, no. 1 (1983): 17–34.

———. *Theological Highlights of Vatican II*. Translated by Henry Traub, Gerard C. Thormann, and Werner Barzel. New York: Paulist Press, 1966.

Raven, Charles Earle. *Natural Religion and Christian Theology*. Vol. 2. 2 vols. Cambridge: Cambridge University Press, 1953.

Reichenbach, Hans. *The Rise of Scientific Philosophy*. Berkeley: University of California Press, 1951.

Rice, Daniel F. *Reinhold Niebuhr and John Dewey: An American Odyssey*. Albany: SUNY Press, 1993.

Ricoeur, Paul. *Interpretation Theory: Discourse and the Surplus of Meaning*. Fort Worth, TX: Texas Christian University Press, 1976.

Robinson, H. M. "Prime Matter in Aristotle." *Phronesis* 19, no. 2 (1974): 168–188.

Rogers, Carl, and Burrhus Frederic Skinner. "Some Issues Concerning the Control of Human Behavior." *Science* 124, no. 3231 (November 30, 1956): 1057–1066.

Ross, Thomas W. "The Implicit Theology of Carl Sagan." *Pacific Theological Review* 18 (Spring 1985): 24–32.

Rowland, Tracey. *Catholic Theology*. Doing Theology. New York: T&T Clark, 2017.

———. *Culture and the Thomist Tradition: After Vatican II*. New York: Routledge, 2003.

Ruse, Michael, ed. *Evolutionary Naturalism: Selected Essays*. New York: Routledge, 2014.

Russell, Bertrand. *Our Knowledge of the External World*. London: The Open Court Publishing Company, 1914.

Russell, Robert J. *Theology and Science: Current Issues and Future Directions*. Berkeley, CA: Center for Theology and the Natural Sciences, 2000.

Russell, Robert John. "Assessing Ian G. Barbour's Contributions to Theology and Science." *Theology and Science* 15, no. 1 (January 2, 2017): 1–4.

———. "Bridging Theology and Science: The CTNS Logo." *Theology and Science* 1, no. 1 (April 2003): 1–3.

———. *Cosmology: From Alpha to Omega*. Minneapolis: Fortress Press, 2008.

———. "Curriculum Vitæ." Last modified 2009. Accessed December 6, 2017. http://www.ctns.org/BOBCV%209%2009.pdf.

———, ed. *Fifty Years in Science and Religion: Ian G. Barbour and His Legacy*. Ashgate Science and Religion Series. Burlington, VT: Ashgate Publishing, 2004.

———. "Ian Barbour's Methodological Breakthrough: Creating the 'Bridge' Between Science and Theology." *Theology and Science* 15, no. 1 (January 2, 2017): 28–41.

———. "Ian Barbour's Methodology in Science and Religion." Edited by Andreas Losch. *Dialog Theologie & Naturwissenschaften*. Bonn: Evangelischen Akademie im Rheinland, June 2014. Accessed February 16, 2018. https://www.theologie-naturwissenschaften.de/startseite/leitartikelarchiv/barbours-methodology.html.

———. "Life and Significance of Ian Barbour." Interview by Joseph R. Laracy. Email, December 23, 2017.

———. "The Paraelectric Resonance of Lithium-Doped Potassium Bromide." PhD, University of California at Santa Cruz, 1978.

Russell, Robert John, Nancey Murphy, and Arthur R. Peacocke, eds. *Chaos Complexity: Scientific Perspectives On Divine Action*. 2nd ed. Vol. 2. Vatican City State: University of Notre Dame Press, 1997.

Russell, Robert John, and Kirk Wegter-McNelly. "Science." In *The Blackwell Companion to Modern Theology*, edited by Gareth Jones. Malden: Wiley-Blackwell, 2007.

Ryan, Michael James. "Character (in Catholic Theology)." *The Catholic Encyclopedia*. New York: Robert Appleton Company, 1908. Accessed November 8, 2018. http://newadvent.org/cathen/03586a.htm.

Sacred Congregation for the Doctrine of the Faith. "Communiqué of the Press Office of the Holy See," July 20, 1981. Accessed January 15, 2018. https://www.ewtn.com/library/CURIA/CDFTEILH.HTM.

Sacred Congregation of the Holy Office. "Warning Regarding the Writings of Pierre Teilhard de Chardin." Last modified June 30, 1962. Accessed February 17, 2018. https://www.ewtn.com/library/CURIA/CDFTEILH.HTM.

Sagan, Carl. *Cosmos*. New York: Random House, 1980.

Sala, Giovanni B. *Lonergan and Kant: Five Essays on Human Knowledge*. Edited by Robert M. Doran. Translated by Joseph Spoerl. Buffalo, NY: University of Toronto Press, 1994.

Sauvage, George. "Analogy." *The Catholic Encyclopedia*. New York: Robert Appleton Company, 1907. Accessed April 4, 2018. http://www.newadvent.org/cathen/01449a.htm.

Sawyer, Joseph Dillaway. *History of the Pilgrims and Puritans: Their Ancestry and Descendants; Basis of Americanization*. 3 vols. New York: Century History Company, 1922.

Scannone, Juan Carlos. "El Papa Francisco y La Teología Del Pueblo." *Razón y Fe*, no. 1395 (2014): 31–50.

Schaff, Philip, Alexander Roberts, James Donaldson, and Arthur Cleveland Coxe, eds. *Ante-Nicene Fathers—Fathers of the Second Century: Tatian, Theophilus of Antioch, Athenagoras of Athens, Clement of Alexandria*. Vol. 2. CreateSpace Independent Publishing Platform, 2017.

Schillebeeckx, Edward. *The Eucharist*. New York: Burns & Oates, 2005.

Schilling, Harold K. *Science and Religion*. New York: Charles Scribner's Sons, 1962.

Schindler, David L. "Theology, Science, and Cosmology." *Communio* 15, no. 3 (Fall 1988): 270–273.

Schleiermacher, Friedrich. *On Religion: Speeches to Its Cultured Despisers*. Translated by John Oman. New York: Harper & Brothers, 1958.

Schmaus, Michael. *God and Creation: The Foundations of Christology*. Translated by Ann Laeuchli, William McKenna, and T. Patrick Burke. Vol. 2. Dogma. New York: Sheed and ward, 1969.

Schmidt, Ulf. *Secret Science: A Century of Poison Warfare and Human Experiments*. New York: Oxford University Press, 2015.

Schönborn, Christoph. "Schöpfungskatechese un Evolutionstheorie. Vom Burgfrieden zum konstruktiven Konflikt." In *Evolutionismus und Christentum*, edited by Robert Spaemann, Reinhard Löw, and Peter Koslowski, 91–116. Weinheim: Wiley-VCH, 1986.

Schrödinger, Erwin. "Die Gegenwärtige Situation in Der Quantenmechanik." *Naturwissenschaften* 23, no. 48 (November 1, 1935): 807–812.

Schwarz, Hans. *Creation*. Grand Rapids, MI: Eerdmans, 2002.

———. *Vying for Truth—Theology and the Natural Sciences: From the 17th Century to the Present*. Göttingen: Vandehoeck & Ruprecht, 2014.

Scola, Angelo. *The Nuptial Mystery*. Grand Rapids, MI: Eerdmans, 2005.

Second Vatican Council. *Dei Verbum*, 1965.

———. *Gaudium et Spes*, 1964.

———. *Lumen Gentium*, 1964.

———. *Optatam Totius*, 1965.

———. *Sacrosanctum Concilium*, 1963.

———. *Unitatis Redintegratio*, 1964.

Seibt, Johanna. "Process Philosophy." Edited by Edward N. Zalta. *The Stanford Encyclopedia of Philosophy*. Stanford: Metaphysics Research Lab, Stanford University, October 26, 2017. Accessed January 23, 2018. https://plato.stanford.edu/archives/win2017/entries/process-philosophy/.

Sellars, Roy Wood. *Critical Realism. A Study of the Nature and Conditions of Knowledge*. New York: Russell & Russell, 1916.

———. "What Is the Correct Interpretation of Critical Realism?" *The Journal of Philosophy* 24, no. 9 (1927): 238.

Selvaggi, Filippo. *Filosofia Del Mondo: Cosmologia Filosofica*. 2nd ed. Rome: Gregorian University Press, 2008.

Selya, Roger Mark. "George Brown Barbour." *Geographers Biobibliographical Studies* 23 (2004): 14–33.

Shannon, Claude. "A Mathematical Theory of Communication." *The Bell System Technical Journal* 27, no. 3 (July 1948): 379–423.

Shen, Guanjun, Xing Gao, Bin Gao, and Darryl E. Granger. "Age of Zhoukoudian Homo Erectus Determined with 26Al/10Be Burial Dating." *Nature* 458, no. 7235 (March 12, 2009): 198–200.

Shipway, Brad. "Critical Realism and Theological Critical Realism: Opportunities for Dialogue?" *Alethia* 3, no. 2 (2000): 29–33.

Shuyun, Sun. *The Long March: The True History of Communist China's Founding Myth*. New York: Anchor, 2008.

de Sitter, Willem. *Kosmos*. Cambridge, MA: Harvard University Press, 1932.

Skinner, Burrhus Frederic. *Science and Human Behavior*. New York: The Macmillan Co., 1956.

Slater, Peter. "Parables, Analogues and Symbols." *Religious Studies* 4, no. 1 (1968): 25–36.

Slattery, John P. "Dangerous Tendencies of Cosmic Theology: The Untold Legacy of Teilhard de Chardin." *Philosophy and Theology* 29, no. 1 (January 25, 2017): 69–82.

Söhngen, Gottlieb. "Analogia Fidei: Gottähnlichkeit Allein Aus Glauben?" *Catholica* 3, no. 3 (1934): 113–136.

Southgate, Christopher, ed. *God, Humanity and the Cosmos: A Textbook in Science and Religion*. 3rd ed. London: T&T Clark, 2011.

Stenmark, Mikael. *How to Relate Science and Religion: A Multidimensional Model*. Grand Rapids, MI: Wm. B. Eerdmans Publishing, 2004.

Stiver, David. "History of the Graduate Theological Union." *Graduate Theological Union*. Last modified July 5, 2017. Accessed December 6, 2017. https://www.gtu.edu/about/history.

Stoeger, William R. "Key Developments in Physics Challenging Philosophy and Theology." In *Religion and Science: History, Method, and Dialogue*, edited by W. Mark Richardson and Wesley J. Wildman, 194. New York: Routledge, 1996.

———. "The Big Bang, Quantum Cosmology, and Creatio Ex Nihilo." In *Creation and the God of Abraham*, edited by David B. Burrell, Carlo Cogliati, Janet M. Soskice, and William R. Stoeger, 152–175. Cambridge: Cambridge University Press, 2010.

Stoljar, Daniel. "Physicalism." In *The Stanford Encyclopedia of Philosophy*, edited by Edward N. Zalta. Stanford: Metaphysics Research Lab, Stanford University, 2015. Accessed January 17, 2018. https://plato.stanford.edu/archives/win2017/entries/physicalism/.

Stratton, Stanley Brian. "Coherence, Consonance, and Conversation: The Interaction of Theology and Natural Science in the Quest for a Unified World-View." PhD, Princeton Theological Seminary, 1997. Accessed October 10, 2017. https://search.proquest.com/dissertations/docview/304371222/abstract/CDD323051D654D77PQ/3.

Streng, Frederick J. *Understanding Religious Man*. Encino: Dickenson Publishing Company, 1969.

Studtmann, Paul. "Aristotle's Categories." Edited by Edward N. Zalta. *The Stanford Encyclopedia of Philosophy*. Stanford: Metaphysics Research Lab, Stanford University, November 5, 2013. Accessed March 20, 2018. https://plato.stanford.edu/archives/fall2017/entries/aristotle-categories/.

Suchocki, Marjorie Hewitt. "Openness and Mutuality in Process Thought and Feminine Action." In *Feminism and Process Thought*, edited by Sheila Greeve Davaney. New York: Edwin Mellen Press, 1981.

Sullivan, Francis A. *Creative Fidelity: Weighing and Interpreting Documents of the Magisterium*. Eugene, OR: Wipf & Stock Pub, 2003.

Tabaczek, Mariusz. "Thomistic Response to the Theory of Evolution: Aquinas on Natural Selection and the Perfection of the Universe." *Theology and Science* 13, no. 3 (July 3, 2015): 325–344.

Teilhard de Chardin, Pierre. *Letters from My Friend, Teilhard de Chardin, 1948–1955*. Edited by Pierre Leroy. Translated by Mary Lukas. New York: Paulist Press, 1980.

———. *The Divine Milieu*. Translated by Sion Cowell. Brighton, England: Sussex Academic Press, 2003.

Tenace, Michelina. "Incontro Del Dipartimento Di Teologia Fondamentale." Presentation, Pontificia Università Gregoriana, October 12, 2017.

Thompson, Charles Frank. *The Greatness of God: How God Is the Foundation of All Reality, Truth, Love, Goodness, Beauty, and Purpose*. Bloomington, IN: WestBow Press, 2016.

Thompson, Phillip M. *Between Science and Religion: The Engagement of Catholic Intellectuals with Science and Technology in the Twentieth Century*. Plymouth, UK: Lexington Books, 2009.

Tillich, Paul. *Dynamics of Faith*. New York: HarperOne, 2009.

Tirosh-Samuelson, Hava. "Judaism and the Dialogue of Religion and Science: A Personal Journey." *Theology and Science* 16, no. 4 (November 2018): 388–414.

Török, Estée, Ed Moran, and Fiona Cooke. *Oxford Handbook of Infectious Diseases and Microbiology*. 2nd ed. New York: Oxford University Press, 2017.

Torrance, Allan J. "Is Love the Essence of God?" In *Nothing Greater, Nothing Better: Theological Essays on the Love of God*, edited by Kevin J. Vanhoozer. Grand Rapids, MI: Wm. B. Eerdmans Publishing, 2001.

Torrance, Thomas F. *Divine and Contingent Order*. Edinburgh: T&T Clark, 2005.

Torrey, Reuben Arche, and Amzi Clarence Dixon, eds. *The Fundamentals: A Testimony to the Truth*. Grand Rapids: Baker Books, 2003.

Toulmin, Stephen Edelston. *Philosophy of Science*. New York: Harper Collins, 2000.

Trefil, James. *From Atoms to Quarks*. Revised. New York: Anchor, 1994.

———. *The Moment of Creation: Big Bang Physics from before the First Millisecond to the Present Universe*. New York: Collier Books, 1983.

Trimmer, John D. "The Present Situation in Quantum Mechanics: A Translation of Schrödinger's 'Cat Paradox' Paper." *Proceedings of the American Philosophical Society* 124, no. 5 (1980): 323–338.

de la Trinité, Philippe. *Rome et Teilhard de Chardin*. Paris: Arthème Fayard, 1964.

Tugwell, Simon, ed. *Albert & Aquinas: Selected Writings*. New York: Paulist Press, 1988.

Turbanti, Giovanni. *Un Concilio per Il Mondo Moderno: La Redazione Della Costituzione Pastorale "Gaudium et Spes" Del Vaticano II*. Bologna: Il Mulino, 2000.

Uebel, Thomas. "Vienna Circle." Edited by Edward N. Zalta. *The Stanford Encyclopedia of Philosophy*. Stanford: Metaphysics Research Lab, Stanford University, February 17, 2016. Accessed February 6, 2018. https://plato.stanford.edu/archives/spr2016/entries/vienna-circle/.

Ussher, James. *The Annals of the World*. Edited by Larry Pierce and Marion Pierce. Green Forest, AR: Master Books, 2007.

Varian, Russell H., and Sigurd F. Varian. "A High Frequency Oscillator and Amplifier." *Journal of Applied Physics* 10, no. 5 (May 1939): 321–327.

Vattimo, Gianni, and René Girard. *Christianity, Truth, and Weakening Faith: A Dialogue*. Edited by Pierpaolo Antonello. Translated by William McCuaig. New York: Columbia University Press, 2010.

Verschuuren, Gerard M. *Aquinas and Modern Science: A New Synthesis of Faith and Reason*. Kettering, OH: Angelico Press, 2016.

Villajin, Noel Ma. N. "The Universe as a Creation: The Ontological Presupposition of Science." PhD, Universidad de Navarra, 1995.

Vincelette, Alan. *Recent Catholic Philosophy: The Twentieth Century*. Marquette Studies in Philosophy 71. Milwaukee: Marquette University Press, 2011.

Vincent of Lerins. *The Commonitory of St. Vincent of Lerins*. Edited by Paul A. Boer. Translated by Charles A. Heurtley. New York: Veritatis Splendor Publications, 2012.

Viney, Donald Wayne. "Charles Hartshorne." *Dictionary of Unitarian and Universalist Biography*. Unitarian Universalist History & Heritage Society, July 15, 2002. Accessed January 15, 2018. http://uudb.org/articles/charleshartshorne.html.

———. "Charles Hartshorne." *American Philosophers Before 1950*. Dictionary of Literary Biography, 2003. Accessed January 15, 2018. https://web.archive.org/web/20070420043457/http://www.harvardsquarelibrary.org/Hartshorne/Viney/index.html.

Viney, Donald Wayne, and George W. Shields. "Charles Hartshorne: Dipolar Theism." *Internet Encyclopedia of Philosophy*, n.d. Accessed January 26, 2018. https://www.iep.utm.edu/hart-d-t/#H1.

Waggoner, Walter H. "Dr. Roland H. Bainton Dies; Retired Yale Divinity Teacher." *The New York Times*, February 14, 1984. Accessed January 16, 2018. http://www.nytimes.com/1984/02/14/obituaries/dr-roland-h-bainton-dies-retired-yale-divinity-teacher.html.

———. "Rev. R.L. Calhoun, a Professor, Dies." *The New York Times*, September 30, 1983. Accessed October 18, 2017. http://www.nytimes.com/1983/09/30/obituaries/rev-rl-calhoun-a-professor-dies.html.

Wallace, William A. *The Modeling of Nature: The Philosophy of Science and the Philosophy of Nature in Synthesis*. Washington, DC: The Catholic University of America Press, 1996.

Weber, Michel. *Whitehead's Pancreativism: The Basics*. Process Thought 7. New Brunswick: Ontos Verlag, 2006.

Weinandy, Thomas. *Does God Change?* Studies in Historical Theology 4. Still River, MA: St. Bede's Press, 2002.

———. *Does God Suffer?* Notre Dame, IN: University of Notre Dame Press, 2000.

Weinberg, Steven. "A Designer Universe?" *PhysLink: Physics and Astronomy Online*, 1999. Accessed February 28, 2018. http://www.physlink.com/Education/essay_weinberg.cfm.

———. *The Quantum Theory of Fields*. 3 vols. Cambridge, UK: Cambridge University Press, 2005.

von Weizsäcker, Carl F. *History of Nature*. Chicago: University of Chicago Press, 1949.

West, Philip. *Yenching University and Sino-Western Relations, 1916–1952*. Harvard University Press, 1976.

Westermann, Claus. *Creation*. Translated by John J. Scullion. Philadelphia: Fortress Press, 1974.

Whealon, John F. "The Magisterium: Biblical and Pastoral Aspects." *L'Osservatore Romano*. Vatican City State, April 13, 1978. Accessed February 21, 2018. https://www.ewtn.com/library/BISHOPS/MAGPAST.HTM.

Whelan, Gerard. "Evangelii Gaudium come 'Teologia Contestuale': Aiutare la Chiesa ad 'Alzarsi al Livello dei sui Tempi.'" In *Evangelii Gaudium: il testo ci interroga: Chiavi di lettura, testimonianze e prospettive*, edited by Miguel Yáñez Humberto, 23–38. Rome: Gregorian & Biblical Press, 2014.

White, Andrew D. *A History of the Warfare of Science with Theology in Christendom*. Buffalo: Prometheus Books, 1993.

White, Thomas Joseph, ed. *The Analogy of Being: Invention of the Antichrist or Wisdom of God?* Grand Rapids, MI: Eerdmans, 2010.

———. *The Incarnate Lord*. Washington, D.C.: CUA Press, 2015.

———. "Thomism after Vatican II." *Nova et Vetera* 12, no. 4 (2014): 1045–1062.

White, Walter Reagan. "The Integration of Science and Religion: Implications of Process Thought's Dependence on the New Physics." PhD, Southwestern Baptist Theological

Seminary, 1995. Accessed October 10, 2017. https://search.proquest.com/dissertations/docview/304245028/abstract/CDD323051D654D77PQ/4.

Whitehead, Alfred North. *Adventures of Ideas*. New York: The Free Press, 1967.

———. *Process and Reality*. New York: Free Press, 1969.

———. *Religion in the Making*. 2nd ed. New York: Fordham University Press, 1996.

———. *Science and the Modern World*. New York: The Macmillan Co., 1931.

———. *The Function of Reason*. Princeton: Princeton University Press, 1929.

Whitehead, Alfred North, and Bertrand Russell. *Principia Mathematica*. 2nd ed. 3 vols. Cambridge: Cambridge University Press, 1923.

Whitehouse, Walter A. *Christian Faith and Scientific Attitude*. New York: Philosophical Library, 1952.

Wick, Gian Carlo. "Properties of Bethe-Salpeter Wave Functions." *Physical Review* 96, no. 4 (November 15, 1954): 1124–1134.

Wicken, Jeffrey S. "The Cosmic Breath: Reflections on the Thermodynamics of Creation." *Zygon* 19, no. 4 (December 1984): 487–505.

Wiener, Norbert. *Cybernetics, or Control and Communication in the Animal and the Machine*. 2nd ed. Cambridge: The MIT Press, 1965.

Williams, Daniel Day. "How Does God Act?: An Essay in Whitehead's Metaphysics." In *Process and Divinity: The Hartshorne Festschrift*, edited by William L. Reese and Eugene Freeman. LaSalle: Open Court Pub. Co., 1964.

Williamson, Peter S. *Catholic Principles for Interpreting Scripture: A Study of the Pontifical Biblical Commission's The Interpretation of the Bible in the Church*. Rome: Gregorian & Biblical Press, 2001.

Wilson, Edward O. *Consilience: The Unity of Knowledge*. New York: Vintage, 1999.

———. "E. O. Wilson: Religious Faith Is Dragging Us Down." Interview by Penny Sarchet. New Scientist, January 21, 2015. Accessed February 28, 2018. https://www.newscientist.com/article/mg22530050-400-e-o-wilson-religious-faith-is-dragging-us-down/.

———. *On Human Nature*. Cambridge: Harvard University Press, 1978.

———. *Sociobiology: The New Synthesis*. Cambridge: Harvard University Press, 1975.

Wilson, William A. "The Myth of Scientific Objectivity." *First Things* (November 2017): 27–34.

Wimmel, Hermann. *Quantum Physics & Observed Reality: A Critical Interpretation of Quantum Mechanics*. River Edge: World Scientific Publishing Company Inc., 1992.

Wippel, John F. *Metaphysical Themes in Thomas Aquinas*. Washington, DC: CUA Press, 1995.

———. *The Metaphysical Thought of Thomas Aquinas: From Finite Being to Uncreated Being*. Monographs of the Society for Medieval and Renaissance Philosophy. Washington, D.C.: The Catholic University of America Press, 2000.

Wood, Ralph. "Biography of J.R.R. Tolkien (1892–1973)." *Leadership University*. Accessed March 7, 2018. http://www.leaderu.com/humanities/wood-biography.html.

Wright, N.T. *Jesus and the Victory of God*. 6th ed. Minneapolis: Fortress Press, 1997.

———. *Paul and the Faithfulness of God*. Minneapolis: Fortress Press, 2013.

———. *The New Testament and the People of God*. Minneapolis: Fortress Press, 1992.

———. *The Resurrection of the Son of God.* 2nd ed. London: SPCK Publishing, 2017.

Yardley, William. "Ian Barbour, Who Found a Balance Between Faith and Science, Dies at 90." *The New York Times,* January 12, 2014, sec. U.S. Accessed November 14, 2017. https://www.nytimes.com/2014/01/13/us/ian-barbour-academic-who-resisted-conflicts-of-faith-and-science-dies-at-90.html.

York, Carl M. "Ian Barbour's Contributions as a Scientist." *Theology and Science* 15, no. 1 (January 2, 2017): 17–27.

van der Ziel, Aldert. *The Natural Sciences and the Christian Message.* Minneapolis: Denison, 1960.

Zimmerli, Walther. "Ort Und Grenze Der Weisheit Im Rahmen Der Altestamentlichen Theologie." In *Gottes Offenbarung, Gesammelte Aufsätze Zum Alten Testament, Theologische Bücherei.* Vol. 19. Munich: Kaiser, 1963.

"Dickinson, Robert Latou, 1861–1950." *Harvard University Library: Online Archival Search Information System.* Accessed November 14, 2017. http://oasis.lib.harvard.edu/oasis/deliver/~med00073.

"Edward Routh—The Mathematics Genealogy Project." Accessed January 10, 2018. https://www.genealogy.math.ndsu.nodak.edu/id.php?id=101929.

"Glossary: Lay Speaker." *The United Methodist Church.* Accessed February 15, 2018. http://www.umc.org/what-we-believe/glossary-lay-speaker.

"Graduation." *Oriel College, University of Oxford.* Last modified June 7, 2016. Accessed November 22, 2017. http://www.oriel.ox.ac.uk/life-oriel/graduation.

"Histoplasmosis—Symptoms and Causes." *Mayo Clinic.* Accessed January 10, 2018. http://www.mayoclinic.org/diseases-conditions/histoplasmosis/symptoms-causes/syc-20373495.

Liturgia Horarium. Vol. 4. 4 vols. Vatican City State: Libreria Editrice Vaticana, 2000.

"Mission & History | Yale Divinity School." Accessed October 5, 2017. http://divinity.yale.edu/about-yds/mission-history.

"Pierre Teilhard de Chardin, SJ (1881–1955)." *Ignatian Spirituality.* Accessed January 10, 2018. https://www.ignatianspirituality.com/ignatian-voices/20th-century-ignatian-voices/pierre-teilhard-de-chardin-sj.

"Templeton Prize—Purpose." *Templeton Foundation.* Accessed November 20, 2017. http://www.templetonprize.org/purpose.html.

"The Gifford Lectures." *The Gifford Lectures.* Accessed November 20, 2017. https://www.giffordlectures.org/.

"The Nobel Prize in Physics 1933." *NobelPrize.Org.* Accessed November 27, 2017. https://www.nobelprize.org/nobel_prizes/physics/laureates/1933/.

"The Templeton Prize: Rev. Dr. John C. Polkinghorne (2002)." *Templeton Foundation.* Accessed November 28, 2017. http://www.templetonprize.org/previouswinners/polkinghorne.html.

"Verifiability Principle." *Encyclopædia Britannica.* Last modified 2018. Accessed February 6, 2018. https://www.britannica.com/topic/verifiability-principle.

"What Do 'Fine-Tuning' and the 'Multiverse' Say about God?" *BioLogos Foundation.* Accessed November 20, 2017. https://biologos.org/common-questions/gods-relationship-to-creation/fine-tuning.

Index